Vanilla Beans and Brodo

Real Life in the Hills of Tuscany

Isabella Dusi

POCKET
BOOKS

LONDON · SYDNEY · NEW YORK · TOKYO · SINGAPORE · TORONTO

First published in Great Britain by Simon & Schuster UK Ltd, 2001
This edition first published by Pocket, 2002
An imprint of Simon & Schuster UK Ltd
A Viacom Company

1 3 5 7 9 10 8 6 4 2

Simon & Schuster UK Ltd
Africa House
64–78 Kingsway
London WC2B 6AH

www.simonsays.co.uk

Simon & Schuster Australia
Sydney

A CIP catalogue record for this book is available
from the British Library

ISBN 0-7434-0411-4

Typeset in Granjon by SX Composing DTP, Rayleigh, Essex
Printed and bound in Great Britain by
Omnia Books Limited, Glasgow

About the Author

After many years working in Australia in interior design, Isabella Dusi decided to move to Italy with her husband Luigi. Based permanently in Montalcino, they now work in the travel business. This is her first book.

To my daughter, Rebecca

Contents

List of Illustrations

Acknowledgements

This is not my story, and it is not a story about me: this is the story of Montalcino.

I am humbled and privileged that friends have shared with me and entrusted to me their memories, their joy and their pain, but I am burdened with the feeling that there is so much I have left out.

I accept responsibility for all of the material, conscious always that occasionally I was faced with slightly differing records, and on occasions I have had to make decisions for the benefit of the reader.

I trust that my friends will understand that I could only write this story from the perspective of a stranger – a stranger who is passionate about Montalcino, and one who feels the time is right for its story to be shared.

My sincere thanks to all the citizens of Montalcino. Without you, dear friends, this book could not have been written. I remain deeply in your debt.

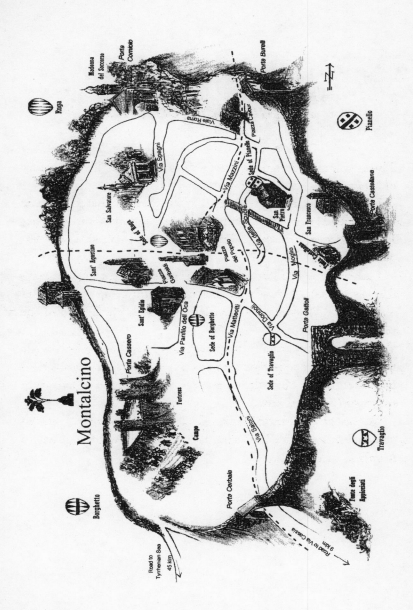

Montalcino

Road to Tyrrhenian Sea 45 Km

Campo

Fortress

Porta Cassero

Sant' Epidio

Via Panfilo dell' Oca

Sede of Burghetto

Via Matteotti

Via Saloni

Porte Cerbaia

Sede of Travaglio

Via Donnoli

Sant' Agostino

Piazza Garibaldi

Piazza del Popolo

San Salvatore

Via Spagni

Via di Ruga

Via Mazzini

Via delle Scudie

Sede of Pianello

Piazza Cavour

Viale Roma

San Pietro

San Francesco

Via Moglio

Porta Gattoli

Madonna del Soccorso

Porta Corniolo

Porta Burelli

Porta Castellana

Porte degli Appiccati

Road to Via Cassia 9 Km

Ruga

Pianello

Travaglio

Borghetto

N

Hidden among the perfumed branches, crowned with
    chestnut trees and vines
Montalcino, beautiful village, reigns on fertile Sienese
    land
Many pages of history, narrated by each stone
Each page a page of glory, a legend that must be told.

Up here, always higher towards the sun
Montalcino's banner rises
First to be kissed by Madonna Spring.

Sig. Nando Ciacci, 1950
Trans. Isabella Dusi

Arrivederci Iron Lady ...
Ciao, Signora Isabella!

A number of years ago we discovered Montalcino; a couple of strangers, Australians, Lou and I were seeking a new home. Both of us spring from migrant families. My parents, with £80 to their name, sailed from war-weary Scotland in 1948 taking us three children across the world to an unknown life in a promising country; and Lou, as a child of six, was taken to Australia by his parents from a troubled Italy torn apart with political strife and foreign invaders. We were all post-war immigrants on our way to the land of opportunity across the sea. The early decades of our young lives in different States of Australia unfolded along entirely different paths but, perhaps from the courage of our parents, sprang a spirit of adventure – and curiosity – about the world beyond Australia.

So, how did this happen? Why am I living in Italy? It sounds simple enough: impulsively selling everything I possessed, I moved to Italy in 1994 with an Italian-born Australian who had just become my new husband. Life, however, is rarely simple. Nor was the tangled road which brought me to Montalcino.

Before my twentieth birthday, soon after I had married my sweetheart, we sailed away from Australia – two precocious Aussies en route to discover the world. Armed with enthusiasm and false invincibility, we managed to get shot at in Spain; to be led – thankfully alive – out of the medina in Marrakesh (where I saw things I cannot yet credit to be true), then blithely travelled through the Atlas Mountains alongside a tribe of dark-bearded herdsmen; spent many nights in a straw and mud hut, sleeping with the goats, in the remote mountains of what was then Yugoslavia . . . finally, in a midnight dash, we were chased out of Italy by the police!

With the confidence of the young, I naively assumed my life would continue along this same exciting path but, within a few short years my handsome young husband was gone. Barely had we reached the safety of our homeland when a tragic road accident left Rebecca, our six-month-old baby, fatherless, and me with a child to raise and a new life to find. These circum-stances influenced the future and, driven by the scary realities of life, I adopted a steely exterior to insulate my inner self from hurt. Possessing little but an unyielding desire to educate Rebecca, I faced an uncertain future. I built a career in interior design, accepting seemingly glamorous commissions which took me up and down the east coast of Australia, so that I was forever on the move. My traumatic circumstances had brought me an insatiable need to search for answers about people and the way they lived their lives in the extravagant dream homes I was creating for them, because I continually wondered why their lives seemed so different, so orderly compared to the turmoil of my own disrupted life. With my vulnerability well camouflaged, I drove myself to Super-businesswoman status by pushing impossible deals, pounding boardroom tables and slamming down phones.

By the time Rebecca gained acceptance into University, I had met Lou who, operating an upholstery workshop, saved me from the wrath of a disbelieving client by delivering eighteen calico-upholstered dining chairs to an Embassy reception ten minutes before the first distinguished Ambassador walked through the doors! Tamil Tigers had hijacked the intended silk. Perhaps I should have resorted to the last line of a designer's defence and said the ship had sunk in the Indian Ocean.

By way of reward for Rebecca's diligence at school, and daring, for once, to look beyond that day, I agreed that the three of us should have a holiday in Italy. My daughter, beautiful, dark-haired and tall at eighteen years old, towered above me. Dragging both her and Lou up the highest mountains to gaze across serene valleys, I then insisted we scramble down a rocky goat track to find an isolated shrine firmly pictured in my mind and never forgotten; a sweet Madonna of benign simplicity smiling into eternal silence. Precious memories rose close to the surface and, blinking away tears, I was astonished at the innocence of my youth.

It was Lou's first re-encounter with Italy, the country of his birth. He was in his own world of discovery, finding himself surrounded by a people and a culture astonishingly familiar to his life in an Italian/Australian family. For the first time he understood his immigrant parents who, during half a lifetime in Australia, had barely spoken English. Now he was able to see the raw life his father had faced. His first job in Australia had been in the woolsheds, awaiting the arrival of the road trains from the outback sheep stations after the shearing. His daily labour was to scour the fleeces on wooden tables to remove lanolin from them before they went off to the wool stapler to be graded.

As we explored Italy, Lou recounted stories of helping his father slaughter a pig in the Adelaide hills. Working together, they would scrub and scrub at the tough skin with stiff brushes to remove the pig's bristles, and afterwards his father would string squat salami and fat sausages from the ceiling of the cellar which he had dug out in front of their suburban home where the lawn should have been – and then, keeping face with neighbours who nurtured springy grass and pretty flowers, he concreted the whole surface and painted it green!

Lou also talked of his mother who, steeped in the ways of the old country, kept her seemingly compliant yet controlling role in the family home, making her own pasta by hand every day, and the bread, too. She would often thread a circlet of garlic cloves around Lou's neck to ward off nightmares. Coupled with the pungent salami rolls she prepared for his lunch, it warded off more than his nightmares; every other child in school refused to come anywhere near him! Sometimes she would pay an Italian sorceress to incant a magic spell to remove a curse she felt was upon her, or a *malocchio*, evil eye, on one of the family. Lou remembered stomping buckets of grapes in the cellar, his father's fermenting red wine and reluctantly sucking on the crude garden hose as the bottles quickly filled, to be stacked in pyramids around the floor. He often awoke at night to the crash of exploding bottles smashing into the cellar walls.

As he absorbed the culture of Italy, looking into the lives of these people so tied to the land, he saw his mother and father, now both dead, through enlightened eyes. They had considered themselves an Australian family, and indeed they were, yet they had lived in two worlds. Embracing their young country but not able to let go of the old culture, they had blended both worlds. The holiday over, it was time to leave, but already Lou wanted to come back, and I understood his inner yearning to find again something which was lost to him.

Back in Australia, it wasn't long before Rebecca moved towards complete independence with her chosen man, announcing she was going west to live in Mount Newman, more than 5,000 kilometres across the barren continent. In my heart, although I could not say the words, I knew she wanted a traditional marriage and to surround herself with a family. Something I had been unable to give her. True to form, I was again tearing up and down the coast directing projects, even ascending five storeys of a construction site in a hard hat and high heels to unleash a volley of condemnation upon a builder who, when he heard I was climbing the scaffolding, was unwilling to face this Iron Lady one more time. Jumping instead into the yellow cement bucket, the crane lowered him to the ground just as I reached the offending office!

On the outside I was tough, but inside I was hurting. Lou had changed direction and was now working long hours in property development but, more than ever anxious to rekindle the culture of the Italian way of life and exhausted with the tedium of sales and marketing, one day, amidst this never-ending turmoil, he rashly speculated: 'Would you like to come with me and live in Italy?'

Meditation and acceptance of this daring proposal occupied roughly three consecutive seconds. My hasty acceptance astonished even me. Shouldn't I be gearing up for the second half of my life? Feigning outrageous flippancy, I was resolute when Rebecca, already 5,000 kilometres distant and probably closer to Africa than the east coast of Australia, suddenly indignant that I would be so far away, told me she was carrying her first child. An iron bolt snapped shut, fortifying my mind against thoughts of encroaching middle age. Incredulous friends were quick to tell me I would get over this impulsive madness. 'But what will you do over there? You don't even speak the language. Get real, it's not the real world,' they counselled.

Ignoring them all, I began to sell the designer furniture. The possessions of the last twenty years were strewn across the carpet in the apartment Lou and I shared, prodded, picked over and paid for by whoever wandered through the door. I sold the refrigerator, the microwave, blankets and pillows, the computer, every kitchen cup, bowl and plate, dinner sets and glasses, the music tapes, even the pictures from the walls, all my excess clothing and my extensive library of interior design catalogues and books – leaving nothing to come back to. I launched into this daring campaign because the real world for me was a wilderness of upheaval and searching, where nothing ever stayed the same, where I moved every two years to another location . . . always ruthlessly cutting ties and running from uncertainty. Disillusioned with my work, I had lived nomadically for more than two turbulent decades. I didn't belong anywhere in particular and, ironically, I possessed no real sense of home. Perhaps this was another opportunity to run away from the harsh realities of life;

or could I find my true home in Italy?

Lou and I dragooned a couple of shocked friends for a fleeting appointment at the office of the Registrar of Marriages – disbelieving witnesses – and then we were gone. We landed in Italy with a bundle of cash and two suitcases. Mr and Mrs Work-a-day Australia, we were not in the financial league to be able to flit back to Australia even if I had left some thread of an existence to return to. We had no idea what we would do, how we could earn a living nor where we might ultimately settle, but first we needed transport. Of course, we didn't intend to purchase an extravagant vehicle when we waltzed into the car showroom of a cousin of someone Lou met in a bar. We were looking for a dependable Fiat; something we could park anywhere and that wouldn't stand out in the crowd, something we didn't have to worry about because it would soon join the majority of Italian Fiats displaying scrapes and bumps inevitably suffered when manoeuvring through medieval passageways, or reversing out of narrow alleys. There were plenty of Fiats, exactly what we had in mind and within the price we wanted to pay – nondescript, bland, knocked-about-a-little Fiats. There was also a Maserati. Lou's Italian blood began revving in time to the throaty gurgle of the bi-turbo engine. I continued checking out the Fiats, but he had lost interest in Fiats.

'Wouldn't you rather drive around Italy in this beautiful bi-turbo two-door Maserati with soft leather interior and original walnut dash?' he appealed to me. I was unmoved, although the Maserati was the same price as the Fiat – plus another few hundred thousand lire for transfer fees. Lou, digging in, was not going to agree to buy a Fiat.

'But if it's so great,' I reasoned, 'why is it the same price?' The dealer logically explained that nobody except enthusiasts and collectors in Italy wanted to own a Maserati because they use more petrol, spare parts are expensive, they are difficult to park and cost more to register. 'Lou! That's exactly why we don't want one either,' I said. It was his turn to be unmoved – becoming an enthusiast and collector on the spot.

We drove away to discover Italy in a burnished gold, two-door, leather upholstery, walnut dash, bi-turbo, very fast Maserati. Excited but confused, not able to remember the last time I had allowed a man to override a perfectly sensible decision, I felt twenty years old all over again.

Weaving our impractical way around seventy-three in-accessible mountain villages over the next eighteen months, we listened, watched, learned, researched, absorbed and lived Italy – sometimes staying only a day or two in one place, sometimes a week, even a whole month. Not really certain what we were searching for, it was proving exceedingly difficult to recognise, but as vague thoughts about how we might earn a living here began to germinate, our excitement and determination soared. We ignored the hollow rattle as the bag of cash dwindled to a dangerous level.

'Lou, do you remember that tranquil valley I took you and Rebecca to see? Let's try there.' We were way up north at the time but, following some instinctive urge, we bundled everything into the Maserati and drove five hours to southern Tuscany. Turning from the superstrada, we began to climb, winding through the hills with vineyards to the left and right, past stone farmhouses, olive groves, occasional chestnut trees and sentinel cypress pines. We were strangely quiet as we threaded the Maserati round the last few bends and, at the top of the hill, as we reached the gates of Montalcino, I turned to gaze across the peaceful valley that had lured me back yet again.

Intrigued with what we found that very first day, we decided it could be interesting to live inside the walls of this medieval village. It was a decision which, contrary to what you might think, did not complicate our lives, but instead opened our eyes to how complicated life had been – and rendered us totally receptive to how beautifully simple life, over the next few years, was to become.

For more than four years the Montalcinesi, whilst polite, obviously held the opinion that this was not to last. Soon, they reasoned, these strangers will go back outside to wherever they came from. But we had fallen under the spell of Tuscan Montalcino and we were patient. There was so much to learn about the ways of the village long before we began to make, at first, almost imperceptible progress, receiving perhaps a subtle nod in acknowledgement of our puzzling continued presence, half a smile as we encountered familiar faces in the piazza every morning, an invitation to share elbow space at the bar counter with a caffè.

Now, after more than five years, Isobel and Lou have become Isabella and Luigi and we have begun to find acceptance within the walls, but we readily admit we have not yet come to fully understand the mysterious ways of Montalcino, nor the complexities of the Montalcinesi who dwell on this hill.

Here, then, I recount the story of our fifth year in Montalcino. Starting with autumn, I shall take you through all four seasons on a journey of joy, hope, sadness, laughter, suspense and surprise . . . as life in Tuscan Montalcino unfolded before the eyes of two anonymous strangers from outside the walls.

AUTUMN

CHAPTER ONE

Under the Holm Oaks

The stone walls encircling Montalcino, first completed in the year 1110, form a defensive band around the village like a stone circle pushed down over the crown of the irregular-shaped hill. It comes to a halt only when it can be pushed no further because the steep slopes begin to creep outwards to the valleys. To learn the significance of the walls I needed to follow them on foot, inside and outside, over many weeks, each time discovering something new; moving closer to understanding the way of life as it must have unfolded in this village through the centuries.

Montalcino straddles a hill some 564 metres above sea level, and the view from the walls, magnificent towards all points of the compass, offers differing glimpses of life over more than two thousand years. Standing looking to the east, my eyes run along the floor of the Orcia Valley, easily picking out the winding road, the Via Cassia, just a handful of kilometres away. Along this strategic road, first laid out by the Romans, I picture in my mind the kings, mercenaries, prophets, emperors, traders, pilgrims and brigands who have all trod or been carried between these famous undulating hills. In the Middle Ages the road was known as the Francigena, signifying the way from Rome to France. Taverns and travellers' inns lined the route, to house pilgrims on their way to kneel in penitent prayer in the holy city as well as merchant traders with mules and horses laden with silks, painted icons or spices, bound for Florence or even attempting to reach France with their goods intact. However, the route was thick with thieves who were quick to lighten the purses of the traders or the pockets of the pilgrims; many travellers, it is well documented, never reached their destinations. From the humble to the mighty, the powerful and the pious, many took their last breath along the Via Cassia.

If you were a traveller today, arriving from Siena or Rome, it is likely your first glimpse of Montalcino would be the same as mine was five years ago – upwards from the Via Cassia. Like me, you would find it difficult to pick out the precise horizontal stone-work of the wall encircling the village because it now blends with the haphazard collection of stone buildings tumbling down the hillside. But the wall is there, well camouflaged by overgrown bushes and enormous clumps of ivy which spread invading tentacles between stone blocks. Nor was I able to see the narrow pathway trodden into the earth which weaves its way around the *outside* of the wall. Once the contadini, peasant farmers from the Orcia Valley, used this pathway to bring beans, corn and a few potatoes up the steep incline to trade in Montalcino on market day. If your eyes were sharper than mine, and you knew exactly where to look, you would be able to pick out the rambling wall where it joins the arched gateway, Porta Gattoli, now sitting alone in the valley through which the contadini could pass into the safety of the fortified village.

It is evident centuries of neglect have left the wall far from straight, caused not only by the severity of the climate, but also the unchecked growth of trees that have pushed their roots into crevices, forcing the stones outwards. Rampant ivy hangs heavily overhead, so that in some places it appears the highest two metres of wall lean dangerously towards the path, bulging forward, about to come crashing down. One day it will topple, but not yet and probably not for a hundred years.

Walking along this path, all I can see, besides the wall, is bushes, trees and sky; I hear nothing but the chirping of birds as they dart between the thickets. I cannot see the bell-tower or any visible sign of Montalcino, and unless the village bell is ringing out the hour I am enclosed in a silent world. I now know the archers of Travaglio use this path; passing through Porta Gattoli they turn towards the valley to reach a small clearing that is their roughly terraced practice range. They are not clothed in medieval costume, only worn during Montalcino's tournaments and pageants, but they will be shouldering curved bows and from their belts will hang leather quivers protecting the delicate arrows. Today's archers do not face the dangers their ancestors did when they crept outside the walls to hunt wild hare or pheasant to feed a hungry family, and they probably give little thought to invaders who trod the same path seeking to find a way through the walls.

Sometimes, when walking along this silent path I meet a small, slightly stooped, thin-faced elderly man coming towards me with, more often than not, a cigarette hanging from his lips. That was how, after a few encounters, I came to know Vasco from Travaglio, although it was some time before we exchanged more than a courteous buongiorno. He uses Porta Gattoli to reach his farm, but lives with his family inside the wall in his quartiere, which is called Travaglio. Every day Vasco makes his way down the slope to the farm, where he checks his rows of vines, watches for any sign of mould on his olive trees, freshens the soil around the vegetables, sees to the feeding of the animals and then, carrying perhaps a handful of zucchini, or sprigs of green parsley tied with a length of straw wound round and round the skinny stems, he returns more slowly up the hill.

Occasionally I meet him on his return and I can see he brings only what his signora needs today, because tomorrow he will go outside again. Vasco, I have learned, is not a landworker, a contadino, he is a village-dweller, a cittadino, but I think he mimics the traditions of peasant farmers who, even a couple of hundred years before the first stone walls went up, more likely as far back as the 700s, brought produce into Montalcino using this now isolated, silent pathway.

If you were to arrive at Montalcino from the coast, through the Ombrone Valley named after the river which runs between the hills, you would find yourself winding through an entirely different terrain: the dense thickets and low bushes of the hunting woods to the west. This approach may be interrupted by the *crack-crack-crack* of rifle fire. Sunday is a popular hunting day when gunfire echoes over the village; often, standing along the wall, I hear the Sabbath fusillade in the Ombrone Valley

6

coinciding with the joyful ringing of the church bells to bring the faithful to Mass. To me the gunfire seems very odd, irreverent, almost as if it will surely offend God, but to the Montalcinesi there is nothing at all incongruous about this.

Looking upwards at Montalcino from the west, I see the encircling wall rising straight and high, a solid band stretching for half a kilometre, broken by two towers which I imagine protected archers and, later, soldiers on guard. Towards the right, immediately past the guard towers, the wall begins to soar as the land is terraced up the hill. In the 1800s a section of the wall was broken and a road cut through, wide enough to allow horses and carts, and now cars, into the village. But the stone wall soon rears up again and the terraces carry the wall even higher until it reaches the arched gateway, Porta Cassero, and butts against the bastions of the fortress. The fortress is a massive pentagonal stronghold sitting on the highest point in the quartiere called Borghetto. From the bastions the surrounding valleys, hamlets and trade routes can be easily watched for more than forty kilometres – which is why the Sienese chose to strengthen a smaller defence post which had been on this spot since 1110, when the first walls went up.

Passing through the fortress gates today, you still walk below the original black and white shield of the Republic of Siena, put there in 1361, which is the same year a retinue of thirty-two of Montalcino's most accurate archers moved into the new fortress.

Turning in the other direction, to the left, the wall curves around the hill until it reaches the rear of the church called Madonna del Soccorso. Behind the church there was once another gate into the village, Porta Corniolo, which in later centuries was built into and became part of the church's supporting wall. You cannot pass through the gate now, although its outline is easily traced. From the valley the apse and bell-tower of the Cathedral of San Salvatore is clearly visible and a few medieval houses cling to each other high on the ridge. All of these buildings have their backs to the west, as if to take the first blows from the freezing wind which sometimes rises from the mountains, or the sultry sirocco which blows sand across the sea from Northern Africa.

For a while I was puzzled about why no buildings, even today, face this enchanting range of hills. The reason is steeped in ancient tradition. The first Montalcinesi thought the hot oppressive wind could carry deadly malaria – which ravaged the Tuscan coast for centuries – from the coast up to their homes. They sensibly turned their backs to it and faced the village towards the more temperate, and healthier, eastern valley.

Standing beside the wall behind Madonna del Soccorso, glancing curiously at the outline of the blocked-in gateway, it is impossible not to turn and to look towards the valley. On the first slope the perceptible changes to the few cherry, plum, fig and almond trees scattered among the farms hint at the turning season. Often when I am standing here, an elderly man and his wife are hoeing between rows of artichokes and onions; they told me the hillside was once covered in orchards that were destroyed by the Sienese after the Battle of Montaperti more than 740 years ago. This battle had a dramatic impact on Montalcino because the orchards were not all the Sienese destroyed in anger. I decided to find out more about this great battle between Florence and Siena, because I sensed it to be a passionate reminder to the Montalcinesi of their unique history.

It was the late 1200s, but even during the previous hundred years the Montalcinesi, through every decade, had struggled for their freedom against both Siena and Florence. Their strategic position overlooking the valuable north–south trade route meant that neither power would leave them in peace. One power would invade the territory, claiming it for themselves, but then the other would arrive with an army and at the end of the fighting take it back, forcing the citizens of Montalcino to alternate their allegiance to survive. There were daring moments of rebellion by the Montalcinesi during those centuries and their defiance meant the Sienese were forced repeatedly to quell the rebellious Ilcinesi, who would not leave the hill.

In 1260 Siena laid siege to Montalcino, which endangered valuable Florentine merchandise being transported up and down the Via Cassia. Provoked, the Florentines raised a fearsome army of 30,000 soldiers, who began to march towards Montalcino because Sienese soldiers were using the mountain settlement as their lookout along the Via Cassia. The battle was eventually fought away from Montalcino, to the north along the Arbia Valley at a place between the hills called Montaperti. Chronicles are sketchy about exactly what Siena expected of Montalcino, but aware that the outcome of this battle was not going to be to their advantage, nor would it restore their freedom, no matter who won, the Montalcinesi decided (prudently, I think) to sit tight and see what happened. Besides, they were very doubtful the Sienese could raise an army to match the Florentines'.

History recounts that the battle was savage, bloody and swift; unexpectedly, the cunning Sienese outwitted the might of Florence – something the Florentines are still smouldering about to this day – and at the end of three days, when the battlefield was strewn with bodies and the exhausted Sienese could barely go on fighting, the panicking Florentine soldiers threw down their arms and surrendered. From what I can gather (because the chronicles become sketchy once more and perhaps the legend has strengthened over the centuries), it seems that it was just about then that the Montalcinesi reached the battleground. To the battle-weary Sienese, the becca morti – those that came to pick over the bones of the dead – had arrived.

Exultant at victory, the Sienese were mercilessly vengeful towards the recalcitrant Montalcinesi and immediately ordered the destruction of their glorious fruit orchards. But that was only the beginning. Their army marched into the village and practically ripped it apart stone by stone. They were so angry that they crashed through stone walls, tore down medieval houses, broke apart the workshops of the artisans and destroyed anything and everything of substance or value. They were determined, once and for all, to subdue these defiant, uncontrollable mountain people, calling them *perfidi*, treacherous rabble. They sought to raze the village from the hill.

Some time later, the label 'becca morte' became a sort of badge of honour, proof of authenticity and a claim to be a true Montalcinese. 'Si, si,' citizens will still declare today. 'I am becca morte, my family was here before 1260. We earned the label which we have carried for more than seven hundred years.' And it was not long before the village pasticceria, pastryshop, was baking delicious meringue biscuits called *ossi di morto*, bones of the dead, to commemorate their defiance.

Walking along the outside of the wall to the left of Madonna del Soccorso, I am faced with the undeniable remnants of Sienese violence; protruding from the base of the wall, later rebuilt, are massive blocks of stone, boulders of granite, irregular and mismatched, which are the lower stone blocks the Sienese could *not* tear down. On many a sunny afternoon men and women from the village wander down to sit along the jutting stones as if signifying to the Sienese, in lingering defiance, that they will never abandon their hill. Even the destruction and violence of the angry Sienese could not make the Montalcinesi leave. 'Come from this direction if you dare,' I imagine the stubborn Montalcinesi declaring, 'you Saracens, barbarians, Longobards, Franks, mercenaries, Florentines and Spanish, but you will not breach the walls here.'

Whenever I walk along here I cannot resist peeping through the split in an old wooden door which opens into a room in the wall. Small windowless rooms like this one were inhabited for hundreds of years by the ropemakers of Montalcino. Their names are borne by some of Montalcino's most ancient families who are still here: Zandoli, Casali, and Bovini. I tenderly run my finger through the shallow crosses scratched into the stone blocks beside the door. It was a way of counting the amount of work carried out by the ropemakers, whose artisan skills were well known.

Turning to the north, I am suddenly facing the most stupendous valley in Tuscany; if the day is very clear, I can see the high tower in Siena forty kilometres away. This breathtaking landscape is a vision etched into the minds of lovers of Tuscany the world over, no matter if they were here in autumn when softly rolling hills were broken by golden vineyards and stone farmhouses surrounded by silvery olive groves; or if they saw rows of golden sunflower heads lined up by the thousand and the still-green foliage hiding clusters of purple grapes ready for harvest. But it was not anything like either of those visions when the walls were built, because around 1110 the hills were densely forested with thick oak woods and chestnut groves, the River Arbia was wide and fast, and agriculture, which was to change the hills for ever, had only just begun.

In 1553 the last great siege in the history of Montalcino took place; Spanish invaders tied lanterns between the horns of goats to guide their men through the steep oak woods to reach the walls, hoping the goats would leap from ridge to ridge and lead them up the incline. But even nimble goats could not leap that high, and besides, archers were lined along the walls and the Captain of the People, Andrea Spagni, with his warrior, Panfilo dell Oca, were ready with their swords.

Only one gate, Porta Burelli, opens through the northern wall;

it was a double gate forming a tunnel and I can still see the low doorway halfway through, leading directly into what was once the guardroom. I sometimes catch a glimpse of an elderly signora peeping through the white lace curtains from inside the narrow window above the arch. In my mind she has taken the place of the sentry; the softest movement of the lace as I pass is my only fleeting glimpse into her snug world above the walls.

Often, though, I watch a white Fiat come bouncing up the hill between the vineyards along the dirt track towards Porta Burelli, traversing the ridges, disappearing round a hairpin bend, then reappearing as it climbs ever upward with a trail of white dust settling in its wake. If the driver is perched on the edge of his seat, his chin jutting upward to enable him to see over the steering wheel, and if I am quick enough to peer inside and see his cheerful face before he races past me with the engine whining through the gears, then I offer a smile and wave to Signor Primo Pacenti, who grows a superb Brunello down in the valley. He told me there were vineyards outside this northern gateway many hundreds of years ago, but it was not today's famous Brunello di Montalcino, more likely the well-documented Moscadello.

With Primo inside, it is now safe for me to venture on, under the arch of Porta Burelli and down the dusty road outside the wall. Looking to the left, the terrain rises almost vertically; at this time of year, the hillside is covered in a mass of foliage from the chestnut trees. The branches are thick with furry balls of chestnut casings which, as the weeks pass, will split open and spill their glossy contents. But having ventured this far, a couple of hundred paces down the white-ribbon road bring me to one of the most enchanting places I have found in Montalcino. I walk down here often, even though I know the walk back up is steep and I need to stay alert, because Primo never stays inside the walls too long and the white Fiat could come hurtling through the gate at any moment. But in this direction, because he is coming down the steep hill, Primo sits well above the steering wheel and usually sees me first, waving and tooting the horn as he hurtles downward to his vineyard.

The abandoned Church of Santa Maria delle Grazie, topped with a delicate bell-tower, sitting alone, hanging over the edge of the cliff outside the walls, is my reward. I cannot get anywhere near the doors because a jungle of rampant blackberry and wretched ivy, long since completely beyond control, blocks my way. From the road I peep through a half-circle window and stare at the crumbling altar, tumbled columns, upturned pews and traces of faded, cracked frescoes on the walls. Fifteen years ago, the grassy square beside the church was a popular weekend gathering point where people would come and listen to the village band; sadly, within a few short years, the roof began to collapse, there was apparently no money for repairs and quite probably the interior was stripped of any decoration. So today Santa Maria delle Grazie is a lonely place, but one full of enchantment for those inclined to see beyond the desolation in a silent grove beneath the chestnuts. I have heard a rumour more than once that the Comune of Montalcino would willingly give Santa Maria delle Grazie to anyone who could find the money for restoration. So far as I know, there have been no takers, and it continues to disintegrate.

Would-be invaders, I am sure, found the final section of the wall along the narrow southern flank the hardest of all to penetrate. Porta Cerbaia, the main gate into the village, is perched on the edge of this steep valley, making any stealthy approach impossible. At the gate, my view is obstructed by the slopes of the highest mountain in southern Tuscany, Mount Amiata; if the mountain was not there I would be able to see down the valley almost to Rome. Invading armies were forced to circle Mount Amiata and funnel up the valley to reach Montalcino, which in 1553 was exactly what the Spanish army did, under the command of Viceroy Don Garzia di Toledo. He was seeking to carry out a vow made by one of his Captains who, a year before, had carved a cross into a stone block in the fortress tower and sworn an oath that he would return to destroy this mountain citadel.

Marching with a mighty army to lay siege to Montalcino, Don Garzia sent an advance party, which included the vengeful Captain, to ride close and scout the way. The party got very close but met with an unexpected encounter at the springs below the gate: waiting for them were Andrea Spagni and his men. The Captain lost his head, thanks to a mighty blow from the warrior Panfilo dell Oca. Facing Porta Cerbaia from the valley, I visualise the horrific welcome Don Garzia must have received, because long picks were apparently hammered into the stones above the gateway arch, and mounted on these were the blood-drenched heads of the Spanish knights cavalieri, including the severed head of the vengeful Captain.

A section of low wall alongside the gate is a popular gathering point and, inevitably when sitting here, I am accompanied by men in dark suits; they have come to watch and gossip, taking the place of archers and soldiers who manned the battlement above, watching who was approaching Montalcino. My elderly companions turn their heads in unison and stare intently at strangers coming through the walls. Studying Porta Cerbaia, my eyes rest on the façade facing the valley, then focus on a dilapidated stone crest. Once this crest would have been overhung by a pointed crown and must have held six round smooth balls, but I notice only one is left; perhaps the other five have simply fallen from it over time. A stone inscription below the crest is obliterated. Again, perhaps it was the elements, but it is worth speculating, as

I do, that the proclamation was one the Montalcinesi would rather not remember. My elderly companions along the wall have told me they do not recall what the inscription said, but they do know that the crest, as well as several others in the village, was attached in 1559, immediately after the Medici of Florence took away their liberty.

When I had worked out the walking route round the inside and outside of the walls to the east, west, north and south, considering the history and relishing the glorious valleys each time, it usually took me three or four hours to complete, but it left me with some puzzling questions unanswered. For instance, where did these Montalcinesi come from? Why did they settle here? How did they get their name? And most puzzling of all, why, in the face of all those hardships, did they refuse to leave?

Turning to the historians once more, it seems that towards the middle of the 700s the crown of the hill on which Montalcino sits was covered in a dense canopy of holm oaks. Barbarians were plundering the lower land towards the sea and, with Saracens attacking coastal villages, frightened peasants from hamlets and primitive settlements between what is now Montalcino and the coast were desperate to seek somewhere safer to live; escaping inland, they found a safe haven on top of this hill under the holm oaks. The ancient name for this hill, derived from Latin and probably used by the Romans, was Mons Ilcinus, and it was not long before the peasants were being referred to as ilcinus, oak tree people, dwelling on Mons Ilcinus, Oak Tree Mountain. A born and bred Montalcinese is often referred to as Ilcinese, an oak tree person, meaning their family and their family's family go back through the centuries as dwellers on the hill of Mons Ilcinus. The most puzzling question of all – why did they refuse to leave? – took a long time to answer. It was really only answerable by uncovering the history and by the life I discovered still unfolding inside the walls.

Merchant traders still come; I watch them leave with trucks loaded with the famous wines of Montalcino, cases of honey and olive oil. Pilgrims, too, continue to find solace in the churches and nearby abbeys. But the powerful soldiers of Florence, the besieging armies of Spain, even the destructive republican Sienese, have finally left the Ilcinesi in peace on their hill, under the holm oaks. The latest wave of travellers up and down the ancient Via Cassia, the tourists, find their way to Montalcino, particularly those who know about the splendid wines. But the curious also come; those that seek, like me, to find out what goes on inside the safety of the walls.

CHAPTER TWO

Twenty Arrows in Half an Hour

This is the day of the annual Sagra del Tordo. The Festival of the Thrush is always held late in autumn, the very last weekend of October. Centuries ago, every autumn, the hunters of Montalcino would go down to the woods with nets to trap thousands of tiny thrush that paused in the woods on their migratory path. After they had presented their catch to The Lady of the Fortress, she

17

would command the hunters to light iron braziers in the fortress keep and the tiny thrush would be roasted over burning embers. With the aroma of woodsmoke wafting around the village, feasting lasted well past dusk. As darkness fell over the mountain, the sentries guarding the fortress would light oil-soaked straw torches and, holding them high, parade around the bastions while the torches flared above their heads casting mysterious shadows which suddenly opened, revealing the citizens below feasting on the delicious little birds. From the surrounding valleys it must have been a magnificent sight. High above the hamlets and farms the fortress of Montalcino was aglow, the flaming torches flickered and crackled as they burned, picking up the rising smoke from the braziers and sending it swirling into the night sky.

Nobody nets the little birds now, but the annual festival is a celebration of thanks for the bountiful supply of food gathered in the woods – not only the thrush which the hunter could trap with his nets, but the wild hare or pheasant his bow and arrow could kill, which were then smoked, dried and hung in the cantina to last through the coming bitter winter. Abundant mushrooms sprang up between the trees, along with autumn chestnuts and berries ready for harvest.

Archery has been part of village life in Montalcino since 1110, and for as long as anyone can remember, being Montalcinese means you understand the importance, the vital significance, of the village archers. In 1361 a retinue of archers took residence in the newly constructed pentagonal fortress, built by the Sienese, which guarded not only Montalcino but also the important trade route south to Rome and north to Florence.

From the bastions the archers kept a close watch on who was passing through the valley where the ancient Via Cassia ran, and it was the hunters with their primitive bows and arrows who went outside the walls into the dangerous woods in autumn to kill wild boar, hoping to return with fresh meat. Sometimes invaders were close; the hunters risked their lives to kill the boar, but if they were successful the catch could be shared amongst the families, smoked and eaten sparingly during times of siege. It could save the lives of their families inside the walls.

Fifty years ago, following centuries of tradition known to everybody, the heritage of defending their territory and hunting for their very survival enabled the quartieri, the four neighbour-hoods of Montalcino, to revive the fourteenth-century festival which displays the ancient skills of the Montalcinesi in the form of an archery tournament. The four quartieri, named Pianello, Travaglio, Borghetto and Ruga, combine the archery tournament with the Sagra del Tordo. The tournament, which takes place today, will reveal the most accurate, finest archers in Montalcino, and will bring glory and honour to their quartiere.

Having lived in Montalcino only a few months when we witnessed our first Sagra del Tordo, Luigi and I were enthralled with the pageantry, the excitement, and the passion of tournament day. We eagerly read the signs posted in the piazza, watched preparations for the archery competition as the range was measured and marked in ever-increasing distances, and even laughed delightedly when we saw a three-wheeler Ape, that practical little motorised work vehicle which has an open tray at the back, race perilously up and down the ramparts in front of the fortress loaded down with timber stands and tables, tents and iron grilles. We thought, as would most visitors who stumbled into Montalcino on the day of the Sagra, that we were fortunate to be able to participate in the fun and celebration. Now I realise how unaware we really were . . . but several years passed before I was fully able to understand what takes place on the day of the Sagra.

It is something not easily distinguishable to a visitor who is captivated, as we were, by the colourful flags, exquisite medieval costumes, stirring drums and heraldic silver trumpets. An overwhelming feeling of emotion and happiness camouflages what is *really* taking place.

Only after I had witnessed several Sagre did I begin to see something far richer, deeper and more meaningful than mere happiness, which I had unwittingly compared to that of a victorious team in any sport, in the eyes and on the faces of village people on tournament day. There was something going on here which was foreign to me, outside my experience – something which, as a straniera, a stranger, I could not penetrate. My curiosity to find it led along a slowly unwinding path to comprehension: it took me many years to unravel the depth of feeling, the passionate emotion for Sagra del Tordo, and eventually to learn what being Montalcinese is all about.

Since early morning the sound of beating drums has drifted across the village as excited quartieri members gather behind closed doors to prepare for the festival pageant before the tournament. At Pianello's headquarters, behind the church of San Pietro, freshly pressed brocade and velvet fourteenth-century costumes trimmed with gold embroidery lie along benches and over the backs of chairs. Michele, Carlo, Cecilia, Maria-Teresa, Francesco and a dozen other youngsters delve into wicker baskets and wooden chests, lifting out coats of chainmail, breastplates, swords and spearheads, locating pointed steel helmets for the Captains and squat round ones for the serfs. Hunting nets are untangled and lie across the floor so the hunters can easily sling them over a shoulder. With just the outer edges being held, the nets will drape along the ground when they parade to the fortress.

'Francesco, here are your gloves,' yells Gabriele, and thick wads of leather that will reach up to his elbows are tossed across the room. From the jewel case come pretty lockets, earrings and a gleaming ruby on a gold chain which will hang from a golden crown and lie gently on the forehead of Cecilia, this year's Lady of Pianello. Outside, the banditore, village crier, rides through the village on horseback looking splendid in his olive-green cape trimmed with fur, which floats out and hangs down the sides of his chestnut. The clatter of the horse's hooves echoing from the stone cobbles magnifies as he passes the vaulted loggia below the ancient village hall, Palazzo Comunale, in Piazza del Popolo where, unwinding a gilded scroll, he reads the proclamation to the waiting crowd:

'*The citizens of the four quartieri of Montalcino are summonsed to each make an autumn offering to The Lady of the Fortress, to meet on the campo at the sound of the trumpets, bringing with you your most accurate and trusted archers . . . there they must display their skills and we will know who has the bravest archers of Montalcino.*'

Alessio, whose job it is to co-ordinate the pageant, bustles around the quarters trying to hurry people into their costumes, anxious to make sure everyone reaches the starting point on time. It is an exasperating job because, inevitably, a button or two is missing or someone's boots have disappeared and, because the medieval costumes are heavy, nobody wants to get dressed too early. A coat of chainmail, thick gloves, a heavy pointed steel helmet and a long spear are not things you can sit down in!

'It's already two o'clock,' he scolds angrily at Ruga head-quarters. 'It's too late to argue about who is wearing what. Assunto, you were knave last year – if the waistcoat fits, let Gianni wear it. Just make sure you are on time, because Ruga is leading the parade – and if you are late the whole thing will be a disaster.'

In less than an hour more than 100 people in an assortment of medieval costumes, soldiers in full armour, hunters with nets, archers with bows and arrows, Lords with their Ladies, courtesans holding delicate cushions, young pages and several rows of drummers and trumpeters will be assembled. Alessio, already hot in his green velvet pantaloons and doublet, clutching sheafs of scribbled notes, dreads what will happen if things go even slightly wrong.

The atmosphere is tense; a tangible air of expectancy and excitement hangs over the four quarters. Cascading down from the highest window of Palazzo Comunale, is a crimson banner proudly displaying the antique crest of Montalcino. Soon two trumpeters will appear at the window facing over the triangular piazza, silver trumpets will be thrust out and, raising them to the sky, they will call for the pageant to begin. Many stomachs begin to flutter at the thought of the archery tournament this afternoon, but there is still the parade to get through and work to be done before the tournament begins. Inside the courtyard the feasting has been going on since early morning; smoke from open braziers is wafting into the sky, carrying the aroma of wild boar and grilling polenta. Soon though, when they hear the trumpets, the food stands will quieten as people begin to take up positions by the roadways to await the colourful procession. Shutters along the roads are already open wide, silver heads poke out and the old patiently sit by their windows to wait, just as they do every year.

At the archery range, everything is ready. Four striped medieval tents are lined up along the grass, each in the identifying colours of a quartiere, and behind them, strung along the fortress wall, fly a dozen quartieri flags. From every tower of the fortress an array of banners and flags wave in the breeze, with the Standard of Montalcino fluttering proudly above them all. The archery range, below the waving flags, is silent and empty. Firing distances have been carefully marked with pegs and ropes, and the four targets at the end of the shooting range, each in the shape of a wild boar, are turned to the side, awaiting the arrival of eight archers. Two of them will bring glory and honour to their quartiere, earning a coveted place in the long history of village archery.

On the field, Carlo and Pierluigi, two archers from the quartiere of Travaglio, explode into a passionate embrace. Arms clasp one another, each archer's bow is pressed tightly into the other's back, they jump and sway until finally they fall to the grass, rolling from side to side, throwing their arms up and thrusting their bows to the sky, disbelieving yet rejoicing in their incredible victory. They scream at each other just one word, over and over: 'Travaglio! Travaglio!' Their faces twist and contort as if in pain, but it is the painful look of joy absolute, the final expiration of months of pent-up emotion. *'Travaglio ha vinto . . . per Travaglio!'* Travaglio has won . . . only for Travaglio! they scream. The eruption from the grandstand of the same chant, 'Travaglio! Travaglio! Travaglio!' is almost drowned out by the blood-curdling cries of the closest Travaglio members as they begin the race towards their victorious archers. They leap over the wall, grab a Travaglio red and yellow banner on the way and at the same time take hold of each other, linking arms as they run. Within seconds, thirty Travaglio quartieranti have thrown themselves on top of the waiting archers in a writhing muddle of arms and legs. They hug and kiss, grab and shake each other, bury heads in the bodies of the archers; tears of joy run down their faces as they throw their fists into the air over and over again. And all the while, incredulous at their thrilling victory, they roar: 'For Travaglio! For Travaglio!'

Even the noble Lady of Travaglio deserts her red and yellow

striped tent; she hitches up her precious velvet and gold brocade gown to her knees and, holding on tightly to her crimson cape and velvet headpiece, she races like the wind across the field. Her dainty hands become weapons as she throws a clenched fist into the air, does a little skip of joy, then quickly clutches at her skirts which not an hour past she had delicately manoeuvred in the discreet space between herself and her noble Lord when they led the Travaglio procession through the village. No sign of emotion had crossed her face then; she was the medieval princess passing her peasant subjects without so much as a glance. But before she reaches the scene, Carlo and Pierluigi have been lifted bodily from the grass, held aloft by the swarm of Travaglio who begin to chant in unison the victory song of their quartiere:

Si viene da Via Donnoli	We come from Via Donnoli
Si canta sempre forte!	We always sing the loudest!
Chi tocca un Travellino	If you touch a Travellino
Pericolo di morte!	You're in danger of death!

'Carlo!' The Lady of Travaglio shrieks reprovingly, as if to remind him she is here too, and then again, this time with urgency and a little desperation in her voice because she is afraid he cannot hear her. 'Carlo!'

From below, the mob sees her need and, effortlessly lifting her slim frame, they push her bodily into the air so that she is able to throw herself across and kiss the nearest archer. The mass of bodies turn in unison towards the gates, but now there are sixty or more with five or six red and yellow banners thrust into the air, swirling above their heads. It is as if each and every one of them has driven the arrows personally. They head through the gates and make their way chanting and singing towards their quartiere, to Travaglio. First they must confirm to everyone in their own territory that their

24

archers are bravissimi, their archers are supremely accurate and have brought glory and honour to Travaglio. The throng disappears around the walls of the fortress with many arms raised to hold aloft the glorious archers, others in a victory salute, and all the time they chant: 'For Travaglio! For Travaglio!'

Vasco, whom I sometimes meet at Porta Gattoli when he visits his farm outside the walls, is Travaglio and, although almost seventy-nine, his passion for a Travaglio win has not dimmed. Along with his energetic son Roberto, who is among those holding the archers aloft, he is in the crowd pressing down towards the quartiere. His body, small and slightly stooped, is already draped in the flag, because Vasco always carries the Travaglio banner, which has a yellow background with a horizontal red bar across the middle and three yellow stars running along the red centre. This is the motif I have seen throughout Travaglio territory on small enamel plaques attached to the walls below each iron ring from which their festival flags fly, and a larger version in the form of an iron crest hangs above the wooden doors of the sede, their headquarters.

'Hey, ragazzi,' Vasco calls like a seventeen-year-old, grabbing the corners of the flag and letting it fly out behind him like a cape. 'Vieni, andiamo. Come on, Let's go.' He is anxious to start the victory march through the village. This procession, returning to their territory, is the first step in a series of celebrations which, starting right now, will last many weeks. Vasco's thin lined face has fallen into deep natural crevices, but it positively glows today, his wide smile only outshone by the pride I can see in his stony grey eyes. The youngsters push him to the front and, carrying the banner, he leads them, on their twelfth victory, proudly home. With their archers held aloft, this joyful walk back to their sede, where they will ring the victory bells, wipes out in an instant all the years of pain when they returned in solemn silence. It only takes one victory for all the anguish, all the disappointment of the times they did not win, to be suddenly gone.

Travaglio has won. Two archers, each with twenty arrows in half an hour, is all it took.

Massimo returns the five arrows to the leather sheath, turns and walks back across the field. His powerful shoulders look too broad for a man of his height; his upper arm muscles are firm and taut, bulging biceps almost bursting through the sleeves of his blue and white medieval costume. And he walks with confidence, each stride an emphatic statement more for himself than anyone else that he has, again this year, done his best for Pianello. Or has he?

'Massimo, you are a great archer, you drove the arrows straight and true,' comforts his Captain, Francesco. 'Five perfect arrows, then another five, and yet again, fifteen arrows and every one driven with an arm like steel into the middle of the target.'

'Yes, yes, I know,' answers Massimo quietly, but his thoughts are elsewhere because the fickle wind had taken one away. 'My eye never moved, Francesco. I watched the arrow fly through the air for forty metres, as straight and true as all the others, but the second or two that it took to cover the distance was an eternity in slow motion.' He had felt his heart sink as he saw it swing to one side; it swayed in the breeze, and then it was gone. Only four of his last five arrows found their target in the boar. He raises his arm and his hand makes an arc through the air as his eye follows the imaginary arrow down the field. His head tilts to one side as if to get a better look, the fingers of his hand making a short wavy diversion mimicking the flight, and then his hand falls to his side. He pulls his head up sharply. There is another arrow! Is that Carlo's arrow flying beside his own? Did he allow Carlo's arrow to enter his line of vision?

'Francesco,' he asks suddenly, 'did you see where Carlo's last arrow went?'

'Si, it followed the others; most went right into the heart of the boar. He shot well, Massimo, twenty arrows into the target.'

After a moment Massimo declares, resignedly: 'I saw his arrow, Francesco,' and both of them know that means he allowed Carlo's arrow to distract him; he had not closed everything out. The replay is like a silent film for Massimo, although thousands of people were screaming and calling his name, the fanatical crowd waving banners and shouting, releasing their own tension, their own desires, their own emotion.

Francesco, Capitano del Arcieri, trying to think what else to say to Massimo, wonders if he did his job properly, or has he let Massimo down? His is the responsibility to care for the Pianello archers during the shoot, which means he has to know when to console, when to threaten, when to flatter, when to pull an archer up with an admonishment. Most of all he has to be at one with the archers, carrying himself to their level and enclosing them in a world where nothing else exists but the bows and arrows and the target. 'Vieni,' says Francesco gently, quickening his step, 'Gabriele is waiting, we must get off the campo.'

As they walk, Massimo considers his training. He had begun the previous February and trained almost continuously through-out the year except for the days he spent with his wife Ofelia and daughter Chiara. He remembers the time his father telephoned and sought his help to stack a load of firewood in the cantina, because he should have practised that day, but hadn't; nor the day his precious Chiara asked him to come and watch her at her dancing lesson; and then there was Ofelia's birthday and the romantic dinner they had shared. 'I don't want archery to become an obligation,' he remarks absently to Francesco, who looks up, puzzled, but remains silent as Massimo continues: 'There were

27

only a few days when I didn't go to the practice range. How big a sacrifice should I have made for Pianello?'

Massimo's shooting partner, Gabriele, just twenty and born the year Massimo started shooting, feels intensely disappointed. He shot his arrows well; five perfect arrows, then four, another five driven straight and, in spite of all the pressure and tension and his own inexperience, his final five drove right into the boar. He is pleased to have made it to the end of four rounds but he knows it is not quite perfect enough. They are second again and soon Dottore Luciano, their trainer, will hear the victory bells ringing from Travaglio and he will know they did not win. Gabriele wanted desperately to win for Pianello, just to see the blue and white banners flying proudly in the village, to be able to chant the Pianello victory song to the rhythm of the drummers and to march or even to be carried in triumph on the shoulders of his friends along the narrow cobbled roads through Pianello. He had imagined this sweet victory in his mind a hundred times in the final weeks leading up to the tournament, but already, his youthfulness overcoming the wayward arrow, Gabriele begins to think of next year. Perhaps next year they can win for Pianello.

Reaching out to him, Massimo embraces Gabriele, congratulating him on an excellent shoot. The long curved bows hang at their sides as, dressed in the blue and white costumes of the Pianello archery team, they follow their Captain from the field. It is an unwritten law – immediately the shoot is finished the campo must be left to the victors, although the three are barely aware of the tumultuous celebrations taking place just a few metres behind them. 'Francesco,' says Massimo softly, despair in his voice, 'I don't know if I can make the sacrifice again.' Once more Francesco chooses not to reply, but leaves Massimo to his melancholy thoughts. Will he shoot next year for Pianello? Can he bring the longed-for victory? It is so long since Pianello won the tournament, but in the end it all comes down to twenty arrows in half an hour.

Within the ring of defensive walls, in the 1300s, Montalcino was divided into terzieri, thirds, or neighbourhoods, and way back then the political and economic life of the citizens was profoundly influenced by the self-imposed laws of the terzieri. Originally there were three terzieri but with the economic development of the village a fourth neighbourhood was divided off, and from that time on they became quartieri, or quarters. Still today, with ancient rituals and rules, each neighbourhood observes a creed decided upon in democratic fashion by the elders of their quarter. The structure of the quarters differs one from the other, although not significantly. For example, Borghetto does not have a President but a Governor, because their philosophy, their creed, is perhaps a little closer to the way a contrada is run in Siena; besides, the Sienese Church of Montalcino is in their territory.

Each quarter elects leaders every three years, plus those who will shoulder certain responsibilities to guide and help the younger members during the year, and of course those who will accompany the archers to the practice range outside the walls week after week. And even today, as it was in the 1300s, the quarters have a role to play in the administration of the village. A representative from each quarter is eligible to attend Comune meetings with the Mayor and Councillors, listening to and commenting on proposals and reporting back to members. The quarters are all self-funding and operate only on voluntary labour from their members, who pay a small annual subscription. However, if a quarter has a large debt to pay, they might borrow from quartieranti, members, and repay it at a later date. There is no interest, no profit, no contract; it is done with faith, and the members will do it to help their quarter.

The citizens of Montalcino live in a tightly-knit community, with those who uphold the values and traditions of their quartiere doing so with absolute and unquestioning loyalty. Although village friendships cross quartieri boundaries, at tournament time the elders and youngsters from each quarter gather and, wearing their colours, display their quartiere loyalty even to their closest friends who may belong to opposing quarters. Husbands and wives born in opposing quartieri will not change quarter even on marriage; they remain divided by their loyalty, wearing opposing colours at the tournaments to demonstrate the extent of their unwavering commitment.

The boundaries of the victorious quarter, Travaglio, begin at Porta Cerbaia and cut along the eastern side of Via Saloni, the main road into Montalcino. This also leads directly to Piazza del Popolo, the heart of the village, but before the road reaches the piazza it has changed its name and become Via Matteotti. The piazza is neutral territory in which everybody has equal rights. Along the eastern side of the piazza is a loggia – a gallery. It is closed in on three sides and roofed over, but graceful columns along the front separate six arches which are open to the piazza. Travaglio's territory finishes right where the arches begin. The loggia is also called the cappellone, and at one time it did have a chapel within the arches, as its name suggests. If you were to draw a straight line towards the Orcia Valley from the arches of the loggia, letting your line fall down the hillside until you reach the encircling stone wall of Montalcino, you would define the border through the hillside which separates Travaglio from its neighbouring quarter, Pianello. At the end of their territory, jutting over the edge of a steep valley, Travaglio have a piazzetta, a small grassed area; already Vasco and a hundred others have swarmed to this little square, where, on a low wall, the two victorious archers Carlo and Pierluigi stand, one each side of Vasco, waving

Travaglio banners. From the piazzetta they can look straight up at the clutch of stone houses cascading down the hill; even from here they can see the towers of the fortress along with the village bell-tower and several of the church towers as well. Their banners fly airily, and rowdy voices, excited and jubilant, easily carry up to the village as their victory song echoes around the valley.

Each of the main arteries in the quartieri is named after illustrious and brave men of history and all of them were Montalcinesi. The main roadway through Travaglio is Via Donnoli, named after Donnolo Donnoli, who was a Franciscan missionary made a saint in 1227 after his death on the mission field in Morocco. Within Travaglio's borders lies a gate through the walls called Porta Gattoli. Travaglio also shares the main gateway into the village, Porta Cerbaia, with its south-western neighbour, Borghetto.

Pianello territory begins immediately on the other side of the arches under the cappellone loggia, but when the road leaves the piazza from the narrow end it has become Via Mazzini, continuing to the northern end of the village and finishing at the neutral territory of the office of the Mayor and the Comune. Pianello's white and blue colours are signified with a diagonal bar and four blue diamonds on a white background and, again, I have seen this insignia on enamel plaques hanging from the walls of the houses within Pianello territory and in front of their head-quarters. Massimo Bovini, the Pianello archer, was born in Via Moglio in the heart of Pianello, and his parents and grandparents were born there too. In fact the first of his family known to be born in Montalcino was Faustina in 1540, the daughter of Sano Bovini, although where Sano came from Massimo does not know; back then, only the churches kept records and a disastrous fire in Montalcino in the mid-1400s destroyed them. The archives are gone, but there is no reason not to believe there were many

31

generations of Bovini born in Montalcino prior to Faustina. Massimo's wife Ofelia can trace her family even further back; the first recorded birth was in 1460, so her ancestors in Montalcino go back at least a hundred years before the Florentines and Spanish came and more than likely many centuries earlier. The latest generation of Bovini, a daughter, Chiara, was born to Massimo and Ofelia in 1989. Of course, Chiara was born right here in Montalcino.

Pianello is the smallest quarter; a handful of narrow lanes wind their way around a huddle of stone houses and I think perhaps it is a little less obviously affluent than some of the other quarters. Via Moglio was named after Fra Giovanni Moglio, another illustrious Montalcinese who followed the Protestant reforms of the Church; but they called him a heretic and he died in Rome in the Campo dei Fiori, where he was burned at the stake in 1553, the same year the Spanish laid siege to Montalcino. Within the borders of Pianello are the eleventh-century Church of San Pietro, the village hospital and Church of San Francesco, two village schools, and two more gates through the walls, Porta Burelli and Porta Castellana.

Travaglio and Pianello share the steeply sloping eastern hillside of Montalcino and the territory of both quarters falls away from Piazza del Popolo towards the Orcia Valley. Ruga and Borghetto share the upper reaches of the village; their territory runs along the western ridge with its back to the Ombrone Valley.

The red and white colours of Borghetto, six white flames on a red background in the form of small enamel shields, signify their territory, which begins at the main gate, Porta Cerbaia, and runs along Via Saloni, but on the opposite side of the roadway from Travaglio. Borghetto headquarters is in Via Panfilo dell Oca, a narrow cobbled roadway descending from the fortress; brave Panfilo was a man of arms, a warrior, who defended and protected the Montalcinesi during the great Siege of 1553. On the western side of Piazza del Popolo, the main piazza, is a steep stairway which forms an arched passageway between the houses, and this marks the boundary limit for Borghetto. Climbing to the top of the stairway you reach Piazza Sant' Agostino, then, cutting a straight line across two smaller roadways, you arrive at a point in the walls about halfway between two thirteenth-century guard towers, the dividing line between Borghetto and Ruga. Borghetto, it seems to me, has a higher proportion of shopkeepers and business people living in its territory. Perhaps it was always so. Also within Borghetto territory is the Church of Sant' Agostino, the Church of Sant' Egidio (known as the Sienese Church), the Church of Santa Croce which is next to their headquarters, the fortress of Montalcino, and the gate called Porta Cassero. Borghetto shares Porta Cerbaia with Travaglio on its south-eastern boundary.

Next door to Borghetto is the fourth quartiere, Ruga, whose boundary runs along the opposite side of Via Mazzini to that of Pianello and similarly finishes when it reaches the office of the Mayor and the Comune. The steep steps which rise from Piazza del Popolo to Sant' Agostino really belong to Ruga, and on these stone steps, which vary haphazardly in height and depth, Ruga youngsters frequently crouch when they chant their victory song towards opposing quartieri in the piazza. The steps lead to their sede alongside the Church of Sant' Agostino where you will find the Ruga crest; yellow transversal diamonds on a blue background.

Via Spagni in Ruga is named after another great warrior who was also Capitano del Popolo, a leader of the people. With Panfilo dell Oca by his side, Andrea Spagni brought Montalcino through the most terrible siege in its history when they held the Spanish outside the walls for eighty days. Marked by Ruga's colours on enamel shields, within its territory lies the Cathedral, the Church of San Salvatore, and the strange architectural clutter of the little Church of Sant' Antonio. The Church of Madonna del Soccorso has a closed-in gateway, Porta Corniolo, built into its rear wall and is the only ancient gate of Montalcino through which you now cannot pass.

As seems to have been common in medieval village architecture, the defensive and civil seats of power are placed at opposite ends of the village; the fortress is on the highest point in Borghetto at the southern end, and one has to walk the length of the village to reach the Comune, the seat of civil power, which leans over the cliff along the northern walls.

The tournament is over. I watch the Pianello, Ruga and Borghetto archery teams move despondently away from the field, and follow behind them as they file through the arch of Porta Cassero alongside the fortress, heading towards their respective quartieri to take off their medieval costumes and put away the bows. The crowd is dispersing, but I see the loyal few from each quarter come forward to shake the hands of their archers, embracing their friends, telling them they are proud of their skills. They are the ones who thank them for their weeks and months of practice and who understand the personal sacrifice each has made for his quartiere. Most of the crowd feel only their own loss and hurt, the intense disappointment. They only want to console themselves. They turn their faces to the side.

'Francesco, what is the value of a great archer?' questions Massimo. 'Is he worth nothing unless he has an ounce of luck on the day and takes the victory?' The weeks leading up to the tournament have been filled with tension, secret meetings and special practice shoots; strategy has been talked through over and over again. Early tomorrow morning, before anyone is up and about, Pianello, Ruga and Borghetto will quietly take down their colourful window banners and festival flags. Only the red and yellow victory flags and banners of Travaglio will fly in the breeze for many weeks, and only Travaglio will be able to leave their flag under the six-arch loggia, the cappellone in the piazza, which will act as a daily reminder of their victory.

Travaglio has won. They did it with two archers, each with twenty straight arrows in half an hour.

CHAPTER THREE

Vanilla Beans and Brodo

As luck would have it, the week we arrived in Montalcino we made friends with a gregarious couple, Maria Pia and Luciano who run a trattoria, Taverna del Grappolo Blu. Maria Pia is a signora not daunted by a seemingly impossible request and she introduced us to Signor Ercole and his wife Lola, from whom we were able to rent – after lengthy negotiations – a tiny apartment which, of no concern at all to us at the time, is in the quartiere Pianello. Signor Ercole was Vice-President of Pianello that year and he wasted no time in introducing these seemingly respectable stranieri to Signora Maurelia, who is President of Pianello and also the wife of the pharmacist, Roberto.

This particular morning, two weeks after the Sagra, the weather has turned towards late autumn and the piazza is suddenly changing appearance because, by mid-November every year, the outdoor seating for Cafe Fiaschetteria disappears overnight. Yesterday I was sipping a warming cappuccino under the weakening rays of the sun, but today all I have found is a line of terracotta plant-holders which were the delineation of the seating arrangements for summer. And some of the shop-owners who, every morning for several months, have been rolling out their beige and white sunshades have surely come stealthily back at midnight and removed the whole shade and its casing from the wall, which is now stored in the cantina where it will be kept dry until next summer. Half-moon terracotta bowls which decorated the walls with blood-red and rose geraniums are now empty; the plants are gone, taken to safety before frost or an icy wind arrives to shrivel and burn them overnight.

Even so, Piazza del Popolo, and by association Cafe Fiaschetteria, is the heart of village life in summer and winter although the glass doors of the cafe which have been cast open all through summer now rattle and crash noisily every time anyone enters or leaves. It means, though, that I can see and feel the very bones of the piazza. The old village hall, Palazzo Comunale, is as dignified and proud-looking as in any Tuscan village. A remarkably thin stone building sitting between two roadways at the wide end of a triangular piazza, the palazzo exudes its own importance yet does not seem to dominate the whole, but rather, blends modestly, harmoniously. The tower which rises on one side houses the bell which chimes the hour and half hour twenty-four hours a day and, because the only change necessary to the palazzo since the thirteenth century, when it was built, was to stabilise the very top of the tower, it represents a perfect example of medieval building; grey stone blocks, more regular in shape at the base, are interspersed with historic family crests.

Business is done on a daily basis in the piazza; you come to make an appointment to see your notaio, notary, or to find Signor Arturo, who knows of every apartment for sale. It is also the place where news and gossip are exchanged. You come daily to meet friends for a caffè, the wine-growers and farmers turn up on Friday mornings to exchange chit-chat and talk about the weather, and it is the focal point of the social passeggiata, that evening ritual of elegantly dressing and strolling around, courteously greeting friends and acquaintances.

To one side of the piazza, along Via Matteotti directly below Palazzo Comunale, lies a sheltered and very beautiful cross-vaulted loggia which, anyone would reasonably consider, would make an ideal meeting-place for the Montalcinesi. For a long time I was perplexed, but I have decided there is a reason why the locals never seem to say: 'I'll meet you in the piazza tomorrow – look for me under the old loggia.' Strangely, the only idlers under this loggia – which is a small portico open on two sides – seem to be visitors on mobile phones or a few young boys kicking a football. Almost hidden in the shadows, at the very deepest point under the loggia, is a lifesize marble statue of a Roman gazing down from a high plinth, wearing a soldier's uniform and with one hand on his hip. The other holds his scroll of office and, with his knee thrust forward, he displays an air of smug satisfaction at his own exemplary appearance. There is no identification on the plinth, not even a date nor the sculptor's name, but it seems to me, because he reminds me of relatively

recent events in the long history of Montalcino – events not held
in great reverence by the Montalcinesi – that he is tucked away
in the furthest shadows of the loggia because the statue is not of
a Roman soldier but a Florentine: Cosimo I di Medici.

Cosimo seems better forgotten by the Montalcinesi because it
was to him, as Commander of the Florentine army on 4 August
1559, that the iron keys to the gates of Montalcino were handed
over to the dreaded Florentines. Portraying clients as Roman
soldiers was a common thing for sculptors to do to enhance a
powerful family, but the Montalcinesi have never been that
impressed because although Cosimo may have been a skilful
administrator, a great warrior he was not. He had no liking for
weapons nor for fighting battles. Nevertheless, he stands alone,
pushed into the shadows and semi-obscurity. I am sure the
Montalcinesi choose not to meet and socialise beneath this dark
loggia because the statue represents resignation to the loss of their
liberty, rather than any honour to Cosimo.

Opposite Cafe Fiaschetteria is the much larger cappellone
loggia with six arches. Four stone steps take you up under the
cappellone, and the graceful columns which separate the arches
are very important to the life of Montalcino because on the front
of each column is the enamel insignia of each quartiere; with the
Sagra only two weeks ago, the red and yellow flag of Travaglio is
flying from the cappellone, a constant reminder to us all of their
victory. But there are six arches and only four quartieri; the centre
column is for the Standard of the Comune of Montalcino and at
the time of the Sagra, or any especially important event, the black
and white flag of Siena flies alongside that of Montalcino. On the
wall above the arches, the crest of the Montalcinesi appears in
sculpted form: six round hills form a small pyramid and at the top
rises a leafy holm oak, forming a canopy over the hills.

The meeting-place in the piazza is, if you are on a business errand, at the foot of the steps below the cappellone; if you are a youngster waiting for your friends, you sit on the steps under the enamel insignia of your quartiere; if you seek shelter from the elements, you move inside the cappellone. But obviously never under the gloomy Palazzo Comunale loggia with lonely old Cosimo!

The stone houses which take up the remaining space in the piazza are typically medieval, mostly three-storey and mostly with shuttered windows or doors leading on to stone balconies which, in summer, are overflowing with petunias and geraniums. Around the piazza is an assortment of shops which exist in most villages in Tuscany, but of a quality which continually surprises visitors. Here you can buy Fendi and Roccabarocca, select the silkiest underwear, browse among antiques, try on fine Italian shoes, and at the Biancheria Pignattai you can furnish your home with exquisite brocades, gorgeous fringed hand towels, white and cream bedlinen, or delicious bobbles and tassels for woven jacquard cushions. And, of course, there are giornalieri, news-agents, the pharmacy of Roberto and Maurelia and one other, the post office, banks, tabacci for cigarettes and bus tickets; there are several alimentari, grocers, and butchers. There are two more bars, Cacciatore and Mariuccia, close by, and a forno where fresh bread is baked daily and pasta fresca is always available. The piazza and a few metres along each road leading to it provide all we need to live comfortably within the walls.

From inside Cafe Fiaschetteria I watch Maurelia step out of the pharmacy to wait for someone. She has put on her thick woollen coat, a warm scarf, her gloves, and has a smart hat pulled down over her head. A wind has risen from the Ombrone Valley and although the temperature is not as low as it will go over the coming weeks, the gusts swirling out of every opening between the houses, and the wind racing through the piazza, have an icy edge.

A red fire brigade truck is parked under the bell-tower in front of Palazzo Comunale; ladders are tucked neatly in place but the hoses have not been unwound because there is no need for alarm, there is no fire. Instead, the vigili del fuoco, firemen, have just dashed into Fiaschetteria for a shot of black espresso. Every now and again the fire truck is in the piazza, not because of a fire and not necessarily because the firemen have stopped for a 'short black', but usually because someone has let the wind slam their apartment door and they are stranded outside without keys. Trying to get back inside is well nigh impossible, because every house is virtually a fortified mini-tower with windows high up the stone wall. If there is a window at road level then it will have an iron grill to keep you out, and as for other entrances – well, most apartments have one way in but often two locked doors before you reach your threshold. All this fortress-like security is not a crime deterrent but a legacy of defence of the territory, unchanged since the walls went up.

Massimo, the Pianello archer, is one of the village firemen. It is his regular job and Maurelia, seeing the fire truck in the piazza, knows he will be coming out of Cafe Fiaschetteria in just a minute or two. The bar is crammed with people but all Maurelia can see is the bleary glow of lights inside, because the windows have misted over. As well as three firemen who have just walked in, Luigi is here with me, chatting with Luciano and Maria Pia who are drinking a habitual morning caffè before starting work at the trattoria. Vasco's son Roberto is here, taking a break from driving the Comune truck, and Mario, a quiet man whose work includes keeping the village tidy with a team of sweepers, is reading the bar newspaper. Negus, who is behind the bar, has plenty to see to.

Massimo, walking straight over to the bar counter, calls out: 'Mi fai un caffè, Negus? Can you make me a coffee, Negus?' 'È pronto, it's ready,' Negus calls in return.

Negus has rows of tiny cups lined up one after the other to quickly dispense shots of hot black espresso. Just as he gets one order out of the way, the door bursts noisily open and in comes Andrea in his immaculate navy-blue and white-trimmed uniform. His cap is pushed towards the back of his head, his spectacles are propped on the end of his nose and a black leather bag hangs from his shoulder. Andrea is one of the village polizia and he too is in the piazza every day, sometimes with two attractively groomed lady polizia, or sometimes edging through in the police car. There is always plenty of work for Andrea. This morning he still has his pencil behind his ear and a ticket book in his hand; someone has probably driven through Porta Cerbaia without a permit and Andrea will be ready to listen to their pleas, but then pass over a L 130,000 fine if the story does not stack up. But now it is time for his regular morning caffè.

'Un caffè, Negus, per piacere,' calls Andrea above the babble, and Negus responds immediately, 'Si pronto,' because he knows Andrea has to be outside again within seconds. Not for the first time, I glance at my watch: the whole ritual, from the moment Andrea opens the door, to when he puts down his cup and turns, calling out: 'Grazie, ciao a tutti,' is barely twenty seconds.

Negus coerces the coffee-machine every morning, making creamy cappuccini and excessively strong short blacks as the daily habits demand. Always dressed in black with a white open-neck shirt, he generally looks serious, but only because his hands are flying from coffee beans to grinder, from milk jug to cups, and he is concentrating on which are macchiato, espresso, orzo or cappuccino. His real name is Angelo, but I have heard he is called Negus after a King of Ethiopia, although the reasons for his nickname are not clear. Perhaps it is because Italians have an affinity with that part of Africa, being a country colonised by Ancient Rome, or perhaps because Negus has dark skin and when he returns from a holiday in Cuba or Tunisia he is *tutto bronzato*, dark brown all over.

Massimo is leaving; through the foggy window I watch Maurelia cross the piazza to speak to him. Maurelia, as President of Pianello, is making sure Massimo knows the date she has fixed for the next quartiere meeting, because she has some very important business to discuss. Head down, neck pulled into her collar, she finishes her brief conversation, says farewell and turns to walk briskly back into the pharmacy, but before she reaches the door someone is calling out to her across the piazza. 'Maurelia cara, wait a moment!' calls Signora Lola as she whirls into the narrow end of the piazza. 'I need to talk to you.' It is much too cold standing in the piazza, so the two women move inside the pharmacy to chat.

Signora Lola, I am absolutely certain, is unstoppable. Even on this bitter November morning when there is hardly another soul about except those on their way to work, Signora Lola can be counted on to make her way to the butcher, or the alimentari. Her kitchen, it is suspected throughout the village, is more than adequately stocked to last through any reasonable siege; from the wooden beams of her cantina hang salami and prosciutto, bunches of onions, and plaits of garlic. There are sacked-up beans and dried funghi ready for winter soups, and chestnuts and walnuts sit in wooden boxes stacked around the stone floor; there is certainly more than enough to last through the coming winter. But Signora Lola is admirably typical of the Montalcinesi's preoccupation with food. Not just the choosing, negotiating, purchasing, preparing and, naturally, the consumption, but also the *freshness*. Italians, and most certainly the Montalcinesi, consider one's ben essere, well being, is closely linked with how you conduct such affairs, and Signora Lola – although she may deny it emphatically – is a devoted disciple.

Montalcino's cucina povera, poor kitchen, was born after the walls went up, somewhere around the twelfth century, and is a way of cooking brought about by the defensive outlook of the village, hardships of the land, seasonal produce which was only available if you grew it yourself, and the creativity of the Montalcinesi to turn a few simple ingredients into delicious, flavoursome meals. The ingredients, repeated endlessly, appear in recipes which have changed little through the centuries with the exception of tomatoes, which did not make their appearance in Italy until Christopher Columbus discovered America and ships began bringing strange produce from the New World.

In fact, to reproduce the cucina povera of Montalcino your basic ingredients are: rosemary, basil, parsley, sage, garlic, capers, celery, carrots, onions, fennel, artichokes, melanzane (aubergines or eggplants) and, a little later, the tomato. Add to these extra virgin olive oil, unsalted Tuscan bread, seasonal mushrooms, honey, chestnuts, plus the recent addition of pine nuts and anchovies, and you have all you will ever need to be able to cook in the way of the Montalcinesi. Of course, you must remember the wine. Brunello di Montalcino may have saved the fortunes of the village in our century but a modest glass of rosso, a younger fine red wine, now, as in the past, inevitably accompanies each meal.

The Montalcinesi endlessly discuss food and it is not considered necessary to stray too far from the cucina povera. It has become a preferred way of eating. It may be perfectly acceptable to travel a handful of kilometres to Pienza to buy fresh pecorino sheep-milk cheese, they reason, or to Castelnuovo del Abate to find aromatic salami hanging in the dark recess of a cantina, but there is no logical reason to travel even as far as Siena, 40 kilometres, where there are several modern and wide-ranging supermarkets. And nobody, I very quickly found out, would be so disloyal as to purchase salami or olive oil from nearby

Montepulciano. Pienza and Castelnuovo del Abate are different, they are local territory and, besides, these villages and their citizens remained loyal with Montalcino in the wars against Siena and Florence that raged in the Middle Ages; but not Montepulciano. Since ancient times and still today, Montepulciano aligns itself with Florence.

The two villages have glowered at each other from their mountain eyries across the Via Cassia for centuries and there will be no joy in inviting a Montalcinese to come with you to a trattoria in Montepulciano. A blank look or incredulous stare will be your answer. Aside from your disloyalty, not only could Montepulcianesi not possibly know what to eat or how to prepare it, but Vino Nobile di Montepulciano may be a wine, yes, and certainly an excellent wine, but it is *not* Brunello! The citizens maintain a respectable distance with less than enthusiastic acknowledgement of each other's respective wines and gastronomy.

The poor kitchen of Montalcino might once have consisted of what could be scraped together from the vegetable gardens within the walls, or gathered in the woods by the hunters, but today's cucina povera is anything but poor, although it is still based on simplicity. Lola's remarkable dedication to fastidious procurement of food could perhaps be explained by the fact that she has served a long apprenticeship, having practically never cooked a meal for her husband until she had been married for fifty years. She is now a lady approaching eighty and, incredible as it seems, Ercole's mother, who lived with them after their first year of married life, controlled the kitchen and did all the cooking until she died at ninety, when Lola was seventy-two. Lola, it seems, was not considered experienced enough to be in charge of the kitchen. But I suspect she is fast making up ground.

The piazza outside Cafe Fiaschetteria is all but deserted because on days like this everybody stays inside as long as possible;

except Lola. Just as Luigi and I step out of the cafe, Lola, on the opposite side of the piazza, walks out of the pharmacy. She sees us and once again calls across the piazza: 'Luigi, Luigi, Signora, vieni qui, I need to talk to you.' Although some locals have begun to call Luigi by his Christian name, it is taking some time to develop the intimacy of anyone offering to call me by my first name. Often I am called La Signora Bionda because of my fair hair, but I have yet to reach first-name status with Lola. It is all a matter of time . . . after all, it has only been a few years. Hearing Lola calling us, Luigi and I hurry straight across the windy piazza and move up the four steps into what scant shelter is offered under the cappellone loggia.

'Buongiorno, Signora.' I greet Lola warmly with a polite handshake, but not too firm as this is not an introduction; it is just a gentle touch to remind us both of our lovely friendship. We exchange greetings and Luigi asks after Ercole who, she predictably explains, is down in the cantina getting things ready for winter. She is just on her way to the butcher, she says, but before that she called in to speak with Maurelia and to see if Roberto, the pharmacist, had brodo, the stock cubes, she needs. 'And anyway,' she adds, 'I had to buy another vanilla bean.'

She is carrying two small parcels wrapped in black and white paper which has a picture of workers concocting medieval herbal medicines with a pestle and mortar and some kind of weird turn-screw. It is the same paper in which Roberto carefully wraps every prescription. I cannot help a little smile, for only in Italy does one go to the pharmacy to buy the very best quality stock cubes – but why? What is in the stock cubes you buy from the pharmacy that is not in the cubes of brodo which come in packets at the grocers? I dare not display my naivety to Lola. As for the vanilla bean – well, that is something totally mystifying.

I was in the pharmacy once when a signora came to buy a

vanilla bean. Yes, Roberto confirmed he did have some, but could she wait a moment? The signora was quite prepared to wait while Roberto went to the rear of the pharmacy, unlocked a door, opened deep drawers and finally emerged carrying a tall glass container with a tight lid. Unscrewing the lid, he withdrew and cautiously unwrapped a foil package which contained three vanilla beans, each about as long as his hand. 'These beans are absolutely first quality,' he told the signora. 'They come from a very rare plant in the jungle in Africa.' The signora was delighted, asked if she might have two and, a little begrudgingly because it would leave him with only one, he let her choose two, carefully wrapped up the remaining bean and consigned it back to the security of the jar. What mystifies me, and seems illogical, is that these precious, hard to get, safely guarded vanilla beans all the way from a rare plant in the jungle of Africa cost L 3,000 each. Perhaps they are safely guarded and only available from a pharmacist because there is some exotic potion in a vanilla bean from Africa which does not exist in the cellophane packets anyone can buy in a city supermarket for $2.99. But L 3,000 is about the price of a cup of coffee! So should they not be L 20,000 each to justify this extravagance? I decide definitely not to ask Lola about the vanilla bean, nor why she needs it. Sometimes, in Montalcino, reasoning about such things as vanilla beans and brodo is obscure. It is just the way things are.

Lola continues: 'Now that autumn is here, and everything is quiet in Pianello because the Sagra is over, I would like to invite you to come to my house for pranzo, lunch. I will cook you a Montalcinese pranzo and do my utmost to make sure it is good.'

'Grazie, Lola, that's very kind,' Luigi politely replies. 'We would really love to come, and I am sure whatever you cook will be just wonderful.' Both of us are a little taken aback, because clearly Lola has been planning this intimate invitation for some time. We have shared many meals with Maria Pia and Luciano at the trattoria but this is the first time in all these years we have been asked to share a meal in someone else's home. It will be an added thrill because we will be sampling a genuine home-cooked meal from Lola based on the cucina povera.

We make arrangements for the following Sunday week and Luigi asks what time we should come. Lola looks at him curiously: 'Mezzogiorno, Luigi, come at mezzogiorno. Pranzo is at mezzogiorno!' It seems Lola considers this a very odd question. When else would you eat pranzo? What perplexing things these stranieri say.

Pranzo on Sunday week at mezzogiorno – noon precisely. No! We have been tripped up on this little anomaly for appointments before. Although Lola is emphatic that pranzo is at mezzogiorno – which is exactly when the village bell will chime the twelfth hour – we know we will not be expected until one o'clock, which is when you *eat* the mezzogiorno meal. Smiling at our own cleverness in making progress when faced with the mysterious ways of Montalcino, we go through farewells, another small handshake, and Lola is soon hurtling through the piazza towards the butcher, preoccupied with her next mission to do with food.

CHAPTER FOUR

Primo – the First-born

Although the vendemmia, harvest, was brought in only a few weeks ago, the vines on the slopes surrounding Montalcino are already limp; only the most tenacious branches, the ones that pushed luxuriant tendrils skyward towards the end of summer, have resisted late autumn winds. A few russet leaves, shrivelling more each day, dance about in the breeze from shrinking stalks.

There is only short respite from work in the vineyards; even though the hillside is unattended for weeks and the vines wander and droop at will, the grower is not resting but in the cantina, where the just harvested grapes demand his daily attention.

The closest Luigi and I had ever been to understanding wine-growing was as citified drinkers; dinner with friends in a glossy highrise apartment overlooking the harbour or a favourite bottle of red when we anchored the yacht, which also belonged to friends, at a hidden beach cove and lazed around sipping wine while the steaks cooked on the barbecue. Yet here we are, making our home in a village in the Tuscan hills renowned for production of an internationally famous wine, il Brunello di Montalcino. In fact, there is little that happens in Montalcino that is not in one way or another, even indirectly, connected with the growing of arguably Italy's finest red wine. At least, it may be arguable in other parts of Italy, and certainly is debated endlessly throughout Europe and as far away as America, Japan and Australia, but in Montalcino we were soon in agreement that there is little need for debate, nor is discussion even necessary.

We wanted not only to enjoy drinking the wines of Montalcino but were anxious to learn about them as well, so we began to read and watch what was happening in the vineyards. Just a few months after our arrival, Luigi happened on a television pro-gramme in which a Montalcino wine-grower was interviewed. A few days later, to my astonishment, he rushed garrulously up to a man who was standing in the piazza, exclaiming: 'I saw you on television! You are Primo Pacenti – how do you do? I am Luigi, from Australia!' This was the beginning of a rich friendship which taught us more about growing wine in Montalcino than we could have learned from a thousand books.

The world is a faraway place; Montalcino's growers do not necessarily know what is being said about their wines, and if they do know, they are usually not greatly disturbed. Not because they have an attitude of smugness, nor of superiority . . . and it is certainly not a result of world acclaim. Many international journalists and wine-writers come and go . . . but I wonder if they really understand that, purely and simply, these Tuscans are at one with the land; it has always been that way, and accordingly, with their hands in the soil, Montalcino's growers produce Italy's finest red wine. When Signor Primo Pacenti jumps into his racy Fiat and leaves his vineyard, zigzags up the side of the hill and hurtles under the arch at Porta Burelli, he has no interest in being hailed as a prestigious Brunello-grower; that is not his way. Luigi once asked him: 'What's the 1995 like, Primo? What do you think of it compared to the great 1990?' Primo benignly told Luigi it was not his place to have an opinion about Brunello, he just does his best to produce a buon vino.

Invited first to visit his vineyard, we followed Primo through the rows as he talked with his hands as much as with words, then to his cantina, where we listened to the wine and tasted one great vintage after another while Primo listened to us, without, I realised afterwards, making any comments; he left it to us to voice an opinion about his wines. Later, we were invited to share a glass of wine in his family home beside the vineyard. That was the first of many occasions. Over the months I pieced together the story of his life and, as it turned out, the story of Brunello as it evolved among growers like Primo.

Primo, the first-born, is a small man, no more than 140 centimetres tall, but his body is compact and astonishingly strong. Bushy black eyebrows set off his ruddy complexion and he has large round protruding eyes, alert and watchful, with broad eyelids that close over them more than is usual. His most noticeable feature is his clipped, black moustache, which has earned him the nickname of Baffino, little moustache. His lack of height is probably as much an indication of lack of nourishment when he was a child as his strong body is a reflection of his life of work on the land. Primo is a contadino, as was his father, and his father before him, back through the centuries. He was born a contadino under the mezzadria, which means his family was mezzadri, bound to a feudal system of farming under a padrone, a land-owner. His earliest recollection is listening to the stories of his grandmother, who was born in 1851; when he was a young child she used to tell him about the life of the family on the land. Primo's story as a Montalcinese contadino under the mezzadria is sad and disheartening; he remembers the pain, humiliation and hunger all too well, but the blackness began to lift in the 1960s and his story, at least in our time, has a happy ending.

The Church of Santa Restituta, a few kilometres outside the walls, is documented from the year 650, which means there was some kind of primitive hamlet there nearly a hundred years before the Ilcinesi came to live on the hill under the holm oaks. Nothing remains of that early temple except a few inscriptions which confirm a later consecration around 1140. Primo was born at Santa Restituta, the first-born son of a contadini family who worked the land surrounding the church under the hand of the padrone, who was also the priest. At that time 90 per cent of priests had a working farm given to them by the Church to supplement their income. They were no different from any other padrone, often worse, because they knew that when they died or moved on, whatever was left on the farm went to the next priest. Nor was it unusual for the Church to control peasant workers. The Church had power and money and, at that time, believed it assisted their cause if the contadini were kept in poverty, subservient and reliant on the mercy of the Church.

Under various titles the peasant farmers of Tuscany have been subject to one form or another of sharecropping or feudal farming since the twelfth century or perhaps earlier, so a system similar to the mezzadria was in existence hundreds of years before Primo was born. Under the statutes, which were lawful until well after World War Two, wealthy and aristocratic owners of farmland could contract a poor family to work their land. In return, the family had somewhere to live and, if they were fortunate, enough food to keep them alive. They worked sun-up till sun-down all year long and the padrone kept a book called a libretto colonico, which was a record of all the expenses of running the farm and a record of the sale of produce and animals resulting from the work of the contadini family.

When Primo was born in 1923, the mezzadria statutes stipulated that the split of the yearly profits, if any, was 43 per cent to the contadini family and 57 per cent to the padrone. At the end of each year a tally was reckoned by the padrone using the records in the libretto colonico. But the contadini family did not just consist of a husband and wife. Primo still has the libretto colonico of his family from 1933, in which his father, Venanno, is listed as the capuccio, the head of the family, and everyone else is listed according to their relationship to him. So the contadini family of Pacenti included Primo's father and mother, who were then thirty-four and thirty years old respectively, their two sons, nine-year-old Primo and his eight-year-old brother, their grandfather and grandmother who were both seventy-two years old, their uncle and his wife who were twenty-nine and twenty-six, and their two small children aged four and two. Altogether the padrone had a family of ten under contract to work the land. And everybody had to work, because at any time the padrone could throw the family out; there was no pity and if they did not find somewhere else to go, they went under. The problem, as Primo explained it, was that the contadini never saw the libretto colonico, which was always in the hands of the padrone. And because, with very few exceptions, the contadini were nulfabetta – they could not read or write – the libretto was a tool which gave absolute power to the padrone. The contadini's only chance for a fair split was if the padrone was honest. Many, unfortunately most, were not.

When Primo talks about his life I hear despair in his voice. His words are punctuated with wild erratic gestures as his grainy hands fly into the air. The words tumble out, barely distinguishable one from the other, but it is as if he wants me to know, wants someone to understand, what really happened to his family and many like them.

'The contadini,' Primo explained with hurt in his eyes, 'no matter how hard they worked, or how well they cultivated and produced, could never ever get ahead. We always got further and further behind because we were never able to get out of debt.' He explained that in the libretto colonico a padrone could write, for example:

Sold: *2 young lambs for the price of 70 lire*
Expenditure: *2 straw brooms for the price of 200 lire*

Because the contadini did not see the book and could not read or write, they did not see that the padrone wrote whatever he wanted in the book. They did know what was happening, Primo told me. Common sense told them they were being cheated but they were powerless to do anything about it.

'At the end of the year the padrone made the tally.' Primo's voice sounded distressed and angry. 'He would tell the contadini family, for instance, that they were 4,256 lire in debt.' I felt my own anger swell when he swallowed his shame, and added: 'That was really my family, and that was the exact indebtedness of the

Pacenti family in our libretto colonico of 1933.'

Seeing my astonishment, he went to a cupboard and fetched a handful of flimsy books, yellowed with age and well-leafed; he showed me the libretto of his family for 1933. The columns were dotted with indecipherable figures, strange additions and sub-tractions, and there on the very last page was the signature of the padrone, under the debit column, showing the crippling debt of the family. I could see the padrone had his talons in them. There was no escape.

Primo, even as a toddler, remembers life at Santa Restituta as purgatory for his family. They were not allowed to burn wood more than two centimetres in width, so in winter his mother was thankful for the animal byre under the stone farmhouse because, she said, the hot breath of the animals helped to keep the upstairs warm. At that time the family grew grain and cereals, which were sown between rows of olive trees; they had calves and sheep to care for, chickens, ducks, rabbits, and a few vines. But the mentality of the priest, the padrone, at Santa Restituta was, as Primo explains, in dietro, backwards. Priests always worked their way in reverse and if a new cow was needed they bought the most frail, cheapest, least productive cow they could find. It would appear as a debit in the libretto and the contadino, no matter how hard he tried, could never make the cow pay its way. Even if the hoes broke and his father asked for new ones, the padrone would tell him he had no money.

The padrone bought seed for the grain, which was a debit on the farm, and the contadino tilled, planted, nurtured and eventually harvested the crop. The padrone would sell the crop then fill in the libretto, but the contadino never really knew whether his share of the sale price was deducted from or added to his debt. All he could do was work so his family had enough to eat. Because the end weight of the harvest was a matter of life and death, every single day Primo's father would go out to the fields and if he found a single stalk bent over in the wind, even trodden on by a field mouse, he would make a splint to lift the stalk back up, nurture and tend it, desperate to keep it alive so it could be included in the harvest.

'Life,' said Primo with a sad shake of his head, 'was incredibly hard. The staple food was bread, which my mother made by grinding a little corn, but because everything belonged to the padrone, if we ate anything else we would sink further and further into debt.'

'For years,' he went on, 'I never had proper shoes to wear. In winter we wrapped our feet in cloths and skins to keep them warm. My mother managed to feed us all but it was a miserable existence.' And every week another village priest would come down to Santa Restituta and put out his hand for an offering to the church. His mother had to give him something even though they were so poor that many times they never had bread on the table, perhaps only a few beans or potatoes, but he would take it just the same.

'When we were young we would go up to the village on Friday, because it was market day, usually with my father to help carry corn sacks for the padrone, or to lead an animal which was to be sold. People in the village would see us with no proper shoes and always hungry; sometimes someone gave me something to take home for my mother.'

I have not been able to work out how he did it, nor what happened to the family debts which must have seemed astronomical at that time, but Primo's father eventually got them out of Santa Restituta. However, they had to go further into the Orcia Valley towards Pienza, still contadini under the mezzadria, where they were to work for the next fourteen long years. Primo's shoulders dropped as he exhaled a long, slow, pain-filled breath.

'I was just a little boy when my family went from purgatory to the inferno! That padrone,' he declared as his eyes widened with easily recollected fear, 'must have been related to Saddam Hussein!' It was unbelievable misery, which the family had to endure for all those years during which Primo passed from childhood to a young man, working from dawn to dusk alongside his father.

'When it was time to harvest the olives, the padrone would send someone down to estimate, by walking around the olive trees, how many gallons of oil the ripening olives would produce, and if we did not produce exactly that amount, we were in debt for the missing oil! And the women, although all of them worked unceasingly on the farm, if the padrone lived near us, and that could mean a few kilometres away, my mother and aunt had to take it in turns to go and attend to his washing and ironing, clean his house, and do whatever he wanted. After fourteen long miserable years at the inferno, my father managed to scrape the caparra together and our family got a mezzadria contract on the slopes of the hill at Montalcino.'

I asked Primo what a caparra was. My indignation at his explanation of this callous injustice made him raise his eyebrows and shake his head vigorously, as if to make me believe it was true. A contadini family, when they were contracted to work the land, had to pay the padrone a caparra, a deposit, as surety. If they walked off the land they forfeited their deposit, or, if a cow was stolen, the contadini's deposit went to the padrone.

Although they were backbreaking years because the land was so steep, and although there was still much misery to endure, Primo describes working the slopes around Montalcino as paradise compared to the purgatory of Santa Restituta and the inferno of Pienza.

And just when I thought I had heard the worst of it, Primo

remembered to tell me how some of his extended family once worked off their debts serving time in the jail which was underneath the loggia, where the statue of Cosimo stands, below Palazzo Comunale. The family was fined a horrific amount after a son was caught using a trap made out of donkey tail bristles for catching a bird in the woods. They paid part of the fine by selling two young calves they had managed to breed, but the rest they worked off by serving a day at a time in jail.

By the late 1940s the split had been improved; this meant the family toiled all year and supposedly received in return a tally which worked out to 50 per cent of their collective effort. Around this time several contadini from Montalcino got together and dared to stage some sort of protest by lining up outside the gates of a padrone. They were trying to get him to agree that their share should increase to 60 per cent of the year's profits. The incredulous padrone, whose name was Pippo, looked down his nose at them, demanding haughtily: 'What do you contadini want? Do you want my very soul?' The contadini fell silent, thinking they had gone too far, terrified they would be thrown off the land. Then Pippo thundered at them, showing disdain at their audacity, 'Il nostro male! It is the worst thing that has ever happened, now that you contadini are learning to read and add.'

At the end of the war the Communist Party began to take steps to dismantle the mezzadria. Primo, now a young man, often came up to the village on foot; in the 1950s there were hundreds of donkeys around Montalcino, so sometimes he hitched a ride. 'But most times,' he stated matter of factly, 'I got belted black-and-blue and was sent stumbling back outside the walls.' Primo would go into Bar Cacciatore or Fiaschetteria; there might be a landowner there, not really a padrone because the mezzadria was being dismantled, who would pay a few lads to hang around outside the bar. When Primo went out they would grab him, give him a good belting and run him out of the village, telling him to get back down with the animals where he belonged. He is philosophical about it now because he realised in later years that those doing the belting were as poor as he was, many even poorer, and they would do anything they were asked for a few miserable lire to take home to their mother. 'At least the contadini could eat, even if it was only a piece of bread,' he says in justification of their actions. 'Up there the poor were starving – they had nothing.'

The dismantling of the mezzadria took decades. Ugly remnants of the system were to linger for many years, even into the 1980s in some areas of Tuscany. During the 1950s and 1960s there were ongoing hardships for the contadini to endure. It was a time of constant humiliation, of insults, of injustice, just because they were born on the land. The dismantling of the system did not bring them instant success, and Italy too was changing. Obviously, the contadini did not own the land which they and their families had worked for centuries; nor did they own the humble stone houses they lived in. With the dismantling of the mezzadria, the wealthy landowners found their source of virtual slave labour drying up. Many of these landowners, some of whom were of aristocratic lineage, simply walked off the land, abandoning it, deciding that their income from agriculture was finished. Instead, these wealthy aristocrats turned to investing in steel plants which supplied car factories, in cement works for building roads, wharves and bridges, in small and large manufacturing plants for the new post-war industrialisation of Italy.

The contadini were forced to uproot their families and make their way to larger villages and cities, hoping to find work in one of the factories which were mushrooming all over Italy, factories owned and operated by their old enemy, the dreaded padrone. So the contadini, certainly the majority, became factory workers or, if they could borrow enough money, escaped this new misery by emigrating to America, Canada or Australia.

That was the time when much of Italy was desecrated. So many beautiful places were destroyed; wonderful monuments of ancient Italy suffocated, irreparably damaged, lost between factories billowing smoke and fumes into the hills and valleys.

There were a few contadini who managed to find a way to stay on the land. They wanted to keep their contadini skills but found their way forward blocked, because there was by now practically no market for their produce. Even if there was a market, they had no knowledge which would allow them to tap into it, because the padrone had always controlled the trade. They did not really know how, or to whom, they could sell a few bales of hay, or sacks of potatoes. Economically, the dismantling of the mezzadria was disastrous for agriculture in Tuscany and the government of the day found itself with an enormous crisis on its hands. The farms had been abandoned and the land was barren, now worthless. Generations of Tuscans who had nurtured and produced were homeless contadini drifting in their thousands to search for work in factories in the cities. The repercussions of this collapse in agriculture are visible all over Tuscany today in the form of crumbling stone farmhouses, grain storage sheds, barns and animal pens which, whilst enchantingly picturesque in today's landscape, were simply left to become dilapidated ruins.

The Government, desperate to re-ignite agriculture, offered farmland at an interest rate of 1 per cent, but nobody wanted it. The offer was aimed at the contadini, but they had just escaped from centuries of virtual serfdom when they were never out of debt, and anyway, they had no money; the idea of going into debt to buy land was a difficult proposition for them. A courageous few, and Primo was one of them, managed to scrape some money together by borrowing from whomever they could. 'But I never dreamed,' said Primo, teary eyes wide, 'that the tiny parcel of land I bought on the hill of Montalcino would return me riches I could never ever imagine.' A few of the aristocrats also held on to their land and, although it was never to be worked in the same way again, they too were enriched on a grand scale.

At last the chain of subservience was broken. In 1962 Primo Pacenti and his family became the lawful owners of a small farm at Canalicchio, a hamlet on the slope leading up to Montalcino. There was no vineyard on the farm, but one hectare was planted with grain and a few vines were strung between olive trees; Primo had no way of knowing that in just a few years it was destined to be land designated for the production of Brunello di Montalcino. The Pacenti family still worked hard seven days a week – in truth they worked harder, because as well as tending their own land which produced a little olive oil, they were forced to continue working as contadini on an adjoining farm for a padrone, because they had to pay off decades of accumulated debts.

By the time Primo was married in the early 1960s, approaching forty years of age, he had a few animals and would occasionally go to the stock sales in Siena. Now a landowner himself, still he could not escape the oppression of the past. If he went into an osteria, others lunching there they would call out to him: 'Hey, look at this contadino – what are you doing here? Get back to the land.' Or they would insult him by saying, 'Look at this contadino who won't work our land any more. Go send your wife home to look after the sheep.' Many times it would develop into an argument. Primo would respond: 'You are still in the mezzadria. It's not up to me to look after your sheep! What about all the money you made out of us? Send your *own* wife out to look after the sheep!'

Most contadini in the 1950s had not even heard of the word Brunello, or, if they had, it held little significance. They tended the vines on the farms, making a generic wine which everybody made a different way; half of it went to the padrone and they sold the other half to whomever they could. The most common method was using a tino, a huge oak vat which, open at the top, would be filled with grapes, any sort of grapes and as many of them as they could get their hands on. The grapes had to be turned every day to create the fermentation. Above the tino, from a rafter, would hang a rope with a handle. Rolling up their trousers past their knees, they would wash their feet in a basin, hoist themselves up, grab the rope handle, lower themselves into the vat and start pressing to move the grapes from the top to the bottom. Although the wine was generic and made without technical winemaking skills, and using primitive equipment, everybody knew the soil on the hill of Montalcino produced a very good red wine.

But the wine story is only now beginning. A number of larger and more sophisticated farms around Montalcino, with great foresight, began experimenting, reviving and planting the clone sangiovese grosso which had been developed in the mid-1800s; from this vine they created Brunello. Many of these vineyards were owned by aristocrats, marquises and counts, who had a hierarchy of foremen to supervise the contadini labouring in the vineyards, mainly because the majority of aristocrats spent much of their time on leisure activities like fashionable hunting expeditions in Africa. There were, fortunately, some forward thinking people among them whose farms were well established, better organised and had more advanced winemaking equipment.

It did not take long for the contadini, especially those like Primo who had a small parcel of land, to realise they, too, could achieve a better income by planting vines rather than potatoes. So they began to plant sangiovese grosso. It was not to be so easy for the contadini. Their old padrone fought strenuously to prevent them, attempting to influence government legislation to make it impossible, even unlawful, for contadini to grow sangiovese grosso. They wanted this much-acclaimed Brunello for themselves, no doubt thinking, 'What do these simple contadini know about wine?' It was true – most contadini had absolutely no technical winemaking skill at all. But they had broken the yoke of subservience and were not going to be denied entry into this enticing new market.

Their fight might not have been won, however, but for the tireless work of Dottore Bruno Ciatti, a scientist with the Ministry for Agriculture in Montalcino, who fought unceasingly for the right of small farmers to produce Brunello. Dottore Ciatti declared on many occasions: 'There is only one place in the world to make this wine and that is Montalcino. It cannot be left to just two or three wealthy aristocrats.'

All through 1965 and 1966 the revered Dottore held meetings with growers, including the contadini, during which, after open consultation and discussion, were formed the disciplines, regulations and statutes which now govern the production of Brunello. People in high places who were able to postpone legislation and freeze reforms constantly blocked his path; wealthy aristocrats, titled gentry, fought it out to the very last, but he wore them down and eventually these powerful people began to lose their sphere of influence. Although Dottore Ciatti has since died, he is held in great esteem by the contadini who owe him so much. With tears in their eyes they will tell you: 'I still have him in my heart. He was like a brother to us, and if it were not for him I would still have nothing.'

By 1968 the Consorzio del Vino Brunello was established and laws passed that it was the land, and only the position of that land, not the blood of its owner, that determined who could produce Brunello.

Primo still lives in the farmhouse on the same parcel of land at the hamlet of Canalicchio, but now it is surrounded by vineyards growing sangiovese grosso. It is a tall, stone house with that natural farmyard look which is nothing more than the practical placement of tractors and tools, neatly chopped wood stacks covered with a layer of straw, plaits of onions, garlic, and red and yellow peppers hanging from rafters, hutches for rabbits and a few wandering chickens which, in Tuscany, never seem to want to leave the farm and make a run for freedom. Primo has renovated another square farmhouse nearby which provides apartments for his family and he has a splendid new cantina where his wine gently matures. He has a very decent olive crop to look after; gnarled trees stand in rows around the farm and he is planting more trees because the oil of Montalcino is highly sought. He has a few fields of grano duro for pasta, and other cereals that he harvests for feed for the animals, or to send away to the north of Italy. From his family holding, about 5.6 hectares are designated for the growing of his precious vines, from which he produces around 14,000 bottles of buon vino, il Brunello.

Every Friday Primo arrives in the village with a leather satchel tucked under his arm. It is market day. The contadini always come to the village on market day, but Primo does not bring potatoes, or corn, or beans in his satchel now, because he is on his way to a meeting of the Consorzio del Vino Brunello. Primo spends much time deep in conversation with enologists, the highly qualified winemakers, and with the Mayor and Consorzio members as they discuss the advanced technicalities of winemaking, this year's harvest, or the long-range weather forecast. Primo, one of the original handful of growers who, along with some of the wealthy landowners, formed the Consorzio and set about ensuring respect for disciplined production of the wine, has given many years working for the Consorzio.

After the meeting, Primo, with his contadini roots, likes to meet friends at his favourite osteria within the walls. Osteria Porta Cassero is just down from the gate of the same name and Lorianna, wife of Piero the owner, specialises in the traditional cooking of the cucina povera. Just the combination of a handful of ingredients, fresh to the table, without complicated sauces and definitely no cream or butter, but plenty of hard Tuscan unsalted bread. The cucina povera's holy trinity, bread, wine, and olive oil, each in moderation, suits Primo well.

Piero himself is a cittadino to every hair on his unruly moustache. His thick Montalcinese dialect cuts off the first few letters of nearly every word, and some words he seems to swallow, so it is difficult for even locals to understand him. The menu is short but genuine; chickpea soup, rabbit in green sauce, and delicious liver and onions. Another of Lorianna's specialities is tripe served with saffron, which was once grown by the monks of Sant' Antimo, an ancient abbey about nine kilometres from Montalcino. Even so, more often than not Lorianna will prepare a plate of pinci for Primo with a sauce of fresh tomato and garlic drizzled sparingly over the top. Pinci is the name of Montalcino's own pasta, which looks similar to spaghetti but is not smooth and even because it is always handrolled, and is usually dressed with the simplest of sauces.

On Fridays we usually see Primo in the village and, like today, we frequently meet him at Osteria Porta Cassero for lunch. Today we find one of his friends, Illiano, is also here having pranzo on his own. Although Primo is the elder by more than ten years, the two men have known each other all their lives. Whereas Primo is short, with a compact and strong body, Illiano is tall, with broad shoulders about which Primo continually teases him. The two men spar with each other across the table.

'Look at him,' Primo turns to address whoever is listening. 'Shoulders like that and he doesn't work on the land. Look at me – I am small, half his size, but I start work at sun-up every day.'

'Yes,' Illiano retorts, 'but I'm not tirchio' – a word which refers to someone who is tight and not free with their money. 'Look, I'll be drinking Brunello with my pranzo and you have ordered Rosso!'

'That may be so,' says Primo with a dry reply, 'but did you look carefully, my friend? Ti ringrazio, I give you my thanks, it is *my* Brunello you are drinking – you will make me rich!'

Contrary to what you might conclude, after half a century under the mezzadria in misery and subservient poverty, in truth Primo is the most generous of men. He shares his wine and warm friendship, in equal proportion, with friends from the land and the village.

Illiano is served a bowl of traditional Tuscan bean soup and as she places it before him Lorianna asks if he wants onions as well. 'Si, certo,' he responds in a low gravelly drawl; she returns a few seconds later with a plate of raw onions, sliced in wedges. Tuscan bean soup is made with many vegetables and a slice of unsalted Tuscan bread is submerged in the bowl, but in Montalcino you are likely to find raw onions as a chaser. I watch Illiano as he pours a sizeable heap of salt next to the onions. Then, spoon in one hand and a wedge of raw onion in the other, he dips the spoon into the steaming soup and, almost in one movement, swallows the soup whilst the other hand swishes the onion into the salt. Immediately he is crunching it in his mouth, so it chases the soup down.

Primo orders his regular pinci with tomato and garlic sauce and Luigi and I decide on the same. He pours a glass of Rosso for each of us. The two men seem just as comfortable in silence as they do talking; one comments on a topic, a little news about the vineyards, or that So-and-so has begun to sow a late crop, and they nod approval without forming an opinion. Their lives, since they were born on Montalcino territory, have been woven together with the seasons, and although Primo might taunt and play the hardworking farmer with Illiano, he has tremendous respect for his family. 'Illiano's father,' he whispers to me, 'was one of the best contadini. He could make his land produce abundantly every single season.'

Illiano remembers the war years when Montalcino was occupied by the Germans. His family, together with five or six other contadini families and all the pigs and sheep, left the farms and went to hide in the woods. They lived in rough shelters and he recalls his mother burying all the household belongings, meagre though they were. His memory of the 1950s is that the village people suffered the most. When he was a boy of ten he would watch the women walk out of the village and go down to the fields, picking up the spigole, tiny ears of grain that fell to the ground. They would take them to the mill, trying to exchange them for a fistful of flour. Although born the only son of a contadino under the mezzadria, by the time Illiano was growing up the blackest days were gone, so he never worked as a contadino.

It is a companionable lunch, but we do not linger. We know Primo wants to get down to the vineyard because there is work waiting for him at Canalicchio.

Only the brave-hearted would follow Primo through Porta Burelli down to Canalicchio di Sopra; on foot it is a slippery, rutted track, but in a car it is plainly treacherous. The wise find Canalicchio by leaving through Porta Cerbaia and winding through the hills on the road to Buonconvento. By 3.30 Primo has changed out of his village clothes and gone straight to the cantina, where enormous wooden barrels are brimming with rumbling wine. He puts his ear to the cask, rubs his hand around the wood a few times and listens to the wine talking to him. The enologist, Primo's consultant winemaker, arrives and together they begin to technically examine and test the new wine. Primo may be the grower, he may be the one who nurtures and tends the vines all year, but he knows the skills of the highly specialised winemaker he engages for this task are indispensable to the production of his wine.

Next February the Consorzio will meet with enologists and other experts, international journalists will come, and prior to a delicious Benvenuto Brunello lunch, this harvest will be awarded its star rating; in four years this wine will be ready. Right now the bottles of 1995 Brunello, harvested more than four years ago, are quietly sleeping at the bottom of Primo's cantina and in just a few more weeks he will be able to release them on to the world market. It is always thrilling when they bring out the wine and are able to examine the result of their work, even though it is four or, for a Riserva Brunello, five years later. The 1995 is an exceptional Brunello; it was awarded a distinguished five-star rating, but Primo is not overly concerned because each harvest has its own special characteristics, its own intense colour and bouquet. He looks forward to uncorking every vintage, gently decanting it and letting the aroma of the terra, his own precious brown earth, rise up to meet him.

The story has finally been told; the centuries of poverty, struggle, humiliation and injustice endured by Primo, his family and his ancestors have culminated in his vineyard – just a handful of hectares – which produces, and there is absolutely no need to argue, a few thousand bottles of Italy's finest red wine: il Brunello di Montalcino.

CHAPTER FIVE

Fooled by the Moon and Tricked by the Wind

The Montalcinesi seem to have soil in their bones. They love to grow something, anything, everything, as close to home as possible. It seems nothing they buy from any shop can equal that which they have planted, tended, nurtured and harvested in the

69

soil of this village. I can see it has always been that way, ever since the walls went up defending not only the village but the vegetable gardens as well. As the last days of autumn draw to a close, the hours of daylight are few, the temperature is dropping and there are only occasional visitors bold enough to face the stiff breezes whirling around the walls. The village begins to face inwards, returning to itself, and the walls become a barrier beyond which, if there is no real need, we will not venture for many weeks. And yet the place is buzzing with feverish activity as if there is a clock ticking away and a date by which all the work must be done, especially in the gardens.

At first glance you could not be blamed for believing Montalcino to be a hard, stony place. Stone walls rise to close in narrow roads, stone stairways ascend through stone arches and descend between stone houses, cobbled paths run beneath your feet. Every building is stone or brick, roofed with terracotta tiles, topped with terracotta chimneys and overhung with stone balconies guarded with iron rails; set within the walls narrow windows and doors are encased in shutters which close out one world and shut in the other. The few trees which line a roadway here and there are sparse, grimly holding on to some lumpy patch of dirt in sheer defiance, fending off the next attempt to cover the earth with stone. Sadly, you could spend a day in Montalcino and not discover a single garden except perhaps the grass below the Cedar of Lebanon at the end of Via Mazzini. But that image is a false one, for with soil in their bones the Montalcinesi have surrounded themselves with abundant greenery. I do not need to go outside the walls to watch the changing seasons; it happens right inside, not only the seasonal growth in vegetable gardens but the olive and grape harvest as well. Everywhere, irregular-shaped plots, some larger than a hectare, produce bountifully, and all within the walls. The secret is working out where to find them.

The main thoroughfares of Montalcino run north-south and each roadway runs along a terraced hillside with a double row of stone houses between it and the next roadway, so when I passed between the houses I could not see that they are separated by hidden vegetable gardens with glorious fruit trees, olive groves and vineyards. To find the gardens was not difficult, but I needed to leave the roads, walk down steep steps, pass through low arches and along narrow paths. Then I understood why Montalcino has withstood the worst of winters and the most brutal siege the Spanish could inflict.

Sunday morning is the ideal time to walk the gardens, because once early Mass is over, gardeners come down to tend the plots and gather whatever they need for the family lunch. Besides, I have found the cycle of work changes quickly and in a week so much happens to make each Sunday morning different. Already it is nearly December. From the gardens below the Church of San Salvatore in Ruga, which run along a hidden terrace, the aroma of feathery fennel, vivid green and half a metre high, wafts into the air. The vineyards are surprisingly extensive here, but by late autumn all that is left are stakes supporting shrivelled vines. The thick green canopy which sheltered the summer crop is gone, allowing every meagre ray of sunlight through to winter vegetables struggling upwards through the soil. Soon the lifeless vine will be cut away in lengths, but the pieces won't be discarded. Next week I will see they have been trimmed into identical lengths and thickness, wound together with another piece of vine and stacked against the garden shed. Tall leaves of Tuscan black cabbage, coarse and straight, sit tightly packed, each plant holding its neighbour upright whilst the spiky leaves of artichokes, set a good distance from each other, allow themselves room to spread. And trees, so many trees; peach, cherry, fig, plum and almond are here, but autumn leaves are gone, pruning is done, the twigs gathered and stacked ready for the wood stove.

In the vegetable gardens of Pianello, snowy cauliflower heads are in bloom. Beds of little broccoletti shot up, then disappeared, and now the first of the winter lettuces, green and crimson flecked with droplets of dew forming pearly beads around their hearts, are ready to be picked. Unruly clumps of rosmarino droop under the weight of their own verdant growth, but caper bushes are spent, just a cluster of drying leaves cascading from a wall.

Looking across to Travaglio, terrace after terrace of abundant vegetables and fruit trees stretch across the valley, and hundreds of olive trees, now silver, now green as the breeze blows, trunks twisting and lurching with the steep terrain. And here more than anywhere else in late autumn I can clearly pick out the round balls of bright red-orange kaki, that strange fruit which ripens when the weather is cold and after every leaf on the tree has fallen. To me it looks peculiar; the fruit dangles like a hundred coloured Christmas balls from twiggy branches. I watch an old man gently sway a branch with a forked stick, trying to coax the fruit to fall just at the moment of its ripeness into the waiting outstretched apron of his signora, standing below. The fruit refuses to fall, clinging until the very last moment and I hear the signora call out: 'Maria-Gesù!' when the fruit misses her apron and splatters on the ground. Her husband raises one hand and makes little waving movements by the side of his head, as if to say: 'Mamma mia, that's another one we won't be eating.' A mushy mound of orange pulp, skin split like a boiled tomato, lies at her feet.

In Travaglio the skinny tomato stakes are still wedged into the earth but the plants now hang in dead ringlets, shrivelling to nothing, the last of the unpicked overripe fruit returning to the soil. The bamboo stakes are laced like scaffolding in a wigwam with lengths of last year's vine binding them together; it reminds

me of a construction site built to take the weight when the plant
climbed high. Next to the dying tomato plants is a round patch of
lively sage, a bushy one of parsley, then a frail line of peperoncino,
chilli peppers, which will soon be picked, dried, put into a small
hessian sack and hung by the fireplace. Some years I see a leafy
plant drawn up tall with stems, coarse and white, encased in a
thick wrapping of brown paper bound round and round with
vine. Asking Travaglio gardeners about this odd wrapped
package, my questions led not only to a lengthy explanation, but
also an exchange of recipes and eventually an armful picked for
me to take home. Cardoon, or cardo, I learned, is hard to grow. It
needs continual protection from the cold, takes time to extrava-
gantly nurture and, if not tended properly, will be hard and
tough. But if you are particularly attentive, this ugly vegetable
repays your work.

Olga from Travaglio says: 'It's delicious cut into slabs. Remove
the thick outer string, lightly coat the slabs in flour and then fry
them in olive oil.'

'Si, si,' agrees Giuseppe. 'But, Olga, the old Montalcinese way
is better . . . peel away the stringy outer layer, chop it into pieces,
add a touch of peperoncino and a few rosy tomatoes and gently
fry it all in olive oil – it's even more delicious.'

Old Giuseppe is determined to have the grandest woodpiles in
Montalcino. I have watched them grow too, one after the other,
several metres long, chopped, graded, stacked and protected from
the elements. Pruned tree branches, some as thick as railway
sleepers, lie haphazardly across the piles, a cosy jigsaw of
protection.

The olive trees in Travaglio disappear over the crest of a hill, so
unless I walk downhill through Porta Gattoli I cannot see how far
they reach. It may not be the largest olive harvest in Tuscany but
it is excellent quality oil. Up until recently it was mostly con-

sumed right here in Montalcino; the secret is out now, and after the harvest people will arrive to buy the piquant, newly pressed oil. This year the olives are ripening with obvious enthusiasm, swelling and changing colour as they willingly mature. Already I have overheard discussions about the volatility of the weather and precisely when harvest will begin. Some groves are ready by the middle of November, others need longer and are harvested in December; sometimes the mills are still crushing at Christmas. The trees do not look like upturned umbrellas now, because savage pruning has done its job, as has the manure which was dug in a wide circle around the roots. Day after day the warm sun of summer and early autumn penetrated into the centre of each tree; late growth is thick, the oil content of the olives is rapidly increasing.

The decision of when to harvest is a delicate one, because overripe olives are useless, become windfalls and cannot be used for the first press. Olives must be just ripe and picked rapidly, the harvest carried out with lightning speed and with great care not to bruise the fruit. And the weather must be clear and cold at harvest, as humidity is the enemy. This grove in Travaglio is ready, and my friend Roberto pushes a tapered wooden ladder into the branches of the first in a long line of trees. A gauze-like net, surprisingly soft, is gently nestled on the grass around the trunk, so when the olives fall they will land on a feathery cushion. They are still picked by hand, the old way; for this long and arduous task Roberto has strapped a half-moon wicker basket to his waist and covered his head with a cloth cap, but once he climbs the ladder he will disappear, lost in the foliage. There is a handy bench alongside the grove here and I think Roberto was puzzled the first time I sat for two hours and watched him harvest, but this morning he grins, offering me a wicker basket and a cloth cap!

In one continuous movement he firmly runs his loosely closed hand down the wispy stems, directing the falling olives into the basket at his waist, where most plop gently in; the ones that miss land on the net, where they gather in growing piles until their collective weight forces them to trickle into a gully in the net. Roberto leaves them in the gullies whilst he picks the tree clean, every now and again moving his ladder into another branch. 'If I have the timing perfect,' he calls to me, his face grave, 'and if the olives are picked tenderly and pressed without delay, the first press is a silky liquid, shining like precious gold. The second press shines like polished silver and is a reasonable oil, but the third press,' he says, breaking into a wide grin, 'è non va un cavolo! Is not worth a cabbage!'

Roberto is content with a moderate crop because the quality is high and the oil will be excellent. Not so a few years back – and he is not the only grower from whom I heard the story. 'That year,' Roberto told me, 'we knew a cold front was coming but we expected a day or two of clear weather and the olives were on the verge of ripeness. We moved the ladders and nets in, keeping a close watch on the moon and knowing we would have to harvest rapidly and with crucial timing. "Tomorrow we will harvest," I said to my wife. "The moon is right, the olives are ripe, everything is ready," and I made an appointment with the crushing mill for five o'clock. At midnight I awoke to hear the wind rustling the trees and I knew we were in trouble, because this wind had risen from the mountains, unexpectedly fierce, and began to whistle and howl. I thought we were going to have too many windfalls by morning and I was worried the swollen oil-filled olives would be blown off and dashed against the ground. Well, I need not have been so concerned about the windfalls, for when morning came, even by the tinny light of dawn, I could see the blanket of soft snow. The unexpected winds hurried the clouds and it snowed for three days, piling up a metre high all over the village. We could not get down to the olive groves. Montalcino was completely isolated, cut off from the outside world. Our street-sweepers tried with their shovels and twig brooms to free the most perilous steep stairways and lanes of snow and ice, sacks of salt were emptied and spread along the paths outside each doorway, but mostly it was in vain. We were imprisoned in our homes.

'On the fourth day the snow stopped, the snowplough made its way up from the valley and the sweepers began to make some dent in the icy mounds wedged against our homes. With heavy hearts we came down to the olive groves. First, all we could see was blinding puffy snow, dark cypress pines silhouetted against the white; then we saw rows of stakes poking above the snowline where the Brunello vines lay hidden. We knew the vines would suffer no damage as they had long since gone into their winter slumber. But the olives, and our ancient olive trees, were not so fortunate. As the snow began to melt and we got to the lower groves we found exactly what we had feared; shrivelled mis-shapen black olives dangling limply. Many trees had succumbed to the bitter cold, harshly burned by the snow. An olive is a long-living, slow-growing tree that rarely survives such bitter conditions. I was one day too late, fooled by the moon and tricked by the wind, which brought the clouds and dumped the snow on Montalcino. My whole year's harvest, all my silky liquid gold, was lost and a third of my oldest olive trees were ruined.'

To trace my steps through the secret gardens this Sunday morning, begin in Piazza del Popolo and walk up the gentle slope past Palazzo Comunale. Turn up the curved steps into the steep pathway called Via Bandi and, at the top of the short rise, pass between the Church of Sant' Agostino and the sede of Ruga. Keep going, turning right into Via Spagni, although, as with many of the smaller roads and paths I take, you will find there is no sign.

The road splits after a few metres, one branching downhill. Take the other, still Via Spagni, which rises to the left, and follow this until you reach the Church of San Salvatore, the Cathedral.

In front of the church is a line of cedar trees; in front of them, stone steps lead downhill to the village. The stairway is flanked by a low stone wall. This is a comfortable place to sit and scan the gardens below. I was astonished to find this much level ground in Montalcino, but medieval road planners had exceptional vision. As well as running the main thoroughfares north-south along the curve of the hill, they terraced the land from west to east. This clever engineering means we can walk the length of the village with hardly a hill to climb and allows us to descend or ascend across the village in bearable stages. The garden bed below the wall has just been sown; there are several fruit and olive trees, wood teepees lean around the wall and underneath my nose is an aromatic rosmarino bush spreading in all directions. The elderly folk turned the soil a week ago; it is finely raked. I will keep an eye on this garden, but I think they have planted onions.

Continue on, passing beneath the columns in front of the church, and walk up the second flight of four stone steps under a row of five gracious holm oaks. This canopy of trees almost conceals a delightful eight-sided covered well. It has circular iron openings cut into the cover, through which buckets can be lowered, and a charming iron wheel mechanism for raising and lowering the buckets. Behind the well is an imposing palazzo, an uncharacteristically grand home in this part of Ruga, but perhaps it once housed some eminent Bishop, since it is right next door to the church. Looking past the well, back across the road, a row of modest medieval stone houses, more typical of Montalcino, face the stately palazzo.

Look for a narrow pathway between the palazzo and the church and, if you walk a few metres along, you may find an old signora working the land behind the church. She is rarely here this late in autumn; in springtime though, when the garden is sprinkled with scarlet poppies, she propagates a vegetable patch, usually peas and beans, right up to the walls of the church. There is also one particular man who I have seen only two or three times, but if you walk to the end of the lane and then to the left, round a bend in the wall to the tennis court, you might see where he has been. A patch of grass about a metre round seems flattened and littered with pieces of dry straw. The stump of a sawn olive tree provides a handy seat, and this is where he sits, weaving half-moon wicker baskets for the olive pickers.

Join Via Spagni again and soon you come to a narrow road called Via del Pino, leading down a steep hill; but before going down, look straight ahead to another of Ruga's gardens. Walking past the garden gate, the wall rises higher, but even from here you will see the vineyard that runs along to the very end of the wall. By walking as far as the broad stairs, you will be rewarded with a perspective of the bell-tower and façade of the Church of Madonna del Soccorso not possible from anywhere else in the village. If your timing is right (although this morning I am too early) and the bells are ringing, you can almost reach out and touch them as they swing towards you, joyfully calling the news to the faithful. Via del Pino is steep and within a few metres the row of houses ends. The smell of feathery fennel wafts into the air and Tuscan black cabbage stands to attention, while carefree artichokes lean everywhere.

Halfway down the hill, turn the corner into an even narrower lane which runs off to your right. It has no name. A stone wall runs either side and the lane is just wide enough to allow you past if a three-wheeler Ape is still loading chopped wood from the garden. Walking slowly along this lane was when I first under-stood how much cultivated land there is between the rows of houses. Spring brings a profusion of growth and colour as the vines come into bud, the trees blossom – first white almond, mandorla, then pink cherry – and the vegetables shoot up. Within weeks the garden is sprinkled with scarlet poppies and carmine tulips bursting open.

I walked to the end of this lane and through an arch many times before focusing on the monstrous bowed timber beam supporting the houses above. Then I noticed the rough brick arches on piers a little further in, because it is really a passageway. Once through the passage, glancing to the right you can see the steps which lead back to San Salvatore, but don't go up. Rather, turn down the slope, cross straight over the roadway and now you have a magnificent panorama of the Orcia Valley. The patterned brick path straight ahead is not signed, but travels rapidly down the hill. There is an iron rail along the wall, which I grip to steady my descent as this pathway emphasises how steeply Montalcino falls. A number of times I have been embarrassed and felt a hundred years old as elderly ladies march steadfastly up the hill towards me with their shopping. They don't seem to need to hold the rail going either up or down, and with both hands full they cleverly traverse the slope like skiers. Holding the rail, I offer them a cheery buongiorno and they pause for a chat – usually to tell me, one more time, that they have been climbing this hill for seventy years.

Reaching the next crossroads, as usual I remember that because of my watchful descent I forgot to look into the terraced garden as I came down, but before stepping on to Via Mazzini I always check the board on the wall, because this is where daily news is posted. Sometimes it announces a concert in the theatre, or a coming festival, but more likely, as is the case this morning, there is a black and white notice telling us, with great sadness, of the death of a citizen and inviting us to share the sorrow of the family at Mass later today.

Make your way along Via Mazzini to the piazza, passing the cappellone, stay to the left and walk through the first archway leading down broad steps. It is called Viccola della Scuola and shortly bends so you can see the first Pianello garden and, in the distance, the villages of San Quirico and Pienza. I love to study the architecture of the upper row of houses lining Piazza del Popolo, trying to identify the balconies of friends, but the huddle of houses clinging to one another as they tumble down the hill looks different from this angle, so it is difficult. This morning I recognise the suspended terrace which juts from the house where Ercole and Lola live. Luigi and I are expected for pranzo at mezzogiorno, one o'clock, today and, staring up, I try to see if Lola is sitting in the sun preparing lunch. She is not there, but hanging on the clothesline are two or three long strings of onions.

Moving on, continue along Via delle Scuole, passing a steep stone stairway which narrows as it ascends and widens as it descends. Stop at the iron gateway with steps leading to a small apartment on the left; the wall inside is thick with cascades of drying caper bushes. It is easy now to tell you this, but it was several years before I recognised these tasty delicacies in the raw. Standing here in autumn it is not unusual to hear the happy chirping of thrushes; the singing comes from two nearby windows which are open for only a couple of months each year to let the caged birds see the light of day. You may be tall enough to peer into the vegetable plots over the wall as you walk to the next corner, reaching the sede of Pianello behind the Church of San Pietro. The walls are still too high for me to see the gardens on the terraces above, but I can see two magnificent kaki trees laden with ripening fruit. There is no sign on the road which travels downhill past San Pietro to the crossroads at the bottom, but there is a wooden bench opposite a water trough where I sometimes meet an elderly signora wearing a floral scarf tied tightly under her chin. She lives in the house above and will usually return a tentative buongiorno if my eyes meet hers and I take the initiative. This morning, resting in the sun, I find a white-haired man with a walking stick. I smile at him and offer a greeting. His response is a doubtful one: 'Signora . . .' but his face looks puzzled as he raises his hat. He is not used to seeing me.

Leaving the bench, take the left fork between the houses, Via Moglio, and within a few metres look up and find a graceful double-mullioned window within a pointed gothic arch. Walking on past Vicolo del Mistero, although 'small road of mystery' sounds enticing, you will soon reach a crossroads. Here I always stand and absorb the astonishing medieval architecture surrounding me. Cross straight over, following the sign to the ospedale, hospital, which takes you more or less straight ahead and up a slope. Already you are halfway round my garden walk. On reaching a row of holm oaks running beside a low wall bordering the valley, you surely cannot resist the temptation to sit on the wall for a while. Looking straight up at the village, a jumble of stone houses tumbling down the hill camouflages the hidden gardens you have just followed me through. From here, Lola's terrace is clearly in view. I check again; she is still not there, but the onions have gone!

You have a splendid view of the bell-tower of Palazzo Comunale, the crenellated towers of the fortress, the twin bells in the tower of the Church of Sant' Egidio, the single bell-tower above Ruga headquarters, the bell-tower of Sant' Agostino and that of San Salvatore, near where you began to walk. Is this not a brilliant place from which to contemplate Montalcino? But back to the gardens in the valley. A crisscross of grapevines forms a sheltering pergola, olive groves run along the ridges and vegetable plots are cultivated wherever there is room to wedge a triangle here, or a square there. You cannot see the encircling wall of Montalcino which encloses these gardens because it is further down the valley; the workers of the land built the meandering stone walls along the terraces long ago.

I retrace my steps to the crossroads below the Church of San Pietro near the water trough. The bench is now empty; the white-haired man has vanished – probably gone home for pranzo. You retrace your steps and continue in the other direction along Via Moglio. Along this road my eyes dart from side to side, resting momentarily on the blue and white enamel Pianello shields attached to the walls. I am sure you can imagine the trans-formation when Pianello celebrates quartiere dinners along this road. Two hundred people sit at wooden trestle tables which stretch as far as you can see; the stone houses are decorated with blue and white flags fluttering from iron holders, twinkling lights cast shadows over everyone, and when Pianello youngsters begin to chant, their voices echo all around the walls. Along this road, in the heart of Pianello, Massimo Bovini was born; many earlier generations of Bovini were probably born here too, maybe even Faustina in 1540.

Few gardens in Pianello have plots set aside for flowers, and apart from jonquils, crocus and tulips which shoot up unaided all over the village each spring, gardens are rarely devoted exclusively for show.

Via Moglio rises and takes you up a slope into Travaglio, identifiable by the yellow and red enamel crests on the walls of the houses. At the top of the slope, turn left at the first crossroad, Via Donnoli, although again you will not find a sign, and you are soon passing the iron crest above the sede of Travaglio. Marvellous medieval architecture forces the road to weave around these oddly angled three-storey homes. Along here, listen for singing thrushes: it is a cheerful chirpy song, but better not to see the forlorn creatures in a line of wooden cages hanging from nails in the wall. Perhaps being kept in the dark for nine months of the year makes them sing so desperately to one another. It is not very far, but a walk full of interest, to a leafy piazzetta at the end of this road and a seat from which to savour the view across the Orcia Valley to the mountains of Umbria. This small piazzetta is where Travaglio youngsters gather to chant their victory song. My gaze wanders to Primo Pacenti's restored farmhouse down in the valley; it is easy to identify because it sits along the road that rises from Buonconvento up to Montalcino. A square stone farmhouse with a hay barn to the left, fields of grain run smoothly away to the rear and rows of young olive trees stand in front of the farm. The vineyards are not all visible because most begin up the rise of the slope, closer to Canalicchio.

Leave the piazzetta, turn left at the first narrow road (which has no name), following a yellow and black sign on the wall directing you to Porta Gattoli. Very soon the lane curves and in front are the olive groves of Travaglio. On the corner is the handy iron seat from where I watch Roberto harvest, but if you are walking after me, just before mezzogiorno, you will not be resting today because this is a favourite gathering point for eight or so elderly citizens who live nearby. For a long time they stared at me suspiciously as I approached – this being fairly off the track for strangers – but now their eyes light up when I walk towards them and they can hardly contain themselves until I offer a buongiorno, whereupon they respond in a lively chorus. An old toothless signora sometimes stretches out her arthritic hand to grab mine. I lightly clasp it, then quickly pull my hand away, because once her friends had to help me unwrap myself from her vice-like grasp. I cannot understand her dialect and although she has long since lost her grip on life, but not her grip on people, she is brought out to sit in the sun with her friends.

Farms are dotted across the valley, vines march like rows of soldiers over a rise and down and straight ahead loom the slopes of Mount Amiata, which will soon be blanketed with snow. As you continue walking you will see Giuseppe's woodpiles stacked high, and sometimes this is where I find cardo wrapped up in brown paper. When the asphalt track turns right, peer into the garden in front of a stone house where a mystical grove of six olive trees is circled by a ring of standard roses. Often begonia and cyclamen flower in pots and multi-coloured pansies bloom between the roses. The signora who lives here takes great pride in this very untypical flowery garden. But now the road bends sharply left, so walk between the houses to the next crossroad, then turn left. A little way along, high on your right, you will see a tangled kiwi fruit pergola in a wonderful terrace garden. At the end of the road is Porta Cerbaia. Cross the road – watch for cars – towards a soaring pine tree, then walk up the stone steps in front of the directional traffic signs. The steps lead up a short stone ramp with an iron railing to a tiny landing at the top, from where you can embrace the dazzling valley.

On the low wall beside Porta Cerbaia, elderly men gather, patiently watching the arrival and departure of the Montalcinesi. If they are still here when you arrive, watch their heads turn in unison with an almost imperceptible nod when friends pass by; their faces will show curious, troubled looks when strangers drive into Montalcino. Behind you, an unnamed stone path between high walls leads into Borghetto. I have seen no sign of work for many months in the garden on the right and fear the worst for the elderly couple who always smiled when I walked past, although the cats I thought were theirs still sit along the wall.

As usual, I pass by the first laneway to the right and divert down the eight broad steps of the second, where a hidden terrace faces me. In summer it conceals a table with a pretty red cloth; a shady green haven beneath the vines. Without descending as far as the terrace, for in reality it is someone's front veranda, turn immediately left and walk up four or five shallow steps to the wall at the top to take in the strange juxtaposition of medieval architecture. Arches have been closed in or opened up, narrow balconies added, doors broken through or windows bricked in, empty roof terraces seem to belong to no one in particular and everywhere the terracotta roofs race away in a sloping mishmash, angled this way and that. Return to the laneway you diverted from and while walking along the cobbles between the houses you will soon see the slender twin bell-tower of the Church of Sant' Egidio. Whenever I walk here, I always envisage the Spanish heads lopped off below Porta Cerbaia by the brave warrior Panfilo dell Oca, in whose memory this road is named. Now you are passing the red and white enamel shields on the wall outside the sede of Borghetto and are just a few steps from where you began this garden walk.

This morning I have just enough time to call in to Gabriela in Pasticceria Mariuccia before I walk home to dress for lunch with Ercole and Lola. Etiquette demands I take a tray of dolci, sweet treats, and Gabriela always opens on Sunday morning because she knows people who are having pranzo with friends will be calling in to collect this mandatory gift. She lifts each oven-fresh biscuit on to the tray, wraps the package in glossy paper and ties it with golden ribbon, spending what seems an inordinate length of time making curly ringlets of ribbon spill down the side. On learning where we are expected for pranzo today and whom the dolci are for, Gabriela nods warm approval and bids me farewell with: 'Buon pranzo, e buon appetito!'

Negotiations to rent our apartment from Signor Ercole and Signora Lola were lengthy and more than a mite bewildering. Having only just arrived, and being unfamiliar with the ways of

Montalcino, we were grateful for help from Maria Pia and Luciano. Each day when we turned up at Grappolo Blu, Luciano would say: 'Come back domani, prima di mezzogiorno, tomorrow, before twelve noon.' The first day, and the second, he had no news. Nor on the third, fourth or fifth days. We were becoming anxious, thinking perhaps there really was no apartment for rent. 'Tomorrow, tomorrow,' he promised with a wave of his arm. We called in at Grappolo Blu on the sixth day and Luciano came rushing to the door to meet us. 'Where have you been?' he demanded. 'Signor Ercole is waiting to meet you.'

My eyes closed momentarily with a sinking feeling of exasperation, but soon Luigi was going through the delicate social introductions, everybody shaking hands with lots of piacere. But nobody talked about an apartment to rent. We were patient, as we knew it would come later. If we were learning anything about negotiating with Tuscans, it was not to talk about whatever we needed to talk about until the person controlling the deal decided they were ready to talk. If they did not talk about it, then we had not got social approval for the first step. We had not passed first base.

After fifteen minutes Signor Ercole announced his departure. He had to get back to his signora, who was preparing pranzo, but as he pulled on his jacket he said, almost as a passing comment: 'If you are not occupied tomorrow, why don't you come and meet my wife? I am sure she would like to know you.'

We had just passed first base! Luigi looked at me enquiringly. 'We'll be free tomorrow, won't we, Isabella? What do you think?'

'Certo,' I responded, trying not to seem over-keen.

'Come after pranzo,' Signor Ercole suggested, 'verso le quatro, towards four o'clock.'

It was unimportant that we did not even know where he lived, and it would have been positively rude to ask, because no Tuscan will give out an address in public. We knew we should discreetly ask someone else and we were sure Luciano would know, which he did. But he did not know where the empty apartment was, although he thought it had two bedrooms. It was definitely in the village, he was sure it was furnished, but he had no idea what it would cost.

The next day at three minutes past four we rang the doorbell of their home. Signora Lola's daughter was waiting to meet us, so we knew we were under close scrutiny. 'Buonasera, buonasera, molto piacere, accommodi.' Slowly we made our way through the social greetings and began to chat. Offered a glass of vin santo or a caffè, we both opted for vin santo, knowing we needed fortifying.

Ercole, who I thought was probably in his late seventies, was dressed immaculately, knife-edge creases down his trousers, a smart blue shirt, and at his neck the soft folds of a cravat. I noticed immediately that he spoke with great purpose, each sentence a contemplative announcement. Signora Lola was altogether different, sprightly and agile, and I liked her instantly. I spied a pristine lace cloth lying over a chair, a needle and thread nearby; she had been mending intricate lacework. Every now and then she interrupted her husband: 'Ercole! Ercole! Move your arm or you'll knock over the vin santo. I have not got time to be washing your clothes all the time,' or, 'Ercole, leave something for me to talk about. I'm not just here to grow old.' Out of the blue she questioned Luigi: 'What is the signora making you for dinner tonight?' Luigi managed to keep a straight face, for we both knew that the answer would raise or lower my standing as a signora of worth. My eyes beseeched Luigi not to tell her we had no idea what we would be eating tonight!

We talked about the village, the last harvest, the weather, but nobody talked about an apartment to rent. We listened attentively to stories about their family, their son who lives and works in Hong Kong, and gazed with admiration at photographs of their granddaughter; still nobody talked about an apartment to rent.

After exactly twenty-five minutes, Luigi, pretending reluctance, rose and said: 'It has been wonderful to meet such lovely people, but we had better get to the butcher before the choicest cuts are gone.' I was taken aback, but went along with this.

As we put on our jackets, Ercole said, 'Signor Dusi, are you still looking for an apartment to rent?' We both gulped and Luigi said, 'Si,' in a very by-the-way, why-are-you-enquiring tone. We had just passed second base! 'If you are free tomorrow, I'll be going down to the apartment at four o'clock. Perhaps you would like to come? It may suit you.' He added, of course, that he would need to speak to his son in Hong Kong, because if he was coming home for Christmas the apartment would have to be free for him. We assured Ercole we understood and would be back tomorrow at four o'clock. With hopes buoyed, we departed.

Ercole's last comment is a very interesting, even endearing, aspect of the Italian character. When making a deal, an Italian must always have an out, there must be a loophole, and the final decision must never be his alone. If a deal goes bad, or if he decides not to go ahead, he has someone else to share the blame. He can pull out and save face and you cannot be cross with him, because it is not his fault. Luigi swears that eventually he will learn this art.

The apartment is well described as tiny. A bathroom, basic but functional and clean, a living room with a one-person kitchen tacked on to one end, but with an open fireplace. Only one bedroom, with shuttered doors opening to a courtyard, terracotta paved, with jasmine growing on the walls and a good number of plants in pots, including bushy chilli peppers and basilico. A passage seemed to ascend into the buildings above, and when I got my bearings I realised we were directly below Ercole's own house. We had come around several buildings and down a long stone stairway and, looking up, sure enough, there was Lola peering down at me from her terrace. 'Buonasera Signora,' she called, grinning impudently.

Although we could have said tiny, we said we thought the apartment was sweet – but nobody mentioned money. Luigi said he thought it might suit us and Ercole said he didn't think his son *would* come home for Christmas. Luigi suggested that if we could come to some arrangement we would certainly consider taking it. Ercole said he would certainly ring his son to make sure he wasn't coming home and he would look into an arrangement. Luigi said he had inspected two or three apartments at prices discreti, discreet, and Ercole knew he had not, but accepted that was a sensible thing to say. On the pretext of re-examining the kitchen I went back through to the living room, because Ercole would not talk about money in my presence. That would not be polite.

The small living room felt friendly. Pushing open the nearest shutter I stared out, skipped two paces and flung open the second. Instantly the room was flooded with that incredibly translucent light that falls on the Tuscan hills in the late afternoon, and there it was, on the Tuscan hills outside those shutters! The apartment overlooks a well-worked vegetable garden and olive grove, across huddled stone houses with terracotta roofs, straight over the glorious Orcia Valley and, in the distance, two villages straddle the hills. 'Luigi,' I called silently, hugging myself. 'Make the deal. I can live small if I can live here.'

We moved in the following morning, and over time have become very close to our landlords. From the very first day there was no doubt Ercole and Lola considered it their duty to attend without delay to anything needed by their tenants – even if these stranieri did not always know themselves what they needed. They naturally felt it only practical to suggest new or alternative things we would need soon. For instance, the apartment has a fireplace, so Ercole felt it his duty not only to provide wood, but also to call at our door one chilly evening to lay the fire. He set to work folding the newspaper into thick bands, laying first wispy kindling and, with only kindness, showing Luigi how to position the folded paper, before finally adding chopped wood. 'It has to be done this way,' Ercole explained patiently, 'so that this particular fireplace works efficiently. When summer comes,' he added thoughtfully, 'I'll bring you a barbecue which you can wedge into the fireplace to grill sausages.' Luigi did not mention that in Australia the last house we lived in had a barbecue as big as the kitchen. Somehow it didn't matter any more.

Lola always kept an eye on the weather, and if I neglected to bring the washing in by four o'clock she would pop downstairs and re-peg it under the shelter of her cantina. Anyone knows, she therefore implied, the air after four is likely to be damp – humid – and you cannot be ironing humid clothes because the damp gets into your bones and will give you a chill. And they both believed there was a certain need for supervision, a watchful eye. 'How can these stranieri know when to stay low, or keep silent, or remain invisible, if we don't guide them?' they reasoned. 'These stranieri seem very naive in the ways of the world, at least the world inside these walls.'

Ercole and Lola show remarkable stamina considering both are approaching eighty years of age. Ercole has been on a pension for twenty years, yet they still seem to be occupied every day. There are one or two sideline businesses, they have an aunt of ninety-two in Siena to care for, and there is plenty of work for them both in Pianello. Ercole has inquisitive eyes, is a man of medium height and lean build and has long since lost most of his thinning hair, but the most fascinating thing about him is that he always has a questioning look on his face. It is as if he is certain you will have something to ask him and, as a retired school-master, he just adores explaining things. He walks with purpose, yet is easily distracted and very happy if you do need to speak with him, especially if you have an interesting question or two. When you do question him, however, he does not reply immediately. His head tilts back, he opens his mouth, chin jutting forward slightly, and at the same time his hands come up and the five fingers of each hand meet each other in a pyramid in front of his chest. 'Ah, caro . . .' He will settle in for an explanation as his joined hands move back and forth in a praying gesture and his head nods. Ercole always thinks deeply before he speaks and phrases his reply in such a way that you will receive the best explanation he can offer. For example, should you telephone Ercole asking simply if you can pass by for a caffè at 10.30 this morning, he will need three or four explanatory sentences before you receive an answer, and every sentence is justified. He is always the schoolmaster, making sure he is understood in a logical, sequential way.

On the other hand, if you were to telephone and pose the same question to Lola she would scarcely wait for you to finish your sentence; sharp, clipped and fast she will reply: 'No, you cannot.' And she offers no explanation. Should you persist, possibly taken aback because of her instant negative response, opening your own mouth too quickly to ask why not, she will briskly retort, as if you ought to have realised: 'Because I will not be here.' Nor will she ask why you want to see her, which is an incredible feat of self-control. She assumes it must be a matter which requires discretion and you cannot talk about it on the phone, so she will ask no questions. Rather, she will simply suggest you come at four o'clock instead and she will be very pleased to offer you a caffè then. End of conversation.

Lola is a neat woman, still with an almost girlish figure, who cares for herself impeccably. Her skin is flawless, her hair always curled and, needless to say, she dresses fashionably and well. Her smile is infectious and her eyes are sharp, but not as sharp as her wit; she always has the last word, and it is usually unexpectedly funny.

In their older years Ercole and Lola are glad of their comfortable life inside the walls, but well remember the time when there was much misery in Montalcino. Ercole, his father and his grandfather were born and raised on Montalcino territory, but only Ercole was raised within the walls; all three generations were born at Poggio alle Mura, a few kilometres from the village. Some time in the 1400s a castle, Poggio alle Mura, was given to Conte Placidi, an honourable Sienese citizen, in reward for his military aid in the medieval wars against Florence. The gift encompassed not only the castle but also thirty-six or so humble houses which were spread around the castle environs for the peasant farmers to dwell in. Ercole's grandfather was born in one of these houses, the son of a contadino. Ercole's father was born in the same place and when Ercole was born in 1920, in one of the remaining houses, after more than 500 years the castle was still owned by the family of Conte Placidi. These days Poggio alle Mura is better known as Castello Banfi, a splendidly restored castle surrounded by rows of vineyards with sophisticated technology producing the brilliant wines of Montalcino, but it was not so long ago that life at the old castello was very different.

In the 1920s Ercole's father left the castle and brought his family closer to Montalcino; by finding work as a labourer he was able to ensure his only son received an education. Ercole qualified as a schoolteacher in 1938, but was immediately called to war. In 1943 he was captured and made a POW in Sicily, later being sent to Africa, where he remained until 1946. When Ercole walks through Montalcino today, I frequently hear people call out:

'Buongiorno, Maestro. Good morning, Teacher.' Back in Montalcino after the war, he taught thirty-four students, all boys, the same class year after year, hence many adult men of the village still call him 'Teacher'.

Lola's introduction to Montalcino was entirely different, and although she has lived in the village more than fifty years she does not claim to be true Montalcinese. Just as Ercole's background explains much about his personality, his logical way of telling a story or dealing with a problem, so Lola's upbringing explains her industrious ways, her quick wit, her ability to surmise a situation instantly. Lola, or Ludovina, was born the last of eight children at Jesi in the province of Ancona. Her mother had no breastmilk so, like her seven brothers and sisters, Lola was fed by a balai, a woman who lived locally, had an infant of her own and enough milk for someone else's baby as well. Lola's mother was a business woman, so she saw little of her as she was busy building up her own silk factory with fifty people working for her, or buying and selling property, so Lola spent much time with her aunts and uncles. She has told me her life as a young girl was completely different to that of the girls of Montalcino because, during the war, Jesi was a busy city full of industry. It was called 'little Milan' and the young never suffered because everyone found work in the aeroplane factory, the silk factory, making matches or jam, or a hundred other things. 'By the time I was nineteen I was working in the office of a silk mill,' she proudly told me. 'I was a very modern young lady riding my bicycle to work every day, and,' she added, expecting this news to really astound me, 'I was even wearing trousers!'

Ercole had been sent to Ancona in 1942 to re-establish a regiment, and that, he solemnly told me, is where his troubles began! Soon enough, modern miss Lola was a wartime fiancée, but Ercole was sent to Sicily, captured, and for the next four years

Lola had no idea if he was alive or dead. 'Then,' she boasted triumphantly, 'after the war he came back to Jesi to get me.'

The Montalcino to which Ercole brought his young bride was, in their own words, a tragedy. It seemed as if the village was forgotten by history, the very last place in all of Italy to begin any restructuring after the war. Ercole was fortunate to have qualified as a schoolteacher and, although there seemed to be hundreds of children and no facilities, he did have reliable work. For the village men it was heartbreakingly hard; some were craftsmen, tailors, shoemakers or barbers, but there was tremendous misery because there was no other work.

'I do remember,' said Lola, 'some of the women sewed, but many women would struggle home from the woods at sunset carrying enormous untidy bundles of sticks and twigs on their heads, little children at their feet. The wood was not for their own fires because there were no ovens in the houses then, it was for the forno, the baker's oven. The women would exchange the wood for a handful of flour, go home and knead the flour into dough, then bring it back to the forno to be baked. And it was a dark, gloomy place because there was little electricity, there were so few lights.' Lola recalled walking up towards Ruga one dark afternoon; her eyes narrowed when she talked and I knew she still pictured it clearly: 'Everything looked so sad, there was so much misery. As I came to a few bushes, the tiny birds flew away, and I thought to myself, "Even God's little birds cannot bear to be in Montalcino." But,' she continued, eyes brightening, 'I loved Ercole and wanted to be with him.'

They lived for a few months in a house outside the walls near Buonconvento; one of the other teachers would walk to their house every morning, bringing the news from Montalcino. 'We had to leave the key outside near the gate . . .' Lola looked at Ercole to see if he remembered. 'Si, si, mia amore,' he finished the sentence for her. 'Yes, my love, because we were always still in bed!' Lola grinned happily. Along with the news, the teacher brought milk for their first baby, so he was called Zio di Latte, Uncle Milk. But at least they had electricity down in the valley, and they had a toilet, even if the well was behind the house and most of the time they could not use the water because it had to be kept for the contadini, who needed it for the animals. Remembering their first year of marriage so fondly, Lola's eyes lit up her face. 'We had nothing, but we were so happy.'

After nearly a year they came to live in Montalcino in a house with Ercole's parents and they were to live with their in-laws until Ercole's father, then mother, died. But Lola cheerfully told me her mother-in-law was a saint, a beautiful person. 'We both looked after the general household work, but Nonna was obstinately and solely in charge of the kitchen. I cannot make sauces the way Nonna did, although I use exactly the same recipe, don't I, Ercole? The same ingredients, but it never tastes the same. I think it is because I still do not know the very moment to add the wine. I know how much of everything, but it is the timing that is important. You have to know exactly when to add the nose of the wine – Nonna always knew.'

Today we are having Sunday lunch with Ercole and Lola. The prospect is a trifle daunting, sends anxious tingles through me, but it is also an exciting and longed-for milestone, because the invitation is an indication of sincere trust and acceptance. Knowing there are wise rules of behaviour we will need to adhere to, we talk about the repercussions of this invitation on our blossoming life here and how we should conduct ourselves. The success of our visit will depend on several things, not least of which will be knowing how to dress. Next to what they eat, Italians place the highest priority on how they look, and it must be right for each occasion, which may mean changing clothes several times a day.

Each morning when the women of the village go out to do the shopping I have noticed they are always well-dressed – not *over*dressed – but well-dressed. The morning round calls for a smart jacket or overcoat, a colourful neck scarf, leather shoes which are low-heeled and sensible for walking, and jewellery is discreet; a semi-precious stone and, if it is chilly, leather gloves. For evening passeggiata a purposeful choice should be obvious, to show you have not turned out in the tired clothes you have been wearing all day.

Lola offered a subtle Montalcinese hint one morning when she met Luigi in the piazza. 'Are you going to the mountains, Luigi?' she asked guilelessly. Clearly, she believed we needed assistance in the ways of Montalcino.

We were fast learning from Ercole and Lola that to become part of this village we needed to adjust our way of thinking, our way of walking and our social etiquette. Dress must show respect for others and ourselves; slightly faded favourite jeans, reversible bomber jacket and Nike footwear went to the bottom of the cupboard. But on this important visit today we must also work out how, without using words, we can reveal to Lola and Ercole how honoured we are to receive this invitation. We know Ercole and Lola will allude to the simplicity of their home, their food, their possessions; that they are not nobles after all, but Montalcinesi living a tranquil, understated life with no pretence of grandeur and, indeed, the honour is theirs completely that we are visiting their family home. This is a courtly game of etiquette and, provided you know how to play, everybody wins!

People in the village do not often entertain at home; many houses are small and the elaborate dining rooms found in modern homes are virtually non-existent in a medieval village. It is more usual to be invited to share a meal with friends at a trattoria. But Lola, after a five-decade apprenticeship under her mother-in-law before taking charge of the kitchen, seems eager to demonstrate she has made up ground fast, and I think she suspects that we stranieri may not be eating wisely, nor at the right time. Lola would not be able to detect any aroma, nor hear the rattling of pots from my kitchen, at any time during the day. In the evening at eight o'clock, when she and Ercole are clearing away their fruit and cheese, she probably hears all sorts of preparations underway. If the aroma of bistecca is wafting upstairs, she will be worrying about us going to bed on a meal like that . . . it just could not be wise. Her concentration on one's wellbeing is an enlightening glimpse into the exaltation of food within the village, the culinary finesse of the cook and, at all costs, the unshakeable priority of Montalcinesi, and all Italians, of eating wisely and well, and at the right time.

For this important occasion we dress appropriately. Luigi wears a crisply ironed shirt, contrasting tie and smart hounds-tooth jacket. His black shoes shine and he insisted on polishing my high heels until the leather gleamed. Having changed my mind twice, I finally dressed in a knitted suit, camel-coloured, with which I wear a favourite antique locket. My skirt is modestly calf-length, and with a duck-egg blue cashmere shawl draped elegantly around my shoulders I think my appearance befits the occasion.

Coats on, bearing the parcel of dolci wrapped so attentively by Gabriela, we set off, knowing full well there are rituals to be observed. Do not imagine for a moment walking into a friend's home at the appointed time, the dining table set with gleaming cutlery and sparkling glasses, aromas emerging from an unseen kitchen down the hall, the wine decanted, and your coat, whisked from your shoulders, vanishing into another room. Rather, imagine us pressing the brass buzzer on the roadway door. Just because we have lived for some time at the bottom of a stairway which connects our apartment with theirs does not mean we approach via this undercover shortcut when a formal invitation has been issued. We are received with courtesy at the front door, where the buzzer is straightaway answered by Ercole: 'Buonasera . . . ciao, caro Luigi, come in, come in.'

Ercole releases the door mechanism which admits us to the ground-floor foyer and we advance up the flight of spotless travertine stairs as the dark timber door on the first landing creaks open. Ercole steps back from the door into the narrow hall behind, and Luigi calls out politely, poking just his head around the door and directing his voice down the passage, so Lola can hear: 'Permesso? May we come in?' She responds: 'Si, Luigi,' as she unwraps her floral apron and joins Ercole in the hall. Social greetings demand an affectionate kiss on both cheeks and a warm handclasp.

We remove our coats and hang them on the crowded coat-stand by the door. Following our hosts down the hallway to the kitchen, the first thing I see is a square table covered with large flat wooden boards. Lying on the boards on cotton tea towels is row after row of tagliatelle made by Lola this morning, ready for the pot. 'Signora, it looks marvellous!' And along with her I raise a handful and let it slide around my palm, examining it attentively but at the same time letting the ends of the long strands rest gently on the board to ensure they do not stretch.

Lola beams, thrilled, but then discloses with a plaintive shrug, 'I am not so sure. There was so much humidity in the air this morning, the rolling was very difficult, so I do not think it is il migliore, the best, I have ever made, but we will make do.' She goes on to explain that she has made a ragù sauce, her mother-in-law's recipe, to have with the tagliatelle. 'Speriamo,' she sighs, 'let's hope we eat well enough.'

How admirably typical. In one short sentence Lola has

incorporated two escape clauses. In Montalcino it is vital to understand how and when to create escape clauses, not only because it can get you out of all sorts of troublesome situations, but also because it is the epitome of politeness, saves one from indiscretion and means nobody loses face. This is another courteous art we have yet to learn. Lola is really saying: 'If this is not the best tagliatelle you have ever tasted, I have already told you it is not the best I am capable of making,' and if the ragù sauce is not to your liking, she has explained it is her mother-in-law's recipe. The weather has been cited as the cause of the first defect – if indeed there is one – and her mother-in-law, well, she died at ninety, she was an exceptional cook and an absolute saint, but perhaps she was too experienced at this particular recipe and did not leave Lola enough instruction. What do you think? Behind these escape clauses is the indisputable fact that Italians, by nature, want everybody to be happy. You may think Lola's escape clauses are her safety net, but this is not strictly so; she is in fact offering the safety net to *me*. She wants me to be blissfully happy with everything, but if I am not, she has politely shown me exactly how I can comment with honesty and still feel at ease. I already know the handmade tagliatelle and ragù sauce are going to be outstanding. I help Lola carry the cotton towels, with the tagliatelle lying on top, to the kitchen, knowing full well it has all been left there just long enough for me to thoughtfully examine it and approve.

The antique dining table is centred on a terrazzo floor in a small extension of an even smaller kitchen. Everything is in its place, meticulously clean, but no obvious extra effort has been made to have the place spick-and-span for our visit. The walls of their home are adorned with paintings and maps of Montalcino, books line the shelves, thermometers and gauges keep a watchful eye on the temperature and dreaded humidity; the cosiness is accentuated with a fire blazing in the hearth. All is friendly and homely, the trappings of life remain in view, and we merge into the scene.

Lola issues a command: 'Ercole, a cloth for the table,' and he scurries about searching for the right one. A square of well-loved pristine cotton with delicate handworked lace edging – the one I saw lying across a chair when we were introduced to Lola – is drawn from an old chest. Lola approves and throws it into the air, letting it float down on to the table. Everyone takes an edge and we pull it into place. A bundle of bone-handled knives and heavy silver forks come from the kitchen drawer and Ercole is sent by Lola to the dresser in the next room to fetch some finely etched crystal glasses. Ercole and Luigi disappear downstairs to the gloomy subterranean warren which meanders beneath these medieval houses to select a bottle of red wine from the cantina. Ercole created this cantina many years ago, digging it out with an iron pick from the very hillside of Montalcino. In several places boulders protrude into the cantina; this is the rocky foundation of Montalcino on which his home rests.

'When I was digging it out,' he explained to Luigi in intricate detail, 'I discovered this massive rock, more than a metre across, sitting in the middle of where I wanted the floor to be. I got some friends together and we tried to break it up with hammers, but after a few days we gave up. Then one day my uncle came and suggested I should dig a big hole and push the rock into it. Gia, a ragionne! I thought he had reasoned well! We had only dug thirty centimetres down when we struck a slab of patterned brickwork, so of course we all got excited, thinking we had found buried treasure. But when we tried to lift the slab it slipped from our grasp and vanished from our hands into darkness. We got torches and lamps and peered down, then descended by rope into a deep well in the shape of a flask, which had pick markings dug into baked clay walls. There was no treasure, but Lola, amore mia, was quick to tell me where to put the rock!'

They reappear with a bottle of Rosso and one of Brunello. Rosso is ideal with pasta, but the Montalcinesi know Brunello comes into its own with a substantial meat dish and the cinghiale we are soon to eat merits nothing less. At last, all is ready for our intimate family meal. Out of a small oven Lola retrieves thin rounds of Tuscan bread. On half of them she has melted mozzarella cheese, allowing an anchovy to sizzle into the cheese as it grilled. The salted anchovy has been drizzled with olive oil and the piquant flavour cuts sharply against the cheese. The other half are topped with salsa verde, a traditional Montalcinese parsley and basil sauce which has its origins in the cucina povera; ingredients I can easily grow on the terrace for most of the year.

'How are they?' she demands of Ercole before he has even got the first one in his mouth. 'Will they do?' We all chorus: 'Yes, they are delicious,' so she immediately pulls out another plateful. Conversation revolves around the possible ways to go about finding buffalo-milk mozzarella and the number of times and places over the last twenty years when they have eaten sublime mozzarella, how they are unlikely to find anything as splendid ever again. And then the discussion turns to what time of year these fresh salty anchovies are available from the fisherman.

Italians in general, and certainly the Montalcinesi, discuss food endlessly; not only the women but men too are constantly concerned with quality. Two or three men sitting in a bar will talk for half an hour about the merits of a certain filling for ravioli, the conversation weaving all over the country. They will recall the particular filling most satisfactory in Lombardia where, only in Mantua, would they eat ravioli with pumpkin, and how only in Piemonte have they eaten a particular ravioli with fondue cheese filling . . . 'But here,' they'll say, 'well, here we know our own ricotta and spinach filling is sublime. But only if you go to Pienza and fetch the ricotta the minute it is setting . . . really, it should still be warm. You will make a buon pranzo.' It is a never-ending conversation, because Italians are constantly thinking about the last splendid meal they had – or the one they hope to eat next.

I suspect that if I were to challenge Lola on her dedication in the kitchen she would dismiss any suggestion she even liked being there, let alone knew how to cook. 'After all,' she once affirmed, 'Ercole is true Montalcinese but I am not, I have only been here fifty years and, anyway, I never cooked at all. Ercole's mother always controlled the kitchen, she cooked in the way of the contadini all her life.' She told me Nonna made sublime bean soup, her pasta with beans was always il migliore, and her tagliatelle and pinci were buonissimi. But Nonna would never cook lasagna, never once in ninety years. She refused because it is not a traditional dish of Montalcino. 'Her real talent,' Lola's eyes sparkled as she remembered, 'her speciality was the girarroste, the open fire with a spit. She was a saint, wasn't she, Ercole? She had patience enough to roast tiny tordi, thrushes, little birds which Ercole brought back from the hunt.' I found it hard not to wince as Lola looked at Ercole, who confirmed the little birds were always roasted to perfection and it needed Nonna's saintly patience because the glowing embers had to be just right or you ended up with dry meat and splintered bones. 'Her baby birds were always juicy . . . so sweet and tender.'

Lola has the water gently simmering on the stove and her freshly made tagliatelle takes only minutes to cook. In no time at all she has two forks between her fingers and is lifting huge mounds into china bowls, gently spreading just enough ragù sauce – a combination of minced pork and veal, a little liver and simmered gently in red wine – over each serving. She moves around the table with a wedge of parmigiano, grating it on the spot over each bowl. The aroma is rich, a delicate balance of meat and wine fills the room, but I can see she is becoming anxious again. This time she demands of Ercole, 'Allora, what is it like, Ercole? Have I done it well?' Again we chorus, 'Yes, you have done it well.' The tagliatelle has a texture and flavour all its own, and dressed with the ragù sauce – spread in moderation – is a scented tangle of simple, first-quality ingredients. She then comments dryly, 'It ought to be – I made sure the ragù simmered on a very low flame for more than three hours.' A second bowl of pasta is essential and resistance is useless, especially since in Italy you do not save yourself for a main course. There is no main course, as the primo and secondo share celebrity status. Each meal is a progression of flavours and textures, but not a progression of size.

Lola seems calm, satisfied with all the sighs, comments and hearty sounds as the second servings of tagliatelle disappear. As we swallow the very last mouthful, she confidently assures us the next time we come she will make ravioli, because it is one of her specialities. Then she adds thoughtfully, 'Would you like us to bring some fresh ricotta back from Pienza for you? Ercole is taking me to buy pecorino for the cantina.' How can one possibly resist? A large pan is bubbling away on the stove and Lola tells me this is the most dependable recipe you can ever follow for cinghiale al' cacciatore, wild boar from the hunter. Because Ercole is one of the Pianello hunters and a member of the Montalcino squad, there is always a piece of cinghiale in the freezer for just such an occasion as this. 'I know this recipe is unsurpassed,' she enthuses with a nod of her head, then cautions with a sense of the dramatic, 'but . . . in reality the success of the plate depends entirely on the quality of the wild boar my husband has brought home.' Identified at once! Another enchanting escape clause is instantly recognisable. Ercole raises his eyebrows, gives a wry smile and by his body language resignedly agrees that everything rests on his shoulders.

We watch as she sets about the finishing touches to serve the cinghiale while Ercole recounts the hunt a couple of weeks ago when this particular cinghiale was shot. We murmur our interest and admiration as graphic pictures of the hunt through the woods to the west of the village rush through our minds. He remembers the details so well that you might wonder whether he didn't know this wild boar personally. He talks with such pride about the hunt, describing the chase by the dogs, the shouts of his friends and the final victorious shoot. It isn't his pride alone, of course, but that of the whole squad – and this particular boar, he points at the bubbling pan, was very clever. 'We had twenty-four dogs with us that day,' he tells open-mouthed Luigi, 'and it took every one of them to flush this cinghiale out.' Taking an astonished Luigi by the arm, he drags him through to the hallway and unlocks a wooden case with his mini-hunting armoury inside. Apparently the boar in this pan was not clever enough.

Tiny white onions fresh from the soil, undoubtedly the ones I saw looped over the clothesline this morning, gently baked in the oven and drizzled with olive oil, accompany the cinghiale, which Lola now serves on to our plates. As is the habit of the Montalcinesi, a modest portion of meat is abbastanza, quite enough. 'Is it tough, Ercole? Have I put too much salt in? Is it as tender as the piece we had last month? Have I destroyed it?' Lola rounds on him theatrically and we cannot help laughing. Of course it is absolute bliss. Just a few simple ingredients which are the mainstay of the kitchen and for the third time we chorus vehement approval. Lola is at last content. I ask if she might explain how she prepared these tasty onions, telling her I had seen them hanging from her clothesline this morning but, as always, quick to respond, she says: 'Explain? No, what would be the point? Bring a kilo of baby white onions here next week and I will show you, there's nothing to it.'

To finish the meal, a wedge of pecorino cheese sits directly on the table with a couple of green pears. Ercole cuts the cheese, which is stagionato, matured for around twelve months; it is coated with charcoal but the round has not turned black nor lost too much moisture. Then he expertly peels and slices a crisp pear and everyone helps themselves directly from the table. When the plates are cleared away, Lola unwraps the tray of dolci which we accompany with a glass of Moscadello. She prepares caffè and sends Ercole back to the cantina to fetch a bottle of grappa. Lola and Ercole have put us completely at ease and my anxiety about rules of behaviour and possible repercussions seem unwarranted. It is all pleasantly simple, genuinely affectionate and, above all, a combination of delicious ingredients prepared with patience and with the love of sharing food at the table.

At the respectable hour of 2.30 we begin our goodbyes, knowing there will be several false departures before we reach the door. Now confident of the success of our visit, we assure Lola we will most definitely be able to tell our friends we ate well at the table of Ercole and Lola, and that she is a very fine cook. Lola, always thinking ahead and never one to miss an opportunity, but with a look of genuine innocence, assails me with: 'That is good, because I am looking forward to visiting you in your apartment soon, just to be sure you are feeding your husband properly.'

My anxiety returns with alarming speed! What she really means is she wants to come for pranzo, and she wants to know if I can cook. How can I possibly respond? What will I do?

'Don't worry,' soothes Luigi under his breath. He has seen me

trying to swallow my panic, choking through our final affectionate farewell. After we have our coats on, are through the door
and on the way down the travertine stairs, he whispers, 'Non
preoccuparti, Isabella. We'll do Thai green curry followed by a
pavlova. That will really confound them.'

WINTER

CHAPTER SIX

Pianello . . . Pianello . . . Pianello!

Maurelia, President of Pianello, is alerting quartieranti of the meeting she has called, because she has important news. On Monday morning a notice appeared in the iron-framed case hanging outside Pharmacy Salvioni next to the cappellone, this being the noticeboard for all Pianello announcements. Any Pianello members passing through the piazza are bound to check the board daily and Maurelia is expecting a good attendance. The notice promises a merenda, a small meal, before the meeting on Friday evening, and the business will be dealt with at nine o'clock.

Luigi and I, because we live in Pianello, were invited some months ago to become members, quartieranti – an invitation we felt honoured to receive and eagerly accepted. I always check the board because it is the only way of knowing what is happening in our quartiere. During the week there seemed to be a lot of mysterious nodding and head-shaking between certain Pianello members, whilst others seemed complacently oblivious about why the meeting is being called. Several times during the week we were reminded by others of the impending meeting. They were gearing up for a record turn-out and were concerned in case we hadn't seen the notice – but there was no way I was going to miss this! Something dramatic is happening.

Pianello sede, our headquarters, is in a stone building attached to the eleventh-century Church of San Pietro. A simple plaque hangs outside on the wall next to a wooden door which leads into a short passage and a flight of steps; before the steps, a low door on the left opens into what seems to be an industrially equipped kitchen. Iron pans line the shelves and stacks of iron trays lie on benches, which house numerous hotplates, with grills and ovens beneath. All of this equipment is essential several times a year, when the Pianello ladies prepare dinner for two or three hundred people. A set of ropes hang in the passage, dropping down through a hole in the ceiling. Above the passage is the slender twin bell-tower of the Church of San Pietro; the two dainty bronze bells are still rung by hand on special feast days, when the priest pulls on the ropes in the passage.

The meeting room upstairs is not large, but has a rustic brick fireplace at one end. The walls are decorated with posters of Pianello territory and blown-up photographs of jubilant scenes of past tournaments showing the joy of Pianello victories. One wall is lined with framed prints of Pianello medieval costumes: the Lady and her Lord, the knaves, Captain of the archers, and the archers themselves. The costumes are not kept here but in a cantina near Porta Burelli, where they are hung and stored through winter because they are extremely costly to maintain. There is a television and video set up so the young people can come and watch football, or on informal occasions members can replay yet again a video of a past victory at the Sagra. In one corner dozens of banners are stacked against the wall; these are the blue and white banners which fly all around the quartiere at tournament time, and on annual feast days.

Beside a narrow window at the rear is a glass-fronted wall-mounted cabinet, no more than forty or fifty centimetres square. The modest dimensions of this cabinet, and its placement, do not really acknowledge its significance. In this cabinet are a good number of medallions and some small silver and golden arrowheads; each one is unpretentiously mounted below a handwritten year and below each arrowhead are the names of two archers. The names of past and present Pianello archers, Arrigucci, Salvioni, Landi and, of course, Bovini appear repeatedly. This is Pianello's victory cabinet. There is no prize for winning an archery tournament, no sack of money for the quartiere, no golden trophy for the archers to swing through the air. There is only honour, pride, and a simple medallion or arrowhead which is mounted inside the cabinet.

The body of the room is taken up with long wooden tables and benches forming a U-shape, but the focal point is the blue and white Pianello emblem emblazoned above the fireplace. The crest

111

of the Comune of Montalcino, the black and white Sienese shield and the emblems of the other three quarters, surround that of Pianello. The sede is a gathering point, a place for social interaction where members share dinners and plan for the future of the quarter. Everything is understated, uncomplicated and, once inside, familiar and friendly.

Tonight the air is touched with loaded anticipation. The ladies, who are now completing preparations for the merenda before the meeting, all work for Pianello on a voluntary basis, bringing their own expertise to the traditional dishes they prepare. Although the roots of the Montalcinese cuisine are all in the cucina povera, ways of preparing and presenting the food sometimes differ between the quarters; some quarters have recipes which are their very own. Today, Friday, several ladies are labouring away, including Settimia, who cannot really remember when she did not cook for Pianello, Maria-Rosa, the elegant wife of Dottore Luciano, and young Fiorella. Luciana is bustling around the room with an air of authority because she is head-cook and, inevitably, Lola is here: always ready to work for Pianello. Although another four or five ladies regularly work in the kitchens, they are not all needed tonight because we are having a light meal.

Fiorella has the tables ablaze with blue and white check table-cloths, blue serviettes and white flowers; everything is in Pianello colours. Just as Settimia lays the antipasto on the tables, Maurelia, the other office bearers and a dozen members begin to file through the door, greeting each other affectionately. Many older members of the quarter arrive, as well as Massimo the archer, his wife Ofelia and their daughter Chiara, Vittorio and Laura who have a farm just outside the walls, and Claudio, a schoolteacher, who is Fiorella's husband. Dottore Luciano who trains the archers is already here, as are ten or more young people including our other archers, Alessandro, Davide and Gabriele. Within ten minutes the sede is crowded and fifty or sixty people are chatting noisily. Maurelia seems satisfied, because the young people these days are generally away at secondary college or university during the week; some work in Siena or even further away and cannot always get home on Friday evening.

There are few formalities at Pianello. Maurelia is in her second term as President and is well supported by the other office bearers. But it is a time-consuming task because there are many obligations each year which the quarters undertake for the benefit of the community, as well as individual quartiere meetings, dinners and celebrations. With a cheerful disposition and a talent for diplomacy, Maurelia orchestrates and keeps things ticking along smoothly; tonight her face is warmly aglow. Clapping her hands and using one of her three favourite words: 'Allora!' she calls loudly for everyone to take a seat. The wine is poured, just a third of a glass each, and it only takes a few minutes for the tasty antipasto of prosciutto and fennel salami to disappear. Settimia is back up the steps and, knowing Luciana has the next course ready, gathers the empty plates and returns to the kitchen. Fiorella, at the kitchen door, calls out to Riccardo, who is slender and tall, and Massimo, who is solid and broad, and instructs them to carry an enormous iron cauldron from the kitchen on to a trolley at the top of the steps. Then, using an exaggerated iron soup ladle she serves copious bowls of steaming zuppa di fagioli, bean soup. As always, baskets abundantly filled with Tuscan bread are on the tables to sop up the juices.

There is plenty of noisy chatter, people are laughing and catching up on news, but the riveting topic of conversation among the men at my table seems to be the hunt programmed for next weekend. This year's hunting season is under way and their capocaccia, leader of the squad, has passed the word that he has

113

been telephoned by the winemaker at Castello Banfi, who has asked if he can arrange for the squad to hunt in the woods close to the castle. Apparently there are many cinghiale there, doing so much damage to vines and crops that it is becoming a matter of some urgency. The worried winemaker says he thinks there must be some fearsome wild boar out there, because a row of vines has been completely uprooted, and not only that, there are practically no pheasant at all in the woods this year. Pheasants will not live in the same territory as cinghiale because the boar destroy the undergrowth where pheasants nest. Cinghiale weigh as much as 120 kilograms and in rampant numbers not only destroy crops and vines but are a hazard to farmers and their dogs, as well as the ecological balance of the woods.

This seems to be a summons for help to which hunting members from all four quartieri are responding with vigour. The men are making plans to register, and it sounds as though thirty or forty Montalcinesi hunters will be out in the woods next weekend. I can tell there is no way Ercole is going to miss out and, glancing at Lola, I can see she certainly knows it is no use seeking to restrain his enthusiasm; even at nearly eighty years of age he will be on every hunt this season. One weekend I asked him how things had gone on the hunt. His face lit up and for once he did not need six sentences to tell me. With a satisfied smile he said: 'Ah, meraviglioso. I have had an enchanting and marvellous day.' It seemed an odd description for a day hunting cinghiale. The hunters have been going to the woods every season since they were old enough to go with their fathers and Vittorio has told me how the comradeship of old schoolfriends, uniting as a team under the capocaccia, as well as accomplishing the task for farmers, is immensely satisfying, even though these days they rarely return from the hunt with meat in any quantity.

Renato, who is sitting next to me, announces that his dogs,

Dora and Dianna, are in prime condition. This I can confirm, because we live next door and every morning when we throw open our shutters, the dogs, as well as Renato, are waiting to greet us. In fact, at first we thought Renato was in his woodworking laboratory waiting to hear our shutters, open so he could pounce, but of course he wasn't, he was simply going about his morning work. But once we are up and about, he instantly appears below the shutters with Dora and Dianna, cheerily welcoming us to join the day.

I am listening to the men discussing who is going to ring the capocaccia to register their names when a curious crashing startles me. Riccardo and the youngsters sitting with him are banging on the table with their spoons in a frenzy of ear-piercing battering. Most people turn round, surprise and shock on their faces, but others do not seem at all perturbed when the youngsters begin to chant: 'Pia . . . Pia . . . Pi . . . an . . . ell . . . o!' – finally breaking into the Pianello song. Riccardo's booming voice leads Pianello singing in the piazza at tournament time, but in the sede his voice is deafening; as the chorus rises, the older people cover their ears and even the hunters give up their conversations. Other youngsters follow Riccardo's lead, knowing exactly when to come in with a chorus or an extra loud 'Pi . . . an . . . ell . . . o!'

Il blu ci s'ha nel sangue	The blue we have in our blood
Il bianco s'ha nel cuore	The white is in our hearts
Del leccio siam l'onore	At the oak tree we have the honour
Ci dovete rispetta'	You all owe us respect
Pia . . . Pia . . . Pianello!	*Pia . . . .Pia . . . Pianello!*
E noi del Pianellone	We of the great Pianello
Si viene da Via Moglio	We come from Via Moglio

| *Del leccio siam l'orgoglio* | We are the pride of the oak tree |
| *Siamo i meglio della città* | We are the best in the village |

| *Pia . . . Pia . . . Pianello!* | *Pia . . . Pia . . . Pianello!* |

They chant and sing eight verses of the refrain twice, then break into rowdy cheers with more spoons crashing before diving into the soup. It is easy to see the friendships run deep; many of the older folk have been sharing a meal at Pianello for fifty years. There are several children sitting with us who are experiencing the enthusiasm of the young adults; they copy Riccardo, already anxious to become part of the singing. The young adults are in turn learning their responsibility and loyalty from the elders; we are among a companionable group which varies from six or seven years to more than eighty years of age.

Settimia, in her high-pitched squeaky voice which can hardly be heard above the din, waddles up the stairs and announces that there will be no secondo plate as this is a merenda and there is too much business to discuss. Young Riccardo hears every squeaky word. He is up from the table in a flash: 'What, no secondo?' He mimics her voice and, grabbing hold of her, with assistance from Michele, they pretend they are going to dump her into a long wooden chest which sits by the wall. Settimia screams and gasps with feigned agitation, but nobody goes to her rescue. Riccardo is 185 centimetres tall and Settimia is no more than 140; she is always trying to box him on the nose when he calls her his little elf or, even worse, tells her the food is terrible. It is a game they often play. He fends off her flailing arms as she struts back to the table and, lifting himself to his full height, towers above her, laughing cheekily.

Fiorella restores order, assuring us there is plenty more soup. Pecorino cheese and mandarancia – a hybrid between a tangerine and a sweet orange – arrive on the tables and after that Fiorella brings caffè and, for those who want it, vin santo or grappa. That is the end of our merenda and at some invisible but timely stroke everybody is on their feet and within ten minutes we have the tables cleared of every plate, cup, knife and fork. Two ladies remain in the kitchen to wash up, but everybody else returns to the tables because Maurelia is ready to commence. Some of what she is about to extol, many people already know, because it has been circulating through the village for some time, but the sequel to her tale is utterly astounding.

Taking on her presidential face, standing confidently, she begins by reminding everyone: 'Allora, the ancient Church of San Pietro has always been considered *our* church because it is in our territory and we celebrate our Saint's Day with Mass in San Pietro. When Pianello wins the tournament, the ropes in the passage are pulled and the bronze bells in the twin towers peal joyfully over Pianello to let everyone know of our victory. Pero, however,' she reflects sadly, using her second favourite word, 'it is some years since the victory bells have pealed.' She recounts a story similar to the one I have heard. Up until a few months ago, anyone could attend regular Sunday Mass at San Pietro, but then the priest died and the church door has been locked for some time. A Pianello family who live near San Pietro has the key, so if anyone wishes to go in to pray they know where to get the key to let themselves in, locking the door when they leave.

He was a kindly enough village priest, who looked after his parishioners for forty-five years, always said Mass on Sundays and carried out his work diligently. But when he died, a scandalous rumour spread quickly around Montalcino – although people are still not absolutely certain if it is true. Word is that the Diocese discovered the church of San Pietro is in debt for quite a substantial sum; not millions of lire, but certainly a notable amount.

What has been happening over the last forty-five years? That was the question everybody wanted answered. What happened to the offerings, money raised by the faithful, for the church in Pianello? Everybody knew the terracotta roof was in disrepair and lacked maintenance, and admittedly, the interior of the faded church has not seen a paintbrush for a couple of decades. But San Pietro is a cosy comfortable church and people like being able to glance from the pews to the sixteenth-century Salimbeni painting with a sputnik in the background. This inexplicable painting regularly brings ufologists to Montalcino, who can but surmise that Salimbeni, having painted a sputnik into his work which is uncannily similar to those launched into space in the twentieth century, must have sighted UFOs in the 1500s.

However, a second rumour was soon circulating, again unconfirmed. This one suggested that the deceased priest had hidden a will, now mysteriously found, which revealed him to be the proprietor of, curiously, several properties around the district. And not only that, he seemed to have been solvent enough to purchase numerous properties in the name of a distant relation to whom he bequeathed everything in his will.

Although everyone was unprepared for such a surprise when this rumour broke, they were not altogether astonished. After all, they only had to reflect on popes through the centuries to understand that the Church hierarchy always looks after its own. The very first thing a newly elected pope often did was embellish his family with property and titles, because he knew he would not rule for long; his duty, even as Pope, was to take immediate far-reaching steps to protect and provide for his family. Every Italian relates to this logic and, although the priest at San Pietro was no pope, if the rumours I heard were true then he seemed to have followed this ecclesiastical strategy.

Maurelia came to the end of her tale, and then reflected: 'The

Diocese has already informed us they are not going to appoint another priest to San Pietro because, although Montalcino has three parishes, these will soon be amalgamated into one, and duties will be shared between the priests.'

Now, flushed with excitement, she announces the dramatic news, the real reason for this meeting. And it is received like a thunderbolt from St Peter himself.

'Comunque – in any case', she uses her third favourite word to prepare us, 'perhaps because of the substantial debt (the existence of which has never been confirmed or denied) and the unsatisfactory maintenance of the church, the Diocese is offering the whole church property to Pianello, lock stock and barrel, and if we agree, the purchase contract will amount to what they prefer to call a very reasonable donation.'

There is stunned silence whilst this news is absorbed. After all these years, can it be true? Will Pianello be able to purchase its own headquarters? The other three quartieri of Montalcino have owned their headquarters for many years, but Pianello is the smallest neighbourhood and, although they have always wished otherwise, there has never been the opportunity, nor the funds, for them to buy the deeds for their sede from the church.

'Allora!' said Maurelia, breaking the spell which is holding everybody captive. She is baffled by our reticence but conversely delighted at the way this astonishing news is being received. 'We need to talk about this.' And talk we do.

The next half hour is taken up with voluble exchanges about this extraordinary possibility, everybody finding their voices at once and wanting to know how much Maurelia thinks a reasonable donation is likely to be. The older people are tentative, not sure if they are pleased or fearful, and call for caution. The young are eager and voice all the positive, exciting benefits, but concede Pianello will need to seek increased interest from the young people in our quarter to make it plausible. Everyone agrees it is going to be difficult for Pianello to raise the money, however much it is, because the only major fund-raising event is the Sagra held only once a year, and that money is needed for the quarter to function through the year.

Even with everybody talking at once, the realisation begins to sink in that first of all we need to know how much it will cost and then, importantly, we will have to consider where the money will come from. Groups of six or seven conduct inquisitions amongst themselves, but everybody is talking at once . . . yelling over the top of one another, which is not at all unusual in Pianello but renders it difficult to work out who is listening.

'Allora!' Maurelia shouts hopefully, but I do not think anyone notices. 'I will advise the Diocese we are interested but want to know how much a reasonable donation is, okay?' Amazingly, this announcement is acknowledged with a chorus of, 'Si, si, va bene,' so our President brings the volatile discussion to a close, asking everybody to reflect responsibly on this fantastic proposition because Pianello has been denied ownership of its sede for so long. She reminds us to be patient and discreet about this news, because although she will write immediately, responses from the Diocese do not arrive quickly. 'But perhaps,' she solemnly concludes, 'this will be the final opportunity to provide for the future of our quartiere.'

As the meeting closes, Ercole, Renato and the other Pianello hunters begin talking about next weekend again. They appoint Renato to ring the capocaccia to make their registrations, agreeing to each contact other friends and meet at the hunting lodge on the morning of the hunt.

We all prepare to leave. The younger ones see the fire safely extinguished, tidy the tables and close the door of the sede. They are heading up to the bar to talk this news over. As we disperse into the streets of Pianello on the way to our nearby homes, small groups of two or three pause to chat, still talking about this extraordinary opportunity which has fallen to Pianello. But will it be possible?

Being capocaccia, the leader of a hunting squad, carries a heavy responsibility – not just for the success of the hunt, which he hopes will render a few wild boar at the end of the day, but also the security of the dogs and the lives of the hunters. It is extremely dangerous out in the woods with a hundred men who have rifles; not only for wild boar. Capocaccia of one of the largest hunting squads in Montalcino is a man of about sixty with a shock of silvery hair. Although his nose at first seems too large for his head, his warm tanned face and gentle eyes reflect a calm disposition, and at a second glance I realise he is still a handsome man in that appealing Italian way. Bruno has the confidence of his squad; he is a bravissimo capocaccia, a great man, a great hunter and passionate that every hunt is carried out with precision, is properly regulated and totally under his control. The hunters do absolutely nothing until Bruno authorises them to move, because he orchestrates everything.

Bruno knows this is going to be an impressive hunt; registrations have been coming in for a week and, rather than the usual thirty or forty, it looks as though there will be nearly one hundred hunters assembled at the lodge in the morning. Bruno had driven out to chat with farmers and wine-growers towards Castello Banfi, and although he knows every lump and bump in the terrain, he meticulously studied the territory where it was thought cinghiale had massed. He examined the damage which had been wrought to vineyards, tramped through furrows dug through the maize and agreed there must be more than a few massive boar in the woods. There was certainly no trace of pheasants, confirming the presence of too many cinghiale. For several evenings he sat with his maps and gradually worked out his plans. Trying to think ahead of the cinghiale, he visualised where to place his men, which ravines and ridges he knew from experience the cinghiale would make for, where were the thickest woods he would have to keep them from reaching.

This morning hunters begin arriving at the lodge around six o'clock, for there is much to be done before the hunt starts at eight, the time regulated by the Provincial Federation. Bruno watches the men tumble from cars and four-wheel drives, which are mostly full, because hunters meet up with friends to drive out to the lodge between Tavernelle and Poggio alle Mura, about six kilometres from Montalcino on the way to Castello Banfi. Livio arrived earlier and already has a fire crackling in the hooded fireplace, heating the first pot of aromatic, tempting caffè. 'Buongiorno, capo,' he greets him. 'The caffè is almost ready. Frescina this morning, eh?' But the blazing fire is already taking the chill from the lodge and formal registration begins straight away.

Seated at a roughly hewn wooden table, Bruno makes up his register as each man presents himself. First he records each hunter's full name and address, then his authorised hunting licence number, then his driving licence as a back-up, thus ensuring he has a lawful and accurate list of his squad. As each man registers, Bruno advises the precise zone they will hunt in and this enables the hunters to fill in their own log. Each hunter is licensed annually and allotted so many days and so many types of hunts. His log must be filled in at the beginning of each hunting day with the date, details of who he is hunting with, where he is hunting and what type of animal he is hunting. If he registers cinghaile for today, he can only hunt cinghiale. Even if a cute long-eared wild hare crosses his bootlaces, he cannot shoot it.

It takes a while for everyone to register, but those waiting check their equipment and guns, browse over maps and everybody tunes their walkie-talkies into the frequency given them by the capocaccia. Bruno is not surprised when he ends up with 103 hunters registered. This confirms his expectation: it is the largest hunt he has led this season. He counts out 106 bags which he lays on the table for when the hunt is over and the catch is divided.

Before he gathers his men, Bruno talks with the canai, the dog handler, to see how he is progressing. Hunters bring their own dogs and hand them over to the canai for the day, but of course not everyone has a hunting dog and, more significantly, not all hunting dogs excel at the same things. Ofelio, canai for today's hunt, looks entirely comfortable with twenty-seven dogs surrounding him. Some are yapping and jumping to receive a pat on the head; others lounge serenely at his feet, stretching their noses in his direction or licking his boots. 'Tutto bene, everything's fine,' the canai assures Bruno, bending to pat a leaping dog. 'Look at the dogs, Capo, they can't wait to get going.'

There is no preferred breed for hunting cinghiale, and often mongrels are selected because they are easier to train. In today's pack there are a few that resemble English setters, one or two beagles and some sleek, svelte dogs, similar to greyhounds, but most are a mixture of breed, size and shape, making a motley group around Ofelio. Some dogs are particularly adept at sniffing out and tracking boar, others excel with an a'bai afferma, which is the elongated, pitched howl they break into when a boar has been found. Some are simply expert chasers that run and run and run, jumping ditches, breaking through undergrowth, keeping on the tail of the boar until it is cornered and stops. The dogs do not get too close to the boar as they are too smart and know that is not their job, so it is rare for a dog to be injured unless a boar becomes unusually aggressive and charges. Ofelio is content, because his crucial role is infinitely easier when he has a reasonable number of dogs which excel in various stages of the hunt. Many years of experience working with dogs in the woods have given him confidence in their important role.

Renato arrives with Ercole and delivers Dora and Dianna to the canai. Both his dogs adore being in the woods, and although Dianna is now ten years old, she still eagerly joins each hunt. Dora is only two and is part of the running team, here for the fun of racing through the woods with her friends – at least, that is what she thinks.

The hunting season commences officially on the first day of November and finishes on the last day of January, but even within this time-frame certain weeks are set aside for hunting animals native to the woods, and other shorter times are allotted for hunting migratory animals.

These days it is forbidden to net thrush, although a few people do maintain licences authorising them to trap small numbers of birds, dependent on numbers during each season, which they sell for a high price to a butcher. There are several houses in Pianello and Travaglio from which I hear invisible thrush singing; these are the traditori, traitors. Occasionally, when permits are obtained for a specific day, traditori birds in their cages are hung in trees in the woods to attract their fellow species while the hunter waits nearby. But, thankfully, it is all but impossible to find a legitimately hunted thrush in a butcher shop in Montalcino.

Hunting was so entrenched as a cultural pastime in Italy that it was not until the 1980s that severe steps were taken to protect thrush and other birds and animals, some of which were close to extinction. Even today a hunter will talk with a gleam in his eye, remembering the good old days when he could hunt thrush, tiny finch and quail. He will sigh with innocent longing: 'I remember we hunted the tiniest bird which had a marvellous song. He could sing and whistle so prettily and he tasted the sweetest, so delicious on the girarrosto, the beautiful robin red breast.' Thankfully, hunts are now tightly regulated, restricted to animals native to the woods such as wild hare, pheasant and particularly damaging cinghiale, which live in the woods all year round.

Bruno calls the men together, waits while they form a circle around him, then takes a cartridge from his pocket and tosses it into the air. Each time the cartridge lands and points to a hunter Bruno gives him a number; the first toss is number 1, the second number 2, and so on. As each hunter leaves the ring he writes his number down, usually on the back of his hand. Next, Bruno moves over to the planning table and begins to call out numbers again. This call gives the men their position in the woods, a position they will hold throughout the day.

'Numbers twelve, thirty-four, ninety-three and forty-five go straight to the narrow ravine on the west side of the second ridge facing the castle; you will be about five kilometres from the lodge. Go halfway up the ravine and position yourselves in the bushes facing the ridge.' The four men locate each other and study the maps to confirm their position while Bruno continues talking: 'Numbers six, nineteen and a hundred and two – you are at pick-up point Nero in front of Piero's farm one kilometre from Tavernelle.'

Each man is given a specific place to be and a specific task to do, so not all, in fact probably only a few, will actually fire a gun today. Cinghiale are hunted in teams, and each team must have a minimum of thirty hunters, so many hunters from other regions are members of the Montalcino squad. To ensure that he has a team of responsible hunters, Bruno reminds everyone that nobody is to move from his position and absolutely nothing must happen without his personal orders, not even the shoot. 'The guns,' he says, 'are to be fired only on my orders.'

Eventually, when 103 men are ready to move out to the woods, they decide, always without dissension, on the precise time when proceedings will come to a halt so they can eat pranzo. Deciding on 12.30, they disperse to take up positions, many several kilometres distant, and wait for eight o'clock.

When Bruno is satisfied everyone is in position and understands the plan of the hunt, he calls the canai on the walkie-talkie. 'Ofelio,' he instructs, 'release your first four dogs.' The dogs tear off into the woods, sniffing, tracking, excited to be digging in the soft earth and knowing exactly what they are looking for. They cross ditches, splash through puddles, clamber up hillsides, sniff the air, snuff the ground and dive headlong into the undergrowth. The men wait; nothing will happen until the dogs get a scent, but it does not take long. In just a few minutes the dogs begin to bark, their barking resounding further and further up the valley as they trail a cinghiale.

Walkie-talkies are activated and everyone listens while Bruno tells the hunters in the path of the advancing cinghiale what is happening, where the dogs are, where he thinks the cinghiale is heading. Now the dogs control the hunt for a few minutes. They have the scent and have begun the chase, barking and running to catch up with the animal. The men are alert, listening for the barking to change pitch, which is why only certain hunting dogs are suitable for this part of the hunt. The lead dogs raise their heads to the sky and howl a long a'bai affermata: 'WooOooh . . . WoooOoh . . . WooooOh . . .', telling the hunters: 'We've found him, we're up here on the ridge, send in the others and hurry up and get here!' Everyone listens to Bruno on the walkie-talkie to Ofelio, who already has his fingers on the latches of the cages. 'Release the dogs,' he orders.

Within seconds of hearing the a'bai affermata, another twenty-three dogs are racing to join their howling friends. Bruno calls up his men in the area of the cinghiale, manoeuvres them into position according to where he believes the animal is trapped, appoints those who will carry out the shoot and waits for the dogs to flush the boar out. Not all the men in the vicinity are shooters; some positions are held by men who are there to help the dogs and report to Bruno but, just the same, what follows next is a sequence better listened to from behind Madonna del Soccorso than witnessed in the woods. The sound of the hunt carries up to the village, and if you are standing along the wall listening, the first noise to be heard changing the tranquillity into frenzied activity is the lead dogs barking. The barks change to the long howls of the a'bai affermata and within seconds the whole valley comes alive as another twenty-three barking dogs race through the hills, sometimes having to cover three or four kilometres to catch the lead dogs. At the same time, from somewhere up the valley rever-berate the oddest sounds; pots and pans slam together, making a hollow tinny racket, drums bang, even horns blow and all kinds of yells and screeches rise. This uncanny din is made by men who are positioned on the perimeters to help the dogs flush out the cinghiale. They must keep heading the animal towards the hunters with rifles. Within minutes of hearing the assorted noise of saucepans and drums, the first reports of rifle fire echo back to the village: *crack-crack-crack-crack*. Then silence.

Renato is with his friend Occhialini – 'small eyes' – up on the lee of a windswept ridge close to where the cinghiale is trapped. He has been hunting with Occhialini all his life. The two were children in school when Occhialini was given his nickname, but it would be pointless asking what his real name is: Renato would shrug, say 'Boh,' and indicate with his hands that he has long forgotten. Ercole is two kilometres away in a sheltered valley, listening with mounting tension as the chase is relayed. The instant the rifles stop, he is on the walkie-talkie yelling impatiently: 'Renato . . . Renato! Di mi, di mi, è stato battuto? Tell me, tell me, have they got him?' Renato's voice crackles back: 'Maestro . . . maestro! Padella! Padella!' and everyone's shoulders drop. A padella is a wide-bottomed saucepan, meaning they shot wide and missed. Fifty walkie-talkies suddenly crackle away: 'How could they miss? Porca miseria! It's as big as a buffalo!'

Bruno is well pleased the hunt proceeded properly, even if the cinghiale is not shot, and the canai is already calling in the dogs so they can start over again. Often during the morning walkie-talkies crackle satisfying news over the hills: 'Stato presso, stato presso! It's been shot!' Morning flies by and already it is time for pranzo, but still the hunters do not break position; they squat beneath trees to see what their signora has put into their packs. Usually there is a Thermos-style container with steaming hot pasta lightly dressed with tomato and garlic, or maybe a bistecca, in which case a fire is quickly lit and the steak grilled. Ercole does not eat a lot of meat and today he has a container of appetising tuna and onions; it is one of his favourite meals. And, of course, another container of white cannellini beans, always fresh fruit – oh, and a flask of red wine, another of piping hot caffè, and plenty of bread. He has no hankering to be barbaric on a hunting trip.

They hunt all afternoon, but at four o'clock Bruno, knowing the hunters and dogs are tiring, closes the hunt and orders everybody back to the lodge. The four-wheel-drive vehicles are directed to the various points where the dead boar have been deposited and they are speedily loaded and brought back too. The butcher has washed down a wooden chopping table, sharpened his knives, and his work begins the moment the first boar is brought in. Each animal is skinned, its head and hoofs discarded, entrails and inedible portions cleaned out, and the liver checked to ensure the beast is free of any disease that would render the meat inedible.

If diseased, the whole animal is discarded; if not, it is butchered and the pieces are put into the bags Bruno counted out in the morning. One part of every animal is put to one side to go into the squad freezer and early in February, after the season has closed, the squad will hold a celebratory lunch and cook whatever is in the freezer. By the time all the vehicles have returned, the cinghiale are piling up behind the butcher, but there are willing and experienced hands to help him.

Bruno is satisfied; it has been a flawless day. But he snaps out of contentment when the canai anxiously radios in: 'Capo, capo, I am one dog short.' Bruno wastes no time in organising dog-owners to rendezvous with the canai to sort the dogs so they can identify which one is missing. Ofelio knows it is not altogether unusual to discover one or two dogs missing at the end of a hunt. He is an experienced canai and knows which dogs occasionally decide to run a few extra kilometres and stay in the woods for even a couple of nights. Those dogs know their way home and will be safe, but he is not sure about the missing dog – he thinks it is young. Renato is relieved to find both Dianna and Dora with Ofelio, although he learns that young Dora did not seem keen to be out in the woods today, which the canai stresses is out of character for her. He suggests she is not well. Renato accompanies the other men to look for the missing dog, which is less than two years old and could have become confused and scampered into the woods, or may have been injured, although nobody had heard or seen any sign of a dog being attacked by a boar.

Backtracking to the positions of the various shoots takes time, and it is an hour before the young dog is heard responding weakly to the whistle of his master. He is bleeding badly, forlornly curled in the shape of a horseshoe at the foot of a ravine. His owner scoops the quivering dog into his arms, wraps him in a sheet and a warm blanket, and edges back up the ravine to a waiting vehicle. Bruno alerts the veterinary surgeon in Montalcino, who opens the surgery to await his patient. As the four-wheel-drive turns in through Porta Cerbaia, the car door swings open and the bleeding dog is carried in to the vet. The hunters are still at the lodge, helping the butcher, so receive the news immediately the vet telephones Bruno. In his judgement, the dog has not been wounded by a boar but has more than likely slipped from a ridge into the ravine. Tagged bushes and trees have torn into his flesh, but they are mostly surface wounds and the hunters are relieved to hear the dog will soon recover.

In the hunting lodge, 106 bags of boar cuts are on the table, because everybody, the dog handler, the butcher and each hunter, takes a share of the hunt, and one bag goes in the freezer. This means that sometimes the hunters end up with a succulent cut, but more often with a lump of dubious meat and a few bones. It is all part of the day. Having given the awaited news about the dog, Bruno brings the occasion to a close, telling everyone about the hunt next week, adding, as if they need any encouragement: 'We are close to breaking our own record. Last season we shot exactly two hundred cinghiale. Magari, we've still got a few weeks to hunt and already we have shot a hundred and fifty-six. Our mission today has been very successful: twenty-two cinghiale. The heaviest is a massive beast weighing a hundred and twelve kilos. We got a few around ninety, but most weigh about forty-five to fifty kilos.'

Ercole and Renato collect their bags of cinghiale, load up lethargic Dora and weary Dianna, the empty backpacks and guns, and head for home. This is when Ercole again focuses his thoughts on Lola who, at six o'clock this morning, lovingly packed his favourite pranzo. 'Husband,' he knows she will demand when he tiredly stumbles through the door, 'bravissimo cacciatore, my splendid and courageous hunter, have you brought me a decent piece of cinghiale from the hunt?' He glances at the bag of dark bloody bones, murmurs a well-tried prayer, and sighs, 'Ah, *amore mia*.' Anyway, he has enjoyed an enchanting and marvellous day!

CHAPTER SEVEN

One Winter's Night

Christmas Eve: the doorbell is ringing. A soft voice through the intercom whispers urgently, 'Signora, it's me, Amelia. Can you come down?' Amelia and her husband Bruno live close by.

Going quickly downstairs, I open the door and am startled to see Amelia, who is eighty-six years old, standing in her house slippers with a fringed woollen shawl draped over her head and shoulders. She beckons me to follow her across the road and up a narrow cobbled path to her house. Her tiny four-room apartment is cosy and warm. A fuel stove is the only source of heating and Amelia rises early every morning to bring it back to life. Two small parcels wrapped in white damask sit on the wooden table.

'Signora,' explains Amelia shyly, 'for Natale I always bake ricciarelli in my wood oven. I made these this afternoon, enough for you and your husband.' She unwraps a serviette to reveal half a dozen diamond-shaped biscuits she has made with ground almonds, orange peel and honey. Bruno fetches a bottle of liqueur he makes from caffè and pours me a gocca – a small mouthful – while Amelia pulls out a chair, fussing to make me comfortable.

I am already thinking all my Christmases have come at once when Amelia gently takes the white damask from the second parcel. It contains ten perfectly shaped figs, each plump and moist and each stuffed with half a walnut. Many months ago I watched Bruno thread summer figs through fine wires and insert them into flimsy frames, which he hung from wooden beams in the cantina to begin the drying process.

Amelia's eyes gleam with pleasure. 'Do you remember, Signora? I put half a walnut into each fig and Bruno hung them to dry – now they are ready.' Amelia's ricciarelli and Bruno's naturally sweetened dried figs, treasured Christmas gifts.

From inside the walls it seems as if, after months of sowing, reaping and harvesting, a lonely slumber has descended on Montalcino. Our work for the year is also done ... the last autumn traveller has flown away and left us to our research. For the first few years in Italy we did not work. There was so much to absorb and learn that we immersed ourselves in books every single day, but we did keep an unbreakable promise to passeggiata in the village morning and evening so that we could talk with our friends, watch and listen as village life unfolded.

This is the second year we have put our learning to profitable use, inviting small parties of international visitors to travel and learn along with us, especially about Montalcino and Tuscany, but also further afield. Luigi continues to develop his interest and knowledge of Italian viticulture, and his cellar houses splendid wines from all over Italy, as well as a tantalising array of great Brunello vintages. I foster my interest in art, architecture, history and culture – delving into the layers of civilisations which have shaped Italy. Guests return as friends because we share rich experiences, even if it is an all too brief spring or autumn encounter. But now our last guest-travellers have gone, the season has turned, all is quiet and, in the wintry weeks prior to Christmas, my steps along the roads leading to the piazza sound hollow. Daylight hours are short, and it is now cold – bracingly cold – and will be for several months.

The frenzied pace of cities like Rome and Florence as they gear up for year's end celebrations and shopping has not been evident here; there is no round of office parties and drinks at eight as the frantic countdown advances. There was scarcely any tangible evidence of the arrival of Christmas at all, until Borghetto decorated Via Panfilo dell Oca with garlands of green holly and red berries and Ruga, just as impulsively, festooned their sede, hanging giant golden bows between their banners and tying them with blue ribbons. At the eleventh hour Mario, a man-in-black who appears from nowhere when there is something to be done for village children, completed a nativity scene beneath the branches of the Cedar of Lebanon at the end of Via Mazzini. And he did it all in a black suit, black shirt and tie, black shoes and black borsolino hat. Bringing in truckloads of soil, he set the nativity in undulating moss-covered hills below the giant tree. He positioned fifty terracotta figures, lowing cattle and bleating sheep, then secluded a holy manger into an alcove. Lit by electric stars sparkling in the tree, several life-size dolls, dressed exactly as modern-day four-year-olds, stand behind a rostrum singing recorded Christmas carols.

Christmas is here, understated, a religious festival fittingly celebrated.

The seasonal change from late autumn to full winter is not only marked and visible with the arrival of winter produce, particularly in the fruit and vegetable shop, but also as neighbours begin practical preparations for many sunless weeks ahead. Loads of chopped wood appear in the early morning outside closed doors, but before pranzo every log disappears up the stairway and the travertine stone steps are swept clean.

All through the last weeks of autumn, Amelia and many of her friends have been walking to the trees below the Madonna and returning with armfuls of thin wispy twigs which they easily snap with their hands. Amelia pushes the twigs into a hessian sack hanging from the wall in the cantina and now she has a supply of dry twigs to feed into her fuel stove in the mornings. Amelia's husband, Bruno, in his ninetieth year, is a lean, tall man. His wiry body has carried him two or more kilometres outside the walls every day for months. With his hand scythe, he expertly chops and trims his chosen wood, then, having wound a rope handle around the branches through which he loops and secures his scythe, he struggles the same distance back through the walls and home. The oak and acacia branches he shoulders are more than two metres in length. He begins work without delay, sawing the logs, then stacking them into wooden crates and placing them on the path outside his door to dry. Soon the sawed lengths take their place, their precise place, around the stone walls of the cantina, which are lined with identical chopped and graded logs.

Before the first snow touches the roofs, all their neighbours hear the winter preparations of another elderly couple – Signora Bruna and her husband Angelo! They have a roomy apartment on three floors and on the ground floor is a day room which leads to a leafy terrace. In summer Bruna and Angelo live on ground level; metre-thick walls surround them and the interior stays fresh and cool. But a month ago, before full winter descended, they manoeuvred a sheet of galvanised iron across the double door and window leading to the terrace. A whole section of the rear wall is boarded up, the terracotta pots of geranium are gone, even the clothesline has been taken indoors – nothing remains in this leafy sun-trap except the herringbone pattern in the paving. This barrier against the common enemy will stay in place until April. Bruna will not be able to wave from her kitchen window or call out 'Buongiorno' for many months. She is in hibernation.

At the fruit and vegetable shop opposite Bar Mariuccia, winter produce is tantalising. Laura has lined up hessian sacks of dark brown lentils, chickpeas and two or three types of white beans next to a sack of semolina and a wobbly bag of couscous. Everything is ready for stomach-warming ribollita, filling bean soup, and hearty minestrone. The top shelf behind the counter is crowded with glass jars containing herbs and spices: freshly grated nutmeg, jars of sesame seeds, poppy seeds, peperoncino and a dozen others. The women buy just a few grams at a time; it is removed from the jar with a measured hand and scooped into a white paper bag, which is folded ingeniously so nothing can escape. On the next shelf are small cloth sacks holding prickly nettles and wispy dragoncello with which to flavour soup, and jars of pine nuts, pistachio, hazelnuts and almonds. But there is only one small sack of deep scarlet saffron threads which, at L 140,000 a kilo, are not easy for Laura to procure. Lower down there is an enormous jar of ever-popular bland pumpkin seeds, trays of fresh dates, moist prunes, plump dried apricots, glazed chestnuts and muscatels.

The narrow shop window, no more than a metre wide, is a picture of squirrel-like wintry anticipation. Baskets of walnuts and Brazil nuts, still encased in shells, sit next to a dozen shapes and sizes of yellow and green squash. Laura has everything balanced on three enormous bronze pumpkins from Chioggia, one sliced in half to show the fiery orange flesh, whilst a crate of crimson radicchio, just arrived from Treviso, is wedged between them. Baskets of sour yellow lemons and sweet orange tangerines from Sicily crowd together, giving off a sunny perfume, while precariously wobbling in a wooden tray are half a dozen brilliant orange kaki, the last from village trees and so ripe they are almost bursting open. Nearby sits a basket of nespole picked from the woods around Montalcino; about the size of a small walnut, nespole are dark and smooth, but the skin becomes crinkly as they ripen. They look pretty piled into the basket but not as if they are something you ought to eat. Unappetising as they look, peel back the soft outer skin and scoop half a teaspoon of mealy pulp into your mouth; the taste is reminiscent of wild custard apple. Nespole are peculiar to the winter woods of Montalcino, and are definitely an acquired taste.

Laura, together with her mother Loridana, operates the fruit and vegetable shop for which her father fetches the produce each day in his van. Italians are always good at working the family business and Laura, a cheerful girl in her twenties, seems to relish the daily contact with village women. This morning she asked her father to bring in two big sacks of polenta, because she feels the change in the air and is sure the snow will fall this week. Laura likes to have this winter staple in the shop well before the village women arrive to buy several kilos. They too know the signs and will want this stomach-warming cornmeal before the first dusting of white powder coats the roofs.

Laura frequently meets friends in Bar Mariuccia to plan a

weekend visit to a discothèque in Siena or a meal out, and together with two or three girlfriends, one of whom is also called Laura, she is an ardent supporter of Montalcino's football squad. This provides a weekly round of entertainment, because Laura and her friends are at every game, outrageously verbal in urging the Montalcino squad to victory in a fashion for which the team's supporters have become famous – some would say *in*famous. She even streaks her hair in team colours, green and white, at decisive games just to emphasise her devotion. Her parents nod and smile, content that Laura takes her responsibility in the shop so seriously. With a shake of her head – Laura is not here – her mother remarks to me: 'Boh! I don't know where she is. Last week she went to Siena, but I don't know why, and her father says he thinks this afternoon she has gone to Florence. Why she needs to go that far is a mystery.' Loridana is puzzled, and I also wonder about Laura's mysterious trips.

Capo D'Anno, New Year, is quickly upon us and we celebrate with dinner at Grappolo Blu. Maria Pia has created a spectacular festive menu and the trattoria is transformed with cobalt plates and co-ordinated blue and gold table decorations. Luciano has rearranged the tables so groups of eight or ten can sit together. We join Maria Grazia and Giacomo, friends who grow Brunello, and Maria Pia's daughter Anna Vittoria and her husband, Bernardo. By the time fifty Montalcinesi have shaken snow from weighed-down overcoats at the door, Maria Pia, wrapped in a white apron with her cook's cap pulled down over her tinselled auburn hair, is elbow deep in a creation of stuffed black cabbage rolls and red pomegranate seeds.

Luciano, on the other hand, appears as if by magic, looking devastatingly handsome in his immaculate black suit. He suavely greets every guest with a charming kiss, glides them to a table, ensuring each one feels the most important person here, and gives everyone a numbered ticket. Maria Pia has wrapped small gifts and, as soon as she has the meal underway, she rushes periodically from the kitchen, calls out a lucky number and presents a gift to the ticket holder.

Bernardo looks churlish with the salt and pepper shaker he has won, calling out: 'Maria! Che sciffo! Maria, this is horrible!' He decides this game lacks spirit. Jokes are Bernardo's forte; they have been tumbling out from the moment he joined our table – jokes about the Pope, carabinieri, the Church, politicians, and there is absolutely no profit in attempting to recall one you have just heard because inevitably he heard it before you. And Bernardo is lightning fast on his feet, always quick to raise Luciano's temperature to boiling point by carrying off hilarious impersonations of Luciano's antics on a night of panic in the trattoria. I notice Bernardo disappears for a few minutes. He returns with a cardboard box, plops innocently into his chair, and waits until Maria Pia calls the next winning number. Before she has time to hand out the prize, he is standing on his chair: 'Allora, allora, ecco!' he bellows across the tables. 'Number twenty-six, here it is, look what you've won, it's fantastico, a bottle of 1985 Brunello!' And the Brunello, reverently trailing cobwebs, is passed through raised arms to the winner. 'Luciano,' he orders bossily, 'direttore! Bring the corkscrew, they want to drink it now.'

Luciano's back is rigid, his face is white and his eyes glint like cut diamonds as they follow the path of his prized Brunello. But Bernardo is not to be halted and in the next hour six winners have cherished, and usually safely closeted, bottles of scarce vintage Brunello – some twenty or more years old – on their tables. As fast as crimson-faced Luciano, trying to smile through weakly concealed fury, removes a bottle, Bernardo has another on the table. This keeps the party rollicking along until nearly midnight. Everybody except stern Luciano thinks it a tremendous joke.

At a few minutes to twelve Maria Pia emerges from the kitchen. We have devoured an exquisite six-course dinner accompanied by Rosso and Brunello. Streamers are ready, whistles tried out and Luciano begins uncorking spumante. Italians being Italians, it is mandatory to embrace every person in the restaurant on the stroke of midnight, and the result is a chaotic scramble over tables and chairs as guests race from one table to another, spilling spumante from streamer-draped glasses. Suave Luciano is reputedly not one to ignore a kiss from a pretty girl, but tonight he clambers desperately round the tables rescuing Brunello. Then, mission accomplished, to an Italian rendition of Auld Lang Syne he struggles down to the cantina, cradling bottles and dangling keys. 'Auguri! Auguri!' he calls, as he descends the stairs.

Befana, Epiphany, a few days later is our third celebration. Again we are shovelling deep snow from our doorstep. Last night was heaven-sent for Befana because, as the snow fell, the dark narrow lanes were sheltering mysterious hunched-over, scarved, black-clad, bespectacled witches who carried straw baskets. These strange creatures trudged round windy lanes knocking only on doors of houses where they knew young children lived, calling their names in disguised shaky voices: 'Lucrezia, Dario, Marlenna.' They went about their mission with complete anonymity. I could not guess the identity of any as I watched them stoop into dark doorways, mutter mystic poems and clutch at their shawls. Perhaps a few children found a lump of ugly black coal in with their gift, yet Befana is not a frightening witch. She is mysterious, secretive, and she knows all the children.

This morning, Epiphany, we awake to a village cloaked in white powder. It is bitterly cold, but evidently Mario-in-black reappeared last night to work on his splendid nativity under the Cedar of Lebanon. The children are gathering, rugged up in capes, wearing gloves and woolly hats. They look to see what Befana has left, gazing wide-eyed at the Nativity which Mario has secretly embellished with several more figures, only they are not Biblical, they are the witches of Befana. Two, mounted on broomsticks and swinging baskets of goodies on their arms, are nestled in the branches of the tree grinning mischievously down on the manger, while two more are camouflaged amongst the carol-singing children, swelling their number to six. How the pagan gift-bearing witch of Befana became entwined in the manifestation of Christ to the gift-bearing Three Wise Men is a mite bewildering but, as is conveniently the way in Italy, Christian and pagan symbols sit comfortably side by side. By the appointed hour of mezzogiorno, Befana has mysteriously left panatone as well as a whole pile of colourful stockings stuffed with caramels and toys. Mario, naturally in black, hands them out. The first thing the children do is run their hand down the stocking, feeling for any bumpy lumps of ugly black coal.

The freezing days of January are creeping past. Snowfalls repeatedly coat the village in white, melt to an icy slush and try again a week later. We have not ventured outside the walls for many weeks. Though the wind is howling and the air freezing, I still walk round the village every day, exhilarated when the ice-cold winds snap at my face trying to blow me inside out. This morning there is hardly anybody around and I have the village to myself. Feet crunching frozen layers of leaves, acorns and chestnut casings, I walk round the walls from the fortress, where a piercing wind is rushing up from the valley. Pushing against it, I shelter behind Madonna del Soccorso looking towards the woods, now sparse and russet-coloured. Chestnut trees on the slope rustle

141

in the wind, the last furry clusters clinging hopelessly to branches, but the clusters are drooping, have spilled their contents long ago, and the most tenacious split casings will soon be carried away now the trees are dormant. Sometimes pheasant fossick below the Madonna; the deep scarlet-brown plumage is easy to identify, but I do not watch long, especially if they are in a distant field, because there will be a few hunters around and too often I hear the *crack-crack* of guns. I do not want to see the plumage flying.

On the other side of the Madonna, the spindly trees facing over the wall toward Siena have shed every leaf; austere, creaking and groaning, they sway in the wind, but silvery spider webs string the branches together, forming a glittering canopy open to the sky. Looking straight up between the branches I stare at the bell-tower, hidden in foliage in summer. Not only had I never paid attention to the elegant belfry, but it had not registered with me that there are four bells in the tower, not one, which explains why the Madonna has such a joyful chime. I must come back before Angelus and stand and listen to four bells ring out the joyful message of the archangel.

Like most days in January, today began with a watery glimmer from the sun. Then a brittle coldness descended that forces the white breath out of anyone brave enough to be outside. On days like this, everything hangs balanced in frozen stillness for several hours until the afternoon, when the already near-freezing temperature begins to drop and the wind rises from the valley that looks towards the sea. At first a stiff breeze whips around the corners of buildings, but it soon forces its way into every stairway and laneway, pushing and shoving until it becomes difficult to walk upright. Sensible citizens retreat to the warmth inside metre-thick medieval walls. As evening darkness begins to close around our mountain eyrie the surly wind subsides back to the valley, which is soon shrouded in mist, and the frozen stillness hovers over

Montalcino once more. But today the wind arrives prematurely, unexpectedly fierce, not waiting for afternoon to strengthen but by mezzogiorno whistling and howling round the village. The roads are soon deserted as people battle their way home against the determined wind; it carries away the tolling of the mezzogiorno bells as if they are from some distant village, wipes away smoke from chimney pots sitting haphazardly on roofs, howls in a rage the whole afternoon, and by the time the village bell begins to toll five o'clock it is almost black as night.

I open my kitchen shutter a crack and look towards the tolling bell-tower. What an unbelievable sight! The ancient tower is shrouded in clouds of swirling mist, bathed in an eerie glow from the street lamps in the piazza. As the tolls ring out, the tower vanishes, swallowed in mist, then reappears as the mist dances away. Knowing I am bound to meet stiff objections, I throw on a coat, grab my hat, scarf and gloves, call to Luigi that I will be out for an hour, and am gone. It is bitterly cold, but convincing myself the wind is abating and with my collar pulled close around my neck, I push through silent empty roads towards the piazza. Not a shred of light escapes from tightly closed shutters; everybody has secured themselves indoors. The piazza is deserted and although the wind is weakening, it still offers me a haunting sight. I stand motionless and stare at the mist enveloping the tower.

Cafe Fiaschetteria, bustling with life just weeks ago, is now a cosy, secluded haven for reading and meeting friends. 'Ciao, Negus,' I call as I enter. There is nobody else inside and Negus is astonished to see me, not really understanding why anyone could possibly need to be out and about. 'What's the matter, Signora?' he asks, thinking there must be cause for alarm. '*Niente* – nothing, Negus,' I say, but before he has time to make my caffè macchiato we both hear sirens. Negus reacts instantly and within seconds is on the phone, chattering rapidly. Whether it is ambulance, fire brigade, or police, I am not certain, because sirens of any sort are rare in Montalcino. Anyway, tonight the wind carries the sound away.

Negus slams the phone down, runs out the back to exchange a few urgent words with Gianfranco, grabs his jacket and, passing through the cafe, calls 'Buonasera' to me as he scrambles out the door. Gianfranco appears to make my macchiato and in three words explains what the sirens are: 'Vigili del fuoco, the fire brigade,' he states matter-of-factly. Gianfranco is generally reluctant to waste words, not into lengthy conversations. He works hard and long through the warmer months and I think he really prefers winter when business is slow and he can play cards and talk football with friends.

Nearly half an hour passes. Gianfranco is staring gravely through the glass door, but this is not unusual because Gianfranco looks grave even when he is happy. It is clear to me that he is at his happiest when playing with his daughter. The month we came to live in Montalcino, the doors of Fiaschetteria were beribboned with pink bows announcing the birth of Francesca, who has now grown into a dark-haired beauty ready for school. I have seen the fatherly joy covering Gianfranco's face when he plays with her, so I understand why he doesn't throw smiles around for nothing; he saves them for Francesca.

Gianfranco announces solemnly, 'Look, Signora, it's snowing.' There is not a soul in the piazza as we both stand and stare at thick fluffy flakes dropping from an angry sky. In no time at all the piazza is transformed, the snow coming fast, clinging to window shutters and iron balconies and soon forming a delicate mantle on the edges of the bell-tower. Within half an hour it is ten centimetres deep and, pulling on my coat, I step outside to a ghostly piazza dressed in settling snow. Setting off through a familiar but now weirdly unfamiliar world, mine are the first footprints.

Andrea is not expecting anyone to be tramping through the piazza and he is not going fast because of the falling snow, but the intrusion of the police car is unwelcome in my magical silent world. He sees me, slows and raises his arm so I can see his closed fingers are pulled upwards into a point, then swiftly moves his hand up and down at the wrist and lightly touches his forehead as his fingers spring open. This is Italian sign language meaning: 'Are you mad . . . what the devil are you doing here?' Or something to that effect. With a questioning expression on his agitated face he drives on, tyres carving ugly black ditches through the snow.

Stepping cautiously down Via Mazzini, I look up to find Negus sheltering in a doorway with two pizzas in his arms. 'Signora! Santa Benedetta . . . what are you doing still out?' he exclaims.

'Ciao, Negus, isn't it gorgeous,' I respond airily. It is clear that Negus does not agree gorgeous is the right word to describe this filthy night. He looks different dressed in blue, the uniform of the Emergency Services, which explains why he rushed out of Fiaschetteria. 'Negus, what has happened?' I ask.

'Everything is under control,' he confirms. 'Fierce winds did some damage in Pianello earlier today; tonight a stone chimney collapsed and crashed through a terracotta roof. Andrea was at the station and took the alarm call and Massimo got there within minutes with the fire truck. Nobody is hurt, the fire is out, we have secured everything, but Massimo is still down in Pianello winding up fire hoses.' I am digesting all this news when his mobile phone rings. 'Pronto, si, sono qui, al Dado. Porca miseria! Si, si, due minuti, subito, subito! Yes, I'm here at Pizzeria Dado. Hell! Yes, yes, two minutes, straight away, now.'

He turns and steps back inside, drops the pizzas into the arms of an astonished Danilo, the owner, and is back out through the swinging door and gone, running towards the piazza. Negus is not one to move that rapidly twice in one night unless he is catching a plane to Cuba or Tunisia.

Backtracking a few metres and stepping gingerly down the stairs, I peek inside the door of Grappolo Blu where a dozen people are having dinner by candlelight. 'Accidente, Isabella! What's happened?' Seeing me on my own, Maria Pia too imagines something must be wrong. I assure her I am fine and, believing I must be the first bearer of just broken news, I ask if she has heard about the chimney collapsing. 'Si, si, I know,' she says nonchalantly, and then excitedly adds, 'Andrea called in five minutes ago, he is proprio esasperato tonight, beside himself. First he had to call the fire brigade and emergency services down to Pianello, now he is racing to an accident at Porta Cerbaia – he only left a couple of minutes ago.' (I should have known not much escapes Maria Pia's chain of information.) 'Guess what's happened?' she goes on. 'The blue bus from Siena was coming in for the final run for the night and, with all the ice and snow on the road, it missed the contra curva, the hairpin bend, and skidded straight across the road into the wall!'

'Accidente!' I reply dramatically, mimicking her expressive exclamation. Everything is happening tonight.' This explains why Negus dropped his pizzas and tore off through the piazza – Porta Cerbaia is definitely where he was heading. A voice calls and Maria Pia returns to the kitchen.

Back out in the snow, I know I should go straight home, but the perfect place from which to see what has happened at Porta Cerbaia is the landing at the end of the stone footpath in Borghetto; it comes out right beside the gate. So instead of turning for home, I cut back up to Piazza Garibaldi, where I plan to take the cobbled road, Via Panfilo dell Oca. I reach the piazza, but the freezing wind has strengthened again and the still falling snow is making it dangerous to walk up the steeply cobbled road, which is icing over and slippery underfoot. Resignedly, I decide to do the sensible thing and walk home, but turning slowly from the hill something catches my eye. Flashing lights? This is curious, because Andrea told Maria Pia the bus skidded into the wall at Porta Cerbaia, but the flashing lights seem to be coming from *below* the fortress, only fifty metres away in front of the terraced park at Bar Fortezza. The wind is gusting and splattering snow into my face, but unable to resist the temptation, I decide to plough on and investigate.

I am completely unprepared for what awaits on the road below the fortress, precisely in front of the enormous Medici crest positioned by the reviled Florentines on the outer fortress wall in 1559. The carabinieri are here with blue lights flashing; so is the police car, Andrea's, but he is standing in the middle of the road. He has a thick cape around his shoulders and his cap has a ruffle of snow around the brim. Standing next to him is the Mayor, il Sindaco. Mayor Mauro, an imposing man, is wearing a dark overcoat, the shoulders of which are caked with snow, but he is unmistakable. As well as his wiry grey beard, I can easily distinguish his Sherlock Holmes pipe hanging from his lips.

Holding my breath, gaping, I watch both il Sindaco and Andrea turn and glance up, worry and shock on their faces, towards the Medici crest and the towering walls of the fortress. Then they peer down to the valley below the road, which I am astonished to see is strewn with stone blocks. My mouth drops open as I realise the road has collapsed in front of the fortress, right below the Medici crest, and the reason the road has collapsed is because the medieval wall surrounding the village, made from stone blocks which were set in place 1,000 years ago, has crumbled and slid down the hill. Poor Andrea, first the chimney collapses in Pianello, then the bus skids into the wall at Porta Cerbaia, and now the road has collapsed below the fortress. Both road and wall are deposited in the valley.

Not wanting Andrea to see me snooping about in the snow for a second time tonight, I abruptly turn for home. I wonder how he is going to organise the traffic tomorrow when people want to go to work. What about the school buses? And the daily buses from Siena – one of which he has only just removed from the wall at Porta Cerbaia? And there are residents inside who need to get out, and people outside who need to get in. Smiling to myself, I need no more convincing. This village does not slip into a lonely slumber at all. Even in the dead of a freezing winter, the place is buzzing. What a winter's night in Montalcino!

'Mio Dio! What a nightmare,' groans Andrea to the Mayor. 'Sindaco, the first traffic will be the butcher's delivery van at about six-thirty, then the school bus for Siena will want to get out at seven, so we have a few hours. I think I know how we can do it.'

Andrea knows that if he is to avoid aggravated bedlam and an unprecedented traffic jam around the fortress he has to think and work fast, so, for the third time tonight, he telephones Negus. By dawn he is in control. With the assistance of the emergency services crew, he has worked all night to rig a one-way traffic light system at the gates into the football ground. All traffic coming into Montalcino will wait for a green light, pass through the gates, bump and scrape around the dirt track between the football ground and the fortress walls, then, after skirting three towers, will emerge at the parking lot in Borghetto. It is complicated and cumbersome, but it will work, and Andrea feels confident as he stands beside the broken wall in the tinny dawn light.

The first car approaches the fortress. 'Andrea, Andrea,' the driver calls to him, raising two hands in a questioning gesture through the car window. 'Cosa hai fatto? What have you done?' Andrea whistles and waves him into the football ground and after the first doubtful drivers have tested the system, all is functioning smoothly. Of course, it means people wanting to get outside have to use the same route, so one of our policewomen is at the other side of the broken wall, directing traffic up to Borghetto to another traffic signal. Italian drivers being what they are, Andrea anticipates they will jump the lights or whizz through as the light changes from green to red, so he allows extra time for each crossover to let these cars through. Unfortunately, this means a ten-minute crossover, so more and more drivers speed through on the tail of a green light. Gradually they learn to wait a couple of minutes after the light turns green, or they will meet five or six cars halfway round, meaning everyone has to reverse and begin again.

Mayor Mauro is grateful to leave the traffic problem to Andrea, as he has to deal with the complex question of rebuilding the collapsed road and what to do about the stone blocks strewn in the valley. 'Perchè? Perchè? Why do these things always happen in winter? There is more snow on the way, and positioning heavy equipment to retrieve the stones, not to mention organising civil engineers and road builders, is going to take weeks, if not months.' Puffing furiously on his pipe, he remembers the Historical Monuments people. 'Madonnina, they will take forever to carry out tests to ensure the fortress has not been undermined, and they will want to examine that infernal crest!'

Taking his pipe from his mouth, he sighs in resignation: 'It will be months before the road re-opens. There is absolutely no way it will be finished before Benvenuto Brunello in February, and to have this land on my plate just when I am trying to tackle the problems of the Sagra with the four quartieri!' He has arranged a conference with the quartieri Presidents because he needs to commence discussion about problems which arose last year. He knows it is not going to be an easy encounter because each quarter is so independent, but he is determined that arrangements for the Sagra will have to change or there will be a catastrophic disaster in Montalcino.

Sitting across the wooden desk from il Sindaco, gazing over the glorious valley to the east, Maurelia can scarcely believe she is hearing all this terrible news. Along with the other three Presidents, Mayor Mauro and a couple of councillors, she is trying to thrash out the difficulties, but none of the Presidents had imagined the meeting would be this terrible. She is dreading having to report back to Pianello members.

'The problem is,' Mayor Mauro continues, whilst the Presidents maintain a hostile silence, 'more and more visitors are coming to the Sagra, not only to the festa and archery tournament but also to drink Brunello and enjoy the day-long feasting. We have cars banked outside the walls for kilometres trying to park, and it's dangerous for people who walk up to the village. You have got to understand,' he pleads with them, 'it's becoming impossible for Andrea to control everything.' The Presidents are visibly distressed, but concur that there are serious problems that have to be confronted. Worst of all is the perilous situation within the thirteenth-century fortress.

On the day of the Sagra, each quarter erects a wooden stand, festooned with their individual banners and identifying colours, inside the fortress courtyard. Members work the whole weekend preparing a veritable feast of the cucina povera of Montalcino for visitors, which is served from the unique ambience of the fortress keep and goes on all day and into the evening. As the quartieri more or less reconstruct complete kitchens inside the fortress for the day, this means four lots of open braziers brimming with red-hot coals roasting sausages and pork steaks, portable stoves to keep the cauldrons of pinci boiling whilst ladies roll and knead pasta by hand hour after hour, and metre-wide slabs of day-old polenta carved up and fried over open fires. Of course, every quarter devotes part of its stand to the sale of Brunello and Rosso; there would be no sense at all in eating Montalcinesi style and not drinking the splendid wines as well.

'Last October,' Mayor Mauro gravely reminds the Presidents, 'we had an unprecedented gathering eating and drinking inside the fortress. We were fortunate, but you know as well as I do, if one brazier or oven had tipped over, or if, heaven preserve us, one gas bottle had exploded, there would have been hundreds and hundreds of people perilously trapped inside the keep.' Everyone recognises this truly horrific scenario, because there is only one exit, through the Sienese gates, aside from a narrow door carved through a rear wall. 'It would not matter if the fire brigade and police were there or not,' the Mayor emphasises, reading their thoughts. 'I am terrified. This is a disaster waiting to happen.'

And so Mayor Mauro tells them he has to step in and ask the quarters to consider alternatives. But, the Presidents argue at each other, the Sagra feasting is always held inside the fortress keep. It is traditional, an integral part of the Sagra, and nothing will be the same if we cannot have the feasting there. Besides, where else can we have it? This is precisely what the Mayor wants everyone to consider.

Someone suggests each quartiere erect its stand within the boundaries of its own quarter, but this is not agreeable to anyone else. It might work out for Borghetto and possibly Ruga because their territory is near the fortress, but Pianello and Travaglio will be greatly disadvantaged and, anyway, the quarters really prefer to stay together. What about down in the car park outside the walls? Nobody likes that idea at all and, besides, there is no power, no water or facilities down there, they would be cut off from the village: 'Che sciffo! Dreadful!' At least the Presidents are in agreement that it is a ghastly idea. There is Piazza Cavour outside the Mayor's office, but the feasting and tournament would be dissected geographically and visitors would be so far from the campo they would be in danger of missing the tournament. 'Besides,' ventures one of the Presidents, 'that is where Alessio gathers the quartieri before the medieval pageant through the village, and before the corteo assembles the farmer will be hitching the white chianini cattle to the hay cart, ready for the dancing.'

'Yes, exactly,' splutters an exasperated Mayor. 'I am worried someone will be trodden on by one of those massive beasts when they amble through the village! Via Mazzini is so narrow, people have to jump into doorways to let them through.' And, as if all this is not painful enough, he dumbfounds everyone by adding: 'And you must also reconsider the practice of selling wine at the festival.' The Presidents are speechless, absolutely aghast!

Maurelia anticipated this was coming next. At last year's Sagra everyone was disappointed to see a number of visitors become drunk, a rare sight in the village. Many Italians are not accustomed to drinking a wine like Brunello, because most Italian wines are less powerful. Brunello is a corposo wine, full-bodied and complex. Residents were unhappy to see empty wine bottles strewn along their roadways and several people had reported to Mayor Mauro that drunken young men clutching wine bottles had slouched on their doorsteps and fallen asleep. But Maurelia feels there is another side to this, which has to be remembered. The four Presidents can justifiably argue that the quartieri of Montalcino were the very first promoters of Brunello. Way back in the 1950s, when the only thing most Tuscans knew about Montalcino wine was its colour, the quartieri had begun the work of spreading the news that Montalcino wines are exceptional. What they did not know was that, in faraway France, knowledgeable wine experts were already talking about the creation of Brunello. But the world outside the walls hardly existed in those days. Montalcino was not even connected with a sealed road down to the Cassia back then; it was a bumpy dirt track. Even inside the walls, many quartieri members were not really aware of the word Brunello, but they did know they were drinking a very good red wine. The quartieri are sensitive about this indisputable fact, because few people nowadays recognise their contribution to the enormous success of the wines.

The quartieri revived the Sagra as a village festival, but soon people were coming from nearby villages to watch the pageant and archery tournament and it was the quarters that began to sell the wine to go with the magnificent feast. As the years rolled by, people began to come from further away, initially from Buonconvento and villages across the valleys, but then they began to come from Siena, and soon after that from Florence. Next, the quarters began to receive telephone calls from Milan and Venice, from Rome and Naples, and they were astonished when people travelled from all over Italy to see the medieval pageant, eat the food and drink the wine of Montalcino and watch the thrilling archery tournament. Soon, everybody was talking about the sensational wines and wanted to take bottles of Brunello and Rosso home with them. Nowadays the quarters have tables of Japanese, Americans, Australians and South Africans, along with plenty of European visitors at lunch on the day of the Sagra. It seems as though the whole world knows about the archery tournament and Brunello.

Maurelia is horrified. Surely Mauro won't do that? He isn't suggesting we should not sell Brunello and Rosso? For a few seconds all four Presidents are silent, and there is a palpable relaxing of shoulders when the Mayor assures them he is not suggesting any such thing. Nevertheless, they must implement changes to protect citizens from any recurrence of unpleasant behaviour. The meeting comes to a close with the Presidents agreeing that all these problems have to be sorted out before the next Sagra. But while everybody acknowledges the dangers and understands the repercussions of what the Mayor is saying, nobody feels disposed to bring about drastic changes, nor are they looking forward to presenting this news to their members.

Being the positive person that she is, before she leaves the Mayoral office Maurelia has already worked out how and when she will tell Pianello members about this meeting. She wants to do it without delay, because if word leaks from one of the other quarters before Pianello members know, she feels she will be letting us down. She has a meeting scheduled with Pianello ladies tomorrow to begin planning Benvenuto Brunello pranzo in February. This is another important yearly appointment when national dignitaries, wine experts and international wine writers arrive in Montalcino to discuss, taste and hear the evaluation of the previous year's harvest. The quartieri combine workforces and share the responsibility, presenting a splendid Montalcinese lunch for more than 200 people. January is a busy time for Pianello, as the ladies also have to finalise a menu for the annual dinner in the sede for the close of the hunt next week. Maurelia calls at half a dozen houses and, within the hour, a dozen women agree they will bring their husbands to the meeting tomorrow. She posts a notice on the board in the piazza, announcing an emergency meeting, and telephones do the rest.

'Allora,' says Maurelia, gathering our attention with the first of her most used words, 'now I have some very interesting and extraordinary news.' She is relieved to be moving on to the next report, because the preceding half hour has been spent in volatile discussion about the unpleasant meeting she had attended with Mayor Mauro and the other Presidents. She explained the grim details as concisely as she could, predicting a certain amount of outrage and screams of doom. We did not disappoint her. This is one of Pianello's boisterous meetings at which everybody yells and nobody listens. Eventually a committee is appointed to liaise with the other quarters and the Mayor, to see if they can find some solutions.

The air is heavy with brooding discontent when Maurelia cleverly switches the atmosphere and brightly tells us she has received a response from the Diocese about the purchase of San Pietro. An unexpectedly favourable figure has been suggested, which the Diocese believes will be a suitable donation from Pianello to acquire the property. Everybody is holding his or her breath, scarcely believing positive news could follow Maurelia's devastating report about the Sagra. She announces the figure, which she asks us to keep to ourselves for the moment, and everyone is stunned. They well know this is a price parents and grandparents paid for property in Montalcino forty years ago. These days you cannot buy a car space for that amount, let alone a delightfully historic church like San Pietro.

'Pero,' continues Maurelia before anyone can comment, 'however . . . there are some conditions. The first is that Pianello must agree to the historic Church of San Pietro remaining a public building, open to visitors and locals who may wish to come in to pray, and properly maintained so Mass can still be said on special occasions.' Everybody nods agreement. This will not present any difficulty, but the next condition certainly will. 'And Pianello,' says Maurelia, 'has to agree to meet the cost of re-roofing the church, because the Diocese has been advised the roof is in such poor condition that repairs could be impossible, and we have to undertake to do this work urgently.'

Instantly deflated, everybody groans, hearts sinking, because it could cost hundreds of thousands of lire to re-roof San Pietro. Even carrying out minor repairs on the roof of a normal home is an astronomical expense, let alone the ancient terracotta roof of San Pietro.

Michele, first to find his voice, points out: 'Scherza, Maurelia! You're joking – that roof has not been looked at for a hundred years, two hundred, maybe even longer. San Pietro has been standing since the eleven hundreds.'

Other young members, Cecilia, Riccardo and Maria-Teresa among them, feel their spirits sag, frustrated. They had felt elated moments ago when they heard the reasonable figure needed to purchase San Pietro, but now, brutally subdued, their hopes are dashed as figures with endless noughts on the end run through their minds.

Not wanting this obstacle to dissolve all hope, Maurelia tells us she has asked Vittorio to arrange for an inspection to be made of the roof, and an estimate prepared of the probable cost. Half an hour of discussion follows. At first, intense disappointment clouds the talk, and negative comments rise angrily to the surface, but a glimmer of fighting spirit persists, especially among the young, and gradually the flicker of hope grows brighter. The youngsters are becoming increasingly vocal and Maurelia senses other members are listening. Their disappointment and hopelessness are subsiding, they begin to gather resolve. 'Maybe it is still possible,' they encourage each other. 'Maybe we *will* be able to meet the conditions . . . but how can we possibly hope to raise so much money?'

One of the elders rises thoughtfully to his feet and, in a melodramatic voice, begins to address everybody. 'What we need,' he booms, 'is not money.' This is met with lots of astonished stares, but he secures everyone's attention. 'What we really need,' he continues more softly, opening his hands wide, 'costs nothing at all.' While we all look at him as if he has taken leave of his senses, he goes on to explain that if Pianello wants to purchase its own sede, what we need is ideas, because we have to think of new ways to raise money. 'Think about this,' he implores, leaving a poignant silence hanging while we wait. 'Ideas cost nothing,' he emphasises each word, 'nothing at all, but if we have *great* ideas, Pianello will find the money to develop them and our ideas will turn into long-term fund-raising. If we do not have any creative ideas, then there is nothing to be gained and we will never be able to raise the money.' Closing his arms across his chest, his face solemn, he sits down.

We all turn to look at each other as if these earthmoving ideas will pop miraculously out of nowhere. Maurelia shrewdly realises this is a fortuitous moment to bring the meeting to a close, adding to the elder's words by emphasising that we need to think outside the box and not be constrained by the past. 'Comunque,' she rounds up our thoughts in her usual way, 'Pianello must move forward, we must prepare for the future of our quartiere. We have to give our answer to the Diocese before the end of summer. Soon we will have the estimated cost of re-roofing, but before summer is over we must find fresh fund-raising ideas.' By the time we file out of the door once more, we are all thinking positively about how we can develop a strategy which might keep our hopes alive.

The calendar is turning towards February. Perceptible to the observant, the village begins to vibrate to a new rhythm. I notice the change in daily greetings between our friends who, for many weeks, have been murmuring sagely: 'Ah purtroppo si, unfortunately yes, more snow tomorrow,' or, 'It's wicked today, eh?' Now they murmur, 'Vero! It's been a long winter but cannot go on for ever.' Anticipating spring, they know in just a few more weeks the temperature will begin to rise, doors and windows will be left open for a few daylight hours and gradually the rhythm of our daily lives will change.

By February, the migratory animals and birds which escaped the hunters take their leave, and the stazionale, the wildlife which lives in the woods all year round, are left to get on with their breeding. More than fifty species of birds and animals live in the hunting woods, which stretch for more than 12,000 hectares toward the Tyrrhenian Sea. As well as birds and animals, the woods hide sanctuaries and ruins dating back to the sixth century, and people come each year to spy on nature's creatures living there; to watch the industrious little bird, for instance, that punches a hole into dead logs to find tiny insects, or to follow the prints of a deer from a muddy creek into the thickets. But, as February rolls around, at last the guns are silent. All that remain are the annual festivities to close the hunt and, symbolically at least, the hunting season and the worst of a bitter winter are behind.

The squad to which Ercole and Renato belong stage a celebration at the lodge at Tavernelle, feasting on the cinghiale which was put into the freezer after each hunt. Ercole invited Luigi and me to meet him at the lodge on the afternoon of the final hunt to see the last cinghiale of the season brought in, and to watch the butchering, an invitation I hurriedly declined. But we eagerly accepted his invitation to join the pranzo for the close of the hunt because absolutely everybody comes. Wives, mothers, sisters, daughters and cousins are here to cook lunch, which is served outdoors at rows of trestle tables – many rows of trestle tables, because there are close to 1,000 people here today. Inside the lodge, every table is occupied with ladies chopping, peeling, stirring or serving because, although the highlight of pranzo is always cinghiale stew and polenta, they are also preparing an antipasto of salami and crostini, then they will serve pasta with tomato and garlic sauce before the cinghiale stew. For almost 1,000 people.

A dozen men hover beside fiercely burning braziers, but they will leave them to burn down to glowing embers before steaks and pork sausages are grilled. We will be eating these after the cinghiale. Wherever they can find flat ground, the men light fires under stacks of bricks that form fireplaces and, balancing tall saucepans, these fires are soon crackling away as well. If you need to cook 120 kilograms of polenta, this is the way to do it. Three men standing above each pan take it in turns to keep the bubbling polenta moving around with flat wooden paddles, while the women pour in the water a little at a time. The polenta has to be cooked on the spot while the cinghiale simmers inside the lodge.

Along the tables, the only topic of conversation is the hunts. Each chase is recollected with intimate detail, and the physical demonstration immediately follows as arms rise across the table, eyes aim down the barrel of an imaginary gun and – *pam-pam-pam* – hunters shoot at each other across tables as they demolish plate after plate. They seem to know the hunt, shooter and boar from which each identical plateful came. Men rise to greet Bruno as he moves among the tables, responding to handshakes and claps on the back. Every now and then he too fires an imaginary gun; arms fly into the air as profanities float about and by the shouts of laughter and derision, I gather he sometimes misses as well.

The only sad reflection of the day is when Renato decides to go home early. It was not really unexpected, because he had made up his mind not to come at all until Occhialini prevailed, insisting he join us for at least a couple of hours. He has done his utmost to enjoy the celebration but is feeling terribly depressed, because ever since the hunt near Castello Banfi a few weeks ago Dora has become progressively unwell. We all remember the canai's report that she had not participated in the way she usually does, by running, jumping and wagging her whole rear end in trembling excitement when she is with the pack.

Dianna, black and white, and Dora, brown and white, look similar to English setters, but their temperaments differ as much as their colour. Dianna is calm and, although pleasure shows in her eyes, her movements are deliberate, she does not waste energy. Dora, on the other hand, is still an inquisitive puppy and exerts every scrap of pent-up energy on every exploration. When Luigi goes downstairs with a slice of salami, Dora is beside herself with joy, not sure if gobbling the salami should come before or after she licks him all over, so she tries to do both at once. As the weeks have passed she has become increasingly listless, and although Renato has taken her to the veterinarian for a thorough examination, and the vet sent blood samples off for analysing, so far he can find nothing wrong with her. Dora and Dianna are like children to Renato, who spends his whole day in the laboratory in their company, and they trot behind him if he walks three paces, never letting him out of their sight. Some days Dora won't leave her box at all now and he has to lift her out and stand her up. Then she will respond with a weak wag of her tail and, with a beseeching look into his eyes, will despondently follow him. He is going home early to make sure she has eaten something, but cannot work out what to do next.

As the meal comes to an end, Bruno receives a mighty cheer when he announces the squad has shot 218 cinghiale, a very successful season, and they have broken their record. The formalities continue as the squad President awards prizes: a ceramic plate with a picture of a grinning cinghiale goes to a youngish hunter who has shot the most boar. Judging by the shrieks of laughter and jeers of contempt, the most popular prizes are for the padella – the widest misses – which receive raucous approval. One is for the hunter who had the easiest opportunity but missed, and the other for the hunter who had the most misses during the whole season. By the time the last prize is awarded, the day is closing in. Hundreds of hunters are on their feet when the President announces a special plaque awarded to Bruno; he has been voted *il migliore*, the worthiest capocaccia in the whole district. The fires are doused and many hands help clean the lodge, because nobody will be back here until September. Trestle tables and benches are stacked, windows boarded and secured with exterior and interior shutters, the chimney flu closed, gas turned off at the mains and the door bolted. That is the end of the hunting season.

'It's the same for all the quartieri,' Massimo says with anguish, 'not just Pianello. There are so many distractions. I understand it is part of the modern world we live in, but what with football and television, not to mention the Internet and a host of terrifying screen games, they sit and play for hours on end . . . accidente, I cannot even pronounce the names of half of them.'

Sitting next to Massimo at the Close of the Hunt dinner in our sede, I am listening to things I do not want to hear, things I do not want to believe, but I have been taking long rambling walks, thinking deeply, trying to understand what it is that happens in Montalcino on the day of the archery tournament. I know I must not push painful realities aside.

Massimo's shoulders are so broad he virtually takes up two table spaces. Turning side on to face me, gesturing pleadingly with his hands as if he has just realised I will know what he is talking about, he continues, 'I used to play marbles, Isabella, marbles! Whatever happened to digging a hole under the Cedar

161

of Lebanon and playing marbles with your friends?' I offer no reply, and he goes on: 'It is so difficult to keep young archers focused enough to want to become great archers, and if we can't do it, if we fail . . . well, I am frightened our archery tournaments will come to an end. It will all be lost, gone for ever, because if we let it go we will never get it back.'

Massimo loves archery and he is dedicated to Pianello – understandably, as he was born in Via Moglio. But more than anything he loves Montalcino, this mountain village where his ancestors raised and protected their families inside the safety of the walls, just as he and Ofelia are doing with young Chiara. But he is troubled and, seeing my look of consternation, he smiles and says, 'Come out to the range on Tuesday afternoon and you'll see what it's all about.'

Quartieri dinners to mark the close of the hunt have a double purpose because, in the first weeks of February every year, archers from each quarter pick up their bows and begin the long months of practice leading to the Sagra in October. The dinner is also to encourage and support the archers as they set out on the yearly quest for victory. In days gone by it was the archers who hunted with bows and arrows, so undoubtedly a similar feast would have been held to celebrate the success of the hunts, the skill and bravery of the archers. In a sense, the quartieri dinners symbolically reach back to the past.

Tonight the wood fire in our sede is crackling away, throwing out welcome warmth. An enthusiastic gathering has come to talk with the archers and our trainer, Dottore Luciano, but instead of wild boar stew the menu for dinner is a variation of the theme. We have eaten our antipasto and primo plate already, and now a whole crackly-skinned spit-roasted pig is carried sizzling into the sede on a long steel tray. Its rigid ears are pointed to the ceiling, a hairy snout stuffed with a lemon pouts as it rests on the tray and yellow eyes stare unknowingly into the fire as Massimo and Gabriele, each with an enormous cutlass, begin to carve into its rear end. The pungent aroma of rosmarino rises as salt-encrusted slices fall on to our waiting plates; the carvers gather up the stuffing, a mixture of the pig's heart, lungs and liver, and we spoon that on too. This is exactly the way Tuscans adore pork.

Maurelia speaks for us all with a few rousing words, complimenting and encouraging our archers. She reminds us practice begins on Tuesday. 'Speriamo, let us hope,' she enthuses, 'Pianello will be able to ring the bells for a victory dinner this year.'

Claudio has secretly warned us all beforehand, and as dinner comes to a close he pours everyone a glass of Moscadello and we sing together:

> *'Buon compleanno a te,*
> *Buon compleanno a te,*
> *Buon compleanno a Lola . . .*
> *Buon compleanno a te.'*

'Ercole! Ercole!' she shrieks instructions at him. 'Don't you dare tell anyone how old I am. I am not as old as you – I deny it.' Then, as we all raise a glass to wish her a happy birthday, she turns defensively, gathers her skirt up to her knees and, pointing her toes into the centre of the room, hotly declares: 'Look at these legs! They cannot be the legs of an octogenarian, can they?' She is absolutely right.

Pianello's practice range is outside the walls, almost impossible to find without a helicopter and even then easily missed. Turning from the asphalt road into a gravel lane, between rows of vines leading to a farm and low-roofed animal sheds, I reach the stony clearing where cars park, but there is no sign of anybody. The range is down a spiralling track between thick bushes and bramble, hidden from the clearing. It winds its way down the side of the hill for twenty metres or so until it spills on to a sandy surface rather like a bocce pitch, on which Italian men play a game of bowls, except the sides are defined by lengths of timber marked in white paint with the distance from the target. The archers arrived early to clear away overgrown grass, and after cutting back bushes which were leaning over the shooting range, they reset the target board which had been covered in canvas and black plastic to protect it through winter. When they pulled off the covering, the clear outline of a wild boar stared back at them from an odd angle, but some gentle manoeuvring took it back to an upright position facing directly down the range. Now they are taking it in turns to shoot a few arrows.

Massimo has finally begun to shed the melancholy he felt at the close of the tournament last year and has thrown himself into working with Dottore Luciano and three young Pianello boys who are showing outstanding aptitude at archery. He seems to be revelling in teaching the boys, helping them set their bows, standing behind and guiding their arms, encouraging with soft words to help them concentrate only on the arrow and the target. They all laugh together when arrows miss. Massimo is making sure he misses the target board now and again too; then they all go tramping through the undergrowth looking for each other's wayward arrows.

I thought back to our talk at the sede dinner, when he told me: 'There are things I miss about being an archer these days . . . it is so hard to have fun now, whereas I can remember when it was all fun. We used to train together, all the archers from the four quarters, and we only began to train seriously a month or so before the Sagra. We would meet at Bar Mariuccia for caffè, last one there would have to pay, then we would go down to the football ground because nobody had a private practice range, and instead of two archers shooting from one quarter, we would make up pairs and shoot amongst ourselves just for the fun of it. We didn't really care who was winning or losing.'

The boys are between ten and twelve years old, yet I know Massimo did not pick up a bow until a year before his eighteenth birthday. He began shooting for Pianello before his birthday came; now he is thirty-nine years old. 'Everything is so serious these days,' he lamented, 'so intense. I can remember when we used to swap bows to learn how different tension suited our build and ability . . . we would adjust our firing technique on the spot, depending on the pound per square inch of tension. We helped each other – joked about our skills.'

Massimo is wondering if he is getting too old. Standing with Dottore Luciano, watching the boys intently, he understands about the distractions in their lives, but also wonders if Filippo, Samuele and Francesco have their hearts in it, if they will nurture their love for archery. He knows it is his responsibility to help them become great archers, not just for Pianello, but for themselves. He wants to help them develop a feeling of exultation when they fire the arrows, pride in themselves as they progress with their skills.

The young boys watch Gabriele fire his arrows, then Davide, and now Alessandro; arrows whizz down the range into the target, making a humming noise. They try to twist their heads and follow the flight path as arrows fly past their noses; soon it will be their turn again. Filippo, the eldest, kicks the dirt around the timber edging, bending down to run sand through his fingers. He will not be strong and broad around the shoulders like Massimo, whom he adores, but since Massimo explained to him that body build and strength do not necessarily help an archer, he has been working on a technique which suits his slight build.

Massimo met him after school today to bring him to the range, and walking to the car they had talked. 'Filippo,' Massimo asked, his wide hand firmly resting on his shoulder, 'are you prepared to make the sacrifices to get through months of training, so that you can shoot for Pianello? You are only twelve ... you will have to raise your level of dedication every year for another three or four years before you are old enough to begin serious training. You are a good archer, Filippo, but do you want to be a *great* archer?' Filippo had not really known what to say, but answered yes, because he loves being on the range with Massimo.

An archer is like any other athlete and needs to be in peak condition at the time of a tournament. He has to be able to time himself, to train continuously so he gradually works his way up to a certain level, and then he has to maintain that level. If he reaches his peak too early, the plateau will not last, he will begin to lose form, and if that happens it is better that he stops training and starts all over again. If he has not reached his peak at the time of a tournament he will not be ready physically, nor will he be mentally focused enough, because there are only forty seconds in which to shoot each round of five arrows. He will not get through four rounds. Massimo knew he had not reached his peak at the tournament last year; he should not have been shooting for another two weeks.

'I was committed to my task,' he had explained to me at the Close of the Hunt dinner, '. . . dedicated to Pianello, but I let other things interfere with my training and did not make all the sacrifices. But more than anything, I was tired, tired and disillusioned because all the quarters are finding it hard to keep young archers focused enough to want to become great archers. Unless the boys are prepared to make the sacrifice, the tremendous sacrifice, I am afraid our archery tournaments will come to an end ... our ancient skills will be lost.'

'Massimo!' He looks up as Filippo, standing with the other boys, shouts to him. 'Alessandro is finished, it's our turn. Come and show us one more time how to drive five perfect arrows into the heart of the boar.' They are testing him, because a few minutes ago he was explaining how they must learn to close out the world entirely during a shoot. It does not matter whether they are on the practice range or on the campo on the day of a tournament, they have to be centred only on the arrows as if nothing else exists. They have to be able to shoot arrows with such concentration that no matter if twenty Travaglio quartieranti are standing right beside them screaming in their ears: 'Miss, Filippo! Miss, Samuele! You are going to miss!' they would not even hear it.

Picking up his bow, five arrows nestling in the leather sheath strapped to his thigh, Massimo joins the boys at the end of the range. He slowly raises the long curved bow, relaxes his shoulders and selects and secures his first arrow. Focusing his concentration, he lifts his arms and eyes to find his target forty metres down the range. But his face explodes with joy and illuminating laughter as the mischievous boys, gathered around him, jump boisterously up and down, screaming and taunting as loudly as they can: 'Miss, Massimo! Miss, Massimo! Miss . . . miss . . . you are going to miss!' But Massimo does *not* miss, and at that moment he knows that these five arrows, each driven straight into the heart of the boar, are the first of thousands he will shoot in his training that will last from now until the Sagra in October. He will shoot for Pianello again this year.

CHAPTER EIGHT

A Little Bit of Silence while the Bishop Speaks!

By some quirk of nature, the first weeks in February bring balmy temperatures. Everyone cautions it is much too early for trees to be bursting into life because undoubtedly we will have more cold weather; it is not unheard of to wake up to a light coating of snow as late as April. A few impatient almond trees have failed to sense the false alarm and have exploded into frenzied bloom, so seizing the opportunity, walking with only a jacket draped over my shoulders, today offers an early escape from winter. I exchange greetings with Jessica, the attractive signorina in charge of Bar Fortezza and, Campari in hand, pull a chair on to the terrace, which has been desolate for months, and sit down, relishing the warmth but not expecting my simple pleasure is soon to be shattered.

A smart yellow car drives past and parks close to a group of workshops that include a couple of car repairers, storerooms and a gommista – a tyre shop. The driver jumps out and, as he opens the boot, calls to the gommista and holds up what I can see to be a flat tyre, if not a ruined one.

'Porca miseria! Look at that – you will have to buy a new one, it's ruined. Curse those damn Brunello-growers! È tutto colpa di loro. It's all their fault.' These startling words come from the hostile gommista. Curse those damn Brunello-growers! And by his tone of voice he means every word.

My face hardens as I watch to see what will happen next, but worrying doubts are already racing through my head. Who curses Brunello-growers? Isn't Brunello the lifeblood of the village? Haven't the growers brought prosperity to Montalcino? I thought the whole community revered the growers for their contribution in changing the fortunes of the village and I have never heard anybody curse them before. Witnessing this volatile exchange, I am being forced into an about-face. I have to accept a painful fact: something is very wrong. Worst of all, the angry exchange is not taking place between the driver and gommista, one against the other, but both of them, voices raised and bitter, against Brunello growers.

Jessica hears the bellowing and comes out to see what is

169

happening, but does not get involved. She watches and listens from the door with a grim face, gives a despairing shake of her head and, raising her eyebrows to me, quickly retreats inside the bar.

The ruined tyre is carried into the workshop. A minute later the two men reappear and a final verbal assault reaches me. 'Look down there! We haven't even got a road – the whole damn thing has been lying in the valley for weeks. We have put up with this long enough!' The furious voice belongs to the fiery-eyed gommista again. 'It's time to put those growers in their place once and for all. I'm going to see the Mayor.' These are embittered words.

Muttering assurances of support, the driver climbs behind the wheel, reverses right in front of me and roars off. The gommista was, of course, pointing to the pile of rubble below the Medici crest where the road collapsed several weeks ago. Dismayed but curious, I need to find out more and decide to start with Jessica, but I am sure this is a touchy subject. I had better tread gingerly.

Offering her a conspiratorial smile, I begin: 'Someone seems very angry today, eh Jessica?' But she responds without enthusiasm: 'Si, si, molto . . . proprio antipatico. Yes, yes, really anti-social.' I try again, keeping my voice gently inquisitive: 'Is there a problem with the Brunello-growers?' 'No, no!' This time she replies emphatically. 'No! But the gommista is a cittadino – non dimenticano mai. They never forget.'

As she is answering me, a couple of customers come into the bar. Urging the caffè machine into a deep rumble, she adroitly, perhaps diplomatically, avoids the question she knows I am about to ask next. What or whom do they never forget – and what has all this got to do with cursing Brunello-growers?

According to Jessica, the gommista is a cittadino, which means he lives inside the walls. I begin to think about threads of exchanges I have overheard in the past, sometimes in jest, sometimes as a defensive retort. I've heard Vasco, L'Arabo, say he was born inside the walls, but I also remember his best friend, Giancarlo, asking him what he has been doing on a particular day. If Vasco replies that he has been staking vines, or picking zucchini or whatever, invariably Giancarlo taunts him with: 'Oh, a real contadino today, Vasco?' Whereupon Vasco gets fired up straight away. 'Don't you call me a contadino,' he threatens crossly. 'I'm no contadino. I was born inside the walls and I've got my battuto del ferro, iron forge, in Travaglio, where my family has always lived.'

I have heard several stories from other people in the village too – like another Vasco who runs the shoeshop with his wife, Elia. The Mariani shop has been in the family for generations, but it was originally the village cobbler where Vasco's great-grandfather made the shoes by hand. In those days not everybody in the village even had proper shoes. The contadini would come inside the walls on Friday, bringing a few vegetables, and sometimes they would bring an animal skin which Vasco's great-grandfather, after tracing a paper cut-out of the contadino's feet for a rough measurement, would fashion into crude farm boots. Most contadini only had one pair of boots and came in weekly for repairs. I know all this is true, because Primo told me that as a child he came to Montalcino on market day, but never had proper shoes to wear. Surely then, the shopkeepers must all be cittadini?

Recalling conversations about where people were born, it occurs to me some people were direct, but some were evasive: 'Oh, my grandparents were born outside the walls, we had property, but my family moved into Montalcino many years ago.' Thus, they did not actually say if they were born inside or outside the walls. I do not know where the gommista was born, but Jessica says he is a cittadino. But what do they never forget? I wonder if the cittadini remember when the contadini were peasants outside the walls, no more important to them than animals on the farms, and not even as well-fed. Perhaps in the past the cittadini and their families handed out charity to poor contadini to redeem themselves in the eyes of God and the Church. Rousing my mind into sharper focus, I recall a comment some months back, which at the time I thought was spoken in jest. Could it have been serious? Could I have been that naive? The bitter words come back to mind with sudden and haunting clarity: 'If the whole of Montalcino slid off the side of this hill tomorrow, those Brunello-growers would not give a damn. They would not even bother to lift a finger!'

Jessica is not about to offer any more enlightening comments. This terrace, so appealing minutes ago, feels lonely now. My hypnotic mood is shattered and, with my mind in turmoil, it dawns on me that I have been missing something vital, and not only that it is important to recognise who are cittadini as opposed to contadini. I do not know how I am going to unravel this puzzle, because none of my reflective thoughts tells me why the gommista and driver are so angry with Brunello-growers and, more specifically, why the gommista is going to see il Sindaco. Nor can I understand the justification for their accusations and disparaging comments against wine-growers.

Il Sindaco, Mayor Mauro, is barely fifty years old, but either his two terms in office continue to age him or he works strenuously to achieve a sage-like, blinking owl appearance. Tall by Italian standards, he is a striking man. His whole head is swathed in a shiny grey mantle, because his thick bushy hair is streaked with silver and is not cut short but rambles down the sides of his head, meeting first his rampant grey eyebrows, then joining his beard, which is several inches long and wiry. He wears official-looking spectacles that enhance his owlish appearance, and inevitably his hooked Sherlock Holmes pipe is tucked into the side of his mouth.

Il Sindaco dresses stylishly but does not wear a suit except on formal occasions, and mostly his pipe is not alight unless he is in deep conversation or is troubled by some pending mayoral decision. I often study him as he arrives for morning caffè, because I am sure in all of Tuscany there cannot be another Mayor so accurately characterised for the taxing work of this office. He purchases two newspapers, which he cradles under an arm, and although he attempts to open first one and then the other, he rarely gets to read either, because predictably, as soon as he is in the piazza somebody is there to talk with him. This offers my most entertaining moment because, with deliberate ceremony, he then lights up his pipe and puffs and blows clouds of suffocating smoke into the air. This seems to help him concentrate on the business at hand, but I rather think he is aware it will hasten the current encounter and deflect hovering, would-be questioners.

February is a hectic month for il Sindaco, and next week sees the grand occasion of Benvenuto Brunello – Welcome Brunello – when he will be occupied in welcoming dignitaries and wine experts arriving in Montalcino to hear the evaluation of last year's harvest. The preceding weeks have not been without problems and, whilst I have heard nothing to confirm whether the gommista stormed furiously down to his office to get something done once and for all, I can see this morning's questioner raising his arms and posturing about another irksome traffic debate. A petition has been raised, and not one but dozens of people have stormed one after the other down to the Mayor's office to lodge complaints. This morning I am eavesdropping on an elderly citizen reminding him: 'My family has lived in that house for three hundred and fifty-eight years. Why should I pay fifteen thousand lire for the privilege of driving down my own road?'

In the predictable and highly successful Italian way, many Montalcinesi have declared solidarity. 'If we all disobey this new law,' they reason, 'the Mayor will have to abolish it, because we will make it impossible to enforce.' This form of reasoning sets Italians apart. There is probably no other civilised country in the world where citizens decide for themselves the rights and wrongs of a decision, even one bound by law. Italians always find a loophole to assure themselves that a particular law does not apply *to them personally* – which is why, although it has been the law for several years, many Italians will not wear seatbelts. They have simply not adopted that particular law because it does not suit them. This is the logic being applied to the Mayor's new regulations to reduce the number of cars which come in and out of Montalcino so that the piazza, between eleven in the morning and midnight, can be traffic-free.

'Certo,' everyone agrees, 'it is a meritorious plan because we all use the piazza every day, we even let our children play here, so we should keep out as much traffic as possible.' However, shop-owners envisage the nightmare they are going to face receiving deliveries; the Enoteca are distraught because customers buy three or four cases of Brunello or Rosso and, if they cannot bring cars in, they will have to carry it up steep hills and outside the walls. Most belligerent of all are those people whose family apartments face the roadways, because they have to apply for a L 15,000 permit allowing them to drive cars in. Adopting bewildering logic, the Montalcinesi approve the Mayor's decision; it has merit and is justified. But each morning this week has confirmed that everybody living anywhere near the piazza has exceptional circumstances and will not be able to comply. This morning Mayor Mauro, puffing furiously on his comforting pipe, nods sagely and listens sympathetically, but grows increasingly haggard minute by minute.

For some weeks he has had the problem of the collapsed road weighing heavily on his mind because, as predicted, no work has begun and the steady stream of Montalcinesi who stroll down to look into the valley, offering a solution, or discussing the lack of progress, are becoming cynical and difficult to placate. 'Work will soon begin,' Mauro assures his morning questioner, 'but we had to wait for the ice to melt before we could get a crane in, and before we fix the road a solid bulwark has to be built to reinforce the wall, or the road will collapse again.' He wisely does not mention it is going to be weeks, even months, before the cumbersome traffic-light system around the fortress can be dispensed with. At last, he thinks to himself, Benvenuto Brunello is nearly here and I will have a weekend of respite from these onerous traffic problems.

However, two days prior to Benvenuto Brunello, the Mayor has another major function to see safely through. On Wednesday night he will officiate at the grand opening of the Museo Civico e Diocesano d'Arte Sacra di Montalcino, and il Sindaco is determined that all will go smoothly. The official opening will conclude years of work, and it simply must be a success because the Bishop of Siena, priests from Montalcino, Brothers from Sant' Antimo, as well as Mayors from surrounding villages, will be here.

Work began a few years ago to renovate the monastery that is joined by a columned cloister to the Church of Sant' Agostino, for the creation of a new civic museum. Mauro could not count the number of silent pleas he had sent up, praying that workers would not unearth any ancient ruins when they began digging, because he well knew that if they stumbled on some pre-Christian temple which could have been on the site before the monastery was built over the top, it would cause untold delays. Troops of

175

government authorities, historians and archaeologists, not to mention the national Belle Arti, would descend on Montalcino to inspect. That could have even meant the end of the new museum or at the very least a decade of delay. But, providentially, after all those months on tenterhooks, nothing has come to light.

The Mayor has also managed to negotiate through numerous disputes with neighbouring villages whose citizens are displeased that the museum is here and not at their village. Some even succeeded in airing their objections in *La Nazione* newspaper, demanding the return of an ancient relic or piece of art now at Montalcino, but which began life in some chapel in the country-side and had been cared for by their priests and monks for centuries. Fortunately, common sense prevailed, because the other village Mayors understood that relics and precious artwork need, for the sake of conservation, to be housed in a technically up-to-date, clean environment. The Museo Civico e Diocesano d'Arte Sacra di Montalcino will provide that home.

With the litigation and agitation behind him, at least for the moment, the opening night has finally arrived. Hundreds of Montalcinesi have come to participate in the ceremony, which is taking place in the sacral ambience of the sandstone-columned cloister. This is an historic night for Montalcino! Not only is the Bishop of Siena here, but a prominent Bishop has come all the way from Rome to give the blessing of the Church.

By the time Luigi and I arrive, the ancient cloister is packed ten deep on three sides. At the official table sit the two richly gowned Bishops. Mayor Mauro sits between them wearing his official Mayoral sash which offers striking contrast to the red and purple robes, and these three are surrounded by black-cassocked priests, white-hooded Brothers, Armani-clad architects and dark-suited engineers. One after the other, these noted dignitaries address the audience and, not surprisingly, we hear many blessings and prayers of thanks paying tribute to the servants of the Church who conserved and protected these relics since the first millennium. Unfortunately, by the time hundreds of people have listened to six or seven speeches and intoned more than a handful of prayers, it is all going on a trifle too long and, anxious to get inside the new museum, everyone begins to talk. Acoustics being what they are in medieval cloisters, the whispering turns to rumbling, echoing and magnifying around the walls and, within a matter of minutes, nobody can hear anything the eminent Bishop from Rome, who has risen to speak, is saying.

Mayor Mauro, straight-faced and acutely embarrassed, is forced to interrupt the Bishop and, peering over the rim of his spectacles and leaning on the table, sternly implores everybody to be quiet and listen to the Bishop, who will officially declare the museum open. But it is too late. Nobody is listening to Mauro either and everyone is bored. With indulgent eyes but a withering smile, the Bishop resumes, unconvincingly . . . and seconds later Mauro interrupts again. This time he angrily thumps the table with his knuckles, then hunches his shoulders towards the crowd and leans both hands on the table: 'Per favore, amici! If you don't mind, my friends,' he thunders threateningly as he glares at us, 'can we have a little bit of silence while the Bishop speaks?'

Only momentarily halted, the rumbling resumes. Il Sindaco's face is menacing, and I cannot tell if the Bishop concludes or condenses his prayer, but amazingly, nobody misses the moment he raises his arms to the heavens and gives the blessing. At that signal hundreds of people look up and clap him back to his seat. Mayor Mauro, thoroughly exasperated, gathers his papers and, reaching for the consolation of his unlit pipe, signals for the doors to be opened. Whereupon I stare in astonishment, because I listen to the group nearest me turn for home and say: 'Let's come back when it's not so crowded. Too many people here tonight.' I can only gape and ask myself: Why don't distinguished Bishops from Rome and Siena hold great sway in Montalcino?

Last November all the growers, like Primo, spent several weeks walking through the rows of vines, cutting the once energetic but now bedraggled stems of late-summer growth which had collapsed to the ground and lay tangled around roots and stakes. Using his bare hands, Primo stripped off skinny tendrils which had leapt from the trunk in the last days of summer when a final burst of energy pushed them outwards. Even though the harvest was in, vines were still seeking an avenue for growth. Raking it all into an entangled mass, he pulled the waste to the end of each row, then went back through the rows to cut away old growth from exposed branches and gently secured each branch along the wire in straight firm lines. The vines were then left to become dormant. Firmly tied, they would be protected from the vicious winds which he could be certain would whip across Montalcino in the coming weeks. He pruned to the maximum the rose bushes at the end of each row that become his watchdogs in spring, providing early warning of disease developing among the vines. All around the hills, spiralling funnels of grey smoke curled into the chill air for a week as Primo and other growers burned away the cuttings. The snow has come and gone during January and may come again before spring advances, but the dormant vines will suffer no damage even though they may be periodically buried in snow.

But although the vines were entombed in a frozen sleep in January, wide-eyed growers were galvanised to feverish action, because that was the month the Brunello that had been maturing for four years was released on to a waiting world market. The bottles have been resting in dark cantinas for many months and in

January were trolleyed out, ready to be shipped all over the world. Customers, some of whom ordered this wine four years ago, have been ringing Primo almost daily, sending pleading faxes for more bottles, wanting to know when orders will be dispatched, which ship, which port, which customs company, asking questions about the vintage and settling their accounts. Larger growers have administrative departments for handling marketing and sales, but for small growers like Primo, most of whom market their own wine around the world, it is a hectic time. He much prefers to be out among the vines than packing cardboard boxes. Journalists and wine writers have been ringing the Consorzio wanting to taste and evaluate, wanting to know prices because they need to file articles for international wine magazines to tell the world's wine lovers how much they can expect to pay for, and what they can expect from, the newly released Brunello.

By February, last year's harvested wine is well advanced. Since early October, growers have been monitoring the fermentation process, watching and carefully controlling many aspects of this critical time in the cycle of winemaking to ensure the new wine is quietly reaching its desired state in a temperature-controlled environment. The wine is then fed into wooden vats. Primo and his winemaker carry out tests using highly technical gauges; they taste and discuss the properties of the wine, the characteristics it is taking on, the progress of the natural reaction of the grape juice with the wood until, gently nurtured, it reaches the point where it can be confidently left to mature in the enormous wooden casks. But growers and the world's wine lovers do not have to wait four years to discover the quality of last year's harvest, because results of experiments and tests now reveal enough about the wine for winemakers to be able to forecast the quality of Brunello when, in four years, it will be savoured throughout the world.

This is precisely the reason a couple of hundred visitors are here this weekend. Respected dignitaries, enologists and wine experts from all over Italy, Europe and as far away as America and Japan arrive each February, and at Benvenuto Brunello all the world hears the verdict first-hand: the quality of the harvest last September. Planning has been under way since Christmas, involving the Consorzio del Vino Brunello, Mayor Mauro, all growers, of whom 98 per cent are members of the Consorzio, as well as the four quartieri. The quarters join together to plan the menu, and the ladies are at this minute at work in the kitchens preparing pranzo for more than 250 people, to be served at the conclusion of this morning's meeting when the eagerly awaited star rating will be awarded to the harvest brought in nearly five months ago.

When 200 or more people descend on, or ascend to, Montalcino for the express purpose of experiencing splendid wine, the occasion is bound to arouse high spirits, resulting in unpredictable and rowdy theatrical drama. Although everybody here understands the significance of Benvenuto to the future of Brunello and therefore Montalcino, those Montalcinesi not directly involved with wine production go about their business with an air of respectful but distanced observation. Anyway, all of Montalcino already knows what the star rating will be, because they were in the vineyards last September examining the grapes with a practised eye, and if they were not there, then certainly an uncle or cousin was. So while smiles are wide and camera lights flash and city pressmen seem perplexed, seeking comments befitting their magazines, the Montalcinesi take the unpredictable weekend in their stride. This tolerance was demonstrated last night when a party of exuberant visitors, without experience of Brunello, revealed their lack of understanding by swilling and drinking a fine and costly bottle of scarce vintage Brunello before their meals were even served! This brought head-shaking amusement from a restaurant owner totalling the account, and scandalised horror from a witnessing grower who had nursed that wine for four years. Fortunately, the majority of visitors concentrate intently on the serious business and know they have one weekend to plough through some taxing work. They have literally hundreds of Brunello tastings to evaluate for their magazines and markets.

The momentous day is here. We all file in to take our seats in Montalcino's Teatro Astrusi while the Mayor and dignitaries take their places behind a scarlet-draped podium. The theatre is a replica in miniature of any of Italy's wonderful opera theatres. Flowers grace the stage and the atmosphere, tingling anticipation, befits this annual proclamation. I am quite certain Mayor Mauro, recalling the opening of the Museum in the cloister of Sant' Agostino, thinks it wise not to labour overlong. His speech is concise, complimentary and of course congratulatory, but he quickly passes the microphone to the President, who theatrically discloses, while flashlight cameras wink, the awaited verdict, exactly as expected and predicted by the Montalcinesi.

But the highlight of the morning is yet to come, conversely, *un*expected. Each year, the Consorzio commissions a distinguished artist to design a glazed terracotta tile to commemorate the harvest rating and, once unveiled, the tile is taken outside and ceremoniously cemented into the wall above a bench at one side of Palazzo Comunale. After the speeches, accompanied by plenty of handclapping and enraptured comments, 200 or so people file out, standing on the steps to watch as Giulio gives a trowel a turn or two, gently plopping an expertly mixed pail of wet cement around.

A sea of heads turn in unison to the waiting wall where, sitting on the bench under the row of tiles, a stone-faced signora is catching the sun. She finds no reason to vary her midday habit. Staring at two hundred people as if we are senseless monkeys in a cage, quite remote from the world she inhabits, she does not contemplate moving but rather, in a moment of discomfort, just as Giulio leans across to ceremoniously cement the tile, she undoes the bottom button of her black coat and, bending over with two arms outstretched, takes hold of the tops of her black woollen knee stockings one leg at a time. Pointing her feet encased in heavy black shoes, she hitches her stockings up securely, roughly turns down the folds, exposing her wobbly white knees, then fastens her coat button, folds her arms and lets them rest across her generous bosom. She is not at all perturbed that she has just reached the photograph albums of a hundred visitors and will star along with the glamorous tile in magazines around the world. Still she does not consider moving. I imagine her mind ticking over, asking: *Why are all these stranieri photographing me?*

The quartieri ladies soon have the Benvenuto lunch underway. Antipasto of crostini and salami, followed by chickpea soup with angel-hair pasta, next a superb plate of hand-rolled pinci dressed with ragù sauce. Fiorella and Maria-Rosa are in the kitchen and miss the agreeable groans of pleasure from around the tables, because the ragù sauce is absolutely sublime – and before we have half finished, a television personality, well versed in fine Italian cuisine, is on the microphone putting voice to all the sounds of contentment. Eventually he drags the quartieri cooks from the kitchen to accept acclaim; it is unanimously agreed that the finest chefs in the land could not produce a better ragù. The meal continues with delicious roasted game and another Montalcinesi speciality, fegatelli – roasted livers.

The wine is poured, bottle after bottle from producers sitting all around me. Peering over shoulders I identify legendary Brunello names and nod vigorously at friends sitting at surrounding tables. At my table, by my elbow, is dear Primo, whose guest I am. Next to him his friend, also a contadino grower, Livio Sassetti, who grows a velvety Brunello on a tiny parcel of just over four hectares. Opposite is Giancarlo Gorelli, who lives a few doors from me and produces from around one hectare, but from that hectare he releases more than 1,000 bottles of sheer pleasure. Our friends Maria Grazia and Giacomo wave to me; from seven hectares they produce the splendid Brunello of Marchesato degli Aleramici. At the table behind sits gracious Donatella Colombini, chatting comfortably with her party of unconsciously haughty dignitaries; some forty hectares there, different people. But Brunello brings all growers to the level decreed by the Consorzio.

Next to them I watch Carlo, the drop-dead handsome Travaglio archer whose career in wine production is with Castello Banfi. He is engrossed in conversation with a table of politely bowing Japanese guests. With 148 productive Brunello hectares producing some 500,000 bottles of Brunello, Banfi is the largest grower. Back in 1919, when the Italian-American brothers Giovanni and Enrico set up their business to export Italian wines to America, they did not foresee that sixty-five years later the company, named in memory of Aunt Teodolinda Banfi who paid for their education, would purchase a derelict castle a handful of kilometres from Montalcino called Poggio alle Mura, where Ercole was born. Ercole remembers how the castle suffered dreadful artillery damage in World War Two. Although its second owner, Mastropaolo, strived diligently to keep the vines producing and restore the farms, by the 1980s the castle was barely more than a crumbling wreck. It had remained in the possession of descendants of Conte Placidi, the Sienese family under whom Ercole's contadini ancestors laboured, for more than

500 years right up until 1959 and, when it was finally sold by Mastropaolo to Banfi, the bombed-out castle was in ruins, considered irredeemable. Banfi began work to restore the castle in 1985, one year after taking possession, and not only has Castello Banfi provided a prestigious home for one of the leaders of Brunello production, thanks to the foresight of John and Henry, and trillions of lire, but it is restored to the cultural patrimony of Montalcino.

Tomorrow all growers will be behind their stands for the final day of Benvenuto Brunello, an all-day wine tasting, and it makes no difference if your name is Sassetti, Colombini, Gorelli, Marchesato, Pacenti or Banfi, nor if you grow Brunello on one hectare or on a hundred hectares surrounding a medieval castle. There is only one place in the world where this wine can be made; around four million bottles are produced annually on, by international standards, a tiny parcel of land in the Tuscan hills, but the diversity of terrain and personal story of each grower ensure every Brunello vintage is a creation.

After a frantic but exhilarating weekend, Benvenuto is behind us and the growers turn their attention back to the vineyards, as the next cycle of work must be completed before spring. February is slipping away and the sun gathers warmth. Soon, imperceptibly at first, for it will be a month or more before the first tiny green leaf struggles out, the vines will begin to rouse from their self-protective slumber. In the vineyards, growers examine every row to check nothing has been disturbed during winter, then Primo, Livio, Giancarlo, Giacomo, Donatella and Carlo, or their workers, begin to cut back the old vines, chopping away the crinkling thin branches which had been tied so securely last November. Now the grey twisted trunks rise from the ground with seemingly lifeless stumpy arms imprisoned along the wires, the vine is ready for new growth. Keeping a daily watch on the rose bushes which will bud before the vines, growers prepare for the spring cycle which begins the morning the first tiny green bud shoots overnight from the branch.

'Pronto! Si, si, va bene, arrivo subito. Yes, yes, okay, I'll come straight away.' Luigi is on the phone to Luciano, who needs urgent help. He and Maria Pia spent the afternoon in Arezzo visiting a wholesaler to stock up on glasses for Grappolo, but Luciano is ringing from his mobile phone because they are stranded about two kilometres from Montalcino, with a flat tyre. Grappolo opens in half an hour and Luigi, ignorant of my disturbing eavesdropping on the angry exchange outside the bar two weeks ago, confirms he will drive outside the walls to collect Maria Pia, bringing her back in time to open and, of particular interest to me, agrees to drive Luciano and the flat tyre to the gommista.

It is a couple of hours before the mended tyre is back on Luciano's car and Luigi is back home. Concealing my bursting curiosity, I am nevertheless quick to probe: 'How did you find the gommista? I've been told he is antipatico, not easy to get along with.' Comes the revealing reply: 'Okay . . . aside from having to listen to a tirade about Montalcino for half an hour, he is fine, a really nice fellow, but he does not like Brunello-growers.' I make no comment, waiting for Luigi to continue, certain he will reveal more.

According to the gommista, recounts Luigi, every flat tyre is their fault. The foundation of this argument is that Brunello-growers get it too easy, and it is not fair on the rest of us. 'Look,' the surly gommista had him cornered in the workshop, 'the reason my customers get so many ruined tyres is because the roads leading up to Montalcino are in a disgraceful condition and that's because the farm vehicles and heavy transport they bring in and out rumble along roads which weren't designed for them. Sooner or later, everyone ends up with damaged tyres because we cannot keep the roads maintained. And those Brunello-growers don't pay *one lira* towards road maintenance. They don't pay national taxes because they are producers on the land, they don't pay regional taxes because they are exempt, they don't pay land tax or council rates, and' (apparently after hardly pausing for breath) 'I wouldn't be surprised if they employ clandestine workers! But what,' he demanded gloomily of Luigi, 'do they give back to Montalcino? They make all this money from Brunello, so wouldn't you think they would be prepared to give ten centimes for every bottle of Brunello sold back to the Comune, to help keep the roads maintained?'

Luigi indicates here that the gommista paused to inhale deeply before plunging on: 'It isn't fair! My family have run this business for generations and we work from six-thirty in the morning until eight o'clock at night. We have to pay taxes to everybody, the national and regional governments, we are taxed out of our minds. And if we employ someone we have to pay workers' compensation, insurance and a million other things, which is why I have to work from dawn to dusk. Once we were reasonably well off. We are village people and proud of it, but we are getting poorer by the day and working harder.'

As Luigi recites this dramatic oration my head is spinning! Surely potholed roads and government taxes cannot be the cause of all this bitterness? Isn't this an international complaint, a worldwide disease? High taxes and bad roads are on the agenda of every political party in the world.

But Luigi is not finished. An enlightening final salvo, somewhat drawn out, brings clarity and a whiff of comprehension. Changing his embittered tone to that of one unjustly wounded, the gommista went on: 'Some of those Brunello-growers have forgotten the times when my family put bread on their tables. They had nothing. Now they are wealthy and they flaunt it. They use the name of our ancient village for the wine and we are proud of its success, but it is our heritage too, so why aren't they willing to do something for Montalcino? Maybe the Consorzio is generous in other ways, maybe they give thousands of lire to other causes, but this is our village – why don't they want to share their success with us . . . help us repair Sant' Agostino, for example? And what about our hospital? They know we are desperate – we've staved off closure twice, but it's a battle we cannot win without help. And just imagine how they could get behind our quartieri, get involved in the life of the village and the Sagra. The quartieri helped them fifty years ago when the wine was struggling, but they have forgotten, just like they have forgotten our sports association which struggles along from lack of funds . . . and they would never think of supporting our band, or the choral group. I will tell you just how insulting it is. Last year I asked a grower to help my quartiere and do you know what he did? He gave me *one* bottle of Rosso! How generous is that? Aside from two or three who contribute privately to the odd recital or the football team, they do not give a damn . . . they don't care one iota about Montalcino.'

Admittedly I don't know, and probably many cittadini don't accurately know, what taxes wine-growers do or don't pay, or what they give back to the community, whether or not it is in terms of ten centimes a bottle, but it must also add up in employment, tourism and prestige. I don't want to believe they would not offer help to the quartieri when they stage the Sagra del Tordo. But the gommista has made at least one valid point. Italians are taxed at every level without mercy, which is why they spend so much energy trying to conceal gains and pretend losses, and also why the social order from the highest to the lowest is continually on the lookout for a way to move sideways around the perpetually changing laws, which seem designed to strangle private enterprise. Italians have become exceedingly clever at creating then avoiding fluid laws, and everyone blames the next one up or down the line for forcing them into ulterior, often unlawful, behaviour. Behind the gommista's frustration with crushing taxes and potted roads, I can see now why blame is being cast towards growers and why pockets of anger or jealousy are harboured towards some vineyard owners. Have the cittadini struggled through the last century, keeping village businesses running through hard times when contadini were impoverished peasants working the farms? Nowadays many contadini have come out on top by growing Brunello, whilst cittadini continue to suffer a myriad of ever-changing and often vaguely worded laws.

With autumnal clarity the answer is staring at me: the growing and development of the wines of Montalcino has turned an ancient social order on its head! There has been a complete role reversal of a class of people who belonged to an agricultural settlement surrounding an ancient village in the Tuscan hills, living under a system very similar to feudal farming that had remained firmly in place since the 1100s. The feudal system was dismantled after World War Two, but the mezzadria contract labour laws were only removed from Italian statutes in 1992. This tells me that after nearly 1,000 years of virtual serfdom, 1,000 years living as peasants, the poor class under the hand of the padrone disappeared virtually overnight because, here in Montalcino, this astounding social upheaval came about only in the last thirty years. And it is directly due to the world's desire to drink the heavenly Brunello di Montalcino. Every time this splendid red wine is lovingly poured into a glass anywhere in the world, every sip, every exclamation of sublime pleasure, cuts a little deeper, accentuating sharply the transition, the astonishing class change of the cittadini and contadini of Montalcino.

But the final part of the gommista's tirade to Luigi is different. Is it not a hurt plea for help? I am beginning to despair that I will ever fully understand the complexities of the Montalcinesi. There is so much going on, percolating just below the surface and, unless I scratch, I am oblivious. This black shadow is wretchedly painful. I can hardly credit that any ill-feeling or even dis-appointment exists towards the Consorzio, especially as I recall the splendour of Benvenuto Brunello, a dazzling spectacle which brought showers of praise from people who could not find enough superlatives to talk about the wines of Montalcino. Smiling fondly, I recall the stone-faced signora staying put on the bench while Giulio cemented in the commemorative tile. But, suddenly I see her through enlightened eyes. Was she a protestor, after all? How easy of me, and all the other visitors, to stare at her grim face with faintly indulgent smiles. Was she really saying: 'Well, you may think you are important, but this is my village and I am not moving. This fancy verdict does not change a thing; I was drinking this wine before you heard the word Brunello.' And was it really distanced observation I saw on the faces of the Montalcinesi on the weekend of Benvenuto Brunello? Or was it hurt? Would the Consorzio lift a finger if Montalcino slid off this hill tomorrow? I need to believe it would, but it saddens me to have uncovered smouldering discontent, an image tarnished with a tempestuous black shadow. Not everyone agrees with me.

It is less devastating to accept that pockets of anger and jealousy exist now that I have focused on the sensational social evolution which has taken place over just a handful of years. And I accept the frustration of cittadini when taxes are high. There *is* still much to be restored in Montalcino, the hospital is threatened with closure and the roads are still wanting. And with a wider perception, I am slowly beginning to understand the Montalcinesi at a deeper level because I am penetrating the reasons for, and sharing, their joy and pain; not only in the historic past but in the Montalcino of this modern world. Yet scraping away one layer reveals another tantalising lode. Now that I understand the gommista's frustration with wine-growers, lingering discontent with contadini and the simmering black anger with the Consorzio, I want to know who these cittadini are, and what makes them so different. Exactly what *is* a cittadino? Lying just below the surface of the life I too am living within these walls is another part of the story. I decide to scratch and dig.

Sitting along the fortress wall on a Sunday afternoon I often see Massimo and Ofelia, arm-in-arm, stroll through Porta Cassero and up the steep hill past the cemetery into the hills, a route which seems to be their regular lengthy passeggiata. Massimo is a cittadino and, knowing how much he loves this village and how he yearns for the culture of the past to be preserved, I think he will be able to talk with me about the cittadini of Montalcino. Unfortunately for me, but auguring well for Montalcino, Massimo is preserving the dialect of the village and is determined not to lose his Montalcinese vocal sounds, which means his cut-off words and guttural shortcuts make conversation protracted. But if I have guessed right, waylaying him this Sunday afternoon he might sketch for me a picture of the cittadini of Montalcino.

I begin by asking questions about certain people, but he immediately stops me. 'No, Isabella, no! How could he be? You see him only once a week.' Seeing my surprise, Massimo throws my question back at me. 'You know Alberto, don't you?' Alberto is someone I regularly see when he calls at Bar Mariuccia or Cacciatore. He is a short, paunchy man with a ruddy complexion, short grey hair, a closely cropped moustache, and he sometimes wears colourful elastic braces to hold up his trousers. Alberto is a gentleman and does not often raise his voice, but always greets me warmly, our handshake full of expressive pleasure.

I nod, and Massimo continues: 'Well, Terrium – that's his nickname – is a typical cittadino. Have you seen him in the village choir? He has a remarkable baritone voice but, as well as singing in the choral group, he also plays trumpet in the village band. Sometimes he has to quickly jump from one seat to another in the theatre, switching places between the band and chorus on a night of musical entertainment. But the difference is this: Alberto is also an artigiano – he is a fabbro del ferro, like L'Arabo, Vasco, working iron by hand. But that is not all, Isabella. Alberto also sculpts. Everyone remembers the miniature medieval villages and wonderful masks sculpted in wood by Alberto. You see, he can turn his talents creatively to many things. He has lived his life inside the walls because he hates having to leave this hill. You see him every day, don't you? He is a real cittadino.'

'Si, si, I know him,' I tell Massimo. 'He sometimes offers me a drink at the bar and his eyes always sparkle. He is secretly mischievous, Massimo – there is something devilish in Alberto. I never know what he is going to say.'

'Essato, exactly!' cries Massimo. 'And what about L'Arabo? He works in his iron forge but also goes daily to his olive grove and vineyard, but when he is at the bar, well, stand clear . . . nobody ever knows what he is going to say either. Many of these real cittadini are still here today. They live life in complete harmony with the culture of the past, but numbers are dwindling because it's harder for us – the modern world encroaches on our life. Most of them are multi-skilled artigiani like Alberto and L'Arabo; they are lightning quick with a retort. There is a name for this – it's called una battuta, which means it's like a punch, but it is not physical, it's verbal. They hit you with words because they

191

are so reflexive. They cannot pass you by without saying something to leave you frozen on the spot.'

'Massimo, I've seen an old man, do you know him? He sits down by the tennis court on the stump of an olive tree weaving baskets.' Of course Massimo knows him, he thinks his name is Giorgio and he too is a cittadino, an artigiano who, in the traditions of his ancestors, once wove long tapered baskets for the grape pickers; now most vineyards use plastic crates, so Giorgio weaves baskets for olive pickers and mends rush-seated chairs.

'There were some cittadini, though,' Massimo begins again, warming to the memory, 'who lived outside the norm; they were more isolated, more inward-looking. I remember old Cartone, "Box", which is what we called him when we were kids, although his real name was Augusto. He only died a few years ago. Cartone was on the streets of Montalcino every day. He would never spend a day at home because the streets of the village were his home and he collected cardboard, but he particularly liked boxes. "Buongiorno, Cartone," we would yell cheekily to him on our way to school and he would respond with a cheery battuta; we watched him calling at houses one after the other. He was a village person, but wanted to be seen as being different; he wanted to be who he was. Cartone was a character, living outside the norm. His whole world was dwelling on this hill within the sound of the mezzogiorno bell because he would never leave, he was a real cittadino and he stayed beneath the holm oaks. He was *Ilcinese* – a dweller on the Hill of Mons Ilcinus.'

Massimo's memories are flooding back, so I stay silent and listen. 'One guy I remember was old Giuseppe. He used to sell nuts and seeds, all sorts of seeds, but I loved his pumpkin seeds the most.' He tells me Giuseppe carried a wicker basket over his arm and he too went round the houses every day, calling out as he passed the windows: 'Pumpkin seeds for sale, nocciolini for sale!' The signori would push a bowl through the window into which Giuseppe, using an old tin, would scoop a few seeds, receiving a coin or occasionally a couple of artichokes or eggs in return. 'These cittadini were unique characters,' emphasises Massimo earnestly, 'and some, like Giuseppe, carried that identity to the extreme by more or less living unto themselves. For Giuseppe, it was a thing of him, out of the ordinary, he was apart from the rest of us. Now he is gone and there are very few left. But one lives in Ruga – you know him, Isabella! Budzino is a true Ilcinese cittadino. His real name is Adelmo, he is an individual character, an Ilcinese personality of the village. Budzino, little buddha, is his nickname.' Massimo is right again, I do know old Adelmo, but if his nickname was awarded because of a round tummy, it is not obvious now.

'Haven't you heard the story?' an incredulous Massimo wants to know. 'It's legendary. A couple of decades ago, Zeffirelli, the famous Italian film-maker, was here shooting a documentary. Old Budzino came wandering down Via Cialdini and stumbled into the movie set, which he hadn't even noticed was filming in Piazza Cavour, and Zeffirelli saw him. Shrieking to the film crew who started to advance, he raced frantically across the piazza. "Don't touch him, leave him alone, get away . . . don't lay a finger on him. He is perfect just the way he is!"' I bring the image of Budzino to mind. 'Just the way he is' happens to be a short, thin, shrunken man of unfathomable age with vague grey eyes and a deeply furrowed face, but a face single-mindedly determined to carry out his day's work. 'He was perfect for Zeffirelli,' explains Massimo, 'because he represented exactly what an Ilcinese cittadino is.'

Budzino wears an overcoat most wintry days and sometimes a woollen beanie. I have seen him begin each day with a cappuccino at Bar Prato, then, using a shopping trolley, although Massimo says it was once a wooden barrow, from a gloomy cantina up the rise of Via Cialdini he slowly carries out a few packets of potato chips, two or three bottles of iced tea or a sack of flour for pizzas. He loads everything into the trolley and delivers it all to Bar Prato, just a few metres away, working for most of the day. 'And Isabella, have you seen him when he takes a break?' Massimo again makes me do the thinking. 'He walks up Via Mazzini to the barber's. But not to have his hair cut, just to sit in the warmth and chat, because the barber shop is filled with his friends, most of whom are not there to have a haircut either. Budzino is an Ilcinese cittadino, his own man, a character of the village, on the streets of Montalcino every single day.

I am surrounded by cittadini displaying unique character traits. I have been living with them all these years – how could I not have seen? 'What about Memmo?' asks Massimo, although my head is spinning with all these new thoughts. 'You probably exchange buongiorno every day when you pass his shop. Haven't you realised he is Ilcinese?' Memmo is the other barber, whose shop is at the top of the stone steps leading down to Grappolo Blu. 'Ask Memmo where he was born and he will tell you that not only was he born here, but he intends to die here as well,' Massimo asserts, then even more excitedly: 'Have you asked him if he has ever been to Siena? He will tell you he went to Siena once, but only once. Memmo is campanalista – he rarely travels outside the sound of the village bell. Accidente . . . his family is becca morte! Do you know what that means?' Thankfully, this time I nod to signify I know it means he stubbornly carries the badge of authenticity claimed by the Ilcinesi after the Battle of Montaperti in 1260. 'What does Memmo do when he takes his holidays?' Massimo doesn't wait for me to reply. 'He brings an old chair on to the road, closes the wooden doors of his shop and, every day for two weeks, he sits outside. His friends gather around him, chatting, smoking and listening to the sound of the village bell wafting down from the piazza. Memmo is campanalista, becca morte and Ilcinese. He knows there is nowhere better in all the world to take his holiday than inside the walls of Montalcino, listening to the bells.'

The other half of the story: the Ilcinesi. Whilst contadini, people from the land, were born within the territory of Montalcino, the other reason they are different is because, clearly, they can never be Ilcinesi. The people who came to live on the hill under the canopy of holm oaks were the first Ilcinesi and, of necessity, they developed their culture as cittadini, village dwellers. They came around the year 740 and wanted only to be left to themselves, but had to fight countless battles, survive brutal sieges and famines and participate in dreadful wars that were mostly other people's. Recognising, with Massimo's help, the character traits of cittadini, I can see these first Ilcinesi must have been single-mindedly stubborn, defiant, defensive and above all else *inward-looking* – because that was the only way they could ensure their survival. Had they not been inward-looking, their village and their mountain would have been overrun; they would have lost their unique identity and their liberty a millennium ago, because they were continually the pawn in other people's battles. Florence and Siena toyed flippantly with Montalcino for more than 500 years because this hill was the jewel everybody wanted – the Spanish, French, Florentines and Sienese. The Montalcinesi have never forgotten that they lost their liberty in 1559 as a consequence of a diplomatic treaty between invading Spanish and French who were fighting a European war on a far broader front than this tiny mountain village, but even during all the wars the Ilcinesi refused to abandon this mountain.

Because of their insulated life, their chosen inward defensiveness, the Ilcinesi developed talents and character traits which included the ability to do many different things. They became flexible, inventive and creative. Today Montalcino has about

2,000 people living within the walls, but there was a time when 15,000 citizens lived here and Montalcino was a productive, industrious village. Records show there were as many as eight shoemakers, many workers of iron, lacemakers, dyers of cloth, pipemakers, specialist workers of leather, ropemakers, tailors and countless woodworkers. They also fashioned ceramics and pottery, grew what they needed and developed their own cuisine. There were many wine shops and they even created a form of the Tuscan language to suit themselves – which Massimo speaks – known as Montalcinese. They learned to make or do whatever they needed for life within the walls.

Massimo passionately draws it all together for me: 'There are still a few Ilcinesi living unto themselves, a life apart from the rest of us, like Budzino, but sadly, they are vanishing. Montalcino misses them because, heaven knows, the rest of us are all the same. There are a good number of campanilisti like Memmo. You see them in the piazza every day, they are never out of hearing of the tolling bells, but there are more Albertos and L'Arabos – multi-skilled, talented and creative artigiani Ilcinesi who will hit you with una battuta. And there are plenty of cittadini like me, a generation or two younger, who want to keep our Ilcinese culture because we love this village, but the modern world makes more demands on us. We hate to leave the hill and only make the sacrifice when we have no alternative, but we are much happier inside these walls. Do you see, Isabella? A cittadino is a talented, creative but, of necessity, an inward-looking village person. He loves his village with inherited passion and dwells within the walls, on this mountain, beneath the holm oaks. We are Ilcinesi. And we will never abandon this hill.'

SPRING

CHAPTER NINE

Alternative Tea and Jonquils

Rome is 220 kilometres from Montalcino but may as well be on the other side of the globe because, as far as the Montalcinesi are concerned, Romans have their own way of doing things. They are a tribe within a country of countless tribes, and as foreign to them as Tahitians.

Luciano and Maria Pia made their escape from the frenetic

pace of the Eternal City a decade ago, yet when I reflect on the confusing pattern surrounding their life in Montalcino it helps explain why, even after a decade, they are still considered almost outsiders – from Rome. Their baffling life revolves around Taverna del Grappolo Blu and their extended family, which includes several branches in Montalcino and others still in Rome. I am driven to the conclusion that Romans are never happier than when utter confusion camouflages everything. I have learned not to be alarmed at the veiled objectives behind ambiguous words, nor the candour with which they are spoken, for I suspect Maria Pia and Luciano design confusion into each day so that no one can derail their objectives – since no one really understands what is going on! This means they maintain control, and although at first it seems contradictory logic, it works for Maria Pia and Luciano. Possibly it is because Romans have never come to terms with not being at the centre of the world; indeed, they seem sincerely to believe everything in the world still revolves around Rome. Not an unjust claim, considering the brilliance of the Roman Empire.

Our Roman friends have endearing character traits I cannot find in Montalcino, definitely not in the Ilcinesi, and if Maria Pia and Luciano are any indication, Romans must be funloving outward-looking people, truly content when they are in control, when they happily confuse as many issues as possible and when they pull hidden strings.

When Maria Pia moved the family from Rome, Montalcino was a very tight-knit closed village. There was no hope of an outsider, as she was, finding anywhere to rent, so she went nine kilometres away, to Castelnuovo del Abate. There she spoke with an old signora, well into her eighties and immensely wealthy, who agreed to rent her a dilapidated farmhouse. The grand signora had derived her wealth from the mezzadria and was the last remaining direct heir to what then existed of the farms her family had controlled for centuries. Steeped in the old ways, unable to adjust to the changes in Tuscany, she had steadfastly refused to connect the most basic services, saying, 'What do contadini need with such things as electricity and running water? It is not necessary for their work.'

Maria Pia describes the derelict farmhouse, at the end of the 1980s, with pane-less windows, no electricity nor running water, and weedy stone-flagged floors from which, evidently, stabled animals had recently been removed. On hearing that Maria Pia planned to keep chickens on the farm, the wily signora demanded she be compensated with half the eggs laid each day. Maria Pia had to concur with this archaic mezzadria split before she could begin to clean the house where she stayed for a year, establishing the family base.

Maria Pia confided to me that it was several years before born and bred Montalcinesi ventured through the doors of Grappolo Blu. The signora was from Rome, they would shrug. What could *she* possibly know about Tuscan cooking? How could *she* cook a Montalcinese meal? On hearing this, I would look loyally astonished, all the while rolling continuously baffling scenes of a night at Grappolo over in my mind. Maria Pia is a picker-upper; she has room for everybody and people of the oddest persuasion gravitate to her and always seem to end up in the kitchen at Grappolo. For a few months a moustached helper from America lingered; he tied his hair in a long ponytail reaching to his waist, wore one dangly earring and exhibited flowery tattoos on his arms. Then a bronze-skinned youth took his place, bald as a badger, not a hair on his head and totally cleanshaven; this was Noi from Laos. Now she has a Japanese chef in the kitchen because he rang from Florence and asked if she could teach him Tuscan cooking. 'Why not? Of course, Takishi, come whenever you like!'

201

Maria Pia finds it no obstacle at all to have an American with negligible Italian, a Laotian who speaks Russian and German and a bowing Japanese with practically no language but his own all chattering in the kitchen at once. But thankfully for us all, Maria Pia's principal assistant is Mimmo and he is very much Italian. But not Montalcinese, he is Napoletano. Mimmo is hilarious, and sings while he labours and makes weird hand signals when he calls out the orders in a completely indecipherable dialect. Japanese, Neapolitan, Laotian, American and Roman; it possibly explains, I often think to myself, why many Montalcinesi find Maria Pia's outwardness a tad perplexing.

Another confusing rhythm concerns family members who appear for a few days, slipping into the routine at Grappolo as if they have been coming and going all their lives, then disappearing once more. Agatta, Elena, Daniele, Laura, Lorenzo, Marzia, Federica and Giovanna are all tall, slim, young, raven-haired, beautiful Roman cousins with profiles to die for. Sometimes we are introduced and sometimes not. Tonight the woman serving pasta turns out to be Maria Pia's sister.

'This is my sister, Lucilla,' we learn, 'just up from Rome to bring our nephew back to Siena University, to pick up Kika the dog to take her down to Rome because she ate the neighbour's rabbit, and to bring our father to the farm because he wants to dig plots for peas which must be planted on Easter Saturday.'

Farm? What farm? What dog? Who is Kika? Which nephew at Siena University? None of this bewildering information comes out in any logical, conversational way. We simply have to guess, dragging tidbits from Luciano as he rushes past with steaming plates of pinci al ragù.

The priority of La Famiglia is more essentially Italian than anything else; nothing is more sacred than family unity, the protection of which rules Italy powerfully. It is much stronger than any political party, government or even the Church. At any given time, Maria Pia and Luciano are the protectors of various nephews, nieces, cousins, uncles and aunts. Loyalty is absolute, and whilst La Famiglia may be structured to allow several contradictory, even illusive, façades, this is purposely designed so that at any given time, as the need arises, La Famiglia – safely carried in various vessels – can alter course and sail on unharmed through the generations. For Maria Pia and Luciano it is an inherited responsibility around which they weave their work at Grappolo Blu.

Aside from her Roman upbringing, I fancy gypsy longings lurk inside Maria Pia. She has told me her family despaired of her when she was growing up because she was always looking for alternatives. She was unwilling to conform to the Italian ideal of a daughter guided and controlled by her parents in the way her four sisters were. Maria Pia was a rebel. She changed her hair colour with alarming regularity, her clothes were always extreme and trendy, and she stayed out till dawn against her parents' wishes. She moved with the alternative people, climbing mountains and reading about the holy teachers of India – the sort of thing a dutiful daughter did not do. Although she has mellowed through the years, Maria Pia still does not conform and, unlike most village women who dress conservatively according to family expectations, she loves bright orange, yellow and turquoise clothes. Her wrists are always adorned with chains and bracelets, and her neck encircled with holistic charms she picked up on her last visit to India, a country in which she feels completely at home. Her hair continues to alternate in colour but at the moment is that reddish-henna Roman women favour.

Luciano, a tallish, handsome, brown-eyed Roman, functions on a different plane from Maria Pia, orchestrating a dozen manoeuvres at once. He issues instructions, then counters them seconds later. He will be talking on the phone about half-finished renovations to his cantina at the same time as he is totalling an account for a party of twelve; then he will cradle the phone on his shoulder and yell at Anna Vittoria to clear a table while he extracts the cork from a bottle with his free hand. This inevitably ends up in confusion, because nobody knows whether he is yelling to him or her or at the caller. When things are not done, he throws his eyes to the heavens, raises both hands to the sides of his head and moans in his Roman dialect, 'Dai, dai, what a mess – it's a disaster! How can I be expected to work like this?'

Luciano does not always call Maria Pia by her full name, especially if he needs her attention urgently. He'll just call out: 'Oh . . . Pia', whereas most friends leave off the Pia and call her Maria. If I am about to ask something serious, or tell her something I want her to remember, then I know sternly calling 'Pia' will get her attention. One thing Luciano does know is not to interfere in Maria Pia's kitchen. Her delicious cooking is based on the ingredients loyal to Tuscany and she refuses to use butter or cream as part of her policy of preparing genuine local dishes. Eventually the credibility of her delicious cooking infiltrated all but the staunchest households, so now the taverna is a nightly haven for locals as well as visitors.

'I learned the hard way,' she told me. 'One night a table of four born-and-bred Montalcinesi ordered sausages and beans. I wanted to make the dish more colourful, so I mixed white cannellini and red borlotti beans and placed the split pork sausages in the middle. Luciano served the meal. When the plates came back to the kitchen, the sausages and white cannellini beans were gone, but each and every red borlotti sat around the rim like stranded jelly beans. One by one they had been separated and discarded as inedible. Luciano was politely asked to counsel me: "In Montalcino we eat only *white* cannellini beans!"'

Wine is Luciano's domain and he prides himself on a wide-ranging list of Rosso and Brunello, which gives him immense pleasure but also occasional agony, especially if someone arrives for dinner and asks for a jug of Brunello. He throws a tantrum at the kitchen door, pushing two cupped hands out in front of his chest, pleading for sympathy. 'But they are Romans!' he says, flabbergasted. 'They should know better!' He is blissfully content when diners ask about Brunello. If they aren't knowledgeable but, hearing about the wines, have come to explore Montalcino, he spends ten minutes chatting, explaining the harvests and characteristics. If they are knowledgeable, he is just as animated comparing wine experiences. Occasionally his tolerance is sorely tried – as on the night a haughty fur-wrapped signora ordered a bottle of Brunello bianco. His patient explanation that white Brunello could not, by the nature of the wine, exist, was dismissed with a disparaging wave, and: 'Strange you cannot get it here. My cousin sells Brunello bianco in his wineshop!' Understandably livid, Luciano vanished downstairs.

But Luciano's overwhelming, anguished and harrowing tale, which he manages to drag out for an airing whenever he needs to remind us of his pain-filled life, concerns the time a lone diner ordered from Anna Vittoria a single glass of Brunello. This was not unusual because Luciano frequently has an opened bottle ready for tasting by those who cannot drink a whole bottle. However, Anna Vittoria could not find an opened bottle so she hurriedly fetched an unopened one from the cantina, pulled the cork, poured a glass and left the bottle on the bar, where Luciano discovered it the following morning. Luckily for Anna, Maria Pia waylaid her before she arrived at the trattoria, because she had unknowingly opened a bottle of 1985 Riserva Brunello, worth more than L 200,000. This was enough to send Luciano *ballistico*, with streams of verbal violence – but the thought of three-quarters of the bottle lying unattended overnight on the bar brought a second volley of Roman curses. Distraught, he collapsed on the bar and almost wept when he realised the lone diner was blissfully unaware of the greatness of the wine he had been drinking.

On the other hand, nothing fazes Maria Pia and as the evening unfolds people end up in the crowded kitchen chatting to her as she adds a spoonful of chopped tomato and basil to a plate of ravioli. She works on with a sparkling smile that lights up her eyes. When the major part of the evening's work is done, she emerges from the kitchen, her white apron and cap showing signs of her cooking, and moves around greeting and chatting to diners. This is often when Maria Pia and Luciano catch us unawares, because although they work long hours at Grappolo they are night owls – or maybe just crazy Romans. Come midnight during summer, Maria Pia will fling off her apron, declaring it is time we all drove to Bagno Vignoni, an exquisite village half an hour away, to eat gelati while we dangle our feet in the thermal spring which takes the place of the piazza.

One night they left us speechless. We had been home from the trattoria for an hour when a lowered voice below our shutter hissed: 'Isabella, Luigi, vieni, vieni. It's too hot to sleep – we are going to Camigliano. Do you want to come?'

Impulsively, we dressed and by one o'clock were driving into Camigliano. To our astonishment, in the middle of this sleepy ten-house village with hardly more than one bar and an ancient church, admittedly all deliciously medieval, was a wooden dance floor crowded with people and with music reverberating into the next province. Luciano launched himself into the sea of legs, finding and dancing with one pretty girl after another, but as soon as the music turned Latin-American he found Maria Pia and the pair sensually floated across the floor. They are accomplished dancers and left us, once more, toe-tapping, open-mouthed and bleary-eyed. When we returned home at four o'clock we vowed Camigliano was off the itinerary for us.

Tonight Grappolo is packed, even though it is still early spring, and although a vague alarm bell rings and some veiled warning drifts through my mind, I rashly accept when Maria Pia says brightly, 'Listen, Isabella, Grappolo is closed on Friday. I'm going for a walk in the afternoon to pick jonquils – why don't you come with me?' We make arrangements to meet at Bar Prato, from where we will walk together through Porta Burelli to pick jonquils.

Spring advances. For a week or two an almost imperceptible change has taken place. Strong arms grapple with straw brooms and sweep away cobwebs from doorways, dead leaves which have gathered in dark corners disappear, and shutters are swung open earlier each morning to let in the first rays of sunlight. An atmosphere of expectancy and hope anticipates each clear chill day as translucent light begins to filter into every gloomy nook of our medieval homes, changing our daily routine just as determinedly as it changes nature. Terracotta pots mysteriously reappear on balconies. The seeded earth shows no sign of life, but when the moment is right, pointy shoots poke through the soil and within a week or two curly iron balconies will be drenched in purple and crimson petunia. Although most homes have central heating, open fires are still favoured in the evening so the aroma of woodsmoke will linger. The wood piles have dwindled to the last few heaps and nightly puffing chimney-pots stand cold during daylight except in those households where the only means of cooking is a fuel stove. From the walls I watch trees burst into balls of feathery white. The mandorla, almond trees, always blossom first, but brisk breezes soon strip their delicate white petals. The village is then peppered with pink and scarlet as the peach and cherry trees awaken.

Montalcino is inextricably bound to the changing seasons and once the first spikes of jonquils are through, stubbornly rising exactly where they did last year, winter is at last gone. Around the outside of the walls my feet dodge patches of wild jonquils, crocus and lily spires. I have been walking daily behind the Madonna and down the northern slope, coming back up through Porta Burelli, because I wanted to see the first jonquil flower, smell the first crocus, but they had some secret pact and overnight have collaborated, bursting into bloom together. They stand today like lines of erect soldiers, platoons of them gathered round a tree stump or along a stone wall, identical ivory and yellow heads so new they are still packed tight, stiff, unable to wave in the breeze.

Life has moved up a notch. My passeggiatas are longer now, taking me in a wider circle, and on this perfect spring afternoon, right on time, I am sitting below the Cedar of Lebanon in front of Bar Prato anticipating our walk to pick jonquils, watching Maria Pia waltz down Viale Roma. I am wearing new linen pants, a light sweater, a Versace jacket is slung across my shoulders and in the pocket are my smart red leather Moschino gloves. You could say I am sanctimoniously Italianated. Maria, as I have now begun to call her, along with her other close friends, advances wearing baggy tracksuit bottoms, a bright green gym sweater with the number 70 plastered across the front, dubious canvas shoes, and is carrying a stick she has picked up under the trees.

I am debating whether I ought to go home and change, when she says, 'Senti, listen' (and I should have harkened closely right there and then), 'I've told Luciano to meet us at five o'clock, to call Luigi so he can bring the car. We'll all go back together, okay?'

It's a reasonable suggestion, but in the back of my mind I

wonder what Luigi will think of being dragooned by Luciano to collect us, at some place he has never heard of, in his beloved Maserati. Luigi too has learned that our Roman friends like to set the ground rules, to stay in control, so I am sure he will come, because we have agreed that living in the surprise-packed world according to Maria and Luciano is a minor price to pay for a valued friendship.

Setting off, we are soon passing under the arch of Porta Burelli and down the steep hill towards my favourite church, the desolate Santa Maria delle Grazie, where I hurry over to peep through the curved window to see what else has crumbled. But we don't stop for more than a moment, continuing down the white dirt road leading to several farms and vineyards towards Canalicchio di Sopra, where Primo lives.

'Maria, where are we going?' I ask, but her innocuous reply, which keeps me in the dark, is typical. 'To the podere of Stefano.'

I do not know Stefano, nor where his farm is, so it does not make much difference. But now the road is becoming alarmingly steep and we cautiously pick our way over rough stony ground, turning on to an even steeper gravel track where we both begin to slip and slide, grabbing each other as we slither around the bends. Bruno Maglie, the famous and expensive Italian shoemaker, did not intend me to descend this track in his handmade leather shoes, and I am becoming flushed and agitated. My Versace jacket is catching in the overhanging brambles, but I keep silent when I see Maria pull away, letting blackberry snatch viciously at her gym sweater.

This steep hill is hard on our knees because momentum thrusts us forward. We have to quickly sidestep ridges and gouged-out troughs; the stones are loose, spraying about as we walk, not easy to dodge. I am concentrating on the track when Maria stops to examine a sprig of wild herb. Rubbing it between her fingers, she holds it up to my nose. 'Lovely, isn't it?' She pulls off a handful, which she stuffs into her tracksuit pocket. Tomorrow it will dress someone's pasta or, more likely, end up in the washing machine if she forgets about it.

Not daring to look behind, I sense we are making a near-vertical descent. We pass terraced vineyards, thickets of dense woods, a shrine sheltering a faded Madonna, and occasional deserted farmhouses. The world becomes tranquil and silent. After thirty minutes Maria finally pauses and we turn to gaze upwards at Montalcino. The village looks breathtaking. Perched right above our heads is the bell-tower of San Francesco, and the stone houses of Pianello seem to hang precariously over the side of the hill. Rewarded, we push on without talking for another twenty minutes, at times having to grasp a tree branch and slide around a corner on our bottoms as the track descends and twists. Thankfully, we at last approach Stefano's farmhouse. My shoes are caked ghostly white; the legs of my beautiful linen pants are dragging nettles and powdered white; the seat feels indescribable. My jacket is now a scrunched-up rag under my arm and I cannot bear to check in case my gloves have vanished. Maria looks exactly the same as when we set out.

Stefano's farmhouse is anyone's dream of Tuscany – a two-storey stone house blending with the land. A familiar terracotta roof now dips and slopes with the years, small windows encased in peeling shutters hang lopsided here and there, and a sunny columned portico awaits above half a dozen cracked stone stairs. Cypress and olive trees spread themselves haphazardly around the farm and look as if they have made their own choice about propagation over the decades. Two cypresses have outgrown a patch of soil at the foot of the stone stairs leading to the farmhouse door, which has caused the stones to crack and split. Someone has been encouraging all manner of herbs to grow along the walls, and the scent from a bushy clump of rosmarino rises. The white-ribbon track circles the farmhouse and goes on to who knows where. I do not care, because I am so relieved to be here. But there is nobody home.

'Non preoccuparti,' Maria says with a shake of her head – and finally the alarm bells clang, because when a Roman tells you there is nothing to worry about, it usually means this is something outrageous which you should treat with suspicious caution. I suddenly think of poisoned Roman senators, knives in emperors' backs and 4 a.m. at Camigliano! Maria certainly is not worried. She opens the door to the kitchen and walks through to the living room, which has a hooded fireplace with pots and fire-poking implements hanging from the stone mantel. This farmhouse has a noticeably lived-in, if somewhat comfortably dishevelled, 'alternative' feel. Whoever Stefano is, he likes to paint and create sculptures with rocks, wire, terracotta, lumps of wood and sand, and the evidence is everywhere. Dried herbs dangle from the ceiling, curly-edged photographs are pegged to cupboard handles and Stefano drinks an assortment of Indian tea from weird pots with thin curling spouts which line the shelves, and he definitely loves music.

I see no evidence of jonquils around the farm and am curious about what will happen next, but Maria brightly announces she is going to gather wood for the oven. I'm not sure about this either, because chopped wood is stacked up along the outside wall of the farmhouse and anyway, I cannot see any oven, so I assume she means the fireplace. With nothing but her bare hands, she sets off into the thick undergrowth. I call after her: 'I'll just sit on the steps in the sun, Maria,' but she is gone. I soon hear her hacking at the bushes and, every now and again, the snap of a branch. Within a few minutes she emerges carrying an axe and dragging two-metre lengths of hewn clippings from olive trees, evidently pruned some time ago, and then she is gone again.

A small car drives up, the door bursts open and a boisterous, yelping white dog rushes out and races straight into the bushes to find Maria. A tall ponytailed man, who I decide must be Stefano, calls buonasera to me and begins unloading things from the car. Hesitant, I walk across to offer help. Fortunate timing, because just then a gnarled lump of olive tree comes hurtling from the woods. As it sails over the roof of the car, I hear Maria's commanding voice: 'Via, via, go fetch,' and the white dog erupts from the undergrowth. Stefano does not seem at all surprised by my presence – in fact, he seems to be expecting me. Maria emerges once more from the woods and they begin, to my relief, talking about going to pick jonquils.

My rush of enthusiasm wanes when the jonquil search has us walking back along the white track circling the farmhouse, then turning cross-country down through fields. This time there is no white-ribbon track. We jump ditches, clamber over stone walls, squelch through seeping puddles, plough through brambles and stomp through clammy earth until we reach an old disused well. Maria circles the puddles and finds a gap in the corroded stone where water trickles out.

'Isabella, come and taste the water! Fifteen years ago, the ladies of Pianello came here to drink because it contains mineral properties and is connected to the old village spring. It's benissimo for your health.' The water looks algae green, possibly because the surrounding wall is covered in moss, but Maria sips away as it trickles through her hands and spills over her gym top. Tentatively, I give this good-for-my-health water a try. It is icy cold and tastes fresh as a mountain spring, which of course it is.

Another 200 metres on we round a hill to find our glorious field of golden jonquils which must have bloomed days ago. Masses of thick heavy heads dance in the breeze and an intoxicating aroma of new growth and damp soil wafts around. Stepping between the clumps, we pick bunches and bunches of jonquils, two armfuls each. The moisture seeping from the stems on to Maria's wet gym top does not look as disgusting as it feels on my sweater, but it is too late to worry. Anyway, I still have to carry them back.

As we near the farm I watch two vehicles unload their passengers. One is Luigi's Maserati, but not only he and Luciano are here; four other people including Cinzia, Stefano's wife, spill from the cars. Luigi does not seem altogether content, although he is playing with the dog whose name he has discovered by checking her tag. As usual, no introductions are offered; everybody assumes you know everybody else. Stefano unearths a grimy steel bath, the type with a handle at each end, and we unburden our armfuls of jonquils. 'Tomorrow,' Maria positively gloats, 'I am going to fill Grappolo with these golden flowers.'

Joining Luigi and Luciano with a glass of Rosso, I watch Maria hurtling towards the woods again, but I am not feeling inclined to be dragging branches behind the house, which she seems intent on doing. Within seconds her commanding voice reaches me once more: 'Isabella, come and see the oven!' Holding my glass of wine, it being the first feeling of comfort I have recognized for some hours, I walk around the corner of the house. All I can see are the back ends of Maria and Stefano, because their front ends are waist-deep inside an external Tuscan bread oven.

Maria backs out. 'Si vedi? Have you seen it?' Maria loves this. She was made for the farm. Her henna-red hair is caught with olive leaves and twigs, and her cheeks are smudged with sooty cinders she has been raking from the oven. Now she is about to lift olive branches and lay them to prepare the fire. Looking at the state of her filthy canvas shoes, tracksuit pants and gym sweater smeared in slimy juice from jonquil stems, and now black and sooty, I doubt if anybody in Montalcino would acknowledge knowing her.

213

I peer tentatively into the oven. Astonishingly, it is as big as a bedroom, shaped like an igloo, and across the stones logs have been laid; the olive branches will go on top. 'Wait till you taste sausages cooked over olive branches,' enthuses Maria, 'and I'm going to put the bread in here too.' I cannot stop laughing. Shaking my head, I tell her she is impossible, but it doesn't translate well. She thinks I am telling her it is impossible to cook bread this way, which of course she strenuously refutes, and at this moment I realise, with all this talk of sausages and bread, that we must be having a barbecue!

Luciano brought pork sausages and racks of spare ribs and, to my relief, warned Luigi in advance, giving him time to fetch bottles of Rosso and Brunello from his expanding cellar. At least we are not empty-handed guests. After arranging the branches to her satisfaction, Maria moves into the kitchen where she begins scraping dozens of artichokes, and yet again I respond to her orders to come and see, and help. Explaining that they are not Jerusalem artichokes because she can only get those in Rome, she sets them on their heads in vinegar and leaves them to drain, telling me that soon we will stuff them with parsley and pancetta, Italian bacon, line them up in a broad steel tray and slide them into the oven.

As the evening progresses, our numbers grow from nine to eleven, with Maria's daughter Anna Vittoria and her husband Bernardo the last to arrive. Cinzia is trying to find enough chairs to seat us all, because it is still too cold to eat outside. We end up with an old trestle table poking through one of the kitchen windows so two people can sit on wine barrels resting under the sill. The fire in the hooded fireplace is crackling away. I help Cinzia gather up half-finished pottery and some delicately balanced objects which Stefano is turning into artistic creations, because he is soon to have a second exhibition in Switzerland of

214

his much-respected work. We put everything into another room and Cinzia produces white candles in weirdly shaped iron holders, lace napkins appear from a wicker basket and jugs of water join the breathing bottles of wine. At last the table is set; five minutes passes in noisy confusion while everybody argues about where they will sit. At last we are ready.

Peeling off the stiff outer leaves of the artichokes, the soft heart mingles with pancetta and parsley; drizzled with olive oil, they still zing with a tang from the vinegar. Luciano carries in what seems to be a whole carcass of ribs, with the pungent aroma of rosmarino and the silver sheen of sage, and salt, lots and lots of coarse salt, which he poured on before the ribs went into the oven. It brings out a distinctly Tuscan flavour to the meat, making me blink and smack my lips. I recall, with swiftly passing guilt, how we had all but excluded salt from our diet over the years. Now, as if in contrast, everyone launches into dry, unsalted Tuscan bread and Luciano carries in a tray of pork sausages which are singing away in the pan. 'There is nothing like sausages cooked over olive branches,' says Maria again. 'Nothing burns hotter than olive.' Anna Vittoria produces a bowl of insalata, rucola and mixed green leaves with a few pretty flower petals for colour, doused liberally with oil but sprinkled sparingly with liqueur like aceto balsamico. Bernardo, as usual, is regaling us with jokes, but even he is moved to silence when, after Stefano reappears from his cantina with a charcoal-encrusted round of aged pecorino sheep-milk cheese, Luigi begins preparing the glasses for a tasting of brilliant 1995 Brunello, just released from the cantina of our dear friend, Primo Pacenti. I am finding it all completely incomprehensible. How could a simple invitation to gather jonquils end up with this enormous production?

The Brunello is shared around and we examine the colour and bouquet, savouring the moments prior to tasting like distinguished wine judges one and all. Then the wine is sipped with justified satisfaction by very knowing wine lovers and we confirm to each other yet again, but as if for the very first time, that Brunello is indeed an exceptional world-class wine, created right here where we have the good fortune to live.

Just as I am thinking, and hoping, that it must soon be time to go home, Stefano adds music to the scenario and within moments Maria and Luciano are gliding across the uneven stone-flagged paving to their favourite Latin-American music, all sensuous body movement and rhythm. The music changes and so do they, to rock 'n' roll, quickly joined by the others. Stefano and Cinzia cavort in exotic steps until Stefano falls exhausted into a chair. Cinzia yells into Maria's ear, she nods vigorously, and they disappear to the kitchen, returning in minutes bearing loaded trays holding iron pots of insipid aromatic liquid – Indian tea? – which I reluctantly suck inward through a doubtful curling metal spout. Well past one o'clock in the morning, Luigi and I finally succeed in dragging Maria and Luciano away, although 4 a.m. would be more to their liking. We load up the car with iron trays, pots and implements which came from Grappolo. Greta barks madly as everybody kisses everybody on both cheeks and then, to the sound of hushed music which Stefano has finally lowered, we draw away in the Maserati. But Luigi does not turn the Maserati up the hill towards the village and this is when I realise why I sensed his discontent when he arrived all those hours ago.

'We are going home the long way,' he announces. 'Si, si, okay, va bene,' comes a muffled reply from the back seat, and that is the last we hear from Luciano before he falls asleep. With a lowered pained voice, Luigi tells me how Luciano insisted on directing him to the podere via the short cut, and he is aghast at the number of times his precious Maserati bottomed and scraped its way along the white-ribbon road. He is positive he has ruined the exhaust system and pessimistically predicts the descent was so steep he has probably burnt out the brakes as well. We still scrape against the ground a few times on the way to the sealed road, but Luciano is asleep so Luigi can groan his *merdas* and *Santa Marias* without offence.

Back inside the walls at last, we decide not to unload the pots and pans tonight, and when we reach Piazzetta San Pietro, Maria shakes Luciano awake. They step out of the car, then turn back and poke their heads in through the windows, grinning: 'Listen, can you hear the neighbours snoring?' We laugh happily at the intimacy of our medieval lanes. After Luigi squeezes the car into the car park, we clatter home up the paved lane, dropping thankfully into bed at two o'clock. Blissful sleep is overtaking me, I am sinking into that welcome oblivion, but something is nagging at my brain.

'Luigi, Luigi,' I whisper urgently, sitting boldly upright in bed. 'Mamma mia, I don't believe it . . . we left every single damn jonquil in the tub under the portico!'

I can but smile when he sleepily replies, 'Non preoccuparti, don't worry about it, Isabella. Go to sleep. Anna Vittoria has an allergy . . . Maria cannot put jonquils in Grappolo!'

CHAPTER TEN

Quarantesimo

Remembering Easter twelve months ago, I am not alarmed to discover a note in our letterbox delivered on behalf of the Parish of Montalcino. Recognising it instantly, I scan the roughly typed lines and, sure enough, it tells me to expect a visit on Thursday at around 10 o'clock, when a priest will be knocking at my door to bestow the Easter blessing. At least this year I know what to expect. Having been brought up in a devoutly Protestant family stemming from dour Scottish Brethren stock, about as distant from the papacy as it is possible to get, the obligatory Easter blessing was not only foreign to me, but Catholic teachings were anathema. The faithful worshipping their brazen images were destined to their terrible fate, and in my zealous youth I would have countered them with a sanctimonious tongue-lashing of book, chapter and verse of the King James Bible. Living here, I have grown comfortable, if somewhat dubious, with the nightly news which proclaims miraculous liquefying of congealed blood, mysterious teardrops from a Madonna, or a report from some isolated village where the priest walks beneath a canopy with a venomous snake entwined around his neck. I willingly confess their faith is stronger than mine, so I silently observe the rituals and think often of my father in the pulpit and Baptist Sunday School. Last Easter when the priest came I had no idea what he was doing because, like many Protestants, my abhorrence was significant, but my knowledge absolutely zero.

The week before the Easter blessing, the women of Montalcino become conscientious about spring-cleaning, and this morning when the note appears I realise why carpets have been cleverly secured and hung from balconies to air, pillows and even mattresses have been wedged through windows, and dust has been flying from top-storey attics. Brooms and bristle brushes scratch every skerrick of dirt from travertine steps, and sudsy stoops are hosed down, trickling into foamy lathers in the road. Whiter than white lace curtains drip from upstairs windows on passers-by and, lastly, the brass doorknocker is polished to shine like gold. All is ready for the Easter blessing. When Padre Don Gino came to bless our home last Easter, none of this was done, and therefore, immensely embarrassed, he found me half buried in a clutter of books and papers in a home lacking for a servant of God.

Opening the door to this small, bespectacled, slightly bent, black-cassocked priest with a neat black berretto sitting to the side of his head was astonishing enough. Fleetingly overcome with relief, I saw he carried in one hand what I recognised as a Bible. However, I hope he didn't see my shock, for in the other he dangled a jar with liquid in it and, although the cap was screwed tight, from two holes in the lid escaped a length of string which he clasped while the liquid sloshed up and down, because the jar almost touched the floor.

He greeted me warmly, and I think he murmured a soft prayer as he slowly worked his way from room to room, nodding and reciting words in Latin, expertly swinging the jar from side to side without spilling a drop, even, to my despair, in the spare room which had not been cleaned for months, although that did not seem to bother him. He could not see the blank astonishment on my face as he incanted the Easter prayer and asked God's blessing on our home. Then, with the benediction in the name of the Father, Son and Holy Spirit and the sign of the cross, he was off down the stairs and ringing Signora Bruna's doorbell. Bruna must have been behind it, waiting keenly, for I heard it swing open instantly. It was a charming visit and Padre Don Gino was reverently happy to be here, going about his Easter work blessing our household. Afraid of what the answer might be, I asked Luigi what was in the jar, but in the literal sense he did not know, so he told me it was more than likely a special blessing for Protestants.

This morning I open the door to tall, white-cloaked young Padre Giancarlo, one of the Brothers from Sant' Antimo, who is bestowing our blessing with a modern hand, waving a silver phial. All is going well, for I lifted my game this year and the house is shining, but I miss the dangling jar so expertly swung by old Don Gino.

With our spotless home ceremoniously blessed, we take our

morning passeggio and call into Bar Mariuccia, where we tend to gravitate when Fiaschetteria becomes busier with visitors. Often we meet Vasco, the one nicknamed L'Arabo, here with Giancarlo, his friend who taunts him about his contadini labours, but if he is not here we know to find him at Bar Cacciatore. We have grown very fond of Vasco, a wiry man no more than 135 centimetres tall with a hooked nose in a creased face. His hands are callused from working in the iron forge which Luigi visited, reporting an amazing collection of memorabilia of goodness knows how many centuries. Antique keys, old pistols, crumbling altars, horsehair stuffing, broken hunting bows and iron well covers lie haphazardly around the anvils. In one corner a hooded forge gives off a cold, aromatic sooty smell.

Luigi must have looked stunned, because Vasco said to him: 'It looks better today, my wife told me to clean it up for you.' This statement confirmed his bachelor friend Giancarlo's comment that Vasco has to do what he is told or he is polvere, dust, because his wife is not to be messed with.

I remember I first began to exchange morning greetings with Vasco when he returned from his vegetable garden outside the walls, walking uphill through Porta Gattoli when I was exploring the walls, but our friendship was sealed some months later following a poignant meeting. That morning I was hurrying to the post office with my head down, concentrating on my goal instead of enjoying getting there. I thought I heard a few words directed at me and looked up to see this familiar man standing directly in front. He was not in his farm clothes, nor in his Sunday clothes either, but dressed in a woven wool jacket with a newspaper tucked under his arm, and he wore a cap, which he removed when he spoke. He still looked like a man from the land rather than a man from the village, but at that time I did not know his nickname was L'Arabo, nor that his workshop was the iron forge.

I found it hard to understand him, but he was speaking earnestly, and I desperately wanted not to slight him, nor smile without really knowing what he was saying. In my halting Italian I explained I didn't understand and asked him to repeat himself. This time I heard words like *che velocità* and *stai calma*, *tranquillo*, *mura*, *dentro* and *che tempo*. A smile flashed across his mischievous face, his hand rested momentarily on my sleeve and then he was gone, moving off down the road at a steady pace. As he disappeared into Memmo's barber shop I recited his words and wrote them on the back of an envelope, planning to question Luigi when I returned home.

Later we worked out he was saying something resembling: *What speed, why such velocity? Calm down . . . there is plenty of time, you are inside the walls.* I had missed the whole point of being out and about; he was telling me the world inside the walls is vastly different from outside. *Montalcino is a walled village, we have a strong fortress and are well defended*, he was saying. *There is no foe threatening from the valley, we are not under siege; sons and husbands are not away fighting a battle with steel swords and breastplates.* Accordingly, I had no reason to be in such a hurry with my head down, passing him at such speed, such *velocità*. Vasco doesn't know he taught me a valuable lesson in those two minutes. I am safe within the walls.

This morning Bar Mariuccia is chaotic. Vera, who is something of a legend in the village, has been making the coffee here for thirty-two years, although the bar is owned by Angelo, whose wife Gabriela runs the pastry shop down the road. Vera is wearing her creased forehead frown, so I decide that it will be better not to make our order too complicated. Angelo is in the kitchen spreading lumpy fresh tomato on pizza bases ready for the oven. It is after eleven and he knows that in a few minutes his first wave of famished youngsters will be through the door looking for a slice of pizza to tide them over till pranzo. Angelo always looks unkempt in a comfortable way, but considering he rises at 4.30 to make brioche and usually doesn't close the bar until midnight, this is probably justified. His cotton trousers are baggy – it is hot in the kitchen with the pizza oven – and never seem to quite fit. His shirt is always too big for him and he inevitably wears his cook's apron, bib-style, wrapped around his generous self. He raises one corner of the apron and tucks it into the waist tie when he carries food to a table, so the stains from his work can't be seen – like fine chefs in classy restaurants whose aprons are never ever stained.

You have to know when to reach Bar Mariucca, because if you don't know Angelo's habits you will never taste his scrumptious food – his bocconcini, tasty mouthfuls. This time of day is set aside for pizza; sometimes sliced green zucchini circle the rim, then orange carrot makes the next circle, followed by pale artichoke, and he repeats the rhythm, turning out an artistic kaleidoscopic pizza. Halfway through the morning Angelo brings out a tray of open soft panini, small rolls, just three or four bites, and the toppings are vibrant tomatoes, basil, capers, tuna, egg slices and artichoke hearts, with a few anchovies chopped across the top. The pastries which Angelo rises at 4.30 to make are puffy, moist, still warm from the oven for his first callers, the professionals who go outside the walls to work, even as far away as Siena. On the way to cars parked around the walls they breakfast in the bar on an eye-opening shot of thick espresso and a warm brioche.

In the afternoon you will find a different range of bar food. That is the time Italians like something sweet, so around five o'clock there will be freshly baked Torta della Nonna, filled with warm custard and topped with pine nuts, and there is always a tray of Ossi di Morto, the commemorative meringue 'bones of the dead' biscuits, to munch with a glass of Moscadello. At special times of year Angelo makes seasonal treats. This morning his counter is brimming with steaming corolli, a pre-Easter sweet. Corolli are round, with a hole in the middle, and are about the size of a small halo for the Madonna. Angelo adds his secret spices, aniseed, nuts and raisins and, if you eat one straight from the oven, it reminds you of the very first time you ever tasted a hot cross bun.

Vera is offering us a frowning buongiorno and we co-operate by ordering identical caffès so as not to cause her brow to furrow more. She leans round the counter and calls to Angelo – telling him we are here – whereupon he bustles out importantly, his peaked white cap slanted to the side and wiping his hands on his apron. Peering over his flour-smeared spectacles because he cannot possibly see through them, he searches under the counter and produces a small parcel which he hands to Luigi, explaining it was left by L'Arabo. Such a delivery is not a surprise; in Montalcino it is quite common to use the bar as a drop-off and pick-up point and people frequently turn up and ask for their house keys, or the warm jacket their mother left for them. One Friday Luigi, seeing some guests off in Siena, couldn't return in time to reach the bank, so he rang to see what he could do about cash for the weekend. 'No problem at all,' he was told. 'Just call in to Mariuccia, and Angelo will have it for you. How much do you want? Call in on Monday and sign the paper.' Sure enough, Angelo, without the blink of an eye, passed over a wad of notes in a paper bag.

The contents of today's package surprise us. Inside is a large, old, shiny silver coin with the helmeted head of Mussolini on one side and, on the other, a Roman pillar, the head of a roaring lion and some writing which says: *Better to live one day as a lion than a hundred years as a lamb*. When Luigi visited Vasco in his iron forge they had talked about Mussolini coinage and Luigi showed Vasco an ancient Roman sesterce his father smuggled to Australia in 1952. Vasco has brought one of the Mussolini coins for him. We know we cannot thank Vasco straight away, and anyway, we cannot go empty-handed; four o'clock in the afternoon is the accepted time, the only time, to call. After pranzo, after siesta and before passeggiata. We know Vasco is Travaglio – he is their number one quartierante and carries the banner at tournaments – but we don't know exactly where he lives. Angelo suggests we call in on our way past this afternoon and he will give directions. Italians are loath to give out a street name and house number. Mostly they simply do not know, but I suspect it also harks back to the days of subterfuge, when one was always on guard in case some political enemy was listening. Luigi and I are now accustomed to locating people using obscure indications.

We dress for evening passeggiata and Luigi selects from his cellar a bottle of red wine to take to Vasco. We cannot think of anything else, and anyway, Luigi has been saving this fine bottle of Amarone for a special occasion. It is from the Valpolicella and we are certain Vasco has never tasted it because it comes from the cantina of a dear friend, Pierangelo Tommasi, who, along with his father and three uncles, has welcomed us to the family vineyard just beyond Verona several times. At twenty-two, Pierangelo is a vibrant and exciting young winemaker whose wine culture is way beyond his years. He told us that at harvest-time eighty members of his family carry out the vendemmia, the harvest, and every one of them is directly connected with growing and producing Tommasi wines. After one look at the stunning high-tech state-of-the-art cantina, we understood the development of his culture and the dedication of his family.

Angelo directs us down Via Donnoli, round the first bend in the houses, past where the fountain used to be near Travaglio sede and before the thin butter-coloured house, which has just been stuccoed, and tells us we will find a door with an old iron letter-box, which is Vasco's. We pass where the fountain used to be, now a tap for bottling water from the village spring but once a stone fountain where women washed the clothes. To Angelo it is still the fountain, even if it really is a tap. After a bit of ponderous searching we find the letterbox. At first there is no response to our buzz, but a minute later a window shutter crashes noisily open fifteen metres up the road and a grey head pops out: 'Chi è? Who is it?'

Luigi calls buonasera and says he is looking for Vasco, where-upon someone releases the inside mechanism on the door, which Luigi cautiously pushes open to reveal a gloomy internal stairway. At the first landing we turn a corner, follow a passage for ten metres, rise another level and there is Vasco standing at his front door. No wonder the buzzer was answered halfway up the road in this medieval warren behind metre-thick walls and twisting staircases.

Vasco retreats and Luigi calls out permesso, but as we enter someone bustles up the stairs behind us. It is Vasco's wife, she who is not to be messed with. I realise I've been exchanging a polite good morning with this signora for ages. She doesn't seem too ferocious. Vasco's home is unpretentious; antiques are scattered round the room, walls are lined with drawings and paintings, the dressers display silver and glass pieces and the home has, naturally, a centuries-old, lived-in feel.

The signora takes charge, ordering Vasco to bring a bottle of wine, but he retorts that Luigi will have grappa, not wine. She tells him to get both, because the signora – pointing at me – won't have grappa. She vanishes and re-emerges with a bowl of fritelli, placing them on the table while Vasco tries to uncork the wine. He is having difficulty, because he prefers to talk about the grappa, which he made himself. 'Mangia, Signora, eat,' he says to me. Fritelli are another Easter treat; small balls of pasta deep-fried in olive oil and drizzled with Montalcino's own acacia honey. The signora is thrilled when I show her how much I am enjoying them, but I'm beginning to wonder, does she always have freshly-made morsels ready or has someone sent out a warning? Was she expecting our visit? She then produces a tray of triangular-shaped fried pasta coated with sugar and returns to the kitchen. I detect a strange aroma wafting through, and when I sniff the air Vasco tells me she is cooking for a festa at Travaglio.

Vasco pours two generous glasses of grappa and a one-third glass of wine for me while Luigi thanks him for the coin and presents him with the Amarone from Valpolicella. Vasco would never go outside the walls beyond his farm unless there was a family emergency, and confirms he has never tasted it. Luigi explains about his friend Pierangelo Tommasi who makes this exciting Amarone, at which Vasco nods, but then says: 'Certo, certainly Luigi, it is a fine wine, excellent but,' and his head falls to the side, eyes beseeching agreement, 'however great it is, it is not Brunello!' Luigi suffers a pang of guilt but knows it would not only be useless but offensive to defend the brilliant Amarone.

Vasco calls his wife, which is how we learn her name is Elvia, although no introductions are offered. Elvia sits and we begin to chat, first asking Vasco how he earned his nickname of L'Arabo. 'In Africa, because I was a sailor. I joined the Navy when I was sixteen to escape the confusion of Fascism. I was a bit of a lad with the girls,' he confesses cheekily and Elvia smiles, 'and in Africa I borrowed an Arab's garb and dressed up, had my photograph taken and sent copies back to the girls in Montalcino. I didn't even know they started calling me L'Arabo, and they didn't know the agony I went through, because the Arab's clothes were riddled with fleas and I was bitten all over, covered in itchy red sores!'

He goes on to tell us he was listed as missing in action, and when someone here heard the radio report announcing his ship had sunk, the sad news went round the village and the legend of the impudent young sailor in the photograph grew. But he hadn't drowned, and after the war he waltzed right back into Montalcino. 'The legend is saved,' they all said. 'L'Arabo is back!' His parents were shocked, because they had been officially informed he was dead. Shortly afterwards a medal arrived for them from Mussolini, to congratulate them on producing fourteen children, including seven strong young men to fight in Mussolini's wars, although they didn't all come back.

An elderly lady comes quietly in, nods her head at Vasco and props herself on a chair by the door. 'There's just Imola and me left now,' says Vasco, pointing at her. 'I was canalitto,' which translates much less appealingly to the 'runt' of the litter, but explains Vasco's small frame and wiry build. 'My mother really called her *Finimola*, which means let's call it quits, because she was the thirteenth, but then they had me and called me after Vasco di Gama.'

The first thirteen children were named after characters from opera because it was a great love of Vasco's father, who disappeared for two days at a time to visit La Scala. I ask Vasco to tell me everyone's names and he counts them off on his fingers. 'Persico, Ruibrassi, Isabú, Nabucco, Jose, Turiddo, Ernani, Santuzza ... Santuzza, Otello, Josella, Palmira – tutti morti, all dead – and that's Imola by the door.' I ask who the others were, because that only makes twelve, and he gives me one of his famous battuta. 'Signora! Nobody told me I was dead! And you should have listened – I said Santuzza *twice*, because the first died as a child.'

Imola must be satisfied as to our intentions because she leaves as silently as she arrived. Perhaps it has disturbed her to hear the names of all her dead brothers and sisters.

'Otello only died a few months ago,' Vasco volunteers. 'He was ninety-one, lived his whole life at the Vatican in Rome . . . he tried to get me in there too because after the war there was no work and Otello found me a job in the seminary beside St Peter's. I've never forgotten it – what a job! So many creepy priests skulking down long empty corridors, all hunched over like goblins. They scared me half to death. On the fifteenth day I said to Otello: "Get me out of here, I can't stand it. These priests don't even put cheese on their pasta!" He begged me to stay, promised he would bring parmigiano cheese every day, but I sneaked out the next morning and caught a train back home. That was the end of my career at the Vatican.'

Elvia is not ferocious at all; she is quite lovely, but she reprimands Vasco to keep him in hand. It is easy to see they have real affection for each other, so I ask her how they met. 'Well, I was already engaged to another boy from the village, but that didn't stop him. Vasco was home on leave from his ship. My family had a farm outside the walls and one afternoon I was sitting in the sun with my fiancé when Vasco turned up and asked me to come for a walk. I agreed to go, but didn't know he was going to walk me seven kilometres and when we got back my fiancé was angry. A fight broke out and my fiancé got a good bash on the nose from Vasco.'

Vasco joins in. 'Yes, but next morning the carabinieri were at my door because he lodged a complaint. He got me back anyway – he sent a couple of beefy friends. Look how small I am . . . they gave me a dreadful belting.'

Vasco may be small, but he is someone who makes himself seen and heard, and Luigi will confirm the futility of taking up his grinning offer of an arm wrestle across a table at the bar. He has incredible strength, built up from years of bending and twisting lengths of iron. His grandfather taught him his trade and by the time he was nine he was working the bellows in the forge. His father forged the iron gates for Montalcino's cemetery and Vasco's work is all around the village. Under the cappellone is a six-sided iron lantern which displays the emblem of each quarter, and the street lamps and iron frames which hold notices for the quarters are his work too.

After what seems like ten minutes but is nearly two hours, Luigi rises to attempt our first false departure, reminding Vasco we have to meet someone in Ruga, the escape clause he offered when we came in the door. Vasco leaves us both speechless with another battuta: 'Ah, Ruga . . . you must tell me what it's like, I haven't been up there since the war.' Clearly, Vasco's world extends from Travaglio to the piazza, and if he is seen in Via Mazzini it is because he is having his hair cut. He was born in Travaglio, married a girl from the quartiere, his iron forge is here and he rarely moves outside his territory; an artigiano Ilcinese cittadino. Elvia invites me to come to Travaglio tomorrow morning, where she will be preparing the quartiere festa, and then invites us to join them for a merenda next week. As we leave, she bundles me up with a bowl of fritelli and Vasco wraps a bottle of grappa for Luigi in the same paper in which he brought the Amarone. After warm hugs and affectionate kisses, carrying far more than we arrived with, we are walking towards Ruga, which Vasco has not seen since the war!

The forbidding wooden doors to Travaglio sede are not designed to welcome strangers. Nervously, I push one ajar and glimpse ladies ferrying boxes of supplies from one room to another. Several young people are carrying wooden benches to the tables and Angelo's daughter, Maria-Rita, has her hands on the edge of a cardboard box which she drags across the floor to begin unpacking tablecloths, cutlery and serviettes.

'Isabella, cara.' A voice from behind makes me jump and I wheel around; it is Vera from Bar Mariuccia. She accuses me: 'You are in Travaglio – why?' Embarrassed to be caught peering through the door, Elvia's name eludes me, but Vera seems not to notice when I explain I am looking for the wife of Vasco, L'Arabo. 'La cucina,' she raises her head in the direction, takes my arm and in a moment we are in the kitchen where half a dozen ladies are talking noisily as they hover between simmering pots with long-handled ladles hanging from the rims. The aromas are intermingling, making it difficult to guess what is cooking, and when I ask Vera about the festa she tells me it is the quarantesimo. I nod my head but don't understand. Does quarantesimo, fortieth, mean something? The ladies smile and call good morning. I no longer expect introductions and none come.

Soon Elvia has me stirring a tall pot containing something pale, the shape of skinny pasta. The water it is cooking in looks awful, but it doesn't smell too badly. Elvia is stirring a smaller pot brimming with bubbling tomatoes and onions to which she adds a handful of parsley, stirring vigorously. 'I'll see you afterwards,' calls Vera as she sweeps out the door. One minute later she is back: 'Il prete arriva!' she whispers urgently, poking her head round the corner to the kitchen. The priest is arriving! The ladies cast furtive glances at each other, quickly bang the lids on all the pots except the one I am stirring, and I catch under the breath *Madonna*s and *Santa Benedetta*s as they hurriedly unwrap aprons and scamper one after the other into the dining room. I decide to stay where I am, because I can hear what is going on without being seen.

The women effusively greet the priest who, of course, is dressed in black. His berretto sits to the side and stout black sensible shoes poke from the bottom of his gown. 'Good morning,

Padre,' they chorus one after the other and I hear him ask if everything is ready for tonight. 'Si, è tutto pronto, no niente problema, si, arrivano a le otto. Yes, everything is ready, no, no problems, yes, everyone is arriving at eight.' The women speak loudly over the top of one another then lean forward, feigning concentration, when he asks what they will be having to eat. Again they chorus soothingly, 'Oh nothing, practically nothing, really a simple dinner – *un po di trippa* and a handful of tomatoes and onions, nothing much else. This is the right way, isn't it, Padre?' I stare down into my pot. Tripe. I am stirring a gurgling pot of white tripe!

The priest is getting over-excited and his voice is echoing through the room. 'Remember,' he declares, 'this is a dinner for quaresima. Tripe is more than enough.' Heads nod in solemn agreement, and with more soothing words of assurance the women calm him down and in a few minutes guide him gently to the door.

Curious about this agitated exchange, I ask Elvia exactly what quaresima is, to which she helpfully replies that it is a dinner. I persist, asking why they are holding it. She looks at me incredulously: 'Perchè? Il quarantesimo, primo di pasqua. Why? It is quarantesimo before Easter.' I feel a scarlet Baptist blush coming on. Forty days before Easter, the first day of Lent, we are not supposed to eat meat, and are supposed to go without. The Travaglio ladies are cooking tripe, tomatoes and a few miserable onions; poor food for Lent. Elvia tells me not to worry about the priest. He is not really upset but has been berating them for weeks. He knows they always have tripe, tomatoes and onions at the quaresima dinner. That is the sacrifice, she says, but there are eighty Travaglio coming for dinner tonight so the women have to cook a few other things as well. 'The priest is just doing his work,' she nods, 'but we have to eat, don't we? And God knows what's going on, because it's symbolic – He knows we are pure of heart. Tonight when the sacrifice is done, you can be sure our priest will be here for his share of the rest!'

By the time I take all this astonishing information on board, the Travaglio ladies have turned off the stoves and put the lids on the pots. They start saying their farewells, because they are going home for pranzo. I am looking forward to telling Luigi about this pot of tripe – maybe he already knows what quarantesimo signifies – and after I affectionately say farewell to Elvia I walk back through Travaglio into Pianello. There is no one about, because everyone is at home or on the way to pranzo. Reaching the wide stone steps which rise to Grappolo Blu, I see Maurelia waving and coming quickly down, but she lives further up the hill, so if she is descending these steep steps it means she is on her way to Pianello sede. 'Isabella,' she puffs, 'are you right for eight o'clock tonight? I arranged with Luigi this morning, so you are booked in. We are having a small Pianello dinner, more like a merenda really. It's quarantesimo today.' More like a merenda, a little bite, a snack, light lunch, a small dinner.

I smile and think of Travaglio, Pianello, Borghetto and Ruga, each quarter taking responsibility to make a sacrifice for quaresima, Lent. But tonight is not, as I fear, my introduction to tripe, onions and a few miserable tomatoes. That turns out to be a Travaglio sacrifice. The Pianello sacrifice is skinny Lenten soup or, as Maurelia put it: 'A few pebbles in a pot of water with a miserable carrot or two!'

CHAPTER ELEVEN

In the End the Ball is Always Round!

Montalcino's green and whites are a passionate football team with
like-minded tifosi, fans, who, with a history of predominantly
verbal but occasional near-physical abuse at games, are something
of a disappointment to some citizens. Others describe their

displays as being akin to passive violence. Luigi goes along with this description and dismisses the iron-caged walkway to assist the referee and opposition back to the dressing-rooms as purely a sensible precaution. Thus, when his football friends Zampa and Illiano asked why he doesn't bring me to the games he mumbled that yes, I did like football – in fact I had attended a home game earlier in the season – but the reason I had not been going was the 4-degree temperature. Now that spring was here, he assured them, I would come. At the earlier game I met Laura from the vegetable shop. She didn't have her hair striped green and white that early in the season and was with her friend, also called Laura. I felt quite comfortable, because many women from the village support the team. Their shrill voices are frequently piercing the air, encouraging our players or, just as frequently, screaming unintelligible words at the referee, because in their eyes he rarely gets it right.

On several self-indulgent Sunday evenings recently I have been sitting snug, sipping an aperitivo in Fiaschetteria and watching cars speed recklessly into the piazza, horns blaring, green and white ribbons streaming behind, with several young people leaning halfway out the windows, screaming: 'Abbiamo vinto, abbiamo vinto! We won, we won!' They race twice round the walls and dash in and out of the piazza before Andrea catches up with them. By this time their subtle message has let everyone know the team has triumphed in their away match.

Luigi is a regular supporter at both the home and away games, but is particularly happy when the game is on our campo sportivo directly below the fortress. An absolute gem, the ground looks over the hunting woods in one direction, with views to the eastern mountains in the other, and has a sturdy undercover grandstand, much grander, he says, than that possessed by many rival teams. The fans are gripped in football fever at the moment because our team is building on a thrilling climb which began four years ago. In a few short years the squad has risen through three divisions and this season is winning enough matches to be contenders for the coveted Coppa Toscana, the Tuscan Cup, a tremendous effort for a small village like Montalcino. Qualifying games are played amongst all the football clubs in Tuscany, including those in higher divisions than Montalcino. Little by little, surprising everybody, including the sports editor of *La Nazione* in Siena who has been praising the determination of the squad, our team has been creeping closer and closer to a dreamed-of position in the Coppa Toscana, consistently winning matches. With enthusiastic encouragement from Luigi, I agree it is time I roused my interest in Italy's national passion.

At the home game earlier in the season I was surprised to see twenty or thirty people leaning over the fortress walls. Before the game started, the amplifier behind me boomed out the reasonable suggestion that those spectators hanging over the wall ought to pay L 15,000 and join the rest of the fans in the stand, instead of trying to watch the game for free. I realised then that the proximity of the fortress does present a drawback, because not only were people lined along the wall, some fifteen metres above the ground, but more adventurous souls had climbed a shaky timber ladder to watch the game from the highest tower, where swallows soared around their heads. What was puzzling, though, was hearing the loudspeaker refer to them as Portuguese who ought to be ashamed of themselves. 'Who,' I asked Luigi, 'are all these Portuguese who haven't paid to watch the game?' He too was puzzled and questioned Zampa, but his reply left him none the wiser. 'It goes back to Rome – not a Montalcino story really.'

Believing the Portuguese must come from Portugal and live in Rome, Luigi asked Luciano, because he had never seen or heard of any Portuguese people around Montalcino. 'Dai, dai,' responded Luciano with a grin, 'haven't you read about them in the papers? Half the seats at the opera in Rome are occupied by Portuguese who don't pay. Accidente, if all the Portuguese who travel first-class on Italy's very fast trains paid for their seats, the railways might make a profit for once! Listen, Luigi, it's an old story to do with the Pope, St Peter's Square in Rome and the obelisk that has been in the centre of Piazza San Pietro for centuries.'

The obelisk which now rises in Piazza San Pietro, St Peter's Square in Rome, first sat in the Circus of Nero and was moved to the Piazza in 1586. Raising the obelisk posed engineering problems and Pope Sixtus V was adamant the occasion must be treated with the utmost ceremonial respect. Nobody was to say a word, no one was to clap or cheer. The obelisk, said the Pope, must be raised in absolute silence. Jute ropes were tied around the immense stone obelisk, teams of hundreds of men lined up, and at a given signal the obelisk began to rise in reverent silence while the solemn Pope and his Cardinals prayed. One of the men pulling and straining with his team saw the jute ropes drying out, beginning to shred, and foreseeing disaster about to befall himself and his friends, out of the solemn silence his desperate voice echoed around the silent piazza: 'Pour water on the ropes! Pour water on the ropes!'

Because of his timely warning the obelisk was successfully raised, but the worker who broke the sacred silence was singled out and brought before the Pope. He was from Portugal. His friends expected him to be thoroughly disgraced, but the Pope acknowledged he had averted danger, possibly prevented many deaths, and decreed he should have the freedom of the city of Rome. From that day hence he did not have to pay for anything. He could go wherever he liked at no cost, he paid nothing for food or lodging, for any service rendered, nor for entry to any sport or entertainment.

And so, over the centuries in Italy, whenever favours are bestowed on family members, politicians, or Church hierarchy from anyone in a position of authority or power, the recipient of those favours, or anyone who claims them, is known as a Portuguese – a non-payer. The Montalcinese way of dealing with the Portuguese in the fortress is, at the first attempt, reasonably polite and some are so ashamed they climb down immediately, the public exposure too much to bear. The defiant few then suffer the brunt of an explosion of less courteous chants from the grandstand as youngsters hurl abuse and offer derogatory comments about the morals of these freeloaders, what they have bled from Italy through the centuries, while various curses concerning their offspring and family are promised. In the end, only a few are brazen enough to be shameful Portuguese who don't support our team.

Luigi has made friends with many regular supporters but is especially fond of Illiano – the same Illiano whom we met at Osteria Porta Cassero when we ate lunch there with Primo – and Zampa, who is also called Sandro, which is a short name for Alessandro. A Montalcino player himself in his youth and one who managed to slip in a bit of thumping in the course of play, zzamp-zzamp-zzamp, Zampa earned his nickname on the field. He denies its justification, claiming he was a strapping, solid youth and very often an opposition player turned with the ball and unfortunately ran straight into him – an encounter which inevitably flattened the opposition because Zampa's defence was like a brick wall. The humour of this Herculean description is not lost on Luigi, because from the time he was fifteen years old Zampa worked as a brickie's labourer and spent his whole day carrying steel pails of cement up and down ladders. Zampa is still a thickset solid man you wouldn't want to run into. His protruding pale grey eyes rivet attention on his wrinkled fleshy

238

face and he swaggers through the village with his hands in his trouser pockets, his jacket squeezed out behind his elbows. The alphabet he uses contains no hard-sounding letter *c*, which has been substituted by the Montalcinese *h*, so most sentences begin with a long-drawn-out exhaled *hhhhaa* . . . and his voice is musical, uplifted at the end of each sentence.

Zampa doesn't go to every football match. His friend Illiano excuses him by telling Luigi that sometimes he has 'got the moon' – that he is in one of his spells under the influence of the full moon and cannot come. Illiano is Zampa's closest friend. Almost inseparable since they were little boys, Zampa says Illiano's temperament is sempre bello, always beautiful, adding: 'He's a good lad when we are together, except,' he qualifies his statement and looks reprovingly at Illiano, 'except when he has cards in his hands. He becomes a different person and I cannot reason with him because he is so superstitious. Halfway through a game he wants to change chairs because he says the one he is sitting in is bringing him bad luck. And if he loses the hand, he puts that chair away and gets out a new one!'

Illiano gets totally preoccupied with making sure everything is in place for each match and sometimes at the home game he gallops around the perimeter fence to retrieve the ball when it is kicked out of play; but Illiano is nearly seventy and his run around the fence leaves him breathless and crimson-faced. When he tosses the ball back over the fence it doesn't always reach its destination on the first, or even second, throw and when this happens the Montalcinesi in the stand roar jovial abuse at him; he makes signals with his hands and arms that originate from Sicily. Illiano wears a peaked cap, his chins have doubled and fallen on to his neck over the years but the personal attribute which embarrasses even him is his delicious, gravelly, rumbling voice. Each word tumbles out as if it is being churned from a cement-mixer, and I think that is why the youngsters taunt him. They are trying to get him to rumble at them.

The team, desperately needing sponsorship a few years ago, was rescued by Giuseppe Bianchini, affectionately known as Beppe. He, I was particularly interested to learn, is a generous Brunello-grower with a farm and hunting lodge close to Montalcino. Giuseppe has always passionately supported the Montalcino squad, but in 1994, the year he became President, he took the position with aspirations of lifting the team into a higher category. But passion was not enough; Giuseppe is clearly an exception amongst growers because he personally sponsors the squad financially. He soon had the team in new green and white strips, organised training and coaching, sorted out team problems and, most significant of all, started looking for new players and with his own money head-hunted talented players to whom he pays monthly wages. Generously reinvigorated, the squad has moved forward. Angelino, who is also a member of the village band, is the Administrator and responsible for the smooth co-ordination of acquisition and sale of players, publicity and sponsorship drives. With the help of loyal workers like Giancarlo, Enzo, Walther and Bruno, he gives generously in time and effort behind the scenes.

Midway through this season, Montalcino began to draw away from other contenders in their division, matched week by week by a rival team, La Sorba. That is why, with a handful of games left to play, Sunday evening has seen the arrival of horn-blowing green-and-white-ribboned cars speeding through the piazza and passionate reports of heroic battles on the field from our team and verbal battles in the stands from our tifosi. The team includes cute Mirko, who is at university after living in America so he could learn English; we have Fabio who never stops running; our Captain, Giacomo, also called Bocci, is something of a heart-throb and he, along with Fabio and Vito, forms the strength in our attack. Fabio's free kicks from anywhere near the goal square are legendary, as he floats the ball over the wall and around the goal-keeper into the net so gracefully. We have Francesco, Arrigucci and our goalkeeper Lunghini, who intelligently reads the play from the goal square. His booming voice carries all over the field during a game.

Luigi does not have a car to get to away games at the moment because the Maserati dealer in Siena is waiting on several hundred thousand lire-worth of replacement parts for the exhaust system. He was right, it was all but ruined on the descent to Stefano's farm. Illiano apprehended him in the piazza: 'Next Sunday we are playing at Grosseto. You can come with us. Why not bring the Signora and we'll mangiamo pesce, eat fish, before the match.' Luigi was curious, but being accustomed to the association of food with everything of importance in village life, he reasoned that as Grosseto is on the coast it would accordingly be the place to eat fish, and apparently the boys always mangiamo pesce when the team plays near the sea. Luigi enthusiastically agreed to bring me and for the rest of the week was kept abreast of meticulous planning of where we would all eat fish. My enthusiasm did not match his, but curiosity about our football team, and the fish, led me to concur.

Zampa and Illiano waited until Friday, market day, when they talked with the travelling fishmonger, and Luigi, accompanying his friends on this lofty quest, said the conversation in the tiny fish shop ended up involving several signore waiting to be served. Zampa and Illiano secured the phone number of a pescatore who supplies his freshly caught fish direct to coastal restaurants, and they were satisfied he would direct them to where we will mangiamo bene. Illiano rang the fisherman who, without hesita-tion, recommended a certain restaurant and assured Illiano he would make the booking. It seems Illiano and Zampa are anxious to cut a bella figura, having invited Luigi and me to accompany them.

Today is Sunday and eight of us are travelling in two cars to eat fish before the game at Grosseto, forty kilometres from Montalcino. Illiano is driving one car accompanied by Zampa, who sits in the back with Luigi while I am made regally comfortable in the front. Once outside the walls, we set off on the road but have only travelled a few kilometres when Zampa sighs, 'No turning back, that's Pia's bridge.' My ears prick up. What bridge? All I can see is a dip in the road and a few posts guarding a ditch overhung with bushes. I ask what Pia's bridge is. 'Pia used to live in the village. She was a fine signora, but her ill-tempered husband was jealous and one day a story got around that Pia had another man, so her husband accused her of adultery. It was a terrible scandal in a small village and Pia's husband cast her out, saying she had disgraced him. He brought her outside the walls and left her here. Pia started to walk up the road but when she came to that stream she missed her footing on the bridge, fell in and drowned, so this is always called Pia's bridge.'

'What happened to her husband?' I ask breathlessly, trying to picture in my mind men in the village who have no wife and who might be the disgraced husband of Pia.

'Nothing,' responds Zampa flatly. 'Later it was discovered Pia hadn't been unfaithful at all, she never was, but she was dead and it was all discovered too late, which is why, when we cross the bridge, we say, "Too late to turn back now – we are over Pia's bridge." She is dead and gone.'

'Zampa! Is her husband still in the village?' I am indignant and completely shaken that the story should have such a vicious and unjust ending for poor dead Pia. Zampa leans his hands on the back of my seat, then he and Illiano throw their heads back and roar with laughter.

'Madonna!' comes Illiano's gravelly response. 'Magari, if only, Isabella. I don't believe so; that was halfway through the twelve hundreds. They have both been dead more than seven hundred years!' For more than seven centuries people have been crossing dead Pia's bridge and still remember her as a fine, faithful wife, cast outside the walls, victim of a jealous husband. I love the story after all.

We ride through the Tuscan hills passing vineyards, straining our eyes to see the first green bud, but the vines are unaroused. A car overtakes and by the sound of the blasting horn and shrieks as they streak past we surmise plenty of youngsters are heading to the game as well. Within an hour we are nearing Grosseto but do not turn towards the city because apparently the game is not really at Grosseto after all, nor is the restaurant; they are both at Castiglione della Pescaia, another twenty kilometres further on. Soon enough we reach 'big castle of the fishermen' and locate Ristorante La Portaccia, the Ugly Door (!), where we are eagerly awaited by the proprietor, who has been forewarned we expect to eat fresh fish and know our friend the pescatore delivered his catch this morning. We do not discuss the menu with the owner, who is called Pietro, as Illiano tells him we are entirely in his hands and Pietro likes that immensely. I try to smother a grin. Is that really his name? Is there a more likely name for the proprietor of a fish restaurant in Italy than Peter?

Once seated, Luigi asks about wine. 'Si, si,' respond Illiano and Zampa in unison, but Illiano wisely counsels, 'We'll have wine, but it must be white wine because we are eating fish, and this is not Montalcino, Luigi, so don't get too excited about the wine. It will be discreet, and that's enough said.'

Pranzo dismisses all thoughts of football from our heads. Out it comes, plate after plate, tasty morsels of char-grilled gamberi, prawns, lightly dressed in olive oil and garlic, baby octopus stewed in wine mixed with tender rocket and blazing red tomatoes, triangles of barely battered squid that look like white envelopes, light as a feather. Two plates of gleaming black-shelled mussels are borne in, bursting open and drizzled with golden oil. We are speechless because back in Australia we have eaten barbecued barramundi straight out of the river, we have waited by the wharf for the day's catch of king prawns to arrive and have munched our way through Sydney bugs and Tasmanian lobster and it has all been delicious, but how do Italians get these flavours into Mediterranean seafood? The juices dribble down my chin, through my hands and trickle round my wrists, so I tie a napkin at my elbow to catch them. Ample cloth napkins tucked under our chins help, but the tablecloth is evidence of a certain ineptness at keeping everything on the plate.

All this is the antipasto, before the primo piatto, which is pasta, arrives. 'What is it?' I demand, as two steaming platters of wriggly shaped pasta are set down, but I am given an unintelligible name, so am none the wiser. It is sublime, and impossible not to have another plateful because the piquant red sauce is irresistible – possibly tasting of oregano – and barely coated with olive oil. Strange creatures lie hidden in the twists, hard to recognise. Is the flavour crab? And are these miniature morsels vongole, tiny clams? These sea creatures still have legs and feelers, but they all taste scrumptious so I just blink and pop them in my mouth. We are all far too greedy with the pasta, cleaning up both platters and supping up the sauce with dry Tuscan bread, which is why everybody groans as the secondo piatto is carried in. Charcoal-grilled and blackened on the outside, the cavity of this stately fish is stuffed with onions and parsley. Pietro dissects it, lifting out the boneless white flesh while we watch. It is branzino, a superb sea bass, one of the best eating Mediterranean fish. We are determined to squeeze the fish in, then spy two platters of sizzling scampi on the way to our table. Each is 20 centimetres long, grilled to perfection and nestled on a bed of rucola with lime wedges. We all groan again and feign despair, but in the end make a courageous effort and all the scampi and branzino disappear as well. Now I understand why it is so important to mangiare pesce at the coast.

Already it is time to leave, because Illiano is not absolutely certain where the ground is and we do not want to miss the kick-off. He calls to Pietro, 'If there is anything to be paid you had better let me know,' then adds, 'and remember, we are modest contadini from the mountains, so don't be exaggerating!' Montalcino is in the mountains? Certainly it sits *on* a mountain surrounded by valleys, but I think 'from the mountains' is a slight exaggeration. And is Illiano, who has never worked the land, claiming conveniently modest contadini roots?

Now we cannot find the football ground. Laughing overloud, the way one does after excessive food and wine, and all talking at once, urging Illiano to go in this direction or that, does not help, but finally we spy an arrow to campo sportivo, which we follow, parking outside the gates. There do not seem to be many people about, but we are half an hour early and after we unload and walk through the gate, surprised there is no charge to enter, we notice the half-dozen people who are here are staring at us strangely. Do we look like we come from the mountains? Yes! And we are at the wrong ground. This is the playing field for the pulci, little fleas – the under tens!

Zampa hurls declamatory abuse at Illiano, because now we really might be late! 'I'm a simple contadino from the mountains, have patience,' he pleads in defence and, to our embarrassment, a car cruises past just then bursting with young Montalcinesi who scream with laughter, realising immediately our mistake.

We race to our cars, follow the youngsters to the right ground and thankfully make our way in before the game starts. There are plenty of Montalcinesi already in the open stand. Laura is here, sitting right at the front with two or three girlfriends, and they look as if they are warming up for some verbal battles. Young men have claimed the top row and we sit between the groups, along with several rows of very respectable and well dressed citizens of Montalcino. Luigi struggled with it for a while, but has succumbed to dressing up and now wears a tie to the football too. Curiously, once we reach our seats, Illiano nods at Luigi and walks off. I see him take up a position behind the goal square while Zampa, hands in pockets, swaggers down and stands along the wire fence. Montalcino's ragazzi stream on to the field and take up positions around the ground; the game is underway. There seem to be more Montalcinesi supporters here than locals. Our young tifosi sing in unison, making up rhythmic chants of support and a few of abuse as the game unfolds. But always the chanting ends with: '. . . our hearts are with Montalcino.'

Excitement is reaching stressful levels, because with three games left this season Montalcino only need to win one more game to secure top position in our league – which will mean next season we rise again, into a higher division! The team we are playing today is halfway up the ladder, so it is expected to be a walkover and will hand us three points towards our objective. Sitting in the open stand we are joined by Angelino, looking tanned and extraordinarily handsome in a canary-yellow shirt and colourful tie. He offers Luigi snippets about players and the team plan, then adds, 'We'll be busy next week, we've got to slaughter ten pigs.' Slaughter ten pigs? There is no time to ask about this odd news because the game tightens up and his eyes roam the field in search of careless play.

Bocci is having a bad day; the opposition has him well marked and he is not getting a clear shot at the ball. As sometimes happens when teams of unmatched skill contest the ball, frustration results from too much whistle-blowing and not enough free play, leading to yellow cards. Two for us and two for them. A yellow card for Vito is bad news, because he is a great attacker and if he gets another he will be out of the game. The second yellow card a minute later, of course for a foul not committed, is for Arrigucci, our midfield defender. Equally disastrous! He received a yellow card last week too, so cannot play in the next game. And the Montalcinesi, not only the thirty or so youngsters sitting at the top of the open stand, go wild. The women are screaming, the men are out of their seats and streaming down to the fence, which they then climb, rocking back and forth in rage. I watch horrified, rigid with shock, as gentle Zampa's arms thrash wildly at the fence and, hearing a distant rumble, I know it is Illiano's unmistakable voice – fortunately unintelligible – reaching the fence before he does.

The referee speedily attempts to get the game underway again, but the verbal abuse from the normally polite and gentle Montalcinesi signore, not to mention the way their husbands are threatening to crash through the fence, seems to have caused him to forget momentarily from where the ball should be played. Believing they have him rattled, our tifosi batter him with unrepeatable insults, but he ignores them, stops play and takes the ball back. Thunderous discontent shows on the faces of our angry defenders. Angelino roars at them: 'Ragazzi, get your minds back on the game . . . play the ball!' He then adds one or two unprintable suggestions – at least, I think that's what they are.

The opposition sees the opening, form a deadly attack and race up the undefended field. Oh no, how did it happen? The ball is in the net. It is one-nil. Montalcino have lost. Despairing groans come from Angelino, who slumps down next to me. 'We've just won eight games straight! How could we lose? Diamine, Luigi! Promise me you won't bring the signora next week? Look at that, we've lost our first game in eight weeks and this is the first week you've brought her.'

On the way home the car is deathly quiet. 'Oh well.' The ever-bello natured Illiano tries to lift the clouded misery. 'Abbiamo fatto un buon pranzo, we did well for lunch.' But my mind is tangled. I do not know what to make of it all. What happened to the gentle Montalcinesi I know so well?

The next Sunday, for reasons other than Angelino's pleas, I decide not to go. Luigi arrives home grumpy with the result, a one-all draw. Bocci tried a few theatrics in view of the referee and got a yellow card, and our attacker Vito got another, so he will not be able to play in the final match of the season. Not surprisingly, the Montalcino fans are livid, all agreeing there should have been a dead set penalty to Montalcino, which the referee ignored! They console each other with words like: 'Chi ha soldi, eh, he who has the money,' implying someone paid someone off. La Sorba, our closest rival, won their second game in a row and, with only one game left to play, have closed the gap in points.

Out for a pleasant passeggiata during the week, my tentative but budding interest in football is shattered when we meet Illiano and Angelino in the piazza. Fortunately the two men are not together. Ever kindly natured Illiano says: 'Are you coming next week, Luigi? And Signora, you are coming to our last game, aren't you?' But two minutes later Angelino pulls us up. 'Look, Luigi, keep your promise and don't bring the signora. Or at least do not let her in till half time. We are playing our last game of the season against La Sorba.' He is smiling, but I am not convinced he is joking. I have been waiting for an opportunity: 'Why are you slaughtering ten pigs, Angelino, and whose pigs are they?'

'They are for the squad. We are going out to the farm of Beppe the President. Every year we slaughter ten pigs for the spring festival in the fortress. It's our annual fund-raising event for the squad – everybody will be there.'

Fascinated but puzzled by the antics of the Montalcinesi at football games, I am looking forward to today. It is the last game of the season, a home game, and Montalcino will be top of the table if we win and will climb into a higher division; but if we lose, La Sorba go forward instead of us. This is already heady stuff, but equally gripping is that the final tally of the round robin play-offs and qualifying positions for the Tuscan Cup is still undetermined, dependent on the home and away goals scored today in matches all over Tuscany. Montalcino has a chance and the fans are delirious with excitement. Unfortunately we don't have last week's yellow-carded Vito, our quick-thinking attacker, and La Sorba have just as much to play for.

As we go through the gate I hide behind Luigi, trying not to let Angelino see me, but he is relaxed. 'Ah, Signora, you are here, everybody's here today,' and he is right – even Mayor Mauro is here to watch this decisive match, which is underway right on time.

A coach-load of La Sorba fans arrive and begin to chant, but our youngsters noisily drown them out. The teams settle into a tight, well-contested first half, the refereeing is fair, and when play resumes after half time the score is still nil-nil. Well into the second half we are getting anxious, because a nil-nil draw will mean a replay, but the ball just will not go in the net. Both teams are frustrated, which is probably what leads to an opposition defender attempting to knock Bocci's head clean off with a pointed elbow just when he has an open shot at goal. Bocci is in outer space!

Whistle blowing wildly, the referee streaks up the field, all the players race over to either try to shield or get a strangling hand on the offending player, and our medico, Bongo, trots on to get Bocci on his feet. This is not a pretty sight. The Montalcinesi fans are absolutely ballistic! Zampa is thumping the fence ferociously and Illiano, crimson-faced and puffing, runs full pelt to the other side of the goal square to join him. The dramatic displays of two weeks ago are but a shadow of this loaded volatility, but most astounding of all, I am shocked to find myself on my feet screaming my head off, only I am screaming in English! In the end it's a send-off − last man in defence rule − the offending player is shown a red card and whilst his team-mates pack around the referee like angry wolves, he retires to the gate where he slumps to the ground, distraught at the unfairness of it all. La Sorba now has to play with ten men. Embarrassed at my own previously unexhibited fanaticism, I quickly sit down.

When play restarts, Bocci, carrying a bag of ice which he intermittently clasps to the side of his swelling brow, chases the ball, which bounces across the field straight towards the gate where the red-carded player is slouched. Off-balance because one hand is clutching the ice, and unable to contain his pace, Bocci crashes into the gate and the slouched player raises his arm to give him a swipe. Or is it to protect himself? Inevitably, Bocci raises the bag of ice and, undoubtedly in self-defence, clouts the slouched player round the side of his head! This action has not pleased the highly mobile whistle-blowing referee, but it pleases the Montalcinesi fans immensely! Bedlam breaks loose again, but the slouched player cannot escape because a multitude of Montalcinesi erupt from the stand and scream obscenities at him from the other side of a precariously leaning gate. Mayor Mauro, at the foot of the grandstand, with a familiar look of despair on his face, is disappearing into his own puffing clouds of smoke. Bocci glares fiercely at his opponent, then heaves the bag of ice over the fence, but the referee is flashing a yellow card to add to the one he earned last week. The Montalcinesi fans double up in agony, because they have just learned from their radios that the aggregate goals have been tallied and if Montalcino scores and wins they will play in the finals for the Coppa Toscana.

'Mamma mia!' they moan, then they curse everyone and everything in phrases unrepeatable. 'We would have to play the first of the final games without Bocci. A yellow card two weeks in a row means he cannot play!' Down at the fence the fans are screaming: 'Forget about the ice. If you win you are in the Coppa Toscana, go, go!' Lunghini throws his hands to his head and drops to his knees, but soon his booming voice activates everyone: 'Forza ragazzi, via, via! Come on, we're strong – let's go everybody!' Players race into position and the game is under way as the familiar chant goes up from the stands: 'Facci un gol, Bocci. Facci un gol. Get us a goal, Bocci!'

La Sorba are having trouble reforming, but the thrilling news about the Coppa Toscana has put renewed strength and determination into our team. Some clever work in counter attack, a deft pass back to Mirko and then to Arrigucci, who takes the ball up the centre and moves it to Fabio on the wing, who runs on to the ball with precision timing. We all watch this brilliant move in knuckle-biting hushed silence, coiled, ready to leap but not daring to move in case we hex the play. With the ball trickling lightly, defenders on both sides, Fabio elegantly nudges it to a scarcely visible patch of open ground in front of Bocci. He has gathered it in, and sighted, in one smooth movement. Then – *wham*. The ball becomes a missile. It is spinning around inside the net. One-nil! We are delirious!

Everybody erupts from their seats as the roar goes up. We jump all over the place, kiss whoever is next to us, and I hug people I do not know. What joy! It's only a football match, for heaven's sake! Why have I got tears in my eyes? Players race to smother Bocci and then to the grandstand, where they throw themselves face down in homage, sliding towards us. It is not over yet. The referee whistles a re-start, but there are only a few minutes left to play and the game ends with a gallant La Sorba battling the Montalcino team, who are defending like tigers to the unwavering chant from the stand . . . and our hearts are with Montalcino! We have won the last game of the season, we are champions of our division and will move into Promozione next year. And, unbelievably, the unlikely dream has come true: we are playing for the Tuscan Cup.

On Monday I peer over Luigi's shoulders, reading the Siena sports pages of *La Nazione*: 'Montalcino: the mountain men reach for the Coppa Toscana. It's David and Goliath.' The Montalcinesi are David and this is a sobering thought. Our opponents, Prato West, whom we will play twice, are formidable and we have to play the first game without Bocci. Prato West draw from a city of 20,000 close to Florence. They have plenty of fans, plenty of young players and plenty of funds. 'Questa è una cosa proprio dura,' announces Angelino gravely. 'This will be a very hard thing.'

On Friday evening I walk hesitantly through the fortress gates expecting to see ten slaughtered pigs strung along the wall waiting their turn for the spit, but there are no pigs in sight. People are arriving early to watch preparations for the feast, but the only topic of conversation is the thrilling first game contesting the Tuscan Cup, which was played on our ground two days ago. Elisabetta, Alessio's wife, placed a cardboard box outside their shop in the piazza urging donations for choreography, because the girls planned to encourage our team. With excitement at fever pitch we all wanted the team to do well, but knew in our hearts we were demanding, if not a miracle, then at least divine intervention; and we were still agonising over Bocci's second yellow card, because we needed him but he could not play.

Laura – hair striped green and white – together with her girlfriends, choreographed a splendid display and before kick-off jolted us out of our seats and shocked Angelino with a row of concealed rockets which shot into the sky directly below the grandstand. Not all the rockets fired and we watched as, very cautiously, Giancarlo descended to investigate the last two. Eventually, with some nervous coaxing, the last two fired and shot into the sky right over the football field. If it had not been for the soaring fortress walls, which they hit, they would have exploded their fiery parachutes inside the fortress keep. A great roar went up when the rockets smashed into the walls and exploded in tatters. 'Bravo! Bravo! Look, it's impossible to destroy the fortress. You'll never breach the walls – our fortress is impregnable.' Illiano rumbled dryly when the cheering quietened, 'That makes six hundred and thirty-nine years we have been under attack.'

With hearts in our mouths we cheered wildly when our team ran on. 'Go, Fabio! You can do it, Vito, bravo, give it to them!' we encouraged, and they didn't disappoint us. Playing a defiant attacking game against this superior adversary, the result was far better than all but the most ardent fans – whose hearts would not let them doubt our squad – could hope for: a one-all draw, and we didn't have Bocci! When the final whistle blew, we sent the glum-faced Prato West fans scurrying haplessly for their coach with bold prophetic words: 'Wait till next week. We'll have Bocci as well then, and we'll show you how to play real football!'

Tonight, encouraged and proud of the one-all score, a loyal crowd talking only football continues to stream through the gates into the fortress keep, where the delicious aromas of simple cooking, wood fires, wafting smoke and all-night feasting seem little changed since 1361.

Are we really going all the way to Prato to watch our team play for La Coppa Toscana? Yes, we are, and I am unbelievably excited. As well as the fifty-seat coach which the squad booked to travel to the game, ten or twelve carloads are coming as well, altogether more than 100 Montalcinesi supporters in the middle of the week when many should be at work. A quick caffè at Bar Fortezza and we join everyone below the fortress, from where the coach is due to leave at 8.30. This early start is an enormous sacrifice on my part. Nobody counts, but we assume everybody is on board who booked a seat; number one fans Illiano and Zampa, green-haired Laura and her friend Laura and all the girls, Elisabetta and Alessio, Giancarlo, Mario and Olga and their whole family, Bongo, our medico, and his son Bruno, and of course Angelino and plenty of youngsters having a day away from school. A hubbub of excited chatter lowers when we stop about a kilometre outside the walls to pick up two people, one of them one of our own players. The coach drives on to Buonconvento but stops again, this time for another three supporters, and everybody sighs, hoping that at last we have everyone. By the time we reach Siena the early excited chattering has slowed and we are just settling into rhythmic relaxation when we stop for a third time and Lunghini, our goalkeeper, helps his father on to the coach. Suddenly the microphone is passed through the air. Angelino tries to settle a mob of out-of-control middle-aged schoolboys in the front rows who scramble for the microphone, yelling: 'We are never going to get there at this rate thanks to Illiano, who probably arranged all these stops, and if by some miracle we *do* reach Prato, by then we'll probably have all their team on board as well.'

It is a three-hour journey, some of it by autostrada, but when the driver exits at the tollbooth south of Prato he is not sure which road to take. Illiano pacifies our anxious looks and tells the driver not to worry because Negus and Gianfranco are in the car behind. 'I saw them coming up behind us,' he rumbles. 'We'll watch them go by and follow them.' We wait . . . and wait . . . and wait. Ten minutes pass. The driver jumps out of his skin when Negus startles everyone by thumping and banging on the doors of the coach. 'What the devil are you doing?' he bawls, arms and hands making curious gestures. 'We parked behind you ten minutes ago so we'd know where to go. Are you going to the game or what?'

The entire coach load of fans round on poor Illiano like a pack of whining hyenas, showering him in a chorus of hisses, boos, whistles and jeers. Articles are hurled at him from the back of the coach and a couple of punches reach his shoulders. Luckily he is a broad-shouldered man. He jumps up, grabs an umbrella and, tucking it under his armpit like a couched lance, points it down the aisle in a defensive pose, declaring in his rumbling concrete-mixer voice: 'From this moment on I am no longer responsible for any activity concerned with this football match.' A mighty cheer goes up. 'Grazie Dio, grazie Dio! Now we might actually get there!'

A happy crowd tumbles from the coach at Prato West, including me. Merriment accelerates when Giancarlo produces two fat white-skinned sticks of salami and a loaf of Tuscan bread from paper bags and, clutching the bread lengthways to his chest, saws into it with a long clasped knife. 'I told you it was a long way to Prato,' he grins, 'so I brought provisions.' Our smiles are somewhat uneasy by the time we reach the grandstand. It has been roped off with Prato colours on one side and, on the other, green and white ribbons indicating where we should sit. 'Do they think people from the mountains are dangerous?' questions a puzzled Giancarlo as he puts his shiny knife away. Illiano and Zampa stop dead in their tracks, staring, mouths agape. Then Illiano says with shocked emotion, 'Accidente, they must have heard about the San Salvatore game all the way up here in Prato!'

Zampa sees our questioning faces and tells the story. 'It was forty years ago – the 1950s – at a game between Montalcino and San Salvatore, a village halfway up Mount Amiata. We were leading the table in points and they were second. Mount Amiata was covered in thick snow so the scheduled game was postponed. Because there was always bad blood between the teams, the Federation decided to hold the game on Easter Monday, and they wanted it to be a peace game.' Illiano breaks in: 'The teams were always fighting, and so were the fans, so they thought it would bring everybody together in a better spirit.'

Coach-loads of San Salvatore fans arrived in Montalcino. There was not a free seat in the stand or space around the fence; it was one of the largest crowds ever seen in those days. One thousand three hundred people came to watch the game designed to restore peace.

'Illiano and I were both there,' explains Zampa, 'and from memory it was just before half-time when things got a bit heated because Montalcino took the lead. Before too long a bit of a scrap started in the grandstand and spread to hostile taunts between fans down along the fence, where I always stand.'

Apparently the fray went on and on as people scuffled about in patchy encounters, but when Montalcino scored again to make it 2–0, a nasty fight broke out. The brawl soon encompassed everybody at the game and hundreds of people filtered on to the road. By this time the players were agitated, and the referee became nervous and vanished from the field when they began an on-field brawl. His desertion made the remaining fans furious and next minute, as grinning Zampa puts it: 'A thousand fans and players from both teams were punching and screaming their way through the gate as well. What a brawl! It was really spiteful. The mob got closer and closer to Piazza del Popolo, but there was nothing anyone could do to control them. When we reached Via Mazzini at the top of the steps to Grappolo Blu, it broke out into a full-scale war. That was the best of it, wasn't it, Illiano?'

'Si, si,' rumbles Illiano, shaking his head. 'That's where we got them, wasn't it? They were polvere.' Zampa soberly nods his head and, looking at the green and white segregating ribbons, agrees that even Prato West must have heard about the historic peace game. I can easily picture the two passionate youths, and their story, told with affectionate recollection, explains the notorious reputation of Montalcinesi football fans.

Prato West probably had not needed to put a cardboard box in the piazza to call for donations for their choreography, for a twenty-strong brass band marches on to the ground, followed by thirty skimpily clad, red-and-white uniformed, baton-twirling marching girls. All their rockets fire skywards without a hitch and the fence enclosing the playing field lights up with a brilliant cascade of starry waterfalls in Prato colours, while twirling cartwheels spin and a never-ending line of cracker bombs explode. The two teams run on to the field.

Perhaps it is the grandness of the occasion, or perhaps having striven so hard all season to find themselves in the Tuscan Cup has depleted the reserve of our team, but things don't go quite so happily after that. So many times Bocci or Vito slam the ball into the post, then the crossbar, miss by centimetres, fall for the offside trap, or play stops for an insignificant foul, but the ball does not go in the net. Working the ball towards the sideline, a Prato West movement goes wrong. The ball is clearly out of play, but the linesman does not signal. The Montalcinesi are beside themselves in outrage, screaming at this cretino who calls himself a linesman.

As things quieten to a hostile simmer, a Prato West fan near the dividing ribbon raises his voice and dares to helpfully suggest, without detectable malice, that the whole of the ball needs to be over the line before the linesman can call it out. But he should have known better. I look around sharply and see one of Laura's friends on her feet, shrilly piercing the air with a devastating *battuta*: 'If you know so much about balls, perhaps you've got a couple you'd like to put on the line and I'll personally make sure you know when they are both kicked out of play!' It is infinitely wiser not to incite the mountain men, or normally polite young ladies, from Montalcino.

It isn't that Prato West are playing a brilliant game, nor a game significantly superior, but in the way these things sometimes go, they end up with two goals in the net and that's the way it stays. Two-nil – we lost. The coveted Coppa Toscana goes to a joyous Prato West. As we leave the ground to the victors, subdued, the ever kindly-natured Illiano consoles us with deep words I am still trying to decipher. 'Ah well, we have got to remember, ragazzi. In the end the ball is always round.'

Saturday dawns fresh and clear. Andrea stops all but essential traffic from entering the piazza, because Giancarlo will spend hours climbing and descending ladders, and the sound technicians are busy positioning amplifiers and microphones. Trucks arrive with tables and chairs, and Delio and Bruno unpack box after box as everybody sets to work to make this the most magnificent championship dinner Montalcino football fans have ever seen. Thirty-metre lengths of green and white fabric drape languidly from the windows of Palazzo Comunale in wide alternate bands, disguising the front of the palazzo and consigning poor Cosimo under the loggia to darkened shadows. The triangular piazza is lined with four rows of green and white adorned tables and more than 300 of us will sit down to dinner, although I am sceptical because at eight o'clock the piazza is still a scene of utter disaster. However, sure enough, by nine our President, Giuseppe Bianchini, Mayor Mauro, our coach and visiting officials from the Football Federation file in to take their places at the official table in front of the bands of fabric. Tina Turner is the star turn. Unfortunately not in person, but 'Simply the Best' is blasting from the amplifiers, reverberating around the stone piazza in which 300 tifosi in cleverly disguised forms of English sing gustily along to the decibel-bursting chorus. Six hundred legs are vertical as we rise to our feet, clapping and cheering our champion squad into the piazza, patting backs and shaking hands as they pass, slowing their advance. Many watery eyes, including mine, are gleaming as we sing 'We Are the Champions' and, not quite sure exactly how or when I converted to a singing football fanatic, I watch the green and whites accept thanks from their adoring loyal fans.

Before we eat, Mayor Mauro, hitching political expedience to such a patriotic occasion and balancing his unlit pipe in his mouth, announces: 'We are celebrating a great sporting achievement. Money will be available to widen the playing field for next season, and the ground will be re-sown.' Giuseppe, beaming, thanks absolutely everyone, heaps praise on our dedicated players and, as he raises his arms joyfully above his head, we all instantly fill the piazza with a rousing chant: 'Beppe! Beppe! Beppe!' Then we begin a rendition of the Montalcino football song. I sense nobody wants this moment to end, and the chorus starts again in an emotional charge of happiness. Everyone is smiling, laughing, crying, cheering, patting each other on the back, singing, ending as always with . . . 'and our hearts are with Montalcino.'

Giuseppe's arms are still raised skywards when the heavens open! With no warning, it begins to pelt huge driving drops which form rainsheets. The flapping green and white bands behind the official table become handy channels for a waterfall which in seconds drenches the officials. Three hundred astonished diners glance up to see a cloud-filled sky and those same six hundred legs scatter like pellets from a shotgun! Within thirty seconds, platters of designer green and white crostini are floating, green serviettes and white tablecloths are sodden, chairs are lying collapsed half under tables, flung aside as everybody runs. The rain pelts down in relentless splattering drops. But where do they run to? In those few seconds, everything I had lost is found again. I don't care about the soaking rain because these modern fanatical football-loving Montalcinesi are the same ancient faithful after all. To a man – and woman – three hundred passionate football fans race up the steps and into the cappellone. In all that confusion, with all that crowd trying to find shelter – even with all the tables lined up in awkward aisles – not one person runs for cover under the old loggia, where the lonely Florentine stands knee-deep in cardboard boxes, demijohns and hoses cluttered around his feet. They never even considered it!

We did not win the Coppa Toscana, but we are champions in our league. The climatic championship dinner is one occasion I will never forget, and I cannot wait till October when football starts all over again!

CHAPTER TWELVE

A Woodcutter's Legend and a Woodcutter's Wife

Giacomo and nature become consorts in harmonious but frenzied battle as the growth cycle in the vineyard commences. The pressure is all on Giacomo, because spring waits for nobody. At some celestially inspired signal, a clean bright April dawn heralds the emergence of not one but hundreds of tightly curled buds. They spurt forward in unison, unrolling and flattening with astonishing speed because the buds to follow are forcing their way through. All over the hills grey listless branches thrust out effervescent life; first millimetres, then centimetres.

Giacomo's work begins in earnest and within two or three days the first green bud on each branch is joined by six or eight ambitious heads greedily striving to be part of the cycle. Giacomo, along with Enzo his enologist and his secateur-wielding pruner, begins to walk the rows. Before the growth is too advanced, the pruner must carry out his crucial work. The form of training imposed on Brunello vines is called cordone speronato, which involves severe short pruning so that only two buds from the eight or more which shoot from the crown of the root stock are permitted to grow. This is the first step which enables Giacomo to ultimately contain the yield of his crop. Consorzio regulations safeguard the quality of Brunello by restricting the weight per hectare which Giacomo is able to harvest, and another step in yield control will be carried out in summer. Walking together, Giacomo and Enzo inspect each trunk, snipping unwanted nutrient-embezzling buds and leaving only two to carry out the work of each plant. The two selected are enriched, energised and now saved the fight with scavenging buds to find the nutrients that will result in strong growth.

The vineyards around Montalcino are dotted with cars parked on the brow of a hill or at the foot of the rows, because pruning must be done quickly to give the two chosen buds the utmost opportunity for an early healthy spurt; secateurs snip and chop ruthlessly but wisely. Dawn air is clean and chill. All danger of a late frost has not yet passed, but is unlikely. The sun pours down for five or six hours every day, drenching the vines and soft earth with warmth, frequently followed by a soaking afternoon shower – perfect spring growing conditions. The two energised buds sprout on, outwards, upwards, and within a week are twenty or thirty centimetres long. Giacomo and his workers are in the vineyard for weeks on end, because each of the two tendrils must be trained to grow as he and Enzo decide, long before the first tiny balls of fruit form. Leaping tendrils are firmly restrained along the lines. They will continue to trap maximum warmth through spring and, when the fruit forms, the clusters will hang free and clear in the hot summer sun.

Only weeks ago Giacomo was spending day after day hurtling at breakneck speed down northern Italy's ski slopes. Downhill skiing is his second passion and, in his seventieth year, he continues to bring home trophies, at the sight of which Maria-Grazia shakes her head. 'Mamma mia, Giacomo, basta, please stop!' Giacomo and Maria-Grazia are not Montalcinesi. They belong to a new wave of growers and, together with son Filippo and his wife Emma, have invested heavily in the future of Brunello. I was curious to know how they have been accepted as growers. The response I received from Primo surprised me, because I anticipated an insulated negative attitude. Under the aristocratic family name of Marchesato degli Aleramici, Giacomo and Maria-Grazia arrived from Torino many years ago, he a retired engineer and she a public relations whizz. Wine-growing has always been in the family, although I suspect not by personal labour but certainly in titled farm holdings.

I said to Primo, 'Doesn't it concern you when outsiders from Milan and Turin move in and set themselves up as Brunello-growers? This is a small growing region.'

Primo was adamant, explaining it this way: 'In the 1960s there was hardly anything in Montalcino. There was no money for restructuring, the farms were deserted and the Consorzio was striving to change Brunello production into a viable modernised industry. People like Giacomo and Maria-Grazia brought their money – sacks full of money – and their expertise here. They were willing to invest and wait many years for a return. But not only that; people like them were the vanguard, leading the way. They did not destroy the crumbling farmhouses but began to restore them, to build them up again, so now we have dozens of characteristic Tuscan farms dotted around our hills. Seeing what could be done, people here had more faith and, by bringing outside experts into Montalcino, our knowledge grew parallel with theirs. They are part of the Brunello story too.'

The vineyard which Giacomo and his son Filippo – this time with the labour of their own hands – have built up is testament to the sizeable investment which they have outlaid. A splendid farmhouse rambles and sprawls around the property and Giacomo has added agriturismo apartments for visitors who come to absorb a bit of paradise in the Tuscan hills, just a few kilometres from Montalcino. Maria-Grazia is still whizzing round the world on public relations trips, but now she is marketing the wines of Montalcino.

These early weeks of spring bring vibrant growth inside the walls, too. The village is reborn, renewed. Vegetable gardens perform their own miracles, and peas and fava beans planted on Easter Saturday are now leaping sixty centimetres high. Artichokes the size of tennis balls raise elegant purple heads, fields of potatoes and beds of onions grow thick, celery is planted by the paddockful and pumpkins seek mates before rambling too far. My walk around the gardens takes longer because there is so much to see, so many people to talk to. Already cherry trees are smothered with hard green balls the size of marbles, almond and peach trees carry furry pods. Scarlet poppies today wave about where yesterday a spire of green stood tall. Deciding for themselves where they will grow, the poppies scatter amongst the beans and come up beneath the vines, line the tops of garden walls and bloom along the fortress embankments.

At the first Friday market in May, the air is touched with palpable anticipation and everybody is here because the vendors have brought early Sicilian fruit to sell. It will be some weeks before we are eating fruit from village trees. I think more country folk than usual have come to see the stalls, bright with blazing strawberries, vibrant apricots from the south and ghostly white asparagus from the north.

I am searching for the man who brings the spinach. He is not part of the regular travelling market but has a vegetable garden in Pianello and usually props wooden crates in the tray of his three-wheeler Ape and offers whatever vegetable is ready from his garden. For several Fridays I've been buying his spinach, the short-leaf variety with crinkly tight leaves. I know if I do not find him soon I am going to miss out, because the monks from the Abbey of Sant' Antimo will reach him first. Finding the spinach man before the monks has been a devilish game I have secretly played with the unaware Brothers, because I have decided they must have a spinach fetish. Maybe they cannot grow it in the garden at Sant' Antimo . . . yet I've heard they once cultivated saffron, which must have been infinitely harder, so why not spinach?

Monks being monks, the Brothers are up earlier than me. In fact, they rise at 5.15 and by the time they reach the market they have finished Matins and Lauds, breakfasted, been to Mass and had study time. Arriving in Montalcino they stop to talk with people in the piazza, so their tardiness means I have a chance. If they get to the spinach man first, they walk off carrying bulging plastic bags, because they buy every single leaf. As there are just a handful of Brothers at the Abbey, it mystifies me what on earth they do with it all.

This morning I spot the three-wheeler parked at a precarious angle to the gutter on the road to the fortress but I have a sinking feeling I am too late. The man smiles when he sees me coming, then says: 'Ah, buongiorno Signora, purtroppo è tutto esaurito,' and he opens his arms wide to show he has nothing left, looks penitent (although I suspect he has worked out my game), then points up the road. I watch three white-hooded monks shuffling along in leather sandals and each is carrying two bags of spinach – including *my* share – all on its way back to Sant' Antimo! I have been trying to figure out how I can tackle the question of spinach with Padre Giancarlo, remembering our personal encounter when he blessed our home at quarantesimo, but vegetables seem somewhat temporal and perhaps he doesn't need reminding. I think he must be gulping spinach seven nights a week.

Glancing around, I see my neighbour Maria heading my way. She is smiling, but her lips are tight because I have told her about the suspected Sant' Antimo fetish and she must have seen my frustration as the monks shuffled off with all the spinach. Her eyes light up as she threads her arm through mine, our shoulders meeting as she bends close for an intimate chat the way Italian women love to do. It is a sign of trusted friendship to which I react warmly. We exchange greetings. 'How is Renato?' I ask, because I know he had a doctor's appointment. When she responds that he is much the same, I ask if there is any news of their dog Dora, because I haven't seen her downstairs for a couple of weeks.

Maria sighs downheartedly. 'I think this is why Renato is not well. He has been outside the walls, and you know for him it is a sacrifice to go as far as Siena, but he loaded Dora in the car and drove all the way to Pavia in the province of Lombardia, nearly as far as Milano. He stayed in a hotel overnight and took Dora to a highly regarded veterinarian who did a thorough examination but, like all the others, he found nothing wrong.' She grimaces.

'Renato is so worried. Dora is getting weaker and weaker and cannot leave her box. He goes downstairs every couple of hours to coax her to eat. He has had heart tests done, blood tests and bone tests, everything the veterinarians can think of, but nobody knows what is wrong with her. I am afraid Renato will have to make a decision about Dora which he refuses to even talk about.' It is now several months since the hunt around Castello Banfi which signalled the downturn in young Dora's health.

I am really sad to hear this news and feel my heart sink, but then Maria bends closer into our conspiracy of two and, with a little smile, confides, 'Gabriela is expecting a baby. I am going to become a nonna!' 'Really? What wonderful news!' But I am careful not to let anyone hear this private conversation and she adds, 'Pass by and Gabriela will tell you herself – and don't forget about tomorrow evening, will you?' Last year Maria and Renato's only son Roberto married Gabriela, also Montalcinese, at Madonna del Soccorso. The bells rang out joyfully all the afternoon and Renato, looking so handsome, had forsaken the grey dustcoat he wears in his laboratory and dressed in a dark dinner suit for this once-only family celebration. Soon we will have a new baby in Montalcino. This is wonderful news.

Lola is at the market every Friday unless she and Ercole need to go to Siena or some other business gets in the way. Depending on whether or not I have an answer ready, I sometimes need to evade her, because I know exactly what she will ask me. With that disarming glint in her eye, she usually says: 'And what have you bought to make pranzo for that poor husband of yours?' I see her coming, but I am still thinking about the awful news of Dora and the lovely news of Gabriela's baby, and I haven't had time to prepare for this morning's interrogation. Today, Lola surprises me by changing tack. 'Ciao cara, have you been down to buy fish?' Market day is the only day we can buy fresh fish in Montalcino, although for a long time I couldn't find where the fish man parked and eventually had to ask Lola for directions.

'He doesn't park,' she laughed, 'he has a hole in the wall.' She took me by the arm to Piazza Garibaldi, turning into the road following the piazza's retaining wall and there, wedged into the stone wall, is a grey steel door, which on market day opens to reveal a white-tiled and freshly hosed-out fish shop. Women crowd around the door because only three can fit inside at one time, although nobody minds waiting because it is an opportunity to chat about the fish. There are always sardines, barrels of anchovies, stumpy blocks of tuna on bloody wooden boards, shiny black mussels, sharp little swordfish, gamberi, entangled squishy squid, cuttlefish and a few things I have difficulty recognising.

Lola is nursing a parcel, un pesce eccelente, an excellent fish, she tells me, and she is waiting for Ercole, because he has been sent to find baby white onions which she says are essential to have with this particular fish. Lola, as always, is preoccupied with food. Ercole arrives bearing the onions wrapped loosely in newspaper, and tilts the package so we can peer at green spires and white bulbs caked with just-unearthed soil clinging to each other. Just as Ercole is launching into a triumphant five-sentence explanation about how he found Mario's mother and she assured him these onions came from her garden not an hour ago, Lola interrupts. 'Well, it is important to have fish because the Eighth of May festivities start tomorrow. Are you having fish today?' I tell her I'm on my way to the fish man, marvelling at my newfound ability to conjure stories to pacify the Montalcinesi who worry about the correctness of our diet. So! Friday is fish day, but even more so on the Friday before 8 May.

The stallholders who travel around the Val d'Orcia setting up and dismantling their wares in a different village each day of the week bring, as well as colourful fruit and vegetables, a wider choice of all sorts of things; buttons and bows, cooking utensils, fluffy new pillows and rolls of crisp white cotton curtains to fit narrow shuttered windows. Many of the country people live four or five kilometres away and market day brings the opportunity for interaction with village dwellers. Friendly coteries of women gossip, drifting around between the stalls, exchanging news, going through the social ritual and endlessly discussing the produce. Meanwhile, the men congregate down at Piazza del Popolo, where they mill about below the cappellone chatting, smoking and waiting to see who else will arrive. Around 11.30 they stroll up to the market which sets up around the churches of Sant' Agostino and Sant' Antonio. Once up here, the men gather in groups of two or three, mingling and watching until the mezzogiorno bell in the tower begins to peal. That signals it is time for the women to conclude their purchasing and their socialising. Somehow everybody finds each other and it is time to head home for pranzo; the market is over for another week. The mezzogiorno bell begins to toll just as Ercole and Lola are reminding me I must bring Luigi to the procession tomorrow evening.

By 12.30 the stallholders are packing their clever caravans and the sweepers begin to hover. Not the mechanical kind, but three Comune workmen pushing rickety barrows which roll along on spoked pram-wheels. A three-wheeler Ape work truck used to help with the clean-up on market day, but the smart new mini-garbage truck of which the Comune recently took delivery makes market clean-up much faster. Everyone was relieved to be assured the sweepers and their barrows would not vanish when the new garbage truck arrived, because the familiar soft swish-swish-swish as the crudely fashioned twig brooms sweep steep stairways, bending and twisting so conveniently into medieval corners and cracked stone steps, is a friendly way to keep the village clean.

Mario, whose mother secured the onions for Ercole, begins sweeping around 6.30 each morning and his route includes Piazza del Popolo, which he reaches just before mezzogiorno. It was planned that way and he had to be punctual, because not too long ago Mario had to go into Palazzo Comunale, pass through what used to be the Mayor's office, climb into a square window-less room at the foot of the bell-tower, unlock a wooden door in the wall and pull a lever which began the chiming of the mezzogiorno bell! The bell is on an automatic timer now, but his rickety barrow is often standing under the old tower about that time, twig brooms balanced across the top, and Mario will be inside Fiaschetteria for a quick gulp of espresso.

Garbage is an enormous headache in a medieval village, but one Mayor Mauro has been tackling head on. When we first came to live here we had to put garbage into a plastic bag, securely tie it so that nothing could escape and only after 10.30 at night take it downstairs and hang it near the front door. That meant finding somewhere so it wasn't lying on the ground where cats or rodents could scratch into it. Between seven and nine o'clock each morning the three-wheeler Ape would zip around the village and each plastic bag was tossed into the tray. But it didn't take many plastic bags to fill the tray, which meant many trips every morning, so Mayor Mauro ordered the new garbage truck.

By two o'clock today the marketplace is swept and hosed. In fact the whole village has been swept spotless, because the sweepers will not be working tomorrow. Maria, Ercole and Lola did not really need to remind me about tomorrow night, as I have been looking forward to it all spring. Hundreds of country folk will be back to join the village dwellers, because Saturday is the beginning of the annual festival to celebrate and venerate the Patron Saint of Montalcino, Saint Maria of Succour.

*

Once there were as many as thirteen churches in Montalcino and it is still possible to attend Mass in nine or ten, although not all of them are in use every Sunday. One or two always seem to be closed for restoration and others have been swallowed up by later architectural changes and are barely recognisable. Sant' Agostino is undergoing extensive repairs to the roof, partly funded by the Bank of Monte dei Paschi di Siena. This will complete years of work, including restoration of the beautiful cloister along with the Agostinian monastery, where our recently opened Museum is a safe home for artwork, ceramics and sculptures. Sant' Egidio, too, has scaffolding erected inside the small nave; buckets of brick and debris seem to empty out daily, but this work is not expected to take too long. The first resting place for Sant' Egidio was inside the fortress keep, but when the Sienese strengthened the defences of Montalcino in 1361, the church was dismantled stone by stone and re-erected further down the hill. San Salvatore, the Cathedral, is in regular use and contains a chapel which displays the remnants of a temple that stood on the site before the first millennium. On Sundays, four o'clock Mass is said in the chapel of San Francesco, which is helpful for the elderly women who cannot walk up the steep hill to San Salvatore or Madonna. There is no doubt Saint Francis came to Montalcino in 1218, and hence his church is at the bottom of the village and, in the nature of Franciscans, beside the hospital.

On special feast days Pianello always holds mass in San Pietro, whereas the Church of Misericordia seems mostly to be used for funerals. Sant' Antonio seems, sadly, to have been forgotten and not open at all, but I hope it will not fall into desolate ruin like the enchanting Santa Maria delle Grazie, my favourite, hidden amongst the chestnuts, just outside the walls. Santa Maria was dedicated to the Madonna more than 500 years ago and popular belief records the miracle that a mysteriously stabbed raven carrying the plague fell dead from the sky on this spot, and Montalcino was saved from pestilence. Each church is a special place, a sacred link with the past with a story to tell, but the most loved and most used is the Church of the Patron Saint of Montalcino, Madonna del Soccorso.

I learned the legend of the Madonna from my friend Amelia, who narrated the story with simple faith and, being an eighty-six-year-old woodcutter's wife, whose husband Bruno is ninety, the poignancy of the legend is accentuated by her own life. If I were up early enough I would meet Amelia every morning as she makes her way uphill to the cemetery to take fresh flowers and sit with her first daughter who, she told me with pain-filled eyes, died tragically in 1946. Taken into her bedroom in a moment of shared intimacy, she showed me her dresser, which is lined with black and white photographs of a beautiful dark-haired fifteen-year-old girl. For more than fifty-four years Amelia has sought solace in these daily visits. She shared her oven-baked ricciarelli and walnut-stuffed figs with me at Christmas, but more than that, we share a soul-deep hidden pain, because I understand how she longs for the beautiful young life she lost. I have walked to the cemetery a few times to find where Amelia's daughter rests, but without success. Before too much longer I will ask Amelia if I can walk with her one morning, although she may not want my intrusion on such a personal pilgrimage.

Woodcutter Bruno is again tramping into the woods day after day. There were only a few short weeks in January when I did not see him returning with tree branches and his scythe. This month the branches seem longer than before and I watch him return from different directions, even through Porta Burelli and up the steep hill. 'The chestnut woods, Signora,' he smiles softly at me under the weight, letting me know where he has been.

Sipping piping hot caffè in Amelia's tiny kitchen one evening, with the wood-burning stove blazing, our thoughts were hundreds of years away as, wide-eyed, she whispered the legend to me. 'It was in the eleven hundreds when a woodcutter, just like Bruno, in the bosco below the church, came across a corniolo tree which is common hereabouts. It grows red berries; sometimes Bruno brings corniolo home. The woodcutter was terrified because on the face of the trunk he saw an effigy of the Madonna. Because he was so frightened, he tried to set fire to the tree to burn the effigy, but it would not burn. Ever since then, for nearly a thousand years, the image of the Madonna has been the reason for many miracles in Montalcino, especially in 1553 when the Spanish had us under siege.'

In the archives of Montalcino the religious chronicles of the time record that during the siege the Madonna appeared at the top of the walls and the brutal siege was broken when the horse carrying the Viceroy of Naples, Don Garcia di Toledo, who was the Spanish Commander, dropped to the ground, kneeling to the vision of the Madonna. I would never raise the matter with Amelia, but it has to be remembered that those who are not religious claim what Don Garcia really saw was the fierce Amazon-like woman of Montalcino, Donna Ricciarda, who was on guard duty along the wall that particular night! Then again, it doesn't really matter who he saw, because the siege was broken and that *was* a miracle.

Only later did I hear a third explanation from logical historians. They say that after Don Garcia and his vengeful captain, whose head was gruesomely lopped off at Porta Cerbaia, arrived to put siege to Montalcino, a message arrived from Naples informing the Spanish that a powerful fleet of sixty Turkish and twenty-six French war galleys had massed in the Tyhrennian Sea, planning to join forces to combat the port of Naples. The message suggested, somewhat sarcastically, that it might be prudent if

Viceroy Don Garcia ceased playing games at Montalcino. The Neapolitans were quick to remind him that the severed heads of his knights were known to be decaying along the wall at Porta Cerbaia. Not only that, they were surprised he had not noticed that hundreds of his men had already frozen to death in the valley, or starved because he did not have enough food for them. Don Garcia was determined to crush this rebellious mountain citadel, but the Neapolitans forcibly made their point: If you hang around Montalcino waiting for those rebels to come outside the walls there will be nothing left of our Neapolitan port, because it will be destroyed by the encroaching Saracens! So, Don Garcia fled to defend the seaport, and the siege was broken.

I think the Montalcinesi are right. It is irrelevant which series of events caused Don Garcia to leave. The miracle was the Spanish had gone – though it would have been better if he had left sooner, because some four thousand people perished from either hunger or disease during the eighty days of that brutal siege. Four hundred and fifty years later, as I stare at a small silver statue of the Madonna conserved in the sacristy, an offering by the Spanish in remembrance of their sacred vision, it is clear the Montalcinesi are not the only ones who believe a miracle of one sort or another took place.

On Sunday 8 May, a 13th-century painting will be unveiled in the church and the revered Madonna who has been safely hidden in her dark recess for many months, the Protectress of Montalcino, will look down on her grateful people once more. The reason I am particularly looking forward to this weekend is because I have observed one or two irregularities in the spiritual life of the Montalcinesi. For instance, I have not worked out why the eminent Bishop from Rome was given such scant hearing when he opened the Museum, yet the Easter procession had been a moving and clearly sacred event, if not widely attended. I am continually intrigued by the natural inclusion of the clergy in every facet of village life. It doesn't seem to matter what the village celebrates: football, quartieri victories, mountain-bike riding, roulette, the Sagra . . . the priests are there, taking part in everything. I have taken time to study the churches and the faithful, and this weekend offers an opportunity to observe the spiritual life of the Montalcinesi, because on 7 and 8 May the most important religious celebration in the year takes place.

Before World War Two the churches carried more importance because they were central to the administration of the village, upholders of law and order and places of help to the poor and sick. The churches were always full and many contadini families who worked the land from dawn to dusk and who rarely left the farms would walk into Montalcino on Sunday morning to come to church. Since the war, as in many other places, attendance has dwindled. In Montalcino it seems this trend has much to do with politics. People remember the dark times after the war when posters appeared in churches warning people that if they voted for the Communists or Socialists they would be denied absolution. It was a time of disillusionment, and although the propaganda was not widespread, it certainly existed. Mostly, elderly women and the faithful regularly attend Mass on Sundays, but on the weekend of 8 May the whole village turns out. There is hardly a person who does not come to the celebrations to venerate the Madonna.

Padre Don Guido looks after the church which everybody affectionately calls the Madonna. He is a much-loved man in his seventies, well remembered for his kindliness when many Montalcinesi had little but bread with which to feed their children. Nowadays, modern silver-phial-wielding Padre Giancarlo from the Abbey of Sant' Antimo assists Don Guido.

Until recently there were three parishes in Montalcino, which have been amalgamated into one, and the churches share the priests according to the needs of the congregation. As well as Padre Don Guido and Padre Giancarlo, we also have dear jardangling Padre Don Gino who bestowed our first Easter blessing and who frequently conducts Mass at the Madonna. We have Padre Don Crociani and often, as on market day when their mission seems solely to be the acquisition of spinach, we see several other Brothers from Sant' Antimo too. This seems a high number of servants of the Church in Montalcino, but on the weekend of 7 and 8 May, Padre Don Guido is in charge.

This Saturday evening people are gathering in the piazza before dusk. Everyone is well dressed, some more so than others. There are plenty of smart black suits and ties, women are wearing elegant Italian knits with cashmere shawls tossed casually over a shoulder and, particularly noticeable, they have discarded their sensible village shoes for smart leather heels to match their stylish handbags. Young mothers are here, as always resembling catwalk models, with baby and pram colour co-ordinated, the first wearing gorgeous bonnets and the latter adorned with beautiful baubles. Their husbands are dressed in the latest mode, everything looking as if it has been thrown on, yet all fits to perfection. Italians wear their clothes with confidence, the wearer knowingly enhancing the clothes, which is I think the reason Italian couples are so handsome. And they always dress young children well. Tonight, the young boys chasing each other around the piazza in designer jackets, check shirts and cotton trousers are almost as hypnotic as the pert girls in navy and red heart-embroidered capes and shiny patent shoes. Indeed, I detect an air of comfortable prosperity in Montalcino.

Padre Don Gino is here, of course, frocked in black. His

sensible black shoes are shining like sunbeams and his black berretto sits jauntily on his head. In contrast, on the other side of the piazza, Padre Giancarlo is cloaked in white. His simple hooded gown floats around his thin frame, caught at his waist with a knotted rope cincture, and sandals peep from the hem, exposing his ruffled white socks. By eight o'clock, Ruga, Travaglio, Pianello and Borghetto are ready and the drums sound: *Rrrrm-ta-tumm, rrrrrm-ta-tumm, ratututum, ratututum* as one banner-bearer, two young knaves and a row of four drummers, all in medieval costume, leave each sede and work their way to the piazza. Travaglio approach from Via Matteotti dressed in crimson and gold costumes trimmed with white ermine at the neck. Borghetto, in white brocade and red velvet, march down from Piazza Garibaldi; Ruga make their way carefully down the steep steps from their sede dressed in blue tunics with gold trim, and Pianello, in ivory with rich blue cloaks embroidered at the hem, arrive from the other direction, marching up Via Mazzini.

Reaching the piazza, everybody relaxes, mingling with modern-day citizens in their finery making a colourful spectacle, but not everyone is here yet. In Piazza Cavour the village band has congregated and now begins to march up Via Mazzini, trumpets blazing away, beating drums and blowing into saxophones and flutes. Everyone is clapping, joining in, singing along with the music, because everybody knows the words to Montalcino's very own song, written by one of their own:

> *Hidden among the perfumed branches, crowned with*
> *chestnut trees and vines*
> *Montalcino, beautiful village, reigns on fertile Sienese land*
> *Many pages of history, narrated by each stone*
> *Each page a page of glory, a legend that must be told.*

Up here, always higher towards the sun
Montalcino's banner rises
First to be kissed by Madonna Spring.

Among our treasures is the fortress — powerful, proud and
  legendary
So many battles, so many sieges, so much bloodshed, so
  much fervour!
How much glory on our scarlet bloodied bastions?

Up here, always higher towards the sun
Montalcino's banner rises
First to be kissed by Madonna Spring.

As the band joins the throng in the piazza, the traditional 7 May evening gathering is ready for the candle-lit procession to the Church of the Madonna to hear the litany and begin celebrations. At nine o'clock we are off. Ruga takes the lead, drums roll and their splendid flag-bearer, taking long, definite, solid steps, moves solemnly down Via Mazzini. His rich blue tunic is trimmed with fur at the hem, around the neck and at his shoulders; the sleeves of his under-tunic are gold brocade and a blue headdress falls to one side with a length of velvet floating from it. Behind him, two young Ruga knaves are dressed to replicate his grandeur. Fingers hitched into their leather belts, they try to mimic his steps, but the boys of nine or ten need two steps for every one of his. A few paces behind, the four Ruga drummers beat the rhythm, which echoes and bounces stirringly from the stone walls.

The other three quartieri, dressed with equal splendour, banners held high, fall into line and, with drums beating, march one after the other, and in a line behind them walk the Presidents. Now the two priests fall into line, leading hundreds of

Montalcinesi who gather spontaneously. Some link arms, talking quietly, enjoying the closeness; it seems like the whole village is walking four or five abreast. At the tail the procession is joined once more by the band, who begin to play a solemn march. Luigi and I are walking with Ercole and Lola, but soon Zampa edges gruffly up beside Luigi, pushes his arm through his and the three men walk, chained together, as if they have done this for seventy years, which Zampa and Ercole probably have. 'Years ago,' remembers Ercole, 'the Seventh of May procession was truly wonderful, because the farms down in the valley would light bonfires of hay and we walked in procession up the hill to the Madonna watching all the glowing, flickering fires burning in the valley.'

When the quarters are close to the Madonna, the bells ring out a glorious chime of welcome. Looking up happily, I see all four bells swinging, yet the glorious chiming is accompanied by sixteen quartieri drummers continuing their stirring beat and I can still hear the solemn march as the band at the bottom of the hill turns into Viale Roma. The combination of a solemn occasion yet joyful celebratory chimes unites everybody. Arms are thrown across shoulders, I take Lola's arm, and as we reach the church a crackling bonfire on the grassy cliff-top opposite the Madonna is blazing magnificently, lighting our way and sending a million sparks into the sky. Ercole is so thrilled: 'Look, Lola, we've got a bonfire this year!'

The quartieri have brought a votive offering to the Madonna in the form of a wax candle, about a metre and a half long. Stamped into the candle are the four quartieri emblems, the same as they appear on the walls in each quarter. Padre Don Guido places the candle beside the altar while the quartieri flags are mounted into special iron holders inside the church, where they will fly for the whole weekend. With a prayer of thanks, the offering to the Madonna is solemnly accepted and suddenly the church is filled with glorious rejoicing as the village choral group completes a magnificent evening. Their harmony flows over the faithful, echoing into the vaulted ceiling and side chapels, where dozens of candles flicker. This first evening of rejoicing comes to a close and in no more than half an hour everybody begins filing out. Bidding friends buonanotte, we make our way back through the village to our homes. Tomorrow morning, Sunday, everybody will be back for the unveiling of the Madonna.

The thirteenth-century canvas painting of the Madonna with her Child between Saints Peter and Paul, a depiction of the effigy the woodcutter saw in the 1100s, once hung above Porta Corniolo, the ancient gate through the walls which is now built into the rear wall of the Madonna. A copy of the painting is still mounted where the original once hung and is easy to find behind the church where the brickwork forms an alcove in the wall. In the 1300s the painting was called *Madonna della Consolazione*, but after Don Garcia withdrew the miracle of breaking the siege resulted in the painting being renamed *S.S. Maria del Soccorso*.

Dear Amelia, when telling me the legend of the woodcutter, peered at me with childlike mystery in her old eyes, her soft voice transmitting her awe as she finished her story. 'No one remembers exactly when, but hundreds of years ago thieves tried to steal our Madonna, but they were caught. After that the Montalcinesi faithful brought her inside and hid her in our church. For hundreds of years she has been hidden all year, although we all know where she is. She is kept in a dark secret place. So May the eighth is always a happy time, a time of grateful thanks when we roll the canvas back and her beautiful face looks down on all of us inside the church. Just for one day, then we hide her away again.'

*

At six o'clock this morning the bells of the Madonna opened celebrations with a joyful flourish of chimes which must have been heard all over the village. I listened, half awake, but this is not the peal that usually calls the faithful to Mass, nor the peal of mezzogiorno which tells the farmers it is time for pranzo, nor even the resounding Angelus to remind everyone to hearken the archangel announcing the news to Mary of her coming baby. This is a long, joyful sound of four glorious bells whirling round and round. But the next thing I hear is the Pianello drummers outside my bedroom window, beating a stirring rhythm. It is now seven-thirty and Mass, which will celebrate the unveiling of the Madonna, starts at eight, so the quartiere drummers are marching through the village to remind people like me to get out of bed now, or we'll miss the whole thing! As I'm throwing water on my face and a few clothes on my back, I hear the village band and, listening to the trumpets and drums, I can tell the bustling music is moving up and back from the piazza. This is our last chance: a third and final reminder just in case anybody missed the bells at six and the drummers at seven-thirty!

As I am hurrying up Viale Roma, the eight o'clock peals from the village bell ring out but are instantly swallowed by the bells of the Madonna, which carry me into the church on a tide of glorious chimes. The church is packed, every seat seems to be taken, people are standing about at the back, but a couple of the signore squeeze up and make room. I sit down tentatively. I have wandered into the Madonna many times in five years, but this is the first Catholic Mass I have ever attended. During this service the venerated image of the Madonna will be unveiled, and this is the first time I have been here to see her.

I look up to see that Padre Don Gino already has things under way, but my first sensation is one of shock because there seems to be so much movement and noise all around me. A few rows in front I see Delia and Anna, then other neighbours Zaira and Bruna, and close to them sits Amelia, but woodcutter Bruno is loitering at the back. Amelia has been watching for me, waves airily across the church and mouths a friendly buongiorno. Stunned, I cannot reply. A signora leaves her seat, crosses the church, speaks with her friend in the next aisle and then, on her return journey, bobs a little curtsey in front of the altar as much as to say: 'Oops, sorry about that, Gesù. Had to speak to Maria-Teresa!' I don't understand why people wander down the aisles to the chapels, light candles and carry on their own private muttering while Padre Don Gino directs proceedings from the altar.

Sunday church for Protestants is much less flexible. I recall my mother's instructions: 'Don't turn round, don't swing your legs, don't play with your offering, don't fiddle, don't open the hymn book, don't whisper to your sister.' Solemn organ music played and we all faced the front, sitting absolutely still until the minister, very often my own father, stepped up to the simple rostrum and said reverently, 'Let's begin by turning to hymn number 257,' and at last I could move! This morning it has already crossed my mind that my father probably never once sat through Mass and my hesitation is a fear of the unknown passed through the family, but I know he will be serenely smiling from on high this morning.

Everybody stands up and sits down several times, reciting the answers as Padre Don Gino prompts with questions, but not necessarily in unison. I watch Zaira whisper to the signora sitting behind her in the aisle. She looks my way, then bobs across the aisle to me and whispers, 'Don't worry, we can't hear what he is saying either!' I hear enough to know Padre Don Gino is running through the woodcutter legend and the Spanish siege, clearly the same version I heard from Amelia. I manage to join in with a hallelujah and hosanna, then everyone is standing, so I jump up too. Padre Don Gino is praying, covering and uncovering a chalice, and I watch, hypnotised, as the canvas screen which hides the image of the Madonna rolls slowly upwards, first revealing the Christ Child, then the Madonna, Saints Peter and Paul and, at the very top, the holy scriptures. For the Montalcinesi the Church of the Madonna is an extension of their own living room where they come to thank God, via the Madonna. There are people here this morning I have never seen before, the contadini of days gone by, now the farmers and growers who still come to Montalcino on 8 May. They all love this church and everything in it and, typically, the treasured Madonna is unveiled without great fuss but with comfortable familiarity, for the Madonna is really one of the family.

We learn from Padre Don Gino that the Archbishop of Siena has arrived for the Holy Eucharist Mass at eleven o'clock, but before that fifteen children from Montalcino will take their First Communion. Impulsively I decide to stay, because I've just caught sight of Carlo, Maurelia's son, bringing the children in. Chiara, Massimo and Ofelia's daughter, in her white cowled gown, sparkling diamanté in her hair, is amongst them. This time Padre Don Guido orchestrates the service and the children turn in their seats, craning their necks to study the half-moon stained-glass window at the back of the church which depicts the miracle of the breaking of the Spanish siege. I twist round quickly too, because I did not know it was there. Padre Don Guido prepares the children for Communion, wittily explaining the miracle of Christ changing water into wine, adding, as an afterthought, 'Unfortunately, it probably wasn't Brunello . . . but good wine just the same.'

At eleven o'clock I am relieved to find a full house, standing room only for the gold-robed Archbishop of Siena, and I am intrigued to find our uniformed ambulance service, police, fire brigade and carabinieri sitting with the Mayor. As we leave the Madonna I am astonished to see lined up outside the church three ambulances and the fire brigade truck, doors open, life-saving equipment lying about and hoses at the ready. I imagine by their presence they are saying: 'We are ready when you need us, serving the community with the blessing of the church.' The Archbishop completes his blessing and the men jump into the vehicles, switch on flashing lights and, with sirens blazing, roar away in both directions, back to base.

'Armando! Armando! Come down here, help me with the cage. Take one end and we'll lift together.' The cylindrical wire cage is heaved on to the stand, then on to a table and Giorgio gives it a whirl to make sure it spins properly.

'The discs and cards are in the ambulance,' confirms Armando. 'I'll get them and we can set up. Look, the piazza is packed already. When is the notaio, notary, arriving?'

Giorgio responds, 'We'll ring him soon. There are still a few pads of entries to be sold, although it won't be long. It's only five-thirty and we've got a good crowd building.'

Armando jumps down from the stand and opens the ambulance doors, drawing out two cardboard boxes. One is small and contains shiny numbered discs, the other holds numbered cards, each about twenty-five centimetres square. The wooden stand, draped in green, is two metres high and Armando and Giorgio co-ordinated the work to have it erected this afternoon. Once again, the lonely Florentine beneath the loggia ceases to exist. Business is booming. People buy two or three L 5,000 entries, then take up positions around the piazza, some standing five-deep on the cappellone steps.

A mobile phone rings. 'Pronto . . . si, ciao Angelo, si, we'll ring them now.' The phone stays in his hand and Giorgio calls to Armando, 'I'm going to ring Angelino to tell the band to start. Angelo has the pizza ready and doesn't want it going cold.'

To a Protestant, it seems odd that Sunday 8 May, the sacred day set aside for veneration of the Madonna, should also be the day to try your luck at tombola, but to the Montalcinesi this makes perfect sense. If you want to do a bit of fund-raising for the ambulance service, to do so on the day everybody is in the village seems logical. Anyway, if you come to venerate the Madonna and end up going home with a pocketful of money, then God is really looking after you.

Giorgio and Armando begin checking the numbered discs and cards as the band bustles noisily up Via Mazzini. By the time they reach the piazza, Angelo has two trays of steaming pizza waiting for them. He does this every year, because the musicians need extra sustenance on Patron Saint's Day. The notaio arrives, the numbered discs are poured into the cage, and the notaio watches as Armando securely locks the wire door and gives the handle a turn so all the discs race round, tumbling up and down. Hundreds of us have pencils poised.

'Allora,' calls Giorgio. 'Signori, the third prize is L 100,000, second prize L 300,000 and first prize L 600,000. Thanks for your support, and remember, we start with the third prize.'

The tombola rollicks along as Giorgio calls the numbers over the microphone and Armando dives into the box of cards to find the corresponding one, sometimes managing to hold it upside down or back to front, when he is soon put right with jeers and whistles from the crowd. The game becomes tense once the third and second prizes have been claimed. L 600,000 is a very reasonable purse. 'Armando!' someone calls, 'we made a deal. Come on, you're leaving it a bit late!' Armando loves this clowning spectacle, whereas Giorgio is focused on the serious business. Between the two, a healthy sack of money is raised for the ambulance service every Patron Saint's Day.

The four bells of the Madonna have been ringing throughout the day, sometimes overlapping the tolling by the village bell and resulting in a fusion of deep bronze gongs and celebratory chimes. Even as the first prize is waiting to be claimed, everyone is reminded by the bells that Mass is on too, and there is still time to visit the Madonna one more time. At last a winner is clambering down the steep steps which lead up to Ruga and hundreds of people cast their entries into the piazza, which is quickly littered with screwed-up paper. Mario and the sweepers will have plenty of work tomorrow morning.

As Madonna begins the last exuberant call for the day, Armando and Giorgio carry the wire cage back to the ambulance. It is 7.30, people look for their friends, link arms, turn from the littered piazza and begin walking up the hill towards the Madonna. After the Rosary, standing beside the woodcutter's wife, with the same understated familiarity with which she was unveiled this morning I watch the canvas screen roll slowly down, enclosing the image of the Madonna in her dark world. A solemn but uniting candle-lit procession, a bonfire, a wax offering, the veneration and unveiling, First Communion, the celebration of Mass and tombola are over for another year. The Madonna is safe, returned to secrecy once more.

The mystery of the eminent Bishop from Rome remains unsolved and I am no closer to an explanation. The Madonna was packed at eleven, but I am thinking again about the visit from the Archbishop of Siena. Was Madonna packed because of him? Or was it packed with Montalcinesi because 8 May belongs to them, a celebration which is their very own? I do know the spiritual life of the Montalcinesi is safely entwined in the simple belief of an ancient legend of a woodcutter and the miracles of the Madonna, which spells unwavering faith, exemplified in the woodcutter's wife. With dearest Amelia on my arm, her faith infectious, I walk out of the Madonna as the bells ring out their glorious chimes, and I am leaving with far more than I took in with me at eight o'clock this morning.

SUMMER

CHAPTER THIRTEEN

The Next Bus Back to Siena

Lower down the valley, fields of handsome swaying grain which have always been grown around Montalcino have changed the complexion of the Val d'Orcia; a seasonal metamorphosis is transforming the Tuscan hills. For a few weeks in spring, dancing fields of scarlet poppies alternated with waving green grain, the patchwork of a watercolour paintbrush stretching twenty kilometres. Golden rape bloomed, stood boldly for a while, then began to wilt, and now the summer air is heavy with the baked-dry smell of sun-drenched earth. The poppies have gone and green has given way to fields of ripened thick brown grain. The earth is pulling in the warmth, drying, now splitting and thirsty.

Thirty years ago contadini planted only soft grain, grano tenaro, harvesting one crop each season, but with increasingly progressive techniques they began to plant grano duro, which is more productive. Before the summer rain falls, the farmers will harvest the first of the grain which will go off to the factories to make pasta. The air will fill with the smell of newmown hay as pencil-thin strays are whipped into the sky and empty husks fly around. It will be tricky manoeuvring the tractor over the undulating hills because the soil is not yet baked stone hard, which it will be by the time the farmer drives out before the end of summer to harvest his second cut of hay. He may even cut a third time – probably harvesting at night with lights on the tractor, bumping over a lumpy, bone-dry moonscape, trying to stay ahead of the rain.

As if by overnight magic, each dale will be dotted with twenty or thirty cylindrical hay bales, rolled into rigid straight lines stretching across the valley. Stone farmhouses will stand in silhouette, because fields are crisply defined, conveying the notion that a crude summer haircut takes place every few weeks, leaving the houses and cypress pines standing on a scalped hillside. The beauty is dramatic, visual elements appear rough, angular, brittle and unforgiving. Thrice the grain will grow, hard-baked earth will be robbed three times and yet, in inexplicable contrast, fluid energy hangs in the air. Sleek hills creep across a quilted sky, dipping and curving as if drawn with a felt-tipped pen, accepting the punishing summer sun with a graceful face.

There are no buttery crowns on the sunflowers yet, sleepy

petals are folded tightly shut, the oil only now beginning to gather inside the head. But lanky virile stems fight each other to reach the light, pushing higher and higher until they are taller than the farmer. Sunflowers have not been grown around Montalcino all that long, because before the war the largest crop stretching from here towards Siena was tobacco. Many contadini planted tobacco for the padrone, tended the crop and, after picking, stacked it up to dry in timber tobacco sheds. Shrivelled tobacco was loaded on to trains and sent to industrial plants – which is probably the reason many Tuscans will tell you Tuscan tobacco still makes the best cigars. During the war years tobacco crops languished, undoubtedly because the contadini were by then conscripted to the armed forces, but there were many more olive groves. Tobacco vanished after the war to make way for sunflowers and many of the olive groves disappeared too, because it was thought sunflower oil was a new product and offered a better market. After the 1960s, not only the tobacco had gone, but most of the sunflowers and many more olive groves too. They all disappeared to make way for vines. Tobacco, olive groves, sunflowers and vines; only the swaying grain has maintained its stand. An agricultural metamorphosis has taken place, gradually changing the landscape and leaving a glorious patchwork recognised all over the world as simply Tuscan.

The rugged bald beauty of a baking summer is, sadly I think, the only way most visitors see Tuscany, and although I know this unforgettable landscape merits recording, I wish they could be here in winter too, feeling that haunting frozen stillness, a suspension of growth when spiders weave silken nets across the broom and bells echo across a silent valley. Or the opposite, in early spring, when the very first jonquil spire rises and the earth astonishes, thrusting up life in unbelievable lushness of a green so green; or the last days of autumn, when russet leaves crunch underfoot, harvesting is over, the air is limpid, olives ripen, chestnut casings fall and nature prepares for winter. Four equally divine agricultural landscapes remind me that nothing is new. The Tuscan hills I see today have been evolving for a thousand years.

Summer mornings bring cheery buongiornos and too-wide smiles. We have to make the most of it because summer is short, so long-awaited yet fleeting. Days under hot, sunny blue skies at last follow one after another. We rise earlier, but not necessarily as early as this morning's near-dawn start, which is forced upon me and finds me at Bar Prato early enough to sip a cappuccino and chat with dear Adelmo before he starts work. Standing together, we hear the blue bus from Siena chugging down Viale Roma, and we glance over as the driver does his usual three-point turn in the confined space and comes to a standstill beside the wall. Six or eight people empty out and, among them, a couple of tourists. Adelmo loses interest, but I stare, a ripple of discontent passing through me because I watched this scenario unfold many times last summer and my discontent is twofold: terse annoyance and frustration. Six or seven buses a day arrive from Siena, about a fifty-minute ride, and I guess there must be several guide books which help tourists board the bus in Siena to visit Montalcino. Arriving here, they step tentatively from the bus, cameras on shoulders, their faces curious and questioning, guide book in hand. My terse annoyance is with the guide book, but my frown of frustration is because I am afraid they are not going to find what they have come here for.

This morning's couple stand on the roadway, noses buried in the open book, pointing in this direction and that. Finally they follow everybody else past Bar Prato, glancing pensively through the door, and begin walking up Via Mazzini. Even without hearing them speak I know today's colour co-ordinated couple are American, because they have that look about them. Bar Prato is busy in the mornings and not particularly encouraging for two strangers who have just stepped off a bus, so it is not surprising they don't stop. If they had come in they would have found the bar crowded with locals having breakfast before work. Hardly a word passes, but regular caffè orders are plonked on the bar, hands peel a serviette from the container and pass over a marmalade brioche. People stand about tossing down caffè and making only grunts and gasps until the first hit of caffeine does its job.

Adelmo is here every morning and so are other elderly widowers who now have no signora at home to make breakfast. They sit around, leaning on walking sticks, wearing black suits and staring glumly from under black hats. To a local, the bar is comforting familiarity and the hovering old are not really glum, but are respecting the hour. It is not a time for chatter because people are hurrying, breakfasting before work. To a stranger it is unnerving.

As I finish my cappuch I see the couple pause and look upwards, gazing in enchantment at faded trompe l'oeil, peeling shutters and plaster crumbling from the once-palatial structure where Idolina lives. They cannot know about the glorious architecture from another era in Idolina's rooms-to-rent, hidden behind these faded walls. They walk slowly on, traversing the road. In rapt attention she studies architraves while he stops to photograph brass doorknockers; both their faces are concentrated and intent.

Leaving the bar, I too walk up Via Mazzini on my way to see Laura in the fruit and vegetable shop to buy a kilo of red cherries. I have had the urge to taste them ever since yesterday, when I watched the signora at the farm below the Madonna climb her rickety wooden ladder and pick one of the cherry trees clean. She tossed the ripe fruit expertly over her shoulder into a small wicker basket she had strapped to her back. Olive baskets sit at the front, cherry baskets at the back, I don't know why. Somehow all the cherries ended up in the basket.

As I pass the tourists I smile to myself. Yes, they *are* Americans! I have learned to identify visitors from different countries and aside from the summer dress and, thankfully not today's couple, occasional barbarian sandals, Americans are easy to identify. They have a certain self assurance that lets them converse across the narrow road. They are unaware their drawling voices present an odd sound to the morning, like a child who has no conception he might be saying or doing something out of the norm. I leave the couple to their guide book and am walking on towards the waiting cherries when an arm reaches from the doorway of the butcher's shop and taps me on the shoulder. 'Buongiorno,' says Lola. 'You are on the street early – did you fall out of bed?'

This precocious octogenarian has an innocuous expression on her face. She has got me trapped, because she knows full well Ercole buzzed Luigi on the intercom at seven this morning when we were dead asleep and our shutters were firmly closed. Luigi answered, and thinking we must have overslept, he tried to sound as if his eyes were open, breakfast had been eaten and we had forgotten to open the shutters. What else can you do when your landlord has a buzzer right above your sleeping head? Never a day passes but Ercole isn't either on that buzzer or under our window, calling out: 'Luigi, Luigi, sei in casa?' He knows we are at home but loves a daily greeting. 'Is everything all right?' he will ask anxiously, 'Do you need anything?'

Normally Ercole does not buzz or visit until our shutters are open, but at seven this morning his voice was fretful. 'Caro Luigi, I thought I had better let you know because otherwise you might worry if you hear noise on the terrace outside your bedroom doors.' Without opening my eyes I listened to Luigi grunt short responses to what I feared might be a lengthy explanation, then say he understood and he thanked Ercole for calling.

'What's going on?' I wanted to know, by then prepared for almost anything, but Luigi told me it was nothing. 'Ercole is coming down to the terrace before it gets too hot, because we haven't picked the capers and it is going to be too late unless he picks them right now.'

Capers? I didn't realise we had capers. But even if I had known, it disconcerted me, because I did not know what capers looked like, so I stumbled out of bed and crept over to the shuttered terrace doors. Squinting between the slats, I saw a wooden ladder leaning against the wall. Ercole was gently removing tiny green balls the size of a pea from what seemed to be wild bushes that had taken root in the crevices between the stones and cascaded down the walls. Every now and then he rejected one, dropping to the paving any which were elongated and splitting open into a pretty white flower. Summer capers! We have a whole wall of caper bushes and because they have not been picked they are beginning to flower. Ercole must have surmised we did not understand that capers needed to be harvested and judged it time to take proceedings into his own hands, probably urged on by Lola, who would be waiting to bottle the tasty delicacies.

Knowing exactly why I am up and about earlier than usual, Lola's eyes sparkle as she adds, 'Would you like a little jar of caperi?' I just laugh as she grabs my arm and pulls me into the butcher's shop, where her attention is immediately taken up with glancing speculatively at the cuts of meat and, simultaneously, greeting friends. Social life and shopping are very closely linked in Montalcino.

The fit-out for this butcher's shop, with its travertine floors, gleaming marble benches and glossy walls, must have cost a fortune. Massive timber beams stretch across the ceiling; they could easily be laid side by side and safely sailed to Australia. On a solid wooden table towards the rear lies a carcass which looks to me to be the approximate size of a slain buffalo, just waiting for the butcher's expert hand with the machete wedged threateningly into the timber chopping block. Garland after garland of freshly made sausages sway about, brushed by the shoulders of waiting customers, while salted hind legs of prosciutto and lines of fat white-skinned salami dangle from iron hooks in the ceiling.

As we edge in the door, the butcher is farewelling a signora and she in turn is farewelling her friends as she squeezes out the door clutching a parcel. Her departure gives the macellaio, butcher, whose name is Luciano, the opening to welcome Lola, then he turns to the next signora in line to be served. It is Idolina from the fading palazzo down the road. I have noticed Italians are not good at queuing, it somehow seems unnecessary to them. Instead, they mill about, haphazardly changing places and chatting. Once inside the butcher's shop, greetings done, Lola calls out: 'Who was last?' Someone calls back and now she can relax. She only has to watch that particular signora, because once she is served, Lola is next.

The real-life theatre which takes place many times each day between the butcher and his customers magnifies the priority Italians give to eating only the highest quality meat. A signora may only buy 100 grams of minced beef and 100 grams of minced pork to make a ragù sauce, or one slice of veal cut so thinly you can see through it, but the essential thing is that it is fresh on the day it is bought and cooked the same day, because Italians deplore meat lying overnight. This morning the drama is being played out once more, as much for the listeners who are Idolina's friends as for Luciano, who has known her all his life. Lola is watching with a sharp eye, as it will be her turn soon.

298

Idolina begins: 'Allora, Luciano, what have you got today that is fresh?'

'Everything is fresh today, Signora. I have some baby veal . . . excellent for scaloppini, and I have just finished making the sausages this very hour.'

'Well you might say,' Idolina responds, 'but my son said that piece of veal you gave me on Friday was not young enough. He told me straight away it was tough, so I am not going to buy your veal again until I know it is young and fresh!'

The butcher drops his head to one side and his hand moves in short, swift, upward motions as much as to say: 'Well, that is what he might have said, Signora, but it was first-quality veal.'

She demands: 'What will I give him today? Do you have any pork?'

Casting my eyes along the counter I can see the butcher takes great pride and care, continually rearranging the meat and wiping away any drops of blood. Two slender calves, heads overlapping the counter tray, stare bright-eyed back at me. They are only three weeks old; milk-fed baby veal. Next to the calves sit five or six pig's trotters, zampone – stiff white bristles poke between the toes. A dark-textured liver, finely sliced and sitting alone on a spotless tray with not a tube of sinew in sight, awaits someone to make fegato e cipolle, liver and onions, for pranzo. But not Idolina, because now she is thinking about pollo. Only three yellow-skinned chickens sit in the counter, pink crowns still shining brightly and glazed eyes firm. They stare at me as if they are amazed at what has happened to them. At dawn they were blithely pecking grain with their companions in the chook house!

Luciano says: 'This is a beautiful chicken. Look, it is really fat – plenty of meat.'

But Idolina is not convinced. 'Let me see the other one. I am sure that's the same one you had here yesterday. Don't go selling me any more old meat!' She inspects a second chicken. 'Quanto? How much?' He weighs it and gives her the price, which is L 16,000. 'Madonna! Show me that pork again.'

The butcher patiently takes a pink roll of pork fillet and holds it gently in one hand. It has been tied with a lacework of string and there is not a whisker of fat. He tells her it is the leanest pork she will find. 'I'll just cut you one or two thin slices,' he coaxes, 'and all you will need to do is turn it quickly on the fire . . . it will be delicious.'

Reluctantly, she agrees to take two slices. The butcher shows her with his knife exactly where he will cut, she motions him to move the blade an iota, nods, and the slices peel off the knife into his waiting palm. He slides them on to wax paper and takes them to the scale. 'Signora, your son will eat well today,' he comforts her and then tells her the price, which is still L 16,000.

She shrugs her shoulders, more at her friends waiting their turn than at the macellaio. 'He had better enjoy it,' she says dryly. 'It is costing him plenty.' She is soon out of the door and, after only twenty minutes, it is Lola's turn. She states her case plainly. 'Ercole does not want his ragù made with the same beef you sold me yesterday.' Luciano drops his head to the side . . . and so the courteous ritual continues.

Each signora is given adequate time and a sympathetic hearing, both of which enable her to maintain her social standing with her friends and give her the opportunity to discuss her family and their needs. It is not difficult to believe an Italian mother really does place all her love for her family on the table every time she prepares a meal. She participates in a ritual which is vital to the well-being of her family, nursing and caressing each ingredient from the time she brings it home until the time it is eaten by those she has in her care.

Having completed her latest fifteen-minute encounter with the macellaio, Lola says her farewells and, arm still linked through mine because she has been holding grimly on to me throughout her negotiations, we make our way down the steps to the road. We walk together until we reach Lola's doorway, where we part, because Lola, with her usual single-mindedness, must begin preparations for Ercole's ragù.

I resume my endeavours to buy my longed-for cherries. Besides, the morning is passing and I am curious to know how Laura is getting on, because I had a very interesting conversation with her earlier this week. Once through the piazza, walking towards the shop, I can see wooden trays filled to the brim with bright cherries, each bunch attached to twigs from the tree, leaves healthy and firm. There is no doubt these cherries were brought from the trees to the shop this morning. There are two varieties, but the ones I want are glistening in the sun like crimson buddhas, reflecting one fat tummy into another.

There are no customers inside the shop and from the doorway I watch Loridana fix her gaze on her daughter, who is unpacking a cardboard box and stacking jars. Absently, Loridana picks up one of the jars, studies the label intently, then declares, 'Laura, this label doesn't make any sense.'

'Mamma, take those bottles of bleach and line them up out the back on the shelf where I put the toilet rolls,' Laura suggests with a pleading smile. 'And the toothpaste – put the last few tubes over there with the clothes pegs.'

Loridana does exactly as asked, because Laura has told her that in less than an hour a truck will be arriving with more cardboard boxes to be unpacked.

'Where did you buy all these things?' her mother demands from the back room. 'What on earth are they for? And who will we sell them to?'

'To the stranieri, foreigners, Mamma, the stranieri and some of the younger women as well.' From the sound of her exasperated voice she is probably repeating this for the fourth time this morning.

'Laura,' her mother begins again, holding the strangely labelled jar out to her, 'how will they know what is in this jar, let alone what to do with it? The writing is all in Chinese.'

'That's Japanese, Mamma,' corrects Laura, 'not Chinese. I put the Chinese things on the bottom shelf.'

Her mother's eyebrows rise and she makes a clicking noise with her tongue, but she breaks into a relieved sigh when she sees me standing at the door. Yesterday, after months of research and planning, Laura finally explained to her mother and father what she has been doing on all those mysterious trips to Siena and Florence. She has been thinking about it for a year, because although she knows it is only sensible that the sale of fruit and vegetables remains the priority side of the family business, she feels the rest of their stock needs sorting out. It is time for change, because they cannot compete with the supermarket and, anyway, there is practically no profit in selling a tube of toothpaste or a tin of fly spray every few weeks. She agreed wholeheartedly with her mother about the need to keep a reduced supply of bleach and washing powder to service the elderly signore who have been buying it from them all their lives, but nevertheless, the shelves must be cleared to make room for a range of different produce.

'More and more visitors are coming to Montalcino,' she explained to her parents, 'and many people like to stay in the farmhouses and agriturismo outside the walls, or even apartments inside the walls where they can do their own cooking. It is time for Montalcino to offer produce other than Italian for the stranieri, because people are used to eating different foods in other countries.' Laura and her girlfriends occasionally have

302

dinner at a Chinese restaurant in Siena and she has talked with girls who have been on holiday to Thailand and Hong Kong who would like to experiment with new cuisine.

At first her parents were horrified. 'But your friends are all Italian,' her father reasoned. 'Why don't they eat Italian?'

'Babo, they do,' soothed Laura, 'but sometimes they want a change, to taste flavours from another country.' This explanation had not made a great deal of sense to her father, but eventually he had yielded and this morning her mother is helping her re-stock the shelves just in time for the summer tourists. So far as Laura is concerned, it is out with the washing powder and in with the kecap manis, even if she is not quite sure herself what you do with it. She is lining the shelves with Thai spicy bake and satay sauce, lemon grass, hoi sin sauce, Tandoori curry paste, rice noodles, palm sugar, wasabi and even pale squares called wonton wrappers. She had not known what to do with these either, and looked astounded when I told her they had to be dipped in water, then food was wrapped in them and you ate everything, wrapping and all.

Loridana escapes outside to fetch my kilo of juicy cherries while Laura lines up packets of nori on a shelf and winks conspiratorially at me. She is not going to admit to her mother it is definitely weird to even *want* to eat seaweed. 'The next truck will deliver coconut milk, mango chutney, pappadams, fish sauce, tins of pâté and Crowther's Chowder,' she beams at me. 'And guess what – I have sourced peanut butter for the Americans, it will be here soon.' Not today, but when she is into her stride, I will ask her about pavlova mix and surprise Luigi with the news that Ercole and Lola can come to dinner . . . and vegemite!

When we first came to live in Montalcino we couldn't even get fresh milk except on Tuesdays and Thursdays, and deliveries were erratic at that. In the last few years the range of produce has widened markedly, but Laura's venture is mind-boggling and I wonder how the born-and-bred Montalcinesi who, as Maria found out, only eat white cannellini beans, will take to it. I cannot see kecap manis being an earth-shaking seller here, but I agree with Laura. The tourists will love it and, as well, her generation of young Italian women seem eager to experiment.

Exchanging secret smiles with Laura who, I notice, has a glittering diamond embedded in one nostril which I have never seen before, and nodding sympathetically at Loridana, I pay for my cherries and walk out into the hot sunshine just as the village bell begins twelve chimes for mezzogiorno. It will be followed in a few moments by deep bronze gongs from the big bell as it swings across the belfry exactly 100 times. I often count this warning signal which lets everybody know it is time to put the tools down and come in from the fields, or time to put the water on to simmer, because your husband will be coming up the stairs in a few minutes, and pranzo must be ready.

I stand in the roadway and listen for half a minute simply because it sounds so reassuring. When I look up, I am impressed to see the two American tourists are in the piazza and they too stare upwards, watching the bell fling itself across the tower. I am particularly happy to see these visitors standing watching the bell as it begins 100 gongs, because the glorious deep notes fill the piazza and echo around the buildings. The sound symbolises Montalcino and it puzzles me when tourists don't bother to look up to see where all the noise is coming from. They have focused on me watching them. Our eyes meet for a split second, then we turn simultaneously away. As the gongs have reached halfway and will soon begin to recede, I disappear downstairs into the coolness of Osticcio to chat with Francesca, leaving the visitors to ponder the reason why the bell will sound twelve chimes twice.

Osticcio is an enoteca, a wine shop. Inside, Francesca is talking with a dark-eyed handsome customer who has been sampling Brunello and she is setting aside bottles which he obviously intends to purchase. Acknowledging me, she makes a pointing motion behind her back, so I leave her to the customer and step down to the glassed-in terrace at the rear of the shop where she knows I will sit a few minutes to look over the vegetable gardens and see what has been happening this week.

On the first terrace is a cherry tree, picked clean, reminding me to open my own package and eat a few juicy cherries while I wait. Below me, beans trellis skywards with flat pods dangling, carefree fat peas hang from bushes which have long outgrown their stakes, and lower down, zucchini plants meander and creep ever outwards, but there are only a handful of yellow flowers. Earlier this morning a signora would have been there to collect the delicate blooms for pranzo and by now the zucchini flowers will be sitting on her bench. Each sunny interior will be inspected to make sure nothing lurks within and then a dice of mozzarella and a slither of chopped anchovy will be slipped inside. A light batter of flour and water will sit by the stove and just before it is time to sit down to pranzo the blooms will be lightly dipped in batter and fried in burning hot oil. A scrumptious antipasto.

From this window I can pick out farmworkers with tractors rolling over the baking brown earth from here to Montepulciano if the day is limpid and clear, but today Montepulciano has vanished in the heat haze.

Fearing Francesca is going to be occupied with her handsome suited customer – from the look of his imposing profile he is a Roman – for some time, I wander past the familiar bottles displaying rows of famous names of Montalcino growers, nod to Francesca and make my way upstairs to head home for pranzo. Glancing towards Fiaschetteria, I wave and smile at Negus. Other friends have gone, so no other greetings or farewells are needed. Still smiling, I turn back and nearly jump out of my skin, for standing right in front of me are the two American tourists, not half a metre away.

'Buongiorno,' I blurt, trying to dismiss my smile and impulsively deciding not to speak English. They stumble awkwardly through buongiorno and then: 'Are you from here?' The man speaks with that easy American drawl. I nod, responding, 'Si,' but not in a terribly encouraging tone. Probably in their forties, they smile shyly at me and I can see they are eager for communication. The pernicious guide book is under his arm, tightly closed. The next question raises the hackles on the back of my neck, making me swallow in despair. 'Is there anything to see here?' he says. 'We came off the bus a couple of hours ago, but not a lot seems to be happening.'

I am tempted to reply, 'No, there's nothing happening, nothing to see here. Might as well take the next bus back to Siena.' Or maybe, 'Well now, what exactly did you come to Montalcino *for*?' But I resist. I don't say it because I have seen these types of people many times over the last few years and, besides, I see myself in them. They return to Italy time and again, they know there is something evocative here which entices and tantalises them, makes them want more; they want to discover something and they desperately want to take this special something home with them. But Italy does not give up her secrets easily and Italians are illusive, clever mirror images of themselves. It is frustratingly hard to know if you have found the real thing or another glossy reflection.

Recalling in these passing seconds their serious faces as they made their way up Via Mazzini, and remembering my moment of pleasure watching them stare up at the pealing bell, I soften. They seem nice people and I know it is not really their fault to have arrived with nothing more than what I imagine is a less than adequate guide book containing four lines about Montalcino. 'How long have you got?' I ask pleasantly. They tell me they need to catch a bus back to meet friends in Siena. One leaves in half an hour, but they could catch a later one.

Making an instinctive decision, I rush headlong on: 'Do you want to learn about Montalcino? I don't know everything . . . but maybe I can help. Are you good walkers? I know it's hot, but I usually walk each day – why don't we walk together?' Smiling with delight, they agree to wait in the piazza while I take my shopping home although, by the look on their faces as I leave, they are a little hesitant, probably doubtful they will ever see me again.

Announcing to Luigi that I will be gone for a couple of hours because I am showing two Americans around whose names I don't even know, he shakes his head in disbelief. 'You are nuts. Americans wouldn't understand. Anyway, everything is always better in America.'

Back in the piazza the couple are standing exactly where I left them. I decide to deal with my annoyance and ask to look at the guide book to see what it says about Montalcino. As anticipated, next to nothing, except that Montalcino is a medieval village and on the surrounding Tuscan hills produces Brunello di Montalcino, a highly regarded Italian red wine. Under things to see, it says: *Fortress built in 1361 . . . Palazzo Comunale 13th-century . . . Cathedral much changed since the 18th century . . .* and that's it!

We complete introductions and I suggest to Karen and Eddie, who come from California, that there is not much benefit in looking at the fortress or Palazzo Comunale mentioned in the book if they do not understand why they are here. Karen responds: 'Well, we already saw the fortress on the way round from inside the bus, so we decided we weren't going to walk back up.' Oh, really. It flashes across my mind that Luigi is going to be proven right. I *am* nuts!

I decide to tackle it another way, because I realise Karen is trying to be helpful. 'Have you been to see the French barracks yet – or the historic battlefield? Have you been down to the abandoned church in the valley? Did you see the UFO in the painting by Salimbeni? Have you walked around the twelfth-century walls and seen the vegetable gardens . . . and visited the quartieri of Pianello or Travaglio? What about the painting of the Madonna? Do you know that she is hidden behind her secret screen and is rarely brought out? I know you could not have seen the tattered banner carried by the Sienese exiles to Montalcino in 1555 because that is inside the fortress, but did you find the exquisite thirteenth-century wooden sculpted angels in the Museum, in the cloister of Sant' Agostino? Have you tasted Pinci al Ragù or munched Ossi di Morto – bones of the dead? Did you meet Cosimo under the loggia, or Ubert at Cipressi, where you can taste his chestnut and acacia honey? I bet you haven't found the hanging springs and scrambled through the undergrowth to the water source. Being Americans, I am sure you already know about Brunello, but have you been to the Consorzio di Brunello growers' headquarters? Have you . . .' At this point I smile sweetly and stop. Karen and Eddie look at me sheepishly and not a little embarrassed, but then see my smile widen and we burst out in happy laughter.

We set off together towards the western wall facing the Ombrone Valley and I begin to explain the ancient origins of Montalcino. First I tell them about the invading Saracens of the 700s; we walk along the lower path around the early walls, which look across the woods towards the sea where the Saracens landed. Sitting below the wall on the jutting boulders the violent Sienese could not tear down, I talk about the courage of the hunters in the dense woods stretching before us, the necessity for Montalcino to have brave and accurate archers, the sharing of the hunt among village citizens so everyone ate salted wild boar during freezing winter months.

We leave the walls and cut through a narrow lane which brings us out in front of the majestic columns which solemnly guard the Cathedral, and, first walking towards the well, we stand under the cooling shade of the holm oaks and talk about the Ilcinesi, why they came to live on this inaccessible hill under these oak trees which once formed a thick canopy over the hill. Then, as we walk towards the Cathedral I tell them about the monks who were granted this territory and who built the beautiful Abbey of Sant' Antimo, nine kilometres away. We are soon stepping between the columns and into the Church of San Salvatore which, according to the guide book, is noted only because it is much changed since the eighteenth century. I take them over to the chapel to see the remnants of the early temple which stood here from around the end of the first millennium – the year 1000 – and tomb inscriptions which I cannot yet decipher. They bend close to me, cameras and useless guide book forgotten, touching the stones gently as I touch them, running their fingers caressingly along the carved inscriptions and I think they are beginning, just for a minute, to sense the magic of Italy and the beating heart of Montalcino.

Outside again, I tell them San Salvatore is a much-loved church in the quarter of the village called Ruga and, for more than half an hour, we sit on the stone wall above the clump of aromatic rosmarino where I explain the role of the quarters, the cultural traditions, the loyalty and pride of each quarter and the highest honour of having the most accurate archers of Montalcino, an honour contested each year.

Time is passing. I will have to skip two or three hundred years of history, and we amble through Ruga in companionable quiet, passing stone houses with green shuttered windows, red and white geranium safely resting on sills, washing billowing above. Their eyes dart here and there following my gaze, but they do not say a word. They are content to absorb and think. At the bottom of the hill I soften my voice. 'Now we'll go and see the battlefield.' They just nod.

As we reach Bar Prato I greet one or two people and, sitting in the shade, I notice Cesare. Seeing him, my mind leaps ahead. This could be interesting for Karen and Eddie. He asks where I am going, so I explain I am taking these two friends up to see the battlefield. This interests and amuses him immensely, making him smile, because few foreigners understand what happened at Montalcino and most don't seek to know. He knows that to me it will always be the battlefield. His family consider him a trifle eccentric, not only because of his passion for collecting antique books, but because Cesare virtually lives in the 1500s, even transporting himself back further, to the Middle Ages, for hours on end. Cesare speaks English and he has held me captivated more than once, relating the stories of Montalcino. His study is lined with fascinating historical chronicles, some many centuries old, and his collection of maps and military plans describe and recount with credible candour what happened here. It rankles Cesare no end that the true story of Montalcino in the 1500s has never been told. He broods with discontent, startling me once with, 'One day, Isabella, one day I will tell the world what really happened, and I do not give a damn who I upset. It will be controversial, I can promise you that!' If I can get Cesare to talk, Karen and Eddie will hear things no guide book tells tourists.

Cesare stands, saying he is walking home past Madonna, so we walk two by two up Viale Roma and on to the shady earth pathway alongside the old iron fence, until we reach the crest of the hill. The valley stretching below is breathtaking. Swallows dive and dart among the chestnut trees in the up-draught, the air seems fresher, freer, although it is still hot, and we all lean over the iron fence for some minutes, picking out tractors creeping over baked brown fields, absently counting serried ranks of vines and glimpsing twisted olive trees. I point out to Karen and Eddie the village of Buonconvento away down in the valley. We spot a field of bursting yellow sunflower heads and in the far distance the blurry skyline of Siena, barely visible through the heat haze, where their friends await.

Cesare seems not to want to hurry away, lingering with us above the wall. Thinking that if I can induce him to retreat into the ancient world he might talk – in his eccentric way – with Karen and Eddie, perhaps tell them what really happened here, I coax, hoping to draw him out. Pointing down to the valley, I remark, 'This is where the reviled Florentines camped, isn't it? Now which battle was it . . .?' Karen and Eddie look keenly at Cesare and he glances at me. My approach is apparently transparent. Smiling, he turns back to the valley, his eyes focused, but now glazed. First he takes Karen and Eddie, with stirring emotion, back to the very last moments in 1559 when the defiant Montalcinesi declared: 'Having lost everything we could lose, at least we will not lose our honour.' And then he solemnly begins narrating the story he told me.

'Mamma! Mamma! The Sienese exiles are here! They are coming up the hill to Porta Burelli.'

Hearing this, Sabatina, balancing her month-old baby on her ample hip, grabbed her toddler by the hand and bustled down the steps and into the road from where her second daughter was calling. Mother and children sped across the grass and joined the gathering along the northern wall from where they could watch the disorderly lines of Sienese citizens, accompanied by what was left of their armed force, approaching the mountain. The human chain stretched as far as she could see, snaking through hills, disappearing among bushes and trees, but as groups of two or three staggered closer to the hill their pathetic state became obvious; many stumbled into ditches and lay like dead bodies. Montalcino soldiers rode out and lifted untidy cloth bundles from their skeletal backs to encourage them to rise again, but the final ascent to Montalcino from the Plain of the Angels is exhaustingly steep. These miserable weeping exiles had filed through the gates of Siena at dawn, desperate to reach Captain Piero Strozzi at Montalcino.

A dozen mothers peering over the wall exchanged no gossip . . . they stared grimly, clutching their young, a feeling of foreboding descending, although everybody was aware Siena had fallen and exiles were coming. Husbands and fathers were now at Palazzo Comunale trying to come to grips with the implications of this calamity, listening to the arguments and pleas of the magistrates. 'You mark my words, wife,' Sabatina recalled her husband Jacopo's chilling warning this morning as he left for the iron forge, 'this will end badly for Montalcino. We will end up the poorer and it will not end quickly. Those Sienese have no regard for our welfare, nor our liberty. They don't care about Montalcino, they want only to save themselves.'

Sabatina had passed her twenty-eighth year. Already the broody mother of nine children, the last born a month before the Sienese arrived, she was one of eleven herself and her own mother was relieved she had made a sensible marriage with Jacopo, who worked in the iron forge owned by one of his uncles. She was a strong girl, already well-rounded with a mature womanly girth. Her buttocks were thick, but she was not obese and her bosoms were continuously heavy with milk, for she frequently had two babies still at the breast. She was contentedly fulfilling her role in a modest but happy family home with her husband, their own nine children, her husband's brother and his wife and their six children, plus her ageing parents, who were already past forty. Altogether twenty-one people under one roof, somehow they all squeezed into cots at night under warm blankets.

In the daytime the house was quiet, because the men laboured in the artisan workshops and the boys and girls had their own chores, feeding chickens, milking the goat and helping Sabatina in the vegetable gardens, or gathering firewood at dusk outside the walls. Her eldest son left home at dawn along with his father to go to the forge. All the older boys in the village learned a trade and he, now twelve, worked hard helping his father twist red-hot glowing iron into pointed spear-heads, his feet pumping the bellows while Jacopo hammered iron shields. He took after his father – a diligent worker. Like his young friends, the boy was excited about the prospect of this war; at twelve he could remember the celebrations two years ago in 1553, when they defeated the Spanish Siege. Sabatina believed in her heart the Madonna had saved them, yet her elder son talked of nothing but fighting in this unavoidable war, no matter how often his father warned him this would end in blood for Montalcino.

For three years after delivering her first son Sabatina had borne a daughter each year. She began to worry they would have no more strong sons, but then she grew large with the twins – and what joy they brought! The travail of her traumatic labour almost took her to the grave, but although weak and prone to sickliness for a year, her precious baby boys survived and so did she. Now eight years old, Tommaso and Dario had identical facial features, but there the similarity ended. Dario grew the stronger and if it were not for this mobilisation for war he would already be learning to be a fine artisan of wood-carving. But gentle Tommaso was secretly her favourite because he was so much like her. Sabatina was unable to conceive for two years after the twins, as their birth and nursing had taken so much from her weakened body, but then she bore two more boys in a row. The next year she miscarried and her last baby girl, a month old, was feeding well.

'But why are they coming here?' she asked her husband. 'They will bring their own calamities upon us! Why do they think *we* can protect them from the Florentines? And whatever will we do if the Spanish come here too?'

'They are coming to Montalcino because, now that Siena has fallen, we are the strongest city in Tuscany still under Sienese dominion,' Jacopo gruffly replied. 'Although we are only two thousand citizens, we have money to buy arms and to pay soldiers . . . we have grain stores and wheatfields. Among us are artisans who can make leather saddles and war tunics, and we have a dozen iron forges for making weapons and shoeing horses. Don't forget the Sienese strengthened the fortress here after they won the Battle of Montaperti three hundred years ago,' he reminded her. 'They know it has never been breached; our walls are secure. But most of all they know Montalcino has a powerful hospital which, because it owns many farms, will be able to trade grain for artillery and canons. Their own city is in ruins, the population reduced to a miserable few, and the Sienese have been humiliated by the Florentines, yet they boldly talk of proclaiming a new Republic of Siena at Montalcino and call themselves the defenders of liberty! Mark my words, we will end up paying for their pretentious war with our money . . . and we will suffer the consequences. We will pay with the blood of our children, and it is us who will lose our liberty.'

The day the Sienese exiles arrived, Deputies of War were appointed, powerful men who would control the war from inside the walls. Their first ominous decree was posted under the cappellone the very same day: *Every male over the age of twelve years is ordered to enlist in the fighting forces*. Sabatina wept her first tears, chilled to the heart by her husband's prophetic words, for she knew her eldest son would be at the front of the line.

Cesare's voice suddenly changes. Dragging himself back to the present, he breaks into his story to explain to Karen and Eddie about the power-broking which was going on throughout Europe in the mid-1500s, especially between the Kings of Spain and France. Although they were neighbours, the Florentines and Sienese were bitter enemies. The Florentines still smouldered at their disgraceful defeat at the Battle of Montaperti nearly three centuries before, possessed by a simmering hatred so great they would do anything to crush the gloating Sienese – and if that meant an alliance with Spanish invaders or being in league with the devil himself, they would do it. The Florentines sought legitimate sovereignty over the whole of Tuscany. Their Commander, Cosimo I di Medici, was not a fearsome warrior, but he was a wily politician, clever enough to foresee that if he schemed with the Spanish invaders he could escalate his internal power and the potency of the Medici family. The Spanish King was purportedly fighting for a Catholic Europe. He formed an alliance with Cosimo and, once the Sienese exiles came here, Montalcino became the only enclave controlled by Republican Sienese. The Spanish saw – because of their alliance with Cosimo – that if they could take Montalcino, they would have the whole of Tuscany. And if they took the whole of Tuscany, then they could have the whole of Italy – and that could change the delicate balance of power in the whole of Europe.

For their part, the floundering Sienese sought help from the French King, sworn enemy of Spain. A garrison of French soldiers reached Montalcino, but the French proved doubtful allies and as the political scene in Europe oscillated, so the alliance became openly fragile.

Captain Piero Strozzi was an incidental player with a personal score to settle, because he was a Florentine exile; his father had swung from the gallows, executed by the Florentines. Strozzi was a brave Captain and he it was who rode down to the Plain of the Angels with a company of soldiers to meet the exiles from Siena. The once-glorious city of Siena was occupied by the Spanish and 242 noble families and about 400 armed men with their families and servants had exited Siena behind the banner of the Madonna, trudging dispiritedly along the Francigena to Montalcino. The first year of the war did not go well for Strozzi. He marched from Montalcino with his soldiers but lost a battle with the Florentines and was forced to ride to France begging for more troops. That year there were 6,000 Spanish soldiers encamped in the densely wooded valleys around Montalcino and yet the Montalcinesi military forces, alongside the remaining Sienese and French, continued all year to engage in dangerous sorties outside the walls as the first twelve months drifted by.

The civilian citizens of Montalcino, men, women and children, were drawn into a battle which was not theirs . . . and a battle which could never have an outcome to their advantage. They had no choice but to side with the Sienese, who had established their new Republic here in Montalcino, because to side with the despotic Florentines would have been infinitely worse. At least the Sienese were Republicans and fought in the name of liberty . . . yet the Montalcinesi witnessed, month by month, then year by year, the gradual destruction of their village, the pillaging of their churches, the despoiling of their artisan workshops, the squandering of their wealth and the spilled blood of their young men and women until, finally, their conscious victimisation became complete.

There is anger in Cesare's eyes and I dare not speak. He is retreating into the past, taking Karen and Eddie with him.

*

Sabatina fought desperately to keep her family together, trying to maintain some semblance of normality at home even though the months dragged interminably on through two years of war. It was all so confusing, she could not really understand, especially when French soldiers garrisoned in Palazzo Nerli – who were supposedly here to fight against the Spanish and protect Montalcino – became excessively insolent. They showed no respect nor loyalty, they did not know the meaning of chivalry and the Deputies of War were forced to send an ambassador to Rome complaining about their intolerable conduct. But it had made slight difference. Before long their presence in Montalcino was looked upon with reviled disgust. 'We might as well fling open the gates and let the Spanish in,' muttered Sabatina's husband. 'They cannot be worse than these barbarians.'

Living with the French became one of the more hated aspects of the war. The citizens of Montalcino were forced to lodge complaint after complaint about their despicable behaviour until, finally, a murderous ultimatum was issued to the Sienese Governor:

'Either you keep those French soldiers to their duty – lock them in Palazzo Nerli where they are supposed to be garrisoned – or we citizens of Montalcino will see to it that as many heads of French soldiers are chopped off as the number of our fruit trees they chop down. Do you understand? Allies or not, they are destroying our trees and our village, and if you do not want us to rise against you and to find the severed heads of those French soldiers in the gutters, you had better look to controlling them.'

But as the stakes rose and the months passed, the atrocities continued. The manipulative French posted Montalcino soldiers on distant and lengthy engagements, then billeted additional French troops here, swelling their numbers and therefore their authority. They then audaciously demanded access to the village strongbox, the cash assets of Montalcino which were deposited in the vault under Palazzo Comunale. But the Montalcinesi would not relinquish guardianship. Instead they doubled the duty guards, knowing the French would squander their dwindling wealth. The month the much-loved carved and inlaid timber choir stalls in the Church of San Francesco were chopped to pieces and burned, the sacred crucifix broken down and all the church icons and precious gold and silver chalices stolen, everyone knew the barbaric French were responsible for the violent despoliation and theft. It was only by good fortune that the distraught priest managed to save two wooden painted angels which stood beside the altar. Almost everything else was gone, but he had hidden the angels.

In the third year Sabatina watched her eldest son go downstairs one morning and the fear of his approaching death welled up inside her, stabbing her in the heart. Would he return again tonight? His post in the fighting forces included exercises with horrible weapons, canons and gunpowder, and he had told her the Spanish had mounted six canons facing the walls. But that night he had returned safely home, now a brash battle-hardened fifteen-year-old, laughing at his petrified mother. 'Mamma! Did you hear the canons? It was the Spanish. They tried to explode the bastion but they do not know how to fire their own canons – and they backfired, Mamma. The mangled corpses of their own soldiers sailed through the sky instead of us. They blew themselves to pieces . . . and they never even dented our bastion.'

She had known he was riding with his uncle outside the wall at dawn next morning. The forges needed more iron to keep up the supply of weapons and a small party of mounted troops were riding towards the coast to gather arms. They needed steel picks, hatchets, long spears and axes, anything which the foot soldiers could fight with or which could be melted down to make armour and canon balls to hurl over the walls at the Spanish.

All day and into the night, hour after hour, Sabatina sat at the top of the stairs nursing her youngest child, now nearly three years old, offering silent prayers of supplication as she waited. At first she rendered tearful thanks to the Virgin Mary when her husband walked through the door and told her the party had returned, but she saw the anguish creep across his sunken face as he climbed the stairs and she knew her eldest son was not with them. He had not travelled as far as the coast but had been hacked to pieces by a Florentine axeman as the party tried to slip between a company of soldiers manoeuvring for battle in the dense woods. Jacopo repeated over and over as if it would stop her falling tears: 'My uncle made sure the Florentine followed him into the grave.'

'Virgin Mary,' she wept and prayed, 'Madre di Dio, ti prego, I pray of you, let this be over before Tommaso and Dario are old enough to fight.' The twins were already ten, would soon be eleven. They worked hard clearing stinking ditches and ferrying supplies, but next year they would have to enlist.

Each evening she and Tommaso sat together leafing through the silky pages of a precious book which her family had guarded for a hundred years. It had come into her great-grandmother's possession last century because Pope Pius II, as a child of ten, came to Montalcino to learn from this book . . . there had always been men of letters here. She could not read the book herself, of course, but her uncle said Tommaso was clever enough to learn and he promised to pay the schoolmaster to teach her son letters. Dear little Tommaso was a thoughtful, intelligent child who desperately wanted to learn to read, especially his mother's treasured book. 'My son will be a fine scholar,' Sabatina dreamed. 'His head is not filled with fighting and killing. Holy Mother of

God, take away this evil war and spare my sons. One day my Tommaso will be a great teacher.'

As the third year dragged on, a state of desolation spread around the countryside outside the walls. What was once tilled fertile soil between fruit and olive trees was now a barren wasteland devoid of greenery, bare hills where nothing could grow and where even birds no longer flew; only scavenging black crows sat expectantly on truncated branches. Centuries-old oak trees lay splintered across ditches, recklessly hewn when trenches were dug by the Spanish. Sabatina peeped through the slit in the guard-tower wall when Jacopo was on duty and all she could see were ugly mounds of brown dirt, leafless tree stumps and hundreds of bones, which poked up from the earth at awkward angles. Soldiers from all the armies lay where they had been slain, but these were mostly soulless Spanish corpses. Hovering crows, oblivious to the stench of rotting intestines curling out from festered wounds, pecked out their eyes and tore the meat from bones so numerous the earth was becoming calcified. Sabatina was astonished to see so wide a field through such a tiny slit in the wall and Jacopo assured her that the soldiers in the valley were far worse off than him, because they could see nothing. 'It is as if they are blind; they never see their enemy behind the walls but I take patient aim. My bow follows his moving body and the soldier does not even know I am watching him. I drive an arrow straight into his heart. He slumps to the ground and I fire another as he tries to crawl away, but he is soon dead. The crows begin to circle and that is one less foreign invader creeping around our walls. We have to guard the walls like falcons. We cannot let anyone pass because they are trying to reach the springs to poison our water.'

I do not know which is worse, thought Sabatina angrily, barbarian French who violate our village or Sienese who threaten that if our men don't guard the springs well, if the water becomes contaminated or poisoned, they will punish us by chopping off the heads of our husbands. All this we have to suffer, Virgin Mother of God. Preghiamo! They have been inside our walls for more than three years, dwelling in the fortress out of harm's way, eating our bread and drinking our wine – and my first-born son is dead. Oh, Signore, have mercy! My husband is so weak from going without, sparing the food, he can barely fire his bow and arrow, my daughters are rudely threatened by French soldiers and stay hidden at the hospital mending sheets and sewing blankets. Blessed Mother and Immaculate Virgin, intercede for us. Soon Dario and my precious Tommaso will be twelve. Look not upon my sins, Blessed Virgin, but upon my faith. Could the Spanish be worse?

Cesare, shaking his head from side to side, signifying he agrees the Spanish could not have been worse for Sabatina, refocuses his glazed eyes, releasing the tension. He interrupts his story to explain that the political situation in Europe had changed. The King of Spain had abdicated in favour of his son and for many months both Spain and France had been strategically moving enormous numbers of troops, colossal amounts of liquid wealth, artillery and supplies, because a vicious war was threatening to engulf all of Europe. This was like a battle of the giants compared to the war at Montalcino – a comparison of little consequence to Sabatina – yet this besieged 2,000-strong mountain citadel had now become an international byword around the dinner tables and royal courts of Kings and Princes, the powerful rulers of all of Europe. *Can the Spaniards topple Montalcino and take the whole of Italy?*

Sabatina, growing weary and thin, knew none of this. Only that her life and that of her whole family had been turned inside out and upside down. She could not decide who she despised the most, the pretentious money-grabbing Sienese or the destructive, insolent French. She thought little about the Spanish other than that they were outside the walls, piling up their dead. So far as she was able to determine, the arrogant Sienese had brought about their own ruin, gloating at the Florentines for 300 years, but now they were destroying Montalcino too. Their stupid war had taken her first-born son and in a few months the twins would have to go to war. Her Tommaso was destined to be a man of letters, not a warrior with steel. But this was not to be the source of her ensuing agony, for as she silently kneaded a ball of dough for the next day's bread on a wooden table by candlelight, she heard scuffling downstairs and, stepping over the sleeping bodies of her children, she carried a candle to the dark stairway.

Her heart plummeted and she shrank against the wall in fear, realising this sickening ordeal was far from over. Her uncles carried Jacopo through the door. Her husband's chest was bandaged and so was his arm. There were few beds at the hospital and fortunately her daughter had been summoned and insisted Jacopo was better at home, where Sabatina could feed him nourishing soups and bathe his wounds. Sabatina could not move, frozen on the landing as they carried him past, seeing instantly the life-threatening implications this brought for her and the children. Their life was now destroyed. Jacopo had no hand at the end of his arm, just a blood-soaked bandage crudely wrapped around a stumpy wrist. He would never work in the iron forge again. 'What has happened?' she demanded. 'He was not on duty tonight.' As her tears began to flow, at that moment she knew she despised the French the most.

Jacopo had been at San Francesco. He and his friends often gathered outside the church in the evenings when one of them was on extra guard duty. Inside San Francesco was the granary, a life-saving stockpile of golden grain which had been harvested from the fields of Paganico, enough to ensure that Montalcinesi soldiers would eat, albeit only bread, for months to come. When French and Sienese soldiers arrived demanding their own key to the granary, the Montalcinesi guards had refused. The French became angry and their Captain insisted on taking control of the grain deposit, but the Montalcinesi remained steadfast, whereupon the French drew swords. As Jacopo gestured with his hand, attempting to halt the fray, a razor-sharp sword came down on his wrist, severing his hand. A vicious fight followed. The French retreated to their barracks in Palazzo Pieri Nerli and the grain reserves were safe for the moment.

Looking into the sunken stone eyes of her mutilated husband, Sabatina's hatred grew. Despising them all, she searched for understanding. 'Omnipotent Father, why did You let them come to Montalcino?'

The twins turned twelve in May 1559, the fourth year of war, the fourth year of Sienese Republican occupation of Montalcino, and through all those years Sabatina unceasingly implored the Sacred Virgin Mary with her prayers. Every night her head was filled with dreams of approaching death. She grew sullen, resentful and reclusive: 'We have harboured the Sienese and suffered the barbaric French, thousands of Spanish are dead, cut down like devils, but thousands more are camped outside the walls. The wicked Florentines care only for despotic power, they supply canons and artillery to the Spanish. My son was hacked to death by a Florentine, my husband is maimed for life by the French, one of my daughters has died in the hospital of a disease caught from a Sienese soldier and now, Sacred Mother of God, a few days after their twelfth year, my worst agony is here: Tommaso and Dario became men of war. Liberate us from these terrors, Blessed

Virgin! I feared my heart would break watching them leave the safety of the walls. They are so small their leather tunics drag on the ground. The French will use them to scout round villages, to cut down bushes so they can ride their horses close to the walls of Siena. My sons will be easy targets for Spanish weapons. And they are not even Sienese, they are Montalcinesi! Mother of Mercy, please, for the love of a mother . . . spare my sons. Tommaso is to be a great teacher . . . bring my sons home.'

Even if Sabatina had known what was happening in faraway Europe, Cesare tells us, a look of hopeless despair covering his face as he again breaks into our thoughts, she would not have been able to change the war duty of her twin sons. The Spanish and French were waging war; it was always about power, religion, political alliances, family marriages, territory and trade. But Sabatina did not know that weeks before her sons turned twelve, in February 1559, the Spanish and French Kings resolved their differences and agreed on a European peace treaty at Château Cambrese. All that remained was to settle the terms of peace. It was to be some months before news of the terms of this treaty reached Montalcino.

Sabatina, heavy with a coming baby, roused her four-year-old daughter at dawn. Wrapping her child in a blanket, she waddled across the barren earth to lean against the northern wall and lifted her eyes towards Siena. She came here every morning to search the desolate hills, waiting for her sons to come back inside the walls. Even as the high tower in the Campo of Siena came into focus, her eyes dropped to the valley floor, distracted by movement. A terrifying fear gripped her heart like a cold stone. Masses of Florentine soldiers were encamped, hundreds of ranks of hostile menacing spears rose from what seemed like the moving shell of several gigantic armoured beetles. Cavalry in light armour, brandishing lances and pistols, rode between the infantry, manoeuvring the crawling mass of humanity across the valley, creeping closer and closer to Montalcino. Jacopo had heard a rumour that the Florentine army was on the march, but even he could never have imagined the awesome power, the terrifying sight of 9,000 armed soldiers swarming across the valley.

On 1 July 1559, a messenger rode up to the gates of Montalcino and delivered the dreadful news to the ashen-faced Deputies of War: 'Spain and France have settled their differences. The Kings have agreed, and all territory which was known as Sienese has already passed into the hands of Cosimo di Medici, including the Republic of Siena at Montalcino.'

'Not the Florentines!' anguished the sickened Deputies. 'After four years of this bloody war, why the Florentines?'

The messenger callously explained, 'Because in four years the Spanish have accumulated an enormous war debt to the Medici – two million ecus – and instead of repaying their debt to Cosimo, the Spanish have ceded the whole of Tuscany.'

The Deputies refused to accept this dreadful treaty, saying, 'We will stay on our mountain and fight to our deaths rather than be ruled by that grovelling despotic Florentine.'

Within the hour a second messenger was at the gates with a letter from the King of France to Piero Strozzi, ordering him at that exact moment to demobilise the French troops protecting Montalcino. *There is nothing more to fight for*, the letter said. *We have made our agreement. The Sienese will go back to their city, the Republic is finished, the territory belongs to Cosimo.*

On the cobbled roads leading to the piazza there was an air of death and painful resignation in the hearts of the citizens. 'How simple they make it sound,' said wise Jacopo. 'The Sienese will go back to their city, the French got what they wanted and are abandoning us, the Spanish are in debt up to their ears to the wily Florentine and Cosimo di Medici has won the whole of Tuscany. See how neatly they have packaged this peace treaty? Each violent player is accommodated, but Montalcino, after four years of struggle, siege, destruction, pain and death, is the victim!'

Handing over six iron keys to the gates of Montalcino, the Deputies of War cursed them all. 'Having lost everything we could lose, at least we will not lose our honour. Not one of you Medici has earned the title of victor. You have been camped on our territory but a few days, with never a battle with which to claim victory over us.'

The war was over. Piero Strozzi lowered the flag of liberty from the highest tower of the fortress. Jacopo's bitter prophecy had come true; this had ended badly for Montalcino. 'Between them all, Sienese, Florentines, Spanish and French, they have destroyed Montalcino. Not one nor the other cares one scrap for the future of our village. They have stolen all the tools from our workshops, everything of value, every one of our precious icons have disappeared, and they have spilled the blood of our sons. They are each of them consciously content to make Montalcino the victim of their war and now, after suffering their flippant game for four years, they have taken away our liberty.'

Sabatina, refusing to give up hope, came to the northern wall at dawn for many weeks, which stretched into months, but her twin sons did not come back. Tommaso and Dario died violently, side by side, at the walls of Siena. The reviled Cosimo commissioned a great statue of himself – dressed as a Roman soldier – to be placed in the piazza, and Sabatina swore on her death: 'So long as I breathe I will never raise my eyes to so much as glance upon he who murdered my children.' She bore Jacopo two more sons but became increasingly wary, protective and introspective, often spending days on her knees in silent prayer to the Madonna.

Her heart was broken, and she never again walked outside the safety of these walls.

Karen and Eddie have listened in absolute silence. As Cesare falls silent, all of us have our eyes far away in the valley. Eddie turns away, fumbling with his camera bag, and as Karen glances nervously at me, welling tears in her eyes escape on to her cheeks. She is not embarrassed because she sees the same in mine. Perhaps they now understand this mountain village served so poorly with four lines in a guide book. Cesare, not yet able to drag himself from the past, wanders vaguely off, muttering about people who distort facts. He is completely immersed in his own brooding thoughts about Montalcino's victimisation. One day he will tell the real story. When he does, historians in France, Spain, Florence and Siena will go scuttling back to their archives. 'Come on,' I encourage cheerfully, 'let's see the Montalcino of today.'

Threading our way through narrow lanes and down steep stairs, we come out in the quarter of Pianello. 'We have talked about the four quarters. Let's walk through Pianello and I'll explain more, because they are really important to the life of the village today.' We pass the elementary school and I pause to explain how the quartieri Presidents visit the children and talk about the cultural heritage of each quarter, and about the ragazzi in their late teens who will show the children their responsibilities in their quarter when they are older. 'The children already know about the archery competitions, the honour victory brings to their quarter, but the Presidents tell them it has nothing to do with money, nothing to do with getting something – and there is no prize other than the honour of having the greatest archers of Montalcino. Even by four years of age the children have experienced the delirious joy of tournament day.'

At the school gates children are coming out and waiting to

meet them are a few mothers and fathers, but more grandparents.
The children are six or seven years old; they kiss each other lightly
before going straight to Nonna or Nonno, and some walk with
arms draped around each other. Affection amongst Italians, the
need to physically embrace and touch, commences very early. We
watch a small boy march authoritatively up to his grandad and
hand his backpack over. Nonno takes the backpack and they
clasp hands and start off together up the hill. 'Nonno does not
object to being the bag carrier for his grandson, it is his job. And
this is a steep hill. Nonno looks close to eighty, the boy's short legs
don't take big steps, so it is comfortable for them both. They will
stop at Bar Prato and buy a slice of pizza on the way home.'

The point I am trying to make for Karen and Eddie is that
Nonno and Nonna have purpose, a responsibility, but they don't
take it as a burden. Rather, it is the right of a grandparent to be
part of the upbringing of the children, and the children learn
Nonno and Nonna are not old and useless, they are an essential
part of the tight protective circle of an Italian family. Their role is
a daily one.

Karen and Eddie ask me if many wives work, if there are two-
income families. I confirm most do, especially since child-raising
and education in Italy is an expensive business, as is the cost of
living compared to many other countries, but the family network
is such that children have the security of the extended family.
Everybody is responsible for the family and nobody feels
embarrassed looking after the young ones.

Suddenly there is a torrent of questions, of comparisons, of
exasperation with modern society. I am anxious to put this outcry
into perspective, as I have had to do for myself over the years. 'We
cannot compare, it is too late for that. Besides, all of modern
society is not bad and not all of today's Italy is this good, but this
is the way it is in Montalcino. If your ancestors had fought bloody

and fierce battles from these walls, if your ancestors were the mutilated husbands and dead sons who struggled to protect their families and defend their freedom inside these walls, then you would comprehend what Montalcino is all about, understand the network, the sacredness of La Famiglia, not only here, but in the whole of Italy.'

Next we walk to Piazzetta San Pietro so I can show them the sputnik in the painting by Salimbeni which ufologists from around the world come to stare at. They are deeply engrossed in talking with each other, discussing the things we have heard and witnessed, so I stay silent and walk a few steps to the church, but find the door locked. They look up, disappointed, so I use Maria's perilous phrase, 'Non preoccuparti! Nothing to worry about!' I turn to cross the road to the house where I know the key is kept. Giving a firm knock, I stand on the roadway and watch the two upstairs shutters, where, sure enough, in a matter of seconds, one is pushed open and a grey head appears above the terracotta troughs overflowing with purple and lilac petunia.

'Buonasera, Signora, may I please have the key to San Pietro?' She returns my greeting but then says: 'Just a moment, I'll ask my husband, he is in the cantina.' Eddie and Karen are staring upwards at windows around about, because my request has disturbed nearby residents and shadowy movements at the windows tell us we are under observation.

While we wait, I begin to tell them a little of the history of the eleventh-century Church of San Pietro and then remember the scandalous story and the reason the church is locked, but I don't tell them about the rumours or Pianello's desperate hopes to buy it, nor about the roof being in such bad repair. 'Look at the open tower with twin bells. They only chime on special feast days. Can you see the ropes coming down from the bell-tower, through the roof to the inside? The bells are still rung by hand to call the faithful to Mass.'

This is an inviting corner in Pianello and for Eddie and Karen, waiting for the key, this old stone church has taken on a personal perspective. 'I hope we can get inside,' Eddie says wistfully. A few minutes pass and there's movement up at the shutters. 'Signora, unfortunately no, the key is not here. My husband thinks Settimia has it – she is working in the sede kitchen.'

'Va bene, okay, I'll go and see if she is still there. Grazie Signora, buonasera.' She returns my farewell, disappears in the shadows and pulls the green shutters closed. I am thankful Eddie had the sensitivity not to photograph her whilst this polite exchange took place, although I know he was probably aching to do so because it is all so naturally Italian.

It is only a few steps to the door of the sede behind San Pietro and of course I know Settimia well. Well enough to have asked her if she is really the seventh child as her name implies, which she is. The door is ajar and hearing voices inside I knock and call out, 'Permesso, may I come in?' 'Chi è, who is it?' someone responds. I walk up a couple of steps and hear, 'Ah, Isabella, are you here to help?' It's Lola! And she is not alone. Sure enough, Settimia is here, as are Maria-Rosa, Carlo and Ercole; in fact, there is frenzied activity.

'Ciao, ciao,' I address everybody. 'What help could I be to you experts? No, but I have two friends with me from America and the door was open, so I wonder if you would mind if I brought them in for a minute or two?'

'Certainly, come in, come in, but we are making preparations, so everything is upside down.' It certainly is, but I think Eddie and Karen believe I orchestrated the whole performance on their behalf. Luciana, head cook for Pianello, is noisily clanging iron pots in the kitchen, where one bench is piled with tomatoes, and another with shiny purple melanzane, aubergines. Three ladies wearing wraparound floral aprons are standing behind the dining table wrist-deep in rolling pinci. Ghostly smears of flour are smudged across their foreheads and it coats their aprons. 'A small dinner this evening,' they explain, 'just twenty people, a meeting of our office bearers.'

Ercole and Carlo, Maurelia's son, are clearing out a corner which is stacked with Pianello banners. Carlo pulls one out, holds it upright and proudly unfurls it, the blue and white emblem bold and bright in the sunlight streaming in the window. He asks Eddie if he would like to photograph it. Would he! Taking turn about, Eddie and Karen pose with the banner, then with Ercole beneath the banner, then with Carlo, then the ladies. I take the photographs. I then show them the Pianello trophy cabinet with rows of small arrowheads and the names of our archers printed below each one, signifying the years Pianello has won the tournament. They ask about the golden arrowheads, so I have to explain that every ten years we have a golden arrow tournament, more significant than the silver. They peer at the framed prints of our quartiere costumes, the medieval dress of our Lady and Lord and the costumes our archers wear during the tournament, but I have not had time to begin to explain about the Sagra.

Not wanting to be too intrusive when I have visitors with me, I begin our farewells, but don't manage to exit until Eddie has photographed Pianello sede from every possible angle as well as every strand of pinci falling from the ladies' swift hands. Both of them have to go to the kitchen to wash the flour from their hands, because Lola had them trying to roll pinci on the table. 'Tonight,' she rattles at them, 'I'll have to make sure our President does not get your ugly pinci.' On the way out, screams of laughter come from the kitchen as Eddie pushes the camera through the door and snaps Luciana and Settimia with their arms full of gleaming purple melanzane.

As soon as we are out on the road I realise I forgot to ask Settimia for the key to San Pietro, but I notice it is many hours since we set off on this journey and, apart from anything else, I am starving. When I tell Eddie and Karen the time, they are astonished. 'If we get back to Bar Prato in the next twenty minutes we will just have time for caffè and pizza before the evening bus back to Siena.'

'Oh, no!' wails Karen. 'We can't – we haven't seen everything. What about all those other places? We haven't even seen inside San Pietro – and I want to go to the fortress. I have *got* to see that banner and climb the high tower.' My face is all smiles as I recall their words: 'Is there anything to do here? Nothing much seems to be happening.' But I resist the temptation to remind them.

On the way to Piazza Cavour where the bus will soon be arriving, Karen is adamant she must take something home from Montalcino, something for herself. Eddie wants to purchase two bottles of Brunello; one to drink in Siena with their friends when they recount the story of their day in Montalcino and one to take back to America. As we only have a short time if we are to drink a caffè, I divert towards the piazza and introduce Eddie to Antonio in Enoteca Pierangioli, leaving him to savour the enticing array of wines which line the walls.

'Come on, Karen, we'll go and see Massimo, it's only a couple of doors away.' Handsome Massimo is in the Biancheria, the well-stocked shop in the piazza which hides a treasure of fabulous things for the home. Luckily no one else is here and Karen watches Massimo quickly unravel rolls of exquisitely coloured cloth, laying them along the counter with just a metre hanging over the edge so she can feel and see each one. Karen is dazzled and settles on two fabrics, one a blaze of terracotta pots with greens, blues and yellows in lemons and grapes, the other a gorgeous woven white jacquard. I convince Massimo he does not have time to wrap the parcel in glossy paper, bind it with ribbon and add his personal card as he usually does. He is more than a little put out when our arms thrust the precious fabrics into carrier bags and he gasps when Karen stuffs in two ivory damask hand towels with long fringed edges. He feels he is not doing his job properly. We fly out the door laughing like schoolgirls having executed some prank, calling our thanks and goodbyes to Massimo. Eddie is waiting for us and looks sheepishly at Karen; he is cradling six bottles of Brunello instead of two. Then we are rushing down Via Mazzini.

We have ten minutes at Bar Prato in which to eat pizza and swap names and addresses. 'We will be back, you can be sure of that,' says Eddie warmly. 'This is the fourth time we have come to Italy. We always love it but we never really understood before – we didn't look properly.' I promise to find a comfortable apartment in the village, or a farmhouse outside the walls, whichever they want, provided they agree to come for at least a week.

The bus driver starts the engine. Eddie thrusts a brown paper bag at me and they both give me warm hugs and kind words of thanks. All three of us show signs of moisture around the eyes because it has been a truly emotional and provocative afternoon. I wave the bus off, then walk behind it up Viale Roma, not wanting to go straight home, although I am bursting to tell Luigi that I think they really did understand. Instead, I return to the iron fence on the crest of the hill and sit down to look over the battlefield once more. The cool evening air is refreshing and ten minutes later I am still there. A couple of tourists wander up, photograph the spectacular valley, turn and walk uncomprehendingly away. Another holiday snapshot, when they get home they won't recall where they were, because they do not understand.

I glimpse a smudge of blue away in the distance on the road to Buonconvento and smile contentedly, watching the bus as it weaves its way through the bald clay hills carrying Karen and Eddie back to their friends in Siena. They are going to have a lot to talk about tonight over a bottle of splendid Brunello. Just as I am wondering if I will ever hear from them again, I remember the brown paper bag, which I absently open. The guide book falls gently into my lap.

CHAPTER FOURTEEN

A Prophet, A Sweeper and A Winemaker

At last Illiano can take a break and head over to the marquee for dinner. What a night! Half the village has turned up for the opening of Festa della Unità, Festival of Unity. A sultry evening has enticed people to walk up the steep hill to seek the cooling breezes under the Pineta, and Illiano cannot remember a bigger first night turn-out. The last week has been frantic as he and other committee members raced against the clock. Officially, his job is to supervise the operation of the games once the Festa begins, which means he will be at the Pineta for ten nights, making sure things function smoothly.

For weeks the Labour Committee has been negotiating the delivery of the stage and tents; the marquee in which dinner will be served on ten nights only rose yesterday. Stoves and wood were carted up the hill, tables and chairs unloaded and set out, while electricians worked to string lights between the trees. Only yesterday, when the major part of the work was finished, could they give the signal for the women to come up and arrange the kitchens, bringing the food. By that time the wine tent had been erected and also Bruno's tent, in which he will cook piping hot donzelline, slipper-shaped fried pasta. Angelino, the same one who administers the football squad, not only plays baritone horn in the village band but also plays and sings in a band of his own, and tonight they are first up on the entertainment programme, playing a tango. People are crowding around the open-air dance floor watching, so Illiano is taking the opportunity to have dinner with Zampa, who has completed his work for the evening.

I have been looking forward to attending this festival because last year it was all over before I even knew it was on. Since Luigi and I frequently travel in the north of Italy in August, we had not even known of its existence in previous years. As usual, there had not been any announcements because, as Zampa sensibly suggested, announcements are not necessary as everybody knows the festival is in August. We did not, so we always missed it, which made me determined this year to be here on opening night.

Illiano explained that Festa della Unità is staged annually at the Pineta, the park beneath the pine trees a few hundred metres, all uphill, outside the walls, with fervent co-operation between the comrades of parties to the left: the Partita Democratici della Sinistra and the Partita Socialistici. 'A decade ago it was more of a political rally. We used to have creative artisans working and we had visiting political speakers. We carried placards and did a bit of flag-waving, but it has become a festival for the people. Anyway,' he added reasonably, 'there isn't really any cause to wave flags and argue doctrine because politically speaking things are under control with a government of the left holding the reins in Rome.'

Having just arrived, I am still out of breath. The steep climb up to Pineta is muscle-jarring, even though I did pause several times, gasping, to look down at the village twinkling along the curved hill. Political banners waving between pine trees have trans-formed the park, and their message confirms the Democratic Party of the Left and the Socialist Party thrive under a brotherhood of solidarity in Montalcino. Wandering between the pine trees towards the dance floor, I greet friends and sidle up to a group to watch, intrigued to find many of the signore I know well whirling around with men I have been talking to for months, although I hadn't made the connection of which husbands belong to which wives. Angelino's band is playing from an elevated stage to one side, which is lit with flashing disco beams. Monstrous amplifiers blast the sensuous tango rhythm between the trees into the night, where the serene face of Italy's head of Government, Massimo D'Alema, beams down from floodlit red banners that declare, under the recently reborn rose insignia of the PDS, the solidarity of the left.

Observing the dancers and onlookers more attentively, it filters through my mind that most signore are not dressed for a festive evening; rather, they are clothed the way you might expect to find them at home preparing dinner, or attending to the family. It is as if they have just unwrapped their aprons, stepped out of the kitchen and come on over, thoughtfully draping a cardigan over their shoulders. I watch for half an hour, envious at seeing people of all ages move on to the dance floor. Most seem to know how to tango. Mothers dance with young daughters, patiently teaching the tango steps as if it is as vital as knowing how to prepare a ragù sauce, and the teenagers show no embarrassment stumbling over complicated steps, trying again.

The lights snap off and applause breaks out as Angelino and his band lay down their instruments and, as the stage lights up in a blaze of red, green and white, everyone deserts the darkened dance floor. Most walk across to sit on benches in front of the stage, because the next act is setting up. Large boxes are being dragged onstage and an unseen microphone announces that: 'The fabulous Otello will now entertain us with his miraculous tricks!' Otello bounces onstage to a trickle of applause. Otello is a magician, a regular rabbit-in-the-hat scarves-up-the-sleeve magician, and the black boxes are part of his act. He begins by magically extracting colourful scarves from his sleeves, a rabbit from nowhere and white doves from his hat, and by the looks of things, will soon saw his bespangled and shapely assistant, poised nearby, in half.

It is already past eleven o'clock, but giggling children sit in the front row watching Otello's tricks. Mothers with babies in prams, and grandparents, smile contentedly, anticipating each well-known trick in this old-fashioned style of entertainment. Considering the revolution in entertainment options over the past few decades, this magician feels comforting, sensing the mood of the audience remarkably well. The atmosphere is soporific, everyone participating voluntarily in an entrancing but unspectacular show. Knowing there are nine more nights to go, I can feel myself becoming detached, as if by some magic outside myself I have become invisible. Up here, on this intoxicating summer night, tripping over fallen pine cones with the heady perfume of tinder-dry pine needles filling the air, the people I know so well do not seem the same. Ephemeral; I can't quite put my finger on it, but it is as if they are on holiday in another world. They have been able to forget themselves, to let go of who they usually are down in the village.

Leaving the magician to his conjuring, I wander past the donzelline tent to see how Bruno is coping, but can only peek between the shoulders of people waiting to eat his fried pasta treat. He lifts each one from the frying pan, drops it on to a tray of salt which is sprinkled in liberal handfuls, then with the bottom half wrapped in a serviette people walk away munching from the top down. The thought runs through my head that even this is a reversal, because Italians do not normally eat on the run but prefer at least a plate, if not a table to sit at.

Illiano has finished dinner and is again supervising the games tables. A crowd is building up in front of the tent, so I leave the tempting cholesterol-laden donzelline and head that way to see what they are playing. Illiano has told me the games are not only meant to be fun but are part of the annual fund-raising for the Party, as are the nightly meals served during the Festa in the marquee. 'Our pinci is hand-rolled by the ladies every day,' he confidently told me, 'and served with ragù or tomato and garlic sauce.' His proud declaration describing these always-desired sauces is no surprise.

Armando is at the games table, which is no surprise either, because he is always where the fun is. Black-moustached Bino and he are selling tickets and, yet a third non-surprise, the prizes are whole legs of prosciutto or fat white-skinned salamis. Nearby is a stand displaying stuffed green dinosaurs, but it is evident a prize in that category is poor consolation. The games are charmingly quaint; lucky numbers, tossing sand-filled bags at a pyramid of tins, rolling tennis balls into skittles. But my eye catches sight of a horizontal roulette wheel about two metres in diameter, for which people are buying tickets at L 5,000 each, so I stand with them to watch. In the centre of the roulette wheel sits a cardboard box and attached to it, with a fifty-centimetre length of string, is a broom handle. Nothing is happening, because Armando and Bino still have tickets to sell, and they are boisterously soliciting business with the offer of both a leg of prosciutto *and* a salami as first prize. This is too much to resist.

'Brava Signora, buona fortuna, good luck,' Armando laughs as he hands me two tickets and I part with L 10,000. A rope fence restrains us a metre from the roulette wheel, but I am among familiar faces. Illiano is leaning against a tree to the side, Memmo the hairdresser is here, and Ofelia is standing with Chiara at the front. Vasco and his friend Giancarlo are watching, and the huddle willingly make a space to let me nearer the wheel.

'Allora!' shouts Bino. 'All the tickets are sold, in bocco al lupo, good luck everyone. There are three turns of the wheel. The first prize is a prosciutto and a salami, the second prize a prosciutto and third prize a salami.'

Armando leans to the side, positions both hands on the wooden rim and, with an exaggerated heave from him, the wheel begins to turn. People seem uninterested, absently chatting, not watching as it whirls swiftly round and round. But once it is up to speed, Armando puts his hand on the broom handle and raises it so the string becomes taut, whereupon conversation dies and every eye is riveted on the cardboard box. Lulled into my complacent detachment, what happens next is all the more astonishing. Armando chooses his moment, then swings the broom handle high into the air. As it rises, surely the shocked screams which alarm everyone are coming from someone other than me?

Liberated from the darkness of the cardboard box, and now spinning helplessly round and round in dizzy circles, races the cuddliest tan and white cross-eyed guinea pig!

Fifty people turn, frowning, distracted by my screaming, but I am fixed on the guinea pig, which does not seem to know where to go. Clearly, he is the dice, and everyone who has a ticket wants him to scamper to the hole on the wheel which holds their number. Hand over my mouth, I watch transfixed as the circling creature attempts a few steps in one direction, then, as the wheel begins to slow, he cautiously creeps against the spin. 'No, no,' someone whispers. 'Number forty-three, can't you see, piccolo cieco maiale! Little blind pig!'

Just as the confused pig is about to dive into the black shadows of box fourteen, he falters, standing stock still for twenty seconds. Out of the silence comes the next comment: 'It's dead, Armando. You have got a dead pig here and it cannot count.' The pig seems to have heard, turns and bolts across the table and vanishes into the darkness offered by cavern thirty-five. Thank goodness. Grazie Dio. It is not my number.

Two more spins and the game is finished and so am I, and so is the guinea pig. Armando lifts him tenderly from the table and carries him to a cage that holds a dozen of his cuddly friends, who evidently take it in turns to go for a spin. As soon as there is a gap in the crowd I slip through, not wanting to meet anyone's eyes, least of all Illiano's. Scarlet-faced, I cower into the shadows, mortified.

I had not known that this particular game is something of a tradition, only played in Montalcino at Festa della Unità. The tradition carries on because someone takes responsibility for the guinea pigs, and it occurs to me there had been no shouting or cursing at the innocent creature; instead, people had coaxed, whispered gentle encouragement. The squeals of my shock had frightened the wits out of him and everybody watching. Enough damage for one night. Rudely awakened from my detached mood, I head back down the hill.

Inside the walls along Via Ricasoli is Bar Arci, Circolo, although there is no visible evidence of the existence of Circolo from the roadway because you find it through the wooden doors leading to the courtyard of Palazzo Nerli. There is a crumbling stone crest higher than the doorway, and the inner courtyard contains a magnificent well behind which rises a two-storey cross-vaulted loggia. I wander in at nearly midnight and only Ilio Raffaelli is here, but this is normal. For ten nights while the Festa is on, there will only be one or two people sitting in this courtyard, as everybody else is up at the Pineta. On other summer nights, in fact most of the year, village men stroll up after dinner to socialise and frequent Circolo. I am comforted to have found Raffaelli here, as I'm still smarting after my embarrassing faux pas and stealthy retreat from Festa della Unità. His reassuring presence, for he is absorbed in reading a book in the corner, offers a quiet opportunity for my grateful reflection on our discussions about the political left in Montalcino, whose lively presence at Pineta I have just encountered.

Bar Arci, Circolo, is different from others in the village, because as well as the dilapidated crest above the doorway there is another emblem – the political insignia of the Partita Democratica della Sinistra, the Democratic Party of the Left. Circolo, in Palazzo Nerli, headquarters of the PDS and the Socialist Party, is one place few visitors discover. This is a gathering point to play cards, watch football and be among friends. A decade or two ago you would have needed to be a card-carrying member of the Party to come to Circolo, but the atmosphere is more relaxed these days because, as Illiano says, there isn't any need to wave flags and argue doctrine. Never-theless, the regulars who frequent the bar nightly pay annual fees and have membership rights; Illiano and Zampa often pass an evening playing cards here. Montalcino's branches of Italy's two major parties of the left, the PDS and the Socialists, share facilities at Palazzo Nerli and, although not long ago the parties differed from each other, the differences seem less significant now. And anyway, anybody is welcome at Circolo – far left, left, centre left, and even slightly right.

After the Communist Party briefly rallied during the turbulence following the war, the combined forces of the Church and the Christian Democrats kept the left out of government until the scandal of tangentopoli, clean hands, decimated the Christian Democrats early in the 1990s. Since then Italy has lurched to the right and left, usually called centre-right and centre-left. In 1998, without the formality of a general election, the reins were handed to the PDS who, in coalition with the Socialists and an array of argumentative parties, returned to govern under the leadership of young, charismatic Massimo D'Alema. No lurching has taken place in Montalcino, left is still left, but the doors of Circolo are open to everyone. You are unlikely to see red banners and flags unless you are here for Festa della Unità.

It can be argued, convincingly, that the left made Montalcino what it is today. It often is argued, again convincingly and repeatedly, that because of this Montalcino has a tremendous responsibility on its shoulders. 'This part of the world,' says Ilio Raffaelli, a modern-day warrior who continues to guard and defend Montalcino with dramatic words as emphatic as any razor-sharp sword which cut the head off a Spanish knight, 'has been called upon to maintain quality. The world has come to expect that Italian means quality and Montalcino has a great weight to carry.' I have frequently heard my solitary midnight companion vehemently proclaim in the bars: 'Montalcino is a village preserved in an exquisite environment. We have a gastronomy which is one of our greatest ambassadors, our honey and oil – all our agriculture – is quality product and we have created a world-class wine. And,' he softens his compelling voice whenever he secures the attention of passers-by or people of influence, for I have noticed all are equal to Ilio, and, almost whispering as if this listener is the first person to whom he has ever said it, 'we have yet to offer our bountiful woods, another resource that people, armed with their cameras, will soon rediscover, to be a world-class natural environment hiding a thousand marvellous secrets.'

Ilio Raffaelli is not one to mince words. He entered political school when he was twenty-five, after his formal education to fifth year elementary, which, he readily admits, was made up of twenty months out of five years at school. He explained it to me this way: 'I took a few bites at my education. I was hungry to learn, but could only gulp a month or two here and there.' The rest of the year he was needed by the family to cut wood around Montalcino, because he came from a family of boscaioli, woodcutters.

Ilio became Vice-Mayor of Montalcino in 1951, was elected Mayor in 1960 and for the next twenty years he led the Comune. He finally retired in 1980, whereupon, he says with a grin, for he has a dry sense of humour, he finally got to know his dear wife whom he had married in 1959. 'We had no children,' he told me, 'there was never enough time.' Having been Vice-Mayor and then Mayor of Montalcino for a continuous period of thirty years postwar, he speaks with tremendous emotion of the village he loves. His reign at the head of a Comune of the left in an era when the country was governed, for more than forty years, by doubtful

Christian Democrats, did not make for an easy life. He, and many others in Montalcino, some of whom were with him and some against, remember decades of struggle. 'I have left my mark on Montalcino,' he says with a satisfied nod of his head. When I asked him why he retired, he replied, 'Well, I had to know when to put up my gloves as a winner, because you get to a point where you begin to annoy even the stones.'

Ilio had to contend with bitter fighting and was not always popular, but he was stubborn; he was fighting for the future and he is an intelligent man. At the time he became Vice-Mayor in 1951, he describes the village with the very words Ercole and Lola have used: 'This was a tragic place. There was no running water, next to no electricity, medieval houses were collapsing, and for the population, most of whom had all but starved through the war, the future looked grim. Worst of all, there was no work, because Montalcino had been forgotten by history.' The race was on to industrialise Italy, and Ilio, with a torrent of words, arms moving in despairing and dramatic sweeps, recalls the attitude which swept the country. '"If you love Italy," the radio blared out to us, "and if you want jobs and riches, you have got to build factories, big ones and small ones. You have got to *make* things. Forget the land – people who talk about agriculture are behind the times, they are pulling Italy back. If you want work, you must industrialise."'

Raffaelli knew what it was to have no work, to be hungry, for he had been raised with the boscaioli who worked dawn to nightfall cutting timber. This was the work of hundreds of Montalcino families and the life he was born into. His earliest memory is of when he was three years of age, being sat on a cart drawn by black oxen and driven into the woods to a rough shelter where his family stayed from October to April every year, cutting wood through every freezing winter. Holding out his hands to me and smiling at the smooth wrinkle-free skin, he told me how he had twice fallen into the fire at their camp. He was only a toddler, but can still remember the smell when his mother plastered his burns with a paste of olive oil and flour. Boscaioli were paid according to the amount of wood they cut, measured by the cubic metre, and in 1930 this meant that if the Raffaelli family worked from sun-up until the stars were out at night, they earned ten lire. At that time a loaf of bread cost one and a half lire per kilo, so mostly Ilio's family ate brodo, a soup of boiled beans or potato. Occasionally there would be a dollop of polenta, but a piece of boiled meat was an almost unknown luxury. 'Except for wild berries from the woods, we never ate fruit.' He shook his head at me, dismissing the thought, then turned his head to the side as if that too would negate the very idea. 'As for other vegetables, we will not even talk of it.'

During the 1930s and 1940s this was the life of 90 per cent of village people, the boscaioli, because this was not just the men, this was hundreds of families! Learning about the boscaioli from Raffaelli, I have finally been able to solve the missing chunk from a puzzle which has hovered in my mind for months. I had learned from several people that cittadini, village dwellers, were terribly poor, not just in the 1920s, 1930s and 1940s, but also after the war, in the late 1950s and 1960s, but I could not unveil the reasons why. I could not work out what had happened to leave them so poor, and it bothered me. Primo had referred to this poverty even whilst revealing his own struggle against travesties of justice to the contadini on the land, and he virtually justified the village lads beating him up and throwing him outside the walls by saying: 'Up there the poor had nothing, they were starving. At least the contadini had a bit of bread to eat.' As well, I remember Illiano's words. He is a decade or more younger and his family took the pigs and sheep to the woods during the war. He told me, 'The village people had the worst of it – they suffered the most. The women went down to the fields to pick up spigole, stray ears of corn, trying to trade them for a fistful of flour.' I had never established why the cittadini suffered the most.

I listened silently while Ilio told me there were nearly 800 families of Montalcino who were boscaioli, thousands of dependent people and, in order to allow for re-growth, it was forbidden for them to cut wood other than in late autumn and winter. All through the freezing winter the families camped out in the woods: mothers, fathers, aunts, uncles, grandparents, children and babies, scratching out a wretched living cutting timber and hoping to cut enough to eke out funds so the family would survive the following spring and summer, so that in autumn they could start all over again.

Ilio's father, also called Ilio, brought the family back to Montalcino every spring. He was known as Ilio il Terrore, Ilio the Terror, and it was not hard to visualise, from Ilio's description, that the family, living in the woods through icy winter months, did not have many niceties of life. The day the bedraggled Raffaelli family straggled into the village with two black oxen dragging their meagre possessions, children would see them coming. 'Ilio the Terror is back!' they would scream hysterically, rushing about to gather friends, hiding round corners and in doorways to get a tantalising glimpse of this legendary terror back in the village. After months in the woods, Ilio's father's hair was long and matted, his face black and eyes red from the smoke of the fires and he looked to the children like a filthy, sooty, wild creature from the bosco. Even today, if people need to distinguish one Ilio from another in Montalcino, they will say, 'Do you mean Ilio, figlio di Terrore, son of Terror?'

At seventeen, Ilio was a partisan fighting the Germans in the hills around Montalcino. He remembers the exploding bombs, the echoing rifle shots and hiding for months in the woods with his young friends, some of whom died. But more than anything else, Ilio has never forgotten, and says he never will forget, the indescribable hunger. 'It was,' he told me, screwing up his eyes and pursing his lips, making a clicking sound with his tongue, 'unbelievable famine and still makes me sick to think of it.' There was a black market for food, but nobody wanted money; you had to have something to trade. Boscaioli had nothing to trade, as they only cut wood; they were not shoemakers, or contadini on the land, or charcoal-makers, so they went hungry because everybody cut their own wood. At last I could see that for these cittadini families it was a miserable existence before the war, then in just a few years the poor life of the boscaioli was ruthlessly destroyed, because Italy, and the world, turned to electricity, gas and oil. Their humble livelihood was swept away in the rush to industrialise Italy, and decades of poverty degenerated into decades of suffering.

When he became Vice-Mayor, and ten years later was elected Mayor, young Ilio understood the anguish of hundreds of young men from Montalcino who were forced to go elsewhere to find work in factories to feed their families. Many boscaioli reinvented themselves, becoming muratori, bricklayers. Some went to the cities, some to France, even to Switzerland, which is where Zampa went, and some, like the dispossessed contadini, if they could scrape enough money together, left their homeland and emigrated to the New World.

The propaganda and pressure on the Comune was intense, because a large proportion of the population of Montalcino wanted to build factories here, they wanted to be done with agriculture. 'Via, via,' they would shout. 'Out with the old, be done with it. We need jobs, Ilio – we have got to industrialise.' Ilio Raffaelli, his face grave, eyes half closing and with his arms folded stubbornly across his chest, looked these desperate, hungry people in the eye and said, 'No! That is not the way we will go.'

Every day there were endless arguments because people did not believe in the direction he and the Comune thought Montalcino should take. 'Every-single-Sunday,' Ilio pronounced each word individually for dramatic emphasis, 'someone would come back with a pocketful of money from a job in a car factory. They would go into the bars and stir up the locals, saying: "What are you doing here? Are you mad? The place is dead. Come on, listen to the radio, watch television – it's factories now, everybody is making money, that's how you will get rich."' At that time a factory worker earned L 500,000 a month while Ilio, as Mayor, earned a lowly L 130,000.

Zampa remembers coming home from the High Alps in Switzerland, where he earned three times as much in one month as he could earn bricklaying in Italy. He and a few friends got a bit het-up about it in Bar Cacciatore. He recalls their frustration as if the intervening fifty years were but a day. 'Diamine! This is intolerable . . . let's go and see il Sindaco.' Next morning, with three friends, he went to see the Mayor. 'Ilio,' he said reasonably, 'tell me, why it is that I have been forced to work away from Montalcino for eight years and there is no end in sight? Every time I come back nothing is any different. There is still no work, there are no new buildings, nothing has been done, the place is exactly the same.'

'Alessandro, sit down with me,' Ilio patiently replied. 'I am going to tell you why, and the way I think we should go.'

Zampa remembers the calm, logical explanation Ilio gave and, above all, the unwavering belief in his eyes and his certainty that, if they could just be patient, the day would come when cars would be lined along the roads to Montalcino with people who were coming here to work. I will never forget the goose pimples that

349

prickled my neck as Zampa looked into my eyes and said, 'Isabella, he was a prophet.'

'Zampa, if they want to build factories,' Ilio reasoned, 'let them build them down in the valley, because in ten years they will be ugly useless ruins, closed up and gone. But they are not building them at Montalcino. We are not called upon to be factory workers, Zampa. We are called upon to do the things our forebears did.'

Ilio remembers there were others who had a vision for the future, who mistakenly thought they were on the same wavelength as him. They thought he was right, there *would* be a revival and boom in agriculture, and they wanted to be ready. They came to his office and said to him: 'Ilio, look at these plans. I can build a thirty-room modern four-storey concrete hotel so that when the farms are producing again and the traders come back, we will be ready for them. I want to build it right in the centre where those old stone houses are falling down near the piazza, what do you think?'

'No! Never!' Ilio glared at them, sending them from his office with a wild wave of his hand. 'Go and build your concrete hotel somewhere else, because I promise you, it will not be built in Montalcino.'

'Ilio,' a family of bricklayers implored him, 'we have had everything drawn up. If you will just give us permission we will build seventeen brand new apartments on the slope below the Madonna and every one will have a neat square concrete balcony overlooking the stupendous valley. Our families will live in modern apartments with proper bathrooms. Just sign here. We will make you look good, Ilio, because we will employ twenty people for a year while we build them.'

I could well imagine Ilio's horror then, as he thumped his hand on the table between us, just as he must have done on his Mayoral

350

desk all those years ago when, looking them straight in the eye, scornful at their lack of understanding, he shouted scathingly: 'No! No! No! That stupendous valley belongs to *all* of Montalcino. Why can't you understand? There will be no factories polluting our air, there will be no concrete hotels ruining our village and we will reconstruct the homes we love.'

This passionate man told them all, as the years crawled painfully by: 'Montalcino has a heart and a soul. This hill is our life, we have our roots in the land, and that is how we will stay.'

'But Signora, at the time we had nothing!' Ilio let these dramatic words sink in. 'I cannot tell you what it was like in the rest of Italy because I never saw it, but here we had to start from zero.' First the Comune brought in a reliable electricity supply, and I could imagine the task of wiring a huddle of metre-thick medieval walls cascading down a mountain. And then came running water, and the construction of a communal wash-house so the women did not have to lower buckets into the wells. 'And the schools!' Ilio threw out the phrase, his eyes wide open in horror as if the very way he emphasised the words would give me an idea of what he was up against. 'There were so many children, but so few teachers, and we had nothing in the way of facilities. We had no sealed road down to the Via Cassia, only a dirt track, and practically every single building in the village needed to be restored.'

People like Zampa had to work away from their homes, sometimes in another country, for nearly twenty years. But month after month they sent money back to their families, and over the years the medieval homes they loved were slowly restored, and for the first time with running water, electricity, basic kitchens and bathrooms. Experts were brought over from Sardinia, or from wherever else the Comune could draw them, who were able to advise and direct experimentation with different types of grain and olive trees, and helped by studying the micro-climate and analysing the soil. Almost imperceptibly, year after painful year, Ilio continued the battle and Montalcino crawled along.

Once in a while, Ilio remembers, someone would come down to his office and say: 'Keep going, keep going, you are on the right road.' More promised to take to him with a pitchfork. They were out to get him. But he kept going because he believed he was right.

Of course, the Comune did not win every battle, and when Ilio told me this story I felt sick in the pit of my stomach. Ilio recalled that when he was Vice-Mayor in 1956 there was talk of building a post office in Montalcino, which was not Comune expenditure, but State. The Mayor of the time, and the Comune, did not want the post office to be built into the loggia beneath the cappellone, but a Bishop got involved and decided that was where it should be. Although politically the Church was not a difficult opponent for the left in Montalcino, it nevertheless wielded power, immense power, especially on a State level. Arguments went back and forth for two years, but on 10 May 1958 a telegram, still in Ilio's possession, was sent by the State Minister of the time to the Bishop, approving the construction of a new post office and stipulating that it was to be built wherever the Bishop wanted it to be. He wanted it under the cappellone, so that is where it was built.

Intrigued by this chain of events, and alerted by revelations of a Bishop lurking in this story, I pressed Ilio – as he waited for me to do – and asked why the Mayor did not want the post office under the cappellone. Only then could I understand the terrible blunder, the tremendous loss to Montalcino, because before the post office was built, the rear wall of the cappellone was not solid. It was transparent, with a row of sheer glass windows so the population could gaze over the glorious hills of the Val d'Orcia to an everchanging panorama of green vines, swaying grain, red poppies, yellow sunflowers and silvery olive trees. A stubborn Bishop locked the Val d'Orcia out of the piazza! Surely this revelation explains the unexplainable? Is scant respect for eminent Bishops steeped in resentment for past deeds?

Ilio went on to tell me that later Bishops showed more perception, but at that time the Church only wanted to be seen wielding power over the Comune, which fought and argued with the State about the post office for two years, an attitude that explains why the Church was never able to assume control of the people of Montalcino as it had in most of Italy's villages. The Church had power, he said, but in Montalcino the Bishops never showed cultural understanding; they did not go out and sow, they lacked foresight and had no concept of a future. When fire broke out, they called the fire brigade . . . always too late. 'But Ilio,' I wanted to argue, 'it is not too late. Surely it can be undone? The post office must be moved!' But I stayed silent, as it is not my place. I am close to these people and living within these walls by their grace, but I am a straniera. In Australia or America and many other countries, we would raise petitions, organise marches, wave placards, demand to be listened to, and ultimately the voice of the people would lead to action. I believe I may at last have solved the puzzle of the Bishops, but I have no remedy for their misdeeds.

Noting my wide-eyed interest in stubborn Bishops, Ilio added a footnote, but of course did not know how forcibly he confirmed my suspicions. In 1963 the young Communist Mayor of Montalcino was interviewed by *La Nazione*, the leading newspaper in Siena. It was an extensive interview in which Ilio sought to outline the direction he and the Comune projected for the future of Montalcino. Ilio pressed home the point: '. . . from the vine, the olives and our woods, we will rebuild our economy.' Even as late as 1967, when the Consorzio di Brunello was formed and the contadini growers were fighting for their rights, the Church hierarchy in Siena was still warring with the Comune with scathing comments which they blatantly published in *La Nazione*: '. . . the village of Montalcino is all but dead.'

Montalcino has been well served by Mayors who saw further than the problems of the moment, men who had vision – who were willing to fight – and, thanks to the left, Montalcino is an unblemished jewel. 'Now they chastise me,' Ilio resignedly explains, but a wry smile creeps across his face. Everything is reversed and they come up to him and say, 'Si, Ilio, our village is beautiful, we have no factories to billow out fumes and our air is pure, we are proud of our agriculture, our heritage is preserved and the stupendous views are still here. But, Ilio, look what you have done. The houses are so dear we can hardly afford to buy them for our children. And the wine, what about the wine, Ilio? It is so expensive!' But they thank him because he devoted his life to the future.

When this small but striking man raises his voice and begins to enlarge on a line of thought, or some plan for the future, punching the air with a finger and bellowing across the closed-in piazza, it is always going to be something that should be heard, because Ilio has not finished his campaign. 'Montalcino,' he declares, 'is only using its resources to twenty-five per cent of their capacity. We have twelve thousand hectares of bosco where forty-two species of birds and seventeen species of mammals live, but we are not looking after it and we are not using it properly. Hidden in our bosco is the still-standing ruins of a church of the Longobard era, sixth century. That church, called Sammichele, is part of our culture, but nobody sees it except a few nature-lovers, because we have not got signed paths and we do not help people

354

find it. We have fifteen hundred hectares of cleared land which should be planted with flowers so our bee-keeping can escalate, but our flowers are finished in the first week of August and the bees stop travelling. If we plant flowers which bloom later, the bees will travel longer . . . and olive trees, we have got to plant more . . . and we have the micro-climate for truffles, but . . . and our Brunello-growers, they are not taking the initiative. Why haven't we set up a Brunello Museum or a Wine Library? This wine is a *creation*, not an accident. People want to learn about it. Why isn't there a film about creating and making Brunello? This wine is part of our culture . . . why don't the Comune and Consorzio protect it? Why? Why? Why?'

Ilio Raffaelli is on the street every day, as reliable as the clock-tower bells he passes down Via Mazzini, usually with two or three friends. Sometimes I see him with Mario the sweeper and Enzo the winemaker. They walk slowly, heads bowed, Ilio with a folded *Repubblica* under his arm, Mario with hands in his pockets, and Enzo with arms crossed pensively across his chest. Pausing occasionally whilst one of them espouses some crucial point, they reach Bar Prato and turn in unison, three abreast, and return slowly to the piazza. Time after time, back and forth; a prophet, a sweeper and a winemaker. If it is raining, they passeggiata back and forth across the closed-in cappellone. It is only thirty-two steps but, still in line, they turn in unison, forming two ranks if there are more than four, without missing a beat. What do they talk about? Probably the past, perhaps the present, but most assuredly the future, because each of them is, in his own way, vitally concerned with what is yet to come in Montalcino.

When the weather is cold, Ilio, who is a neat man, will be wearing his fawn raincoat and a small black beret. In summer he is more relaxed, but generally dresses with a jacket hanging across his shoulders, as if expecting to be called to business at any moment. His eyes are sharp, but he is never intrusive; ready with an opinion but preferring to wait until asked, which, in Cafe Fiaschetteria, he frequently is. He carries the *Repubblica* under his arm and usually a thick book has wrapped inside the folds of the paper. I am always trying to get a look at this book, to see if it is the same one every day, because I have never seen it unwrapped.

Books are something of a passion with Ilio, who has written several, including one titled *Creativita Populare Montalcinese*, a volume recording the derivation of Italian words and phrases the Montalcinesi adopted. Raffaelli is not only a prophet but also a reader and writer of great distinction, which makes me wish I could understand him better. But he is determined to preserve the lingua of Montalcino, which he has documented, and he uses expressions and dialect difficult for me to decipher. Strangely, I have never heard him addressed as 'Dottore', or 'Professore', which is the respectful way to address someone who has attained prominence and served the community. He is 'Ilio', or just 'Raffaelli'; but then again, considering his philosophy and his life's work, he probably prefers it that way. A prophet, a sweeper and a winemaker. The heart and soul of Montalcino.

CHAPTER FIFTEEN

White Canyons in the Sky

Casting his eyes towards Mount Amiata and then upwards to Montalcino, Primo's frown deepens; he does not like the look of this at all. Dark shadows sail way up high, not close enough to worry about, but for days the sky has looked troubled and, more than that, it is the air, the atmosphere, a glassy look around the hills which tells him something is brewing. Towards Siena the horizon is clear, nothing happening in that direction, nor the east, where Montepulciano sits atop its mountain bathed in sunshine – not the bright sun of summer, though; the mountain is glowing with a false halo.

Primo heard tractors last night. Farmers were working in the dark, harvesting the last of the animal fodder, as they had read the signs just as he does. This morning he watches uneasily as trucks load bales of hay, the men working fast to transport the feed north. At his feet, black ants scurry over rocky mountains and vanish into the earth; they agree with him that something is coming. He strolls along the nearest row of vines where clusters of bulging purple grapes hang beneath the foliage. The leaves are curiously still, with not a whiff of wind to rustle even one leaf from its rigid position along the row. He thinks back to his last meeting with the enologist, when they talked about the long-range weather forecast. 'Do not expect any severe weather until October,' they had been told, but summer storms are impossible to predict, fierce and often ruthless.

He glances again towards Mount Amiata, letting thoughts run through his mind, praying the mountain will keep its pact with nature to protect Montalcino slopes from sudden downpours and, scarcely daring to even let the thought filter through his mind, ruinous hailstorms, which can rip through Tuscany in late summer. 'Not now,' he prays silently. 'I hope I am reading it wrongly. Maybe it will come to nothing, pass us by. Anyway, the enologist is here. We must reduce the crop, eliminate clusters.'

Since vibrant growth burst along the rows in spring, the growers have been watching nature work. By June, the two green buds on the crown of the root stock, the ones from which the whole crop grows, had stretched along the rows and the vines became lush with greenery, wanting to spread everywhere. Primo was in the vineyard every day, securing the unstoppable tendrils, training them along the wire. One morning, as if in secret tryst, thousands of pinhead clusters burst from skinny stems, the first tiny balls already forming the shape of the cluster to come. He knew there were too many clusters, as they emerged like extra-terrestrial life in a science-fiction movie. Where one morning barely bulbous pods sat on the end of spiralling stems, the next morning fingers of wiry green had unwrapped the bulbs, which exploded into a thousand pinheads. Primo drove the tractor carefully through the rows, churning up and aerating the soil, cutting down weeds that stubbornly tried to steal nutrients. He was careful not to damage the clusters. They must hang free and clear, fed with goodness through long veins that suck energy and life from the two buds which spurted growth last April.

Through summer the growth has been magnificent, with hot sunny days the growers dream of. Summer storms threatened, but turned to overnight showers which wet the ground, nothing more, enough to refresh the vines as the sun poured relentlessly down and the fruit grew and grew. Primo is in the vineyard daily, securing, watching, nurturing the clusters through critical growth. He cannot leave for even a day, because a fungus could attack one plant, and if that happens it will travel through the vineyard like a plague and could destroy his crop. There is still the danger of insect infestation, which means he walks the rows, day after day, inspecting stems, turning leaves, gently lifting powdery bunches to make sure no parasite attaches itself to a vine. The date beyond which it is forbidden for growers to spray copper sulphate on the vines has expired, and now it is just Primo and nature; science is not permitted to interfere from here on in. Copper sulphate spraying is not always necessary, but failure to adhere to the limitation date bears heavy consequences, including possible confiscation of the crop. Growers are eagle-eyed as the date slips by, hoping they have been sufficiently vigilant, trusting their decision not to spray was right and that the vines are fungus free, but now the vine is on its own. Anxiously, Primo watches.

The closer to harvest we are, the less fruit is left on the vine. Foliage is dense, but clusters are sparse because a ruthless massacre takes place, severe enough to make you wonder if there will be sufficient grapes left to harvest. The enologist and Primo are at work, walking along the rows. 'Buoni, buoni,' the enologist softly intones, nodding. Then, 'Taglia, taglia, cut, cut,' as he points to a bunch of juicy grapes, lifts it with his hand and Primo snips the stem with his clippers, letting the bunch fall to the ground, discarded. In an hour the ground is littered with rejected clusters which shrivel and deflate. Just as severe pruning back to two spring buds along the crown restricted the early growth of the vine, this morning's work is the final step which ensures Primo can contain his yield, because the Consorzio regulations strictly stipulate the yield to a maximum of eighty quintale per hectare. Many growers harvest below that weight, striving only for optimum grapes with which to make Brunello.

Primo and the enologist lift the bunches tenderly, studying the rapid growth in the last week, testing sugar content, acidity, looking for clusters which are swelling and ripening uniformly. If the grapes closest to the dangling tip are puny, slow to mature, and those at the stem of the bunch fat and juicy, it is a cluster they can do without, because the ripening is too uneven. Clusters which grow uniformly, grapes swelling together and the tip of the bunch only days behind the stem, they know these will be optimum grapes, because each milligram of weight will release the highest quality juice.

As they work they hear gunfire. Looking round in unison, they know someone is in trouble with wild boar, another hurdle the grower must overcome in these last weeks and the reason Primo has been up before dawn skirting the vineyard, looking for signs of broken undergrowth, tell-tale hoofprints or droppings. If a wild boar wanders overnight into the vineyard, now that the fruit is on the verge of ripeness, he can destroy hundreds of clusters before his hunger abates.

Primo has 5.6 hectares planted for Brunello; over at Castello Banfi, with 140 hectares, the exacting work is magnified. Teams of workers comb the hills through this crucial cycle, searching for any sign which might endanger this multi-million-dollar crop. The work is the same for everybody, one-hectare growers like Giancarlo Gorelli, a few hectares like Livio Sassetti, Primo, and Maria Grazia and Giacomo, the tens of hectares of Colombini and the largest grower, Banfi. There has been no time since the growth cycle began to sit back and watch the vines come into fruit from the serenity of a Tuscan farmhouse, nor the loggia of a country villa, or even a walled medieval castle. Harvest is only weeks away. There is tension in the air; so much rests on nature, and on man. Will the storms stay away? Will the parasites go elsewhere? Is the quality high? Will it rain and endanger the harvest? Has nature brought them this far only to deal them a dreadful hand?

Thirty more days to wait. Primo glances anxiously up at the sky. Something is brewing . . . he does not like the look of this at all.

Andrea, relaxing out of his policeman's uniform, is listening attentively at Ristorante Il Moro, where half a dozen of us are dining on the narrow terrace which opens from the rear of the restaurant and looks out towards the stunning Orcia Valley. Tonight a Montalcinese is regaling a table of six with a scandalous story to which his friends keep saying, 'Non ci credo, I don't believe it, it cannot be true.' No matter, Luigi and I, Andrea and everybody else dining on Franca's pasta with zucchini sauce are eavesdropping on this entertaining story about carabinieri, who are respected in the community, if somewhat aloof from village police.

Immaculately turned out in black uniforms with a thin red stripe down their trouser legs, carabinieri are invested with the highest level of authority in Italy, seemingly, at times, beyond the reach of lawful statutes of justice. They go about their duties with tangible imperturbability, an unspoken potent air which lesser levels of law enforcement like the provincial or village police cannot hope to emulate. When polizia have one up on carabinieri, it is a moment to discreetly savour. We have discovered over the years that carabinieri, despite being the butt of endless jokes, are extraordinarily effective in solving baffling crimes, particularly terrorist- and mafia-related, or fraudulent, or simmering family vendettas, straight-out evil murders. Admittedly, tactics permitted, employed, and overlooked would leave the makers of civil codes in other countries turning in their graves, so to speak, but in Italy it seems the end justifies the means. It is prudent not to tangle in any way, positive or negative, defensive or offensive, with powerful carabinieri. But is the story we are hearing tonight true?

Complaints had been directed to the police for a couple of weeks about cannons fired to scare away hungry birds and foraging wild boar which wander into vineyards looking for a tasty breakfast. Like everything in Italy which comes within the attention of rubber-stamp authority, the use of these cannons, which are small, wheel-mounted weapons, and the times at which they may be fired, are subject to bureaucratic control. Everything is regulated, even if responsible staff and irresponsible citizens then each spend inordinate amounts of time designing plots to circumvent these regulations. Andrea admits he knows a particular cannon has been firing at the wrong times, disturbing more than birds and boar, but that is all he acknowledges to be true. It seems heated complaints were filed with the carabinieri but, instead of passing the information to the local police, which is the sensible practice with relatively minor complaints, the carabinieri decided to act with their own wide-ranging power.

This morning, two handsome young officers in immaculately pressed uniforms drove in their blue Alfa Romeo to a small vineyard on the south-western edge of the Brunello zone to investigate. The owner is a small grower. He does not come into Montalcino often, except for Consorzio meetings, and although we know his wines, we do not know him. When the officers arrived at the vineyard the grower was absent in Siena, but his wife, wisely complying with their request, told them where they would find the offending cannon. Deciding the right and just course of action was to confiscate the weapon, the young officers loaded it into the back seat of their Alfa Romeo – not without some difficulty – and were driving out of the property just as the grower arrived home. Each car pulled off the dirt track to the grass beside the vines and the aloof carabinieri casually wound down a window, informing the grower his cannon had been confiscated, and that it was now a matter of State.

Furious at losing his cannon, the grower knew he had no hope of seeing it again, because every Italian is only too aware from unfortunate experience that once something becomes a matter of State, you might just as well forget it and cut your losses. Seemingly outraged, he jumped out of his car, arms gesticulating wildly, pleading, but the righteous carabinieri refused to listen and, waving him away, accelerated out of the vineyard. He looked at his watch. 'Miseria!' It was two minutes to mezzogiorno, but he was not thinking about his lunch, he was waiting.

As the twelve chimes of the midday bell rang out across the valley, the Alfa Romeo was still in sight, rounding the curves which would take the carabinieri and his costly cannon to the police station. He knew he would never see it again. The hundred gongs of mezzogiorno began and his fears became reality. The reverberation of the firing cannon exploding inside the Alfa Romeo echoed around the hills and the quaking car careered dangerously about the road. Two quivering officers clutched their heads, deafened by the thunderous noise. The back seat was in tatters, the rear window blown to pieces, glass everywhere, and two crimson faces switched between fury and mortification. The grower retreated inside to his wife and pranzo.

'I tried to tell them,' he argued at carabinieri headquarters later, 'but they refused to listen! I pleaded with them to give me five minutes with my loaded cannon to dismantle the automatic timer.' Red-faced carabinieri will now have to account for one severely damaged Alfa Romeo and two sooty uniforms – not to mention a dent in their mythical egos.

Tonight we are falling about laughing, lapping up the self-destructive story even if we are not absolutely positive it is true. Andrea is sitting quietly, not saying a word as he launches into grilled ribs and pork sausages. Perhaps it is not true; perhaps these stories circulate in wine villages as tension rises and harvest approaches. I think I'll ask Primo tomorrow, market day, although I am not sure that he will be in the piazza when harvest is so close and there is so much work going on in the vineyard.

This morning I detect an air of panic. People are shouting over the top of one another and when Italians do that I lose track of conversation, because the words stream out like machine-gun fire. But something is definitely going on; an atmosphere of outrage fills the piazza. Beneath the cappellone, dozens of men stand about, more than usual for a market-day morning. By 11.30 the men are usually drifting up to the market. I am curious to know why everybody is milling here. Spying Primo in a huddle of men, I pass close by, but he has no time for his usual affectionate kiss and handshake. He does not even see me, because he is engrossed in conversation with an enologist and two or three growers. Judging from the numbers, it seems there must be an extraordinary meeting of Consorzio members. My interrogation of Primo about the canon story will have to wait. But why do they seem so agitated?

Luigi will be waiting for me at Bar Mariuccia, but with Primo out of bounds and a palpable sense of the dramatic in the air, I decide to sit at Fiaschetteria and ask Negus to make me a caffè macchiato. Even he keeps glancing up at the swelling numbers. What is he watching for, I wonder? He lays my coffee down and vanishes inside before I can question him. Nobody has time to talk this morning.

The agitated groups begin to move across the piazza and, as I suspect, disappear through the wooden doors of Palazzo Comunale in which the Consorzio has its headquarters. A moment later Mayor Mauro strides into the piazza with the Vice-Mayor right beside him, both weighed down with satchels, obviously stuffed with documenti importanti. Grim-faced, purposefully acknowledging no one, they too vanish through the doors of Palazzo Comunale. Crikey! Three carabinieri streak down the slope and follow them in, one adorned with helpings of scrambled gold braid around his shoulders and cap. This theatrical performance means something dramatic is up! Surely this cannot be the result of the exploding cannon?

When anything happens to implicate Brunello, the growers, or the vineyards, it is big, really big, and can often have catastrophic repercussions. I am not even sure the cannon story is true, because Andrea gave nothing away, but by the looks of things this morning it *is* true and the carabinieri are furious with the damaged Alfa Romeo and a couple of dented egos. Mayor Mauro looked particularly fearsome, although he always tends to look bookish and unapproachable. Summer rumours seem to be rife in Montalcino right now. I heard the amazing news that Mayor Mauro is not standing for a third term, and we are to have a new Sindaco. Rumour has it that young Massimo Ferretti, the Vice-Mayor, has received the sanction of the parties of the left and will step into Mauro's shoes. In fact, we have been told it is a cut and dried debate, no real need for an election. If young, stylish, non-smoking, sharp-eyed, short-haired Massimo has the sanction of the left, we can be sure he will be our next Mayor.

I will miss bespectacled Mauro, his unwieldy hair and wiry beard, not to mention my entertaining moments at Fiaschetteria when he lights his pipe and puffs clouds of smoke towards would-be questioners. Perhaps two terms as Mayor, negotiating with the growers and orchestrating village life, are enough for him. The year has been punctuated with headline-breaking incidents, because rules governing planting sangiovese grosso, the clone of sangiovese which produces Brunello, are strictly enforced by the Consorzio and Comune. A grower cannot just plant more vines in order to produce more Brunello. Even if he managed to purchase land within the strictly designated zone for Brunello production, and even if he planted the whole vineyard with sangiovese grosso, the proportion of his vineyard which produces Brunello may be only one hectare in ten. The family of one of Montalcino's butchers has been offering an olive farm for sale. It sits directly below the walls, faces south-east, is within the Brunello boundaries and comes ready for habitation, with a characteristic Tuscan farmhouse surrounded by several hectares of productive olive trees. But even if you could afford the millions of lire sought for the olive farm, even if, heaven forbid, you tore out the olive trees and planted vines, perhaps only 10 per cent of your total vineyard will be sanctioned for Brunello.

Whatever is up this morning, knotty grower problems or reprisals for exploding cannons, the forbidding wooden doors of Palazzo Comunale are tightly closed. Mayor Mauro, incumbent Mayor Massimo, Consorzio growers and carabinieri are locked in battle.

By the time I reach Mariuccia, the bar is packed. Vera's forehead creases as she concentrates on how many caffè, how many rosso, how many orzo she has on order and how many people are lined up waiting to pay. Catching her eye, I make a sign to the side of my forehead, meaning: 'Vera, what is all this crowd about?' She lifts her eyes and heaves her shoulders. Luigi is in conference with half a dozen people, among them Luciano from Grappolo, Vasco and his best friend Giancarlo, and Andrea.

Luigi sees me. 'Ciao! Did you hear what has happened?' Not wanting to appear uninformed, I nonchalantly reply, 'Oh yes, it's true, I watched everyone going into Palazzo Comunale.' He looks taken aback, as if he should be telling the story, so I add, 'Well, we heard about the cannon at Il Moro last night, so I put two and two together.'

Everyone in the group is looking blankly at me. 'No, no, no! That's not why everyone is in Palazzo Comunale!' exclaims Luigi. 'Did you see the carabinieri Marshall go in? And Mauro and Massimo? The enologists and all the growers? Isabella, it's nothing to do with the cannon, although it did explode inside the Alfa Romeo. This morning something disastrous has been discovered. Somebody has sabotaged two rows of priceless Brunello vines, sawed through the trunks and, because of the thick summer foliage, nobody noticed until the vines began to wither and collapse. The grapes are ruined!'

Sabotage Brunello? This is unheard of. Who would do such a

thing? My eyes and mouth are open to the maximum as Luigi
rushes on: 'The culprit hacked through peach and plum trees too,
but nobody cares about that. Carabinieri have been called in to
investigate. The news will be plastered on the front page of *La
Nazione* tomorrow – the place is buzzing with journalists planning headlines like: *Brunello savagely cut down!*'

The huddle turn towards each other. I am still speechless and
Luigi looks up again. 'Did you come through Piazza Garibaldi?'
he asks. 'You will not believe this. Colour photographs of the
sawn-off drooping vines and hacked trees are stapled to the walls
of the shops around the piazza.'

Who is responsible, and why? Heads nod and tongues wag all
day, but no names are mentioned, nobody is talking. I wonder if
the clever crime-solving carabinieri will be able to cut the
mustard on this one. Will we find out who the culprit is? Is this
the silent hand of a village vendetta viciously played a few weeks
before harvest? Is harvest-time always this sensational?

Italians become another race entirely in August. As ferragosto, a
sacred public holiday on the fifteenth, approaches, they put aside
any sense of normality, not expecting anything in August to be the
same as it was in July. Nor will it be until September, including
themselves. In the weeks before and after ferragosto, thousands of
Italians take their annual holidays and the country grinds to a
standstill.

Italy, and Italians, go slightly mad. The industrial plants close
down and factory workers set off for il mare in search of the sun.
Milan becomes a steamy ghost town, the relentless sun reflects
stifling heat up from flintstones, made worse by empty rattling
trams and vacant-eyed shop assistants. In Rome, restaurants and
boutiques pull the shutters for quindici giorni – fifteen days seems
to be the acceptable length of a seaside holiday. The city is

deserted except for skimpily-clad, perspiring tourists who dangle feet into Bernini fountains or seek cool refuge inside gloomy churches where they can barely read their guide books. They cannot understand why half the city is closed down in what is, to them, the height of the season.

Those Italians forced to stay in the cities are irritable and cranky, annoyed they too are not posing half-naked beside a thousand blue and white striped umbrellas on a strip of gritty sand at the seaside. To even the score, they blithely double the price of a half-melted gelato or tepid lemon soda, responding sourly to everyday questions and not caring one iota in which direction they wave their arm, so long as this irritating tourist goes away. Montalcino, too, is bitten by the crazy ferragosto bug. Many locals head for Isola di Elba or visit the Ligurian coast, although, when sweltering heat chokes the cities, Montalcino's altitude ensures moderate temperatures by comparison.

In the first half of August Luigi became curious when he received no mail for a week, but let this abnormality slip by for ten days, keeping an eye out for Maurizio, the postman, who crams the mail into his leather shoulder satchel and marches up and down steep hills every morning, but he did not see him. 'Ercole,' he casually asked, 'have you received any mail lately?' Ercole raised his eyebrows and for several seconds looked back at Luigi, then leaned forward with his two hands forming his questioning praying gesture. 'Caro Luigi, it is nearly the fifteenth – ferragosto. Maurizio is at il mare for two weeks. There will be no normal mail delivery until he returns.' While Maurizio works on his suntan, the mail piles up. Too bad if you are awaiting car registration or, worse, a pay cheque. The post stops for holidays around ferragosto.

The magical fifteenth is almost here and this morning Maria and her sister Lucilla tooted and pulled the car to the side of the road when they saw me walking round the walls. 'We are leaving for Mount Amiata in half an hour, taking the whites,' they call through the wound-down window. 'Why don't you bring yours and come with us?'

Everybody, including me, because I learned about it last summer, knows that in August you pile into the car all your bedsheets, pillow cases and towels and drive to Mount Amiata, where you wash the whites in crystal-clear spring water gushing from the mountain. Nothing, it seems, washes whiter than ferragosto spring water at Mount Amiata, not even your favourite bleach-loaded washing powder. Last year we hung acres of wet linen in trees and laid them on river boulders to dry. I declined their invitation, because we will be lunching with Pianello today.

Ercole has reminded us every day this week that if it rains before the fifteenth, we can forget the rest of summer – that will be it. Summer will finish abruptly, the temperature will drop and will not climb again. But I see no sign of rain today; the sky is cerulean. Down here along the walls, the aroma filling the air is from pots of basil and the stemmy smell of sun-drenched tomato plants sagging on bamboo wigwams. The fruit is full, overripe and begging to be picked, but no matter how many times we launch into mozzarella, basil and tomatoes, another armful, aromatic stems intact, turns up at the door. A glut of tomatoes means we eat them with everything, even on their own, biting into them all day like apples. Wooden boards lie along the tops of walls, where hot sunny tomatoes shrivel, curl and dry. A little peperoncino is sprinkled over them, but I do not understand why birds don't dive and peck, because surely the gauze covering doesn't trick them? Perhaps there are so many in the gardens that the birds are not hungry for more tomato. Summer peaches and plums are gone from the trees, but the figs are ripening, growing fatter, drooping over fences. I would rather not know about the buzzing insects trying to do their work; summer figs are better savoured but not closely considered. By midday on this soporific summer's day we are driving along the bumpy track between vines under the shadow of an old farmhouse. We are not at the vineyard to inspect the fruit, nor to talk about the grapes, which hang in powdery purple clusters, nor about the approaching harvest. We are here to talk about archery.

As each car arrives, we unload plates and glasses, table cloths and cutlery, a demijohn of wine and folding chairs. Even a coffee machine and all the paraphernalia to make the essential espresso sits on a tree stump. Everybody lends a hand to set up tables and chairs for today's traditional Pianello lunch at the practice range, to support our archers who have been coming here week after week since February.

'Who's coming below?' calls Carlo, and three or four people, including Luigi and me, join him as he steps into the under-growth and vanishes down the side of the hill. We pick and weave our way through brambles down the winding path to the sandy practice range, where our archers are taking turns firing arrows into the target board forty metres away, practising for the approaching tournaments.

Maria-Teresa and Fabio unroll white paper which becomes the table cloths then set the tables for pranzo for forty people. The timing has to be just right, because Fiorella will ring on the mobile phone to check everything is ready before she and head cook Luciana pack two cars with steaming food and drive out to the range. Thankfully, they will be able to reach the range in a few minutes because, after more than six frustrating months of oscillating work, repairs to the collapsed road have finally been completed. The road around the fortress re-opened this week. The cumbersome traffic-light system Andrea installed is gone, and so is the grassy verge round the football field, which was quickly disfigured with ugly deep ruts and ditches as tyres relentlessly pounded it since winter. Fortuitously, this is not a cause for dismay at the campo sportivo, because the Mayor's pledge to assist with funds to re-sow the ground has materialised. The perimeter fences have been moved back a few metres so that our squad home-ground accords with Federation requirements, because our team plays in the higher league next season. A sturdy bulwark has been constructed in the valley where the wall collapsed below the undisturbed Medici crest. Faced with new stone which is already beginning to fade, soon it will not be noticeable.

Fiorella zips around the walls confident the pasta will still be hot, and by the time she and Luciana drive into the clearing everyone is seated and chattering about the tournament which precedes the Sagra. The Apertura della Cacce Tournament for the opening of the hunting season is not as well-known as the Sagra but stirs great emotion, because it focuses on the territory of each quarter, raising loyal territorial passion. Being the first tournament of the year, if Pianello performs well at Apertura, it augurs well for the autumn Sagra.

Lunch is on the tables – predictably, basil, tomatoes and mozzarella cheese followed by chilled pappa al pomodoro, tomato soup, and pasta dressed with tomato and basil sauce. Lunch is accompanied by a modest glass of rosso and we are all drowsy because, even though a breeze is wafting, it is uncomfortably hot. Tables hug the shade and we lounge lazily. Hearing raised voices, everyone straightens and turns towards Dottore Luciano, who is trying to calm four or five youngsters. Catching snippets of an agitated exchange, I gather startling news has rippled through Montalcino and our young people are complaining bitterly because this morning accusing stares greeted them from opposing quartieri members across the piazza.

372

'We only heard the rumour yesterday,' says a despairing voice. 'We were the last to hear – everyone else seems to have heard about it before us. It's just not on – they can't do it! It's breaking with tradition, Dottore, outside the accepted rules.' Another voice rises: 'There are only a few more weeks, not many practice days till the Sagra. We don't need this adding to the tension. Everybody's getting angry.'

Rules govern the nomination of archers for tournaments and, although each quarter may have several archers practising at any one time, only three are nominated to represent each quarter in the tournaments. Dottore Luciano makes the decision who the three Pianello archers will be, and a ballot on the day of the tournament randomly selects the two who will actually fire the arrows. The story, which had spread in half a day, is that Travaglio is breaking with tradition. In an astonishing move beyond the accepted rules, they are said to be hiring an outside professional archer to shoot at the Sagra.

'Diamine!' A shrill female voice this time. 'Not only is he not Montalcinese, he is not even Tuscan. I heard it is someone who has won international archery tournaments, a candidate for the Italian Olympic squad!' This is not only outside the accepted rules, it represents a dreadful break with village tradition and opens up the tournaments to all kinds of foreign influences. One of our archers becomes embroiled in the debate: 'Next they'll be bringing in external trainers and all sorts of experts in the wider field of archery. The whole point of the Montalcino tournaments will be lost. Dottore, we have got to stop it.'

The archers are sacrificing so much, and nobody knows better than Dottore Luciano that the responsibility which rests on their shoulders is heightened when the emotional tension rises. Thinking quickly, he makes it his business to quell fears which could aggravate the tension.

'Calm down, let's just think about this for a moment,' he tells everyone. 'Why would Travaglio do that? Their President knows, just the same as Maurelia, that we must maintain quartieri archers because if we don't, if we let it go, the Sagra will be lost. Montalcino will lose its identity, because we would be like any other place in the world, we would become anonymous, generic. No! I don't believe this rumour and I don't think you should either. Let's wait and see what happens. Have you listened to what Travaglio are saying about this?'

'That's the problem,' moans one of the girls. 'They are blaming us. They think Pianello started the rumour, which they deny, but you know Travaglio, they play a closed hand and we are not so sure it isn't true. Anyway, Dottore, there are rules, written and unwritten, which must be observed.'

'Well, common sense tells me we should drop this rumour right now,' he says firmly. 'Carlo and Pierluigi won the Sagra for Travaglio last year, and they are fine archers, proud of their skills and heritage. The Ilcinesi defended this hill with bows and arrows, and all the quarters uphold the tradition which we will hand down to the children.' Seeing many doubtful faces, he adds: 'By tomorrow it will be discarded as a false rumour. Let's forget it. We have the Apertura to contest on Sunday, and the Sagra will soon be here. We need to be focused and united.'

Dottore Luciano is satisfied this rumour has not disturbed the rhythm of his archers but also knows, because it happens every year, that it is unlikely to be the only conflagration he will deal with before the Sagra. He glances at Maurelia, exchanging knowing looks, but she has purposely left the Dottore to handle this unpleasant exchange. Besides, shortly she has to make not one but two disheartening reports, quite enough for one day. Dottore Luciano has told her, but seems to have decided against telling the youngsters, that brand new, exorbitantly expensive bows had been delivered to one quarter the previous week, and he has heard from his friend in the archery shop in Perugia that other archers had ordered sets of world-class competition arrows. A set of five arrows like that is a several hundred thousand lire investment for the quartiere, which hopes for a technical advantage.

Dottore Luciano knows the preparation of the archers, even their technical skill and physical fitness, is secondary to their mental readiness, which is paramount and can win a tournament. All this is far more significant than the acquisition of sensational bows and arrows. His selection of archers to represent Pianello must be based on which archers are reaching the required level of mental training, concentrated, focused, because if an archer is not mentally ready to enter the campo, he will not be able to maintain the exacting discipline. He will lose concentration and will not make it to the end of each round.

Dottore Luciano glances at Alessandro, Gabriele, Davide and Massimo, reassuring himself they have dismissed any rumours of unfair play by Travaglio, and begins to think about who will shoot in the Apertura on Sunday. He decides Massimo is still on the way up, so he will not be selected because the last few weeks before the Sagra are vital for him. Massimo will continue his rigid training towards the autumn tournament.

'Allora . . .' Maurelia is on her feet, launching into the first of her reports. 'I did not want to call a special meeting in the sede this close to ferragosto, but we have to talk about some not so good things today.' Her serious tone makes us all sit up and listen, because Maurelia always addresses us enthusiastically, putting a happy complexion on everything. Today she sounds unusually anxious. 'I am sorry not to have given you this news before, but we needed to wait for three quotes for the repairs to the roof of San Pietro and that has taken practically all summer. Comunque, in any event, today I will tell you the cost, because in two weeks we have to give our answer to the Diocese.' She looks along the row of alert faces, wishing she did not have to give us this news. Then, taking a deep breath: 'From three quotes, two companies have advised that the whole roof of San Pietro will have to be replaced, and their quotes, almost identical, indicate it will cost close to cento milioni, a hundred million lire.'

The sharp gasps and astonished looks are exactly what she dreads. 'Oh Madre di Dio!' comes a faint response as mouths fall open in shock. 'You have got to be joking, Maurelia. It's a joke.' But it is not a joke. The gathering is suddenly wildly vocal, everyone is yelling, expressive gestures going back and forth, with plenty of Madonnas and Santa Benedettas and a few curses scorching the air. 'Well, that is the end of it, we will never be able to own our own sede . . . It's hopeless – we cannot even think of going into that much debt. We could never raise the money . . . No wonder the Diocese was so generous, they probably knew all along . . . Well, the roof will just have to fall in.' Maurelia, hating negativity, tries to lift the atmosphere but cannot be heard above the din, so takes her seat for a few minutes and listens to the anguished cries. As soon as there is a lull, she rises again.

'Pero, the third quote offers a ray of hope and he is coming back again. He thinks maybe he can save part of the old roof.' This ray of hope isn't having much impact, but Maurelia brightens, confidently telling us she wants us all at the sede on Friday after Apertura. 'And it is particularly important you youngsters contact the others at university and college. I need everyone home next weekend, because we will be discussing the future and taking a final vote on buying San Pietro.' Incredulous looks pass up and down the tables, as well as a few negative comments. On the inside Maurelia is not feeling quite so confident, but she refuses to give in and finishes with some tantalising words which raise a few eyebrows, as much as to say: 'Is this supposed to be a rabbit in the hat trick, Maurelia?'

'Allora, everybody must be at the meeting because – I cannot mention any names – one of our members has diligently searched for an answer to this question. This person was at our last meeting and has come up with an idea, a new idea. I don't yet know myself what it is, but we cannot give up hope.'

Maurelia sits down for ten minutes whilst fruit is served – refreshing water-melon slices. Having got through the report of the prohibitive cost of reroofing San Pietro, she still has a most unsavoury announcement to make. This will be controversial and, although not as challenging as the San Pietro riddle, she knows there is going to be an emotional spillover. She has to tell us about the politely framed changes the Mayor and Comune have proposed, and which they want implemented for the autumn Sagra.

The first change is abysmal, but whilst everyone is devastated, we know it is unreasonable to argue with the facts. This year the feasting is *not* to take place inside the fortress keep. The danger of a fire from open coal braziers or, even worse, a gas-bottle explosion, is one the Comune is not prepared to entertain, because the repercussions would be inconceivable for Montalcino. The Mayor has decided the few people in the fortress who drink too much wine are impossible to control. The Comune has sought an opinion and is not prepared to enter into any additional insurance to protect the citizens of Montalcino from possible disasters. 'Staging the Sagra,' said the Mayor, 'is the responsibility of the quartieri, but safety is a Comunal liability.'

'So where are we going to have it?' everyone wants to know.

'That still has to be worked out,' Maurelia replies awkwardly, then moves on to suggestion number two. This is that quarters must take responsibility for visitors by manning not only the two approach roads, but each of the other gates leading down the valleys along dirt tracks. The suggestion is for two quartiere representatives to guard all gates, charging an entry fee of L 10,000 to any visitors who want to come inside the walls to the Sagra.

'How on earth,' outraged voices rise together, 'are we going to differentiate between locals and visitors? This gets crazier as we go along. We don't know everyone who lives within twenty kilometres. Anyway, how is that going to control the people who come not for the Sagra, but just to drink wine?'

'On the contrary, the over-consumption of wine is the whole point of the suggestion,' sighs Maurelia, pressing on. 'Wine is to be sold only *outside* the walls, down in the car park, not in the village itself.'

'What!' A chorus of piercing wails meet her. 'Che sciffo, everything will be ruined!'

The reasoning behind this plan is that if visitors really want to come to the Sagra to see the pageant and archery tournament, they will be willing to pay L 10,000, which will be collected at the gates and applied towards staging the event and the massive clean-up of the village afterwards. On the other hand, people who are not genuinely interested in the Sagra, but only come to drink wine, will stay outside the walls down in the car park. They will not have to pay L 10,000 and, because they won't be in the village, they will not disturb residents.

'But there are only a few of them,' complains Francesco. 'It's unfair – everyone is penalised because of a few selfish people. Selling wine is one of our most profitable fund-raisers. How many people are going to walk down to the car park, knowing that is where the drinkers are, just to buy a glass of wine? And anyway, Maurelia, what's to stop the drinkers staying down there for hours on end, then coming up to the village *after* the tournament? Surely the Comune realises that's really when they cause trouble, after the tournament is finished? This does not make any sense, and we will suffer because we won't be able to raise enough money to keep our quartiere going through next year. This is going to destroy the Sagra!'

The arguments continue. Heated debate of these mammoth problems certainly takes the emphasis away from the financial riddle of buying San Pietro, and the Travaglio rumour pales to insignificance. The question of which archers will shoot in the tournaments is becoming academic.

Maurelia is feeling just as confused as everybody else, but with her final words, an honest response to Michele's direct question, she burdens us with the enormity of our problems. 'It is only a matter of weeks until the Sagra, and I am sorry to say that if all these things cannot be sorted out in time . . . yes, it is possible the Sagra and tournament will be cancelled.' In the agonised silence which descends, Massimo's prophetic words last February rush into my mind. 'If we let it go it will all be lost, we will never get it back. We will lose our ancient skills.' This is unthinkable.

Dottore Luciano is thoughtfully watching the archers. He did not participate in the anguished debate about San Pietro, nor offer his thoughts about the problems which have to be solved before the Sagra. He knows this threat of cancellation will interfere with the training of his archers and damage their concentration, relegating the ridiculous rumour about Travaglio to a piddling hiccup. The archers have been training since February, giving up their time and missing their families, working consistently to reach the level of fitness which great archery demands, physically and mentally. All this talk of raising money and Comune regulations is counter-productive. He feels it is time the four quarters began working co-operatively, solving problems together, like they used to.

The hunters will not go out to the woods for some weeks yet, because the season does not officially begin until late autumn, but Apertura delle Cacce, the opening of the hunt festival, is symbolic of the imminent bountiful season. The Apertura pageant meanders through each quarter and members are able to participate in festivities, whereas at the Sagra those not in the pageant can only close the food stands for an hour and race to the campo to cheer on the archers. The feasting inside the fortress only takes place on the day of the Sagra, not Apertura, so there is less work and quartieri do not have to transport kitchens to the fortress and man the stands all day. Apertura celebrations include an eve-of-tournament dinner in the heart of Pianello, Via Moglio, to honour our archers. Saturday morning traffic is diverted and once the banditore, the village crier, has passed, tables and chairs to accommodate more than 200 people are set along Via Moglio, between the houses.

The banditore rides through Pianello on horseback, carrying the scroll of proclamation. His knaves ride behind him, then come three marching rows of drummers and two rows of trumpeters. Altogether about twenty people in a procession of horses and musicians weave through the twisting lanes with the standard of Montalcino at the front, pausing every fifty metres for a roll of drums and a rally of silver trumpets. Quartiere loyalty is electrified, and this morning I feel my neck tingling as I stand quietly, listening to the procession winding closer. The small piazzetta in front of San Pietro is free of cars and Fiorella has cloaked a table in blue and white and laid a refreshing feast for the banditore and his men. Maurelia is behind the table and a couple of dozen of us, wearing our Pianello scarves, watch the banditore and musicians in fur-trimmed medieval costume round the corner and arrive at the water fountain at the bottom of the slope in front of San Pietro. They pause and, standing in the heart of ancient Pianello, pound the drums and thrust their trumpets skywards, sounding a heraldic burst which is magnified in the confined space. The banditore reads the proclamation commanding Pianello to be at the campo tomorrow for the Apertura delle Cacce tournament. The procession marches for three hours through the quartieri, filling the village with the sounds of revelling trumpets and beating drums, a stirring spectacle of pageantry, accompanied by the sound of horses' hooves clip-clopping over the cobbles. The proclamation is read in each quarter.

By nine o'clock this Saturday evening, 200 people are seated along Via Moglio below Pianello flags, iron street lamps wanly reflecting our blue and white emblems. Dottore Luciano has nominated our archers, but nobody yet knows which two archers will fire the arrows for Pianello tomorrow. Davide, Massimo, Gabriele and Alessandro are being cheered on to victory as equals. As darkness falls, the Cena di Arciere, dinner for the archers, is served by the young people. Maria-Teresa, Riccardo, Caterina, Fabio and a dozen others scurry up and down the slope beside San Pietro, to and from the sede, with pots of pasta, empty plates, trays of roast turkey and bowls of salad and fruit. At last the meal is eaten and caffè is on the table. The young take off their aprons, drape themselves in blue and white flags and split into two groups, squeezing down the sides of the long table and gathering behind our archers, who sit across from each other. Now it is time to stir some passion and begin the chanting. Riccardo's melodious voice leads his side into a vibrant chorus of the Pianello song and Fabio responds on the other side with a boisterous stornello, a singing insult, about what Pianello will do to the opposition tomorrow. I watch, fascinated by their fervour, as their voices echo from the walls. They harmonise so beautifully and voices rise vehemently, becoming boisterous.

The elders smile and look appropriately dismayed at the dreadful curses being cast on the opposition. Most of them finish with Travaglio and Borghetto being thumped, or worse, having their bones broken, and a provocative claim that other archers are scared to death and probably will not even turn up to face the might of Pianello! The elders look offended, but in their eyes I detect a kind of treasured remembrance, a pride to have passed to the younger ones the desire for glory and honour, not for themselves but, through our archers, only for Pianello.

The meal is over, our archers are honoured, the elders know the rest of the night is for the young. Farewells are said and we prepare for home, but I am not really going home because I am determined to find out what happens on this inflammatory night before the Apertura tournament. With energy only the young can muster, they sprint up and down the hill to the sede carting everything back inside. They fill plastic bags with rubbish, clean the tables and stack chairs against the walls, calling, 'Andiamo, andiamo, let's go or we'll be last in the piazza.'

'Come on,' booms Riccardo. 'Is everyone ready? We have work to do tonight.' I follow at a distance as they race to the piazza, and watch them take up position under the Pianello insignia on the steps of the cappellone. Now it is time for the operatic argument to start in earnest. Travaglio is already chanting at the other end of the cappellone, Borghetto is arriving down the slope beside Palazzo Comunale and Ruga will soon be crouched on the stone steps leading to their sede. At midnight I am listening transfixed. The piazza is filled with chorus after chorus of loyal chanting youngsters urging their archers on to victory and, just as fervently, heaping dastardly curses and bad omens on the opposition while claiming glory for their quartiere. Travaglio voices rise in a crescendo towards Ruga as the two quarters compete in a stinging verbal battle across the piazza. Pianello youngsters form a huddle and concoct particularly demoralising prose about the pointlessness of Borghetto archers even turning up. As soon as there is a pause, they are into it, forcing their melodic harmony to rise above the opposition and echo beneath the cappellone. With no bias in mind whatsoever, I am convinced the harmony and melodies of Pianello are the best. My heart leaps with proprietorial pride, but Borghetto youngsters are making horrible hand signals, jeering and covering their ears. It will be their turn in a minute, and they are getting ready to respond with odious stornelli of their own!

In bed at two o'clock, I can finally hear the chanting coming closer and realise the Pianello youngsters have left the piazza and are on their way back to the quartiere. I can still hear Riccardo's beautiful voice, but the volume lowers as they drop from the group one by one, reaching their homes. Demands for victory at Apertura tomorrow have been claimed.

Borghetto had absolutely no business winning Apertura, especially that way. Five decades of tournaments, the wisdom of hundreds of accumulative years of four experienced trainers, six shaken archers and the solid reasoning of a couple of thousand spectators confirm that Borghetto should never have won. They did everything wrong. You cannot win a tournament when you do everything wrong – but they did!

The first five arrows from each archer are worth one point each; fired from a distance of twenty-five metres, this is a warm-up round. But an archer from Borghetto missed the target twice – at that range! We all bellowed and jeered as Borghetto quartieranti buried crimson faces in their arms. In the second round, thirty metres, with their confidence destroyed, Borghetto floundered and missed three more arrows. The other archers had not missed one single arrow, and in that round each accurate arrow was worth two points. An embarrassing shooting disaster is one thing, but the display of dramatics from Borghetto was unheard of.

As his fifth arrow in the second round sailed past the target, hit the fortress wall and ricocheted into the bushes, a Borghetto archer did exactly what an archer must never do. He threw a tantrum and stalked angrily back up the campo towards his Captain. In amazement, we watched him slam his expensive bow to the ground in self-disgust, raise his arms and shout horrible curses back at the screaming crowd. He put his hands on his hips and glared. Everybody in the crowd responded wildly. 'Borghetto is out of it,' we screamed. 'You have lost the plot!'

I watched Marco, the Borghetto Captain, intently, but he did not move one centimetre in the direction of his exploding archer. He stood frozen, arms folded firmly across his chest, legs anchored apart, as only his shoulders rose and fell. Posing like a rock, he waited. The other archers retrieved their arrows and were poised for the third round. The wayward archer at last raised his sullen eyes towards his Captain, who did not flinch. I could not see Marco's face but I imagine a silent penetrating exchange took place. The archer turned on his heel and bolted down the campo to extract two arrows from the target. He had to borrow the missing three for the third round. From my discussions with Massimo, I knew that the archer's concentration would now be in tatters. He was not mentally fit to be on the campo and a couple of thousand people in the grandstand agreed that he would not be able to make it through the final two rounds.

As the forty-second rounds speed by, the rewards increase; three points an arrow in round three and, in the final frenzied round, four points at forty-three metres for every arrow driven into the wild boar. Arrows ripped through the air and our eyes darted from target to target, trying to see the moment the blurred missiles sank into the board. The heart-stopping tension was palpable. Archers were trying to close out the disturbing vision of Borghetto dramatics, but in the third, amazing, round only Borghetto's archers shot five perfect arrows each. Surely they could not catch up!

Five arrows left to shoot and the crowd sniffed a sensational finish, sending shockwaves through the air. It was going to be a tight finish between three quarters whose scores were level, and the archers were also aware that the scores were tied. Hearts were racing. Could Borghetto get back in? In the last sensational round, surrounded by hysterical screaming and palpitating hearts, Borghetto never missed a four-point arrow, but everyone else missed at least one. Borghetto pulled off an unheard-of, miraculous victory. But everyone agreed, they had no business winning Apertura that way!

My eyes were riveted on the Captain, who had not moved, standing solid as a rock as he waited at the end of the range. The victorious Borghetto archers raced across the campo, their Captain opened his arms, and the three locked in an embrace way beyond mere joy. Tears trickled down their faces. Borghetto is celebrating.

Only now am I aware of a translucent light weirdly filtering across the campo. Looking up, I see dark clouds hurrying, but piercing shafts of light burrow through here and there and the space between me and the clouds seems suspended. Nothing moves, the trees are strangely still. I walk away from the campo through an ominous light sphere locked in time, a surreal world in suspended animation. This happened one evening last week too, as if some omnipotent power was relaying a cautionary warning. Spellbound, I had watched, but nothing happened that night. Darkness fell and the following morning dawned sunny and clear. Nearing home, I glance up to see scudding black clouds travel fast overhead, carrying themselves away to some other place. White lightning forks across Mount Amiata twice, and again, but that is forty kilometres distant. It seems as if darkness is falling early and the heavens have lowered, squeezing the fading dusk into the ground. Primo is right, something is brewing.

As the sky cracks open, rent in two by a phosphorescent flash which splashes ultra-violet light across our faces, we instinctively rise from our chairs in shock. The fear of the unknown. An unheralded crash, so terrifying as to seem supernatural, breaks the storm and we shudder, moving towards each other, seeking mutual safety from this uncontrollable phenomenon. When an electric maelstrom crashes and flashes around this mountain eyrie, it is as if the gods, finding Montalcino closer to Heaven than anywhere else, have searched us out for destruction. The lights flicker. Luigi and I stumble to the windows and look upwards into black fury. The sky is splitting with lightning forks so near we marvel open-mouthed. Stunned, we listen as the thunder pours out its terrible rage, appallingly close. Everything seems suspended, awaiting the decision of this supernatural event. This horrific storm is breaking right over our roof.

Even as the first drops of rain pound against our windows, we watch a shaft of lightning carve a white canyon through the sky which vanishes above our heads. But there is no time-lag, and the gigantic force which carves this white canyon simultaneously explodes a clap of fury from the heavens, accompanied by the clatter of terracotta as half a dozen rooftiles, scorched and smouldering, shatter on the road below our window. We do not know where to run, hardly believing we are still alive, because we smell burning Bakelite – the fax is smoking – yet we are standing frozen, watching the phone connection spit from the wall and hiss across the room. The storm is pouring down merciless rage, torrents of rain fall from the sky as the stillness vanishes, nature's terrible decision has been made and the outside world is savagely attacked by wheeling winds.

The lights go out. In total darkness, black thunder and white lightning arrive together, carving up the sky and pounding Montalcino with pent-up anger, driving the rain into the waiting earth around our trembling hill. We try to pull other plugs from their sockets, but it is too late. Setting a solitary candle on the table, we can do nothing but watch and listen, not believing any rage in the heavens could unleash this power, and not under-standing why the gods have chosen Montalcino, twenty days from harvest, on which to release this appalling violence. The storm refuses to move, but crashes savagely on and on. Booming thunder is preceded by sheet lightning. Alerted by the tinny beating on the terracotta roof, we race for the windows again. *Mio Dio! Madre di Dio!* Hailstones are dropping like balls of concrete. They pile up on the windowsills, split open on the road below and heap around our scorched rooftiles. With this final despicable assault, twenty minutes of concentrated naked power begins at last to slacken. The crashing recedes to rumbles, turns to muttering, the flashes weaken in the distance, far away from our hill at last. All is eerily still, as if exhausted by the tempest. We most certainly are.

Someone is banging on our door downstairs, the buzzer is not functioning. It's the police. Andrea calls: 'Are you all right?' We learn that a single bolt of lightning struck our television aerial, found an inviting conductor and scorched a trail, now charred black, from roof to roof, finally exhausting itself when it earthed in the garden at the bottom of the hill. It has destroyed eight television sets in our road, burned up our fax, spat out the phone line, seized up the hot-water system and washing machine, fried the computer, modem and printer, and melted Luigi's mouse!

We know electrical power will not return tonight, but that is not what is on our anxious minds. 'Andrea, what's happened in the vineyards?' Nobody knows; the village is only able to take stock of its own devastation. Twenty days from harvest, the grapes are on the verge of maturity, a multi-million-dollar crop, but a year's work can be decimated in five minutes, let alone twenty minutes of unleashed fury. The grapes may survive pelting rain, provided the clusters are not dashed about the vine, but icy chips, even small ones, pit the fruit and split the skin, juice oozes and the crop cannot be saved.

We have no phone to ring Primo or any of our other friends. Extinguishing the candle, we head for bed, thankful the lightning bolt on our roof did not penetrate the metre-thick medieval bricks and fry us as well. But we are tense with worry, because Primo has invited us to help his family bring in the harvest at Canalicchio. I am fearful we will not be needed. More than once in the last ten days he has warned: 'I do not like the look of this at all. Something is brewing.'

CHAPTER SIXTEEN

Sailing into Cyberspace ...
Digging up the Past

'If there is anybody here tonight who would abstain from voting
for Pianello to buy San Pietro if we can raise the money, this is
your opportunity to address us all. If you feel there are reasons,
other than financial, let's talk about it now.' Nobody stands, so

Maurelia continues, 'Comunque, well then, let's talk about how we are going to raise the money. We have an innovative thinker in Pianello, who for the moment will remain nameless. I have hardly been able to restrain myself since hearing this idea – it has been a personal torment for me to suppress the news all week.'

'Maurelia! Get on with it – tell us, for heaven's sake,' calls out Riccardo, but our President seems to want to hold it in as long as possible so it will be all the more astonishing. She shakes her head. 'First there are some things I have to say, otherwise you will not understand.' Riccardo groans. 'Oh Dio, Maurelia, don't do this. Just tell us before we burst!'

'Riccardo, it will only take a couple of minutes. Allora, the Diocese has offered us San Pietro at a price we can afford and we do not have to hand over the money right now. It is a discreet amount and the Diocese will accept payment over a longish term. We also have to remember that the transaction still has to be ratified by the Vatican, which should be a formality. But there are some aspects we did not consider appropriately and something which opens the way for us to increase revenue with this new fund-raising idea.' We all remain silent, knowing it will only delay the agony if Maurelia is halted once more. Besides, this sounds interesting. 'Comunque, the Diocese does not want to deconsecrate San Pietro, which is why we will still have Mass on our Saint's Day, why the Diocese wants the church kept open to visitors, and why we must agree to maintain San Pietro as a functioning Christian church.'

The continued silence which meets these reminders indicates to Maurelia we understand everything she is saying. But where on earth is this leading? She closes her eyes, probably offering up a silent prayer, takes a deep breath, presses her lips resolutely together and then, as our eyes widen and one by one our mouths drop open, she pours out a torrent of words, knowing that only this way will she be able to finish what she has to say. If she leaves half a second for interruptions, forty wailing people will drown her out. These wailing words are quickly forming on lips but finding no avenue for sound, so we are forced to stare open mouthed and hear her out.

'This idea is all about getting married, about getting married in Montalcino and having a wedding breakfast at Pianello.' As Riccardo tries to get out his booming, 'Who is getting married?' Maurelia ignores him and bolts on. 'What we are proposing to do with this idea,' she boosts herself with a broad smile at everyone, 'is set up a marriage package. We are going to offer a Montalcinese feast for a wedding lunch or dinner, and it will mean we can offer weddings in San Pietro and receptions in our sede, here in Pianello . . . We propose to offer this to stranieri who come to Tuscany and want to get married in Montalcino!'

Two seconds of silence is all Maurelia pauses for. This bomb-shell leaves us temporarily dazed and speechless. Astonished stares race from person to person and back to Maurelia, and just as half a dozen voices are on the verge of screaming, 'What!' she dives in again.

'This project is the culmination of ideas, and the package is to be offered to Americans, Japanese, British, Germans and who-ever else in the whole world would like to get married in Montalcino. It is no problem for us to have a priest at San Pietro, so they can have a Christian wedding service and afterwards we can prepare a Pianello feast for their wedding reception. These stranieri will be very happy to contribute a donation for the use of San Pietro, which will go towards restorations, and Pianello will suggest a reasonable donation per head for the wedding breakfast.'

Seeing arms begin to rise and questions forming in minds and mouths, Maurelia waves her hands to halt them. 'Yes, I know you have plenty of questions. Some of them we will not be able to answer tonight, but we will talk about them in a minute. The ultimate objective to focus on tonight is that every wedding and celebratory meal we have in Pianello will help towards paying for San Pietro and the repairs to the roof. Each wedding will pay for about one square metre of roofing and, year by year, as the news gets out, we will be solvent enough to pay for the repairs. And think about this – in less than ten years we will own our own sede outright!'

She finally stops, and forty people are poised for assault. The questions pour out. 'What will the other quartieri think? Isn't this breaking with tradition? Is it within our charter to do this? But Maurelia, we do not speak English, let alone Japanese or German! And what if they are not Catholic? And what about Signora Gloria at the Comune? What will she think of all this? We would have to mend the roof temporarily so it doesn't leak, Maurelia, and the stairs need a—'

'Ascolta! Listen! Un momento di silenzio!' shouts Maurelia in the loudest voice I have ever heard her use. 'Yes, I know you have many questions and there are many things we do not yet have answers for, but your questions tell me you are already thinking about *how* we can bring this about, rather than *if* we can bring this about, so the primary question to answer is this. If we can cross all these hurdles, if we have found a way to raise the money to buy San Pietro and meet all the conditions, are we confident enough to move forward, to vote on buying San Pietro and plan for the future of our quartiere?'

Everyone quietens down and Maurelia begins to answer a few questions. 'I am sure it is within our charter to open our sede to public use. Don't forget, Ruga staged a concert last year, open to the public, and it was very successful. Our wedding package will probably raise a few eyebrows, but each quarter must find ways to raise money through the year and provide for the future. As for the language differences, well, that is really not a problem, because there are people in Siena who can act as interpreters. And you are right, Michele; not everyone in the world is a Catholic. But that's no hindrance either, because couples can be married in Palazzo Comunale in a civil ceremony and still have their wedding breakfast at Pianello, can't they? The paperwork for Signora Gloria will be taken care of by the stranieri themselves, but Signora Gloria is used to it because many couples come to Tuscany to be married. She has had to facilitate Japanese weddings before now. Provided the legal paperwork is in order, exactly as Signora Gloria requires, there is no hindrance.'

Maurelia is one step ahead of us and stays on the front foot with: 'It seems to me the stranieri come to Italy to be married because if they stay in their own country they feel obliged to orchestrate a wedding for two or three hundred people. But if the couple and their parents and friends come to Tuscany, they can have a romantic wedding in an enchanting place and a holiday and honeymoon at the same time. I think we will be looking after parties of between ten and thirty people, not too large for us to handle. All they have to do is attend to the legal paperwork for Signora Gloria and arrive in Tuscany. We will look after all the rest!'

'Maurelia,' interrupts Maria-Teresa, 'we will have to dress San Pietro up a bit – I mean with flowers and things. In spring we can fill the church with blossom, or tulips, and if it is a summer wedding then we could use sunflowers and sheaves of wheat . . . and grapevines – it would look lovely. Whereas for autumn we can use olive branches and baskets of chestnuts, with white ribbons tied to the pews.'

Before Maurelia can respond, Fiorella joins in with: 'We could make the feast a seasonal one, couldn't we? Because we cannot have porcini mushrooms in spring but we can in autumn, in spring we can have wild asparagus. Ragù we can cook all year round – wild strawberries in June . . .'

'Brava!' butts in Lola, who is animated by all this talk of seasonal flavours. 'And Fiorella,' she suggests thoughtfully, 'if these stranieri are so interested in our gastronomy, do you think they would like it if we offered to teach them? I mean, we could organise cooking lessons in the cuisine of Montalcino, couldn't we?' Every head turns to stare at Lola, astounded at her leap forward in thinking. This octogenarian works fast.

Maurelia is ecstatic. 'Si, Lola! Look, now we have a second brilliant idea for raising money. Yes, I think it is more than possible people will want to learn to cook in Montalcino, especially the Montalcinese way.' Lola sits back, glowing with her own cleverness.

By this time Luigi is exchanging not one but half a dozen astonished glances with me, and I am responding with equal amazement. It is all happening so fast and spontaneously that we have not passed a word between us.

Maurelia is talking again. 'I have made a list of things we will need to sort out. Accommodation is no problem because we have all categories of hotels, apartments and agriturismo. And bridal flowers and photographs we can work out – oh, and we can offer genuine Italian wedding cakes.'

Others take up her enthusiasm, adding: 'We can ring the bells of San Pietro every time we have a wedding – the stranieri would like that. And bon-bons, Maurelia, I don't think stranieri have bon-bons at weddings in America or England. We can make them in Pianello colours and the guests can take them home!' Francesco suggests wine tastings of Brunello, because we have so many fabulous enoteca where they can learn about Brunello, and anyway, the food and wine must go together. 'And Maurelia,' bursts in Fabio, 'what if they want entertainment? Could we ask Angelino and the band? Or the choro? Imagine having our choro perform in San Pietro – wouldn't it be marvellous?'

Maurelia is thinking she will never be able to stop all these brilliant suggestions tumbling out, but Ercole is rising slowly to his feet with a reproving, schoolteacherly expression on his face. I had been watching him sitting solemnly, thinking, and now, taking up his familiar enigmatic, head-nodding stance, he cautions: 'Ragazzi, listen a moment. This is all very well – tremendously exciting – but Montalcino is an isolated village in Tuscany. How are we going to tell people in America, or Japan or Australia? Magari! We do not have money to spend on advertising and it will take years for information to filter through. Let's think about that aspect for a moment, because we will need more than two or three weddings a year to make this work.'

Frowns appear as everyone realises we are being swept up by the enthusiasm of the young and the speed with which all these brilliant ideas are flowing. Ercole is right; the practical side of the equation has to be considered, not just the happy execution. Maurelia is strangely silent, letting the seconds tick past, and I am wondering what she is waiting for, when Michele suddenly shoots from his chair, yelling to Riccardo and Maria-Teresa. They are jumping in the air together. 'Si, si, it'll be okay,' they shout. 'It's easy, we can do it with the Internet, we can get on the web. Don't worry, Ercole, we will send it through cyberspace!' A dozen of them are rattling in unintelligible jargon about cyber notes, virtual reality, gigabytes, megabytes, pixels and bookings through space. 'Non preoccuparti! Millions of people – the whole world – will know about Pianello weddings and cooking lessons. But we need a name on the web, Maurelia, we'll have to have a web address ... Montalcino something or other ... what shall we call it?'

The elders are shaking their heads at each other. 'What are they talking about?' squeaks Settimia. 'Have they gone mad?' Then Dottore Luciano's mother, a signora into her nineties, makes us laugh: 'If anyone is going into space I'll be in on it, I'm not missing the fun.' Lola shoots a forbidding look at Ercole. 'Do not even think of it, Ercole. We are staying right here.' There is so much laughter in the air one would think San Pietro has been paid for on the spot.

Maurelia is thrilled with the way everyone has latched on to the idea and shrewdly decides this is the time for a vote, so she brings us back to the present. 'Allora,' she rounds us up again, 'now it is time to vote on buying San Pietro. A yes vote means you understand we also have to raise the money for the roof, we have to comply with all the conditions of the Diocese and the whole thing still has to be ratified by Rome, which will take quite a few months. Raise your hand if you are voting yes.' A sea of hands go up and everyone is yelling: 'Si, si, we are buying San Pietro, we will own our own sede at last.'

A unanimous vote carries the day. Maurelia will write to the Diocese and this momentous meeting comes to a close with our President reminding everyone of the work to be done in preparing for the autumn Sagra. She still does not know where we will be having the feasting, but the quartiere Presidents have decided to press on and continue with all arrangements, trusting the difficulties will be sorted out once work is well advanced. After the Sagra we will begin resolving the details for our new fund-raising plans, which are to be kept quiet.

We begin filing out of the door and Maurelia, unseen by Luigi, slides her arm around my shoulders and gives me a squeeze, but we do not look each other straight in the eye. We dare not.

Summer is over. The violent tempest which broke over

Montalcino was nature's signal that we had had enough, it is time to look towards autumn. The temperature has not risen again. Rather, we will have a month of blissful autumn days, but gradually the mornings will be tinged with cold and autumn will take us, at first gently, back to wearing warmer jackets and lighting wood fires. Looking back through a fleeting summer, I can hardly credit so much has happened. The season was punctuated with stories of exploding canons, the mysterious Brunello sabotage – still unsolved – rumours of a new Mayor, washing whites at Mount Amiata and other ferragosto madness, Borghetto's stunning victory at Apertura, Pianello's joy to be purchasing San Pietro, Festa della Unità at the Pineta, glorious concerts from our band and choro in the cloister of Sant' Agostino – and then the summer ended with that electrical maelstrom, the fury of which I pray never to witness again.

The morning following the storm, we jumped in the car to drive to Canalicchio and found the road around the walls littered with debris and broken branches which the Comune Ape was already carting away, as Mario and the team of sweepers began the clean-up. Mario told us the first report back to the village had come from Castello Banfi. From the castle walls they had watched the storm gather over Mount Amiata and followed the advancing path of the lightning, easily visible from the castle tower, towards Montalcino. But Castello Banfi is ten or twelve kilometres to the south-west, and although the vineyards were drenched with rain, making it hard to get into the rows to inspect them, the wine-growers there are confident they will dry out quickly, as already it is clear and sunny. So far as they know, they did not lose a grape, hardly a leaf.

Canalicchio is one kilometre from the village, at the bottom of the slope where several smaller vineyards face north-east, lying directly in the path of the advancing storm. Primo's story was tinged with dramatic descriptions of what happened that dreadful night.

'I watched this tremendous blackness, like something hovering in the sky. It moved slowly towards us, lit by shafts of lightning which seemed to be showing it the way, and it sailed through the darkness straight for the village. I could feel the electrical tension in the air. Concentrated power had built up over time and the blackness rested like some alien form, then lowered itself onto the hill. The village vanished and we could only see an eerie formation of charcoal brushstrokes streaking through the sky, lit by forks of lightning as the torrents of water drove down in wide rainsheets. I knew it was destructive, as the thunder rolled like something possessed by evil. I said to my grandson: "If it moves from the mountain we are gone." We secured the animals, but that was all we could do. There is no protection for avenues of ripe fruit hanging from vines, which were swinging perilously for a while. But mostly it remained still, and the wind gusted but whirled away. Swollen streams of water poured into crevices and began to wash down the side of the hill, so the vineyards were soon saturated. We watched forked lightning rend the sky and the thunderbolts crashed like sonic booms. Suddenly the whole village vanished into blackness. We did not know about the lightning strikes, nor about the potentially disastrous hailstones until this morning, when people began to tell us of the fury. It was close, perilously close. I knew it was coming a week ago, there was something brewing in the atmosphere and I was afraid our harvest would be destroyed, but it went to Montalcino and wrought its dreadful havoc there instead. The pent-up fury is released. As long as we have a few days of warm sun at Canalicchio to dry out the vineyards, we will bring in an excellent harvest.'

The unexpected casualty of the storm turned out to be Dora

who, in her weakened state, could not be comforted. Renato stayed in the cantina with the dogs while the fury raged, but Dora had trembled uncontrollably, wretchedly frightened. She would not even accept comfort from Renato, and by the time the storm had rumbled away he had faced the inevitable. Nobody will ever know what ailed Dora; there was no treatment because there was no prognosis. Renato could not bear to see her suffering and knew that she would not recover. It was time to have her put down. He took her to the veterinarian and Luigi, hearing him return, went downstairs to find him standing in the laboratory silently weeping. Dianna sat in her box looking disconsolate, as she knew her friend would not return. The two men stood together, letting their tears fall – Renato for young Dora, and Luigi, feeling Renato's pain, put his arms around his friend and ached with him.

This year I am determined to observe the Sagra through the eyes of village people, rather than the eyes of a stranger witnessing a medieval pageant and archery tournament. I am convinced the Sagra is far more complex than that and, having learned so much about Montalcino and the Montalcinesi, I intend to examine the phenomena surrounding this annual pageant.

The Sagra is nearly here and I am deeply immersed in my own drifting thoughts as preparations begin. I have listened attentively to Massimo all year, and I have stayed silent when I could have questioned Maurelia. I am determined to observe what is happening for myself, even if at times through veiled eyes, preferring that to prompting her or others, because I do not want to be told what people think a stranger might want to hear. I want to see, feel, experience and comprehend this emotion for myself.

I have been keeping track of the other three quartieri too, their Presidents, their faithful workers, the enthusiastic young and the disciplined archers. What pulls this thing together? What knits it into a whole? Quartiere rivalry is part of it, but I suspect not the whole, because rivalry seems to me to be the chosen avenue for the expression of passion, but not the cause of it. I have scraped away layer after layer, people have opened personal doors to me, only made possible because I live within these walls and they trust me. Even as each private revelation comes, it seems I am making gigantic strides in understanding. Yet fascinating, occasionally disheartening, and sometimes incredible as it all is, my puzzle remains disjointed. I know about the heartbreak of the contadino, but can never see his unjustly hard life, nor the centuries which preceded it for his ancestors, through eyes other than my own. The old boscaioli are remote from my world, even though I have been to the bosco and walked among the woodpiles. I have learned how they lost their livelihood, starved and suffered. To starve and suffer is in itself alien to me. Inner pain I know, but I do not know suffering. The cittadini remain protectively inward-looking and defensive. The little I have experienced is with their trust, but it will take many more years, maybe never, even though I am with them every single day, to understand them in the way I yearn to. I am honoured to call many Ilcinesi my friends, people I love dearly who dwell on this hill under the holm oaks and whose lives unfold along with mine in the piazza every day. But this can never be *my* hill and I can only form a charming but scarcely adequate vision of their thousand-year-old culture. I have listened and learned, but cannot see through their eyes, nor feel through their bones, nor think or comprehend with the perception of the centuries.

But I long to discover what binds it all together, because Montalcino is not a village made up of thousands of identical people. They do not agree about everything, and there are many disputes and arguments, but neither do they seem to wish to escape from each other. Nor is this a Tuscan village so steeped in the past that it is dying a slow death the way some once-proud villages do. This is a village that carries the ancient past proudly on its shoulders and, bringing the recent past with it into the modern world, is a thriving, creative, industrious, forward-thinking and prosperous village with a vibrant community spirit, determined to secure for itself a place in the third millennium.

Primo and his enologist are in the vineyard. 'He is like a doctor,' explains Primo. 'He examines the bunches and tests the juice, because even if the fruit looks plump and healthy and the weather is warm and dry, sometimes the acidity has only reached a certain level and he knows we must wait a few more days. Or when we have had late rain, like this month when the storm cleared up quickly but we could not get into the vineyard because the rows were too wet, he monitors the grapes, testing their sugar content, and watching the humidity, which can rise alarmingly after a soaking rain. The critical decision of when to harvest is really his. He is indispensable to the production of Brunello, because this is a unique complex wine.'

Primo remembers the old days when the grape harvest was always on a set date, because afterwards the contadini celebrated bringing in the harvest with a family festa, singing, dancing and, of course, drinking. It did not concern them what the state of the harvested grapes was like, so long as the harvest was in and there was plenty of them. Nowadays the crucial days of harvest are calculated for the uncompromised benefit of the wine rather than the frolicking of the harvesters. There are four geographical zones where Brunello is grown, which means the harvesting of some 200 growers is staggered according to the micro-climate and decision of the enologists working in each zone – and is also why there can be significant differences in styles of Brunello grown in the four zones.

One region may receive a higher rainfall, the area to the south is often dryer, of course altitude makes a difference, and the infinite variations of soil and climate are evidenced in the intensity of ruby colouring, robust tannins and harmonious bouquet.

Although he knows full well our expertise will be severely limited, Primo's invitation to help with the harvest was eagerly accepted. When his telephone call comes, we hang on every word. 'Caro Luigi, the enologist says we start harvesting tomorrow. The acidity level is right, the sugar content high, he is confident the grapes are mature and the weather ideal. The rest of my family arrive tonight and we will be picking for four days. Wear strong shoes, and make sure you both bring something to cover your heads. We start picking at first light, but come down whenever you are ready. I will be at the cantina, because the first grapes go into the press just after dawn. Wine will be filling the tanks by mid-morning.'

Primo has no conception of how excited I am this morning! Today is the culmination of his year's work, which I have followed month by month in the vineyard. More than that, for me this is the culmination of the anguish and pain of his ancestors, the emphatic answer this generous man and others like him can give to the whole world after a life spent mostly under the yoke of mezzadria, on this land. I feel unique, repeating over and over to myself: 'Today I will pick sangiovese grosso for Primo's Brunello on the slopes of the hill of Montalcino. This wine is a creation, this is the only place in the world where it can be made, and I am helping bring in this year's harvest!'

As dawn breaks we edge our way around the fortress to the intersection of the roads from Grosseto and Siena, from which three more roads radiate towards the vineyards. My eyes are darting everywhere as I yell out number plates. 'Luigi! That one is from Perugia . . . he's Grosseto. Look – another from Arezzo.

Even the Florentines and Romans are here!'

As we weave our way down the hill towards Canalicchio, we pass lines of cars creeping upwards. If I were Ilio Raffaelli, I would be up at dawn every morning for the three weeks of harvest, to climb the high tower of the fortress and watch a prophecy come true! 'If we can just be patient,' he had implored Zampa in the 1960s, 'I promise you the day will come when the roads leading to Montalcino will be lined with cars filled with people who are coming here to work. This hill is our life, Zampa, it is our future. Our roots are in the land, and that is how we will stay.'

Hundreds of people have been drifting to work in Montalcino since the spring cycle began, and the numbers increase month by month as the growing vines need more and more daily attention until, resting on the decision of the enologists, in today's fresh dawn-light a workforce of thousands swarm around the hills. For three weeks during harvest, hundreds of workers are needed at Castello Banfi alone. Castelgiocondo needs almost as many, Donatella Colombini will employ dozens of helpers, and the individual growers, who make up the majority of Brunello producers, will work with a handful of helpers and their extended families, just as Primo will, taking anything from two to ten days to bring in the harvest. Sangiovese grosso for Brunello is harvested by hand. After months of painstaking co-operation between man and nature, nothing is permitted to endanger or bruise the fruit.

By the time we reach Canalicchio the first tractor is manipulating crates towards the de-stalker, where Primo is directing operations. He is quietly optimistic with the early quality, picking up and inspecting the clusters, holding them out for us to see the uniform size and even growth. He feels he is bringing in a good harvest, but with his usual modesty does not offer a definitive opinion. 'We will see,' he says. 'This is only the first step.'

The load is tipped into the trough, the giant screw begins to churn the bunches, and gradually the leaves and stalks spit out on to a growing pile at the side. The grapes feed through a fat hose along the ground and into the soft press where, according to the pressure specified by the enologist, the grapes are gently squeezed. The juice and broken skins trickle out and, forming a murky stream, are fed into the first in a line of sparkling fermentation tanks. Primo shows us several gleaming new fermentation tanks he invested in this year. They are astronomically expensive, as are his six brand new Slovenian oak vats. He is not alone in his desire to produce Brunello only with optimum equipment in world-class conditions. Many growers this year will replant twenty-five-year-old vines, ever watchful not to allow the disciplines of their great mentor, the now deceased Bruno Ciatti, to slip. Above all else, the exceptional quality of Brunello, the vinification of a single clone called sangiovese grosso created in these hills, must be safeguarded.

The newly pressed wine is rising in the tank as Marco, Primo's grandson, tips the next load of grapes into the de-stalker. He is learning from his grandfather and, when Primo is no longer able to, young Marco will carry on running the vineyard. The Pacenti family dynasty is in safe hands. Warning yells and instructions rise above the noise and the work is hard and furious, everyone fulfilling their role, keeping the grapes coming and the juice flowing. I stay close to Primo when he moves down to the vineyard and watch closely as he shows me how to lift the foliage, raising the bunch clear with one hand and snipping the stem with the other. He hardly seems to look and cuts through the vine quickly and easily, but when I try it looks as if I have wrenched the stalk apart with my teeth.

The family stops only for pranzo and, just as I am lamenting the state of my broken back, aching arms and stinging fingers, Primo bounces up like a thirty-year-old and announces that the enologist has instructed that as soon as the family is finished at Canalicchio they are to move straight down the hill and harvest the vineyard of Primo's brother. Primo has been asked to supply wine to Japan, but he does not have enough and will not turn his back on loyal customers who have supported him for more than three decades during harder times. Someone must be selling to Japan though, because I remember how, at Benvenuto Brunello, a Japanese importer told a very receptive audience of the astonishing increase in Japanese appreciation and consumption of Brunello.

I like the thought that for the next four years the grapes I am picking right now will rest in sacred silence in Primo's cantina and perhaps end up on a dining table in Switzerland, Germany, France, England, Australia or America. Maybe an appreciative wine lover will lay this wine in his cellar for ten, twenty or thirty years. Maybe I will be gone from this world when he uncorks my bottle and sighs with anticipatory delight as the harmoniously balanced aroma rises up to meet him. He will read on the label: *the terra of Canalicchio di Sopra*. He will not know the disheartening story of Primo's life, but it doesn't matter. Primo's sad story has a happy ending, and there can be no more powerful expression of that happiness than in the splendid development of the aged Brunello my imaginary wine lover will savour.

At the end of the first day's harvest I am more or less asleep on my feet. My legs are wobbly, my arms hang limp and I am extremely light-headed because the musty aroma of newly pressed wine fills the air. Lingering in a soaking bath, which does nothing to remove the purple stains on my hands, arms and forehead, I collapse into bed wondering how on earth I will manage to get up at dawn. Four days sounds like four weeks.

Falling into the dreamless slumber of the physically exhausted, I thank God I am not harvesting at Castello Banfi. I muse through drifting veils: 'Well, dearest Primo, there is absolutely no argument from me. We are harvesting Italy's finest red wine – one of the great wines of the world – it is not a bad drop, dear Primo, il Brunello di Montalcino.'

Maurelia is darting in and out of the pharmacy clutching a pinboard, calling across the piazza and talking in low tones with Mayor Mauro and the other Presidents. All of them are sub-merged in organising the coming Sagra and still searching for ways to resolve the tiresome problems. Meetings have been held almost daily, absorbing Maurelia in administrative decisions, co-ordination of the pageant and tournament, and I had not realised she had even seen me watching her from Fiaschetteria. She waves and calls out, 'Buongiorno, are you coming to the meeting on Saturday afternoon?'

I am not sure how to respond, because I have not been involved in any meetings. Seeing my bewildered stare she adds, '. . . the meeting of the Etruscan Association – Ivo is presenting the latest findings.' I continue to stare, speechless, because it is incon-ceivable that Montalcino has an Etruscan Association about which I know absolutely zero. I have been living here five years. Surely this is not something else I have missed?

My fascination with intriguing Etruscan culture is as highly developed as any stranger who adores Italy. I own shelves of books in English, and have also struggled through complicated Italian chronicles by Etruscologists like Massimo Pallottino. I have visited every major excavated Etruscan city and as many minor sites as I can. I have crawled through dank tombs and black tufa caves on my knees and have walked in the footsteps of the testy D.H. Lawrence, pondering his dreamlike conclusions after his six-day flirtation with Etruscans. Perched on the steps of the painted tombs at Tarquinia I have examined the sumptuous banquets happy Etruscans prepared for their dead. The hairs on my neck rose when I entered the sepulchres at Cerveteri, desolate and empty tombs spilling over with haunting traces of those who lay on beds of stone undisturbed for nearly two and a half millennia, their needs for life in the next world spread around their decaying bones.

Soon, after years of research, I'll be helping six guest Australians explore the marvels of Etruria on a ramble among ancient cities and cemeteries. Today, Maurelia informs me, almost incidentally, that we have an Etruscan Association right here in Montalcino! Rummaging in her handbag, she passes me a letter which invites all members to a meeting at which Ivo Caprioli, the President, will report on the successful findings and preliminary conclusions of a highly specialised team, led by Professor Luigi Donati from the faculty of Antiquity of the University of Florence, on the Etruscan civilisation at Montalcino.

Searching my mind, I am certain not one of the dozens of books I own mentions Etruscans here. Nearby at Murlo, yes, and a little further away the Etruscan cities of Roselle and Chiusi, but never a word about an ancient civilisation here. So far as I am aware, the recorded history of Montalcino began around the year 740, when primitive peasants between here and the sea sought safe refuge and developed their settlement beneath the canopy of holm oaks on this mountain. They became my friends the Ilcinesi, dwellers on the hill of Mons Ilcinus.

Racing home, I wave the letter under Luigi's nose and demand he telephone Ivo at once. 'I have to join the Association before Saturday, Luigi. The Professor is from the University of Florence, and something colossal in Etruria research is going on here.' Is there to be no end to the discoveries I make about this village we have chosen for our home? The richness of the life I am living in this defensive, inward looking, walled medieval wine village in Tuscany is beyond my wildest imaginings, at times beyond my comprehension, and it astounds me to be on the brink of uncovering yet another layer in the civilisation of this mountain stretching back two and a half millennia. I decide to put my Sagra investigations to one side for a few days, join the Association, go to the meeting, talk to Ivo, find out what they have found out. Maybe I will be introduced to Professor Donati. There is so much to catch up on.

Four days later, clutching a numbered white card authorising me as a member of the Associazione Ricerche e Studi Etruschi e Italici di Montalcino, I am stepping through the dust on to the excavation site at Poggio Civitella. Ivo hands me a narrow trowel and a yellow bucket, and his friend Assunto directs me alongside an Etruscan wall curving around the pinnacle of the hill. It has been partially reconstructed after lying hidden for 2,500 years. Taking my place behind a team of university students and a few familiar faces, and imitating Gabriele, the gangly fifteen-year-old son of handsome Massimo from the Biancheria, I drop to my knees and sink the trowel into the brown earth. I am on the excavation site with Professor Donati and his skilled team, who are bringing to light a powerful Etruscan fortress which was constructed on the summit of this hill, the site of even earlier Etruscan habitation, 600 years before Christ was born.

'Buongiorno Signora,' smiles Professor Donati. Recognising me instantly as a straniera, he offers a little information. Although I have spent the last four days poring over the university findings, I listen intently as he explains the reasons this particular Etruscan site is under scrutiny. 'Signora, this is new ground, a point of reference for international archaeologists. We have excavated thousands of tombs of Etruria, many Etruscan cities of the living, and Italy is peppered with necropoli, the cities of the dead, but this is a first. Poggio Civitella is the very first Etruscan fortress we have been able to excavate. This appears to have been a defensive stronghold between two Etruscan cities, strategically positioned. Within this ring of walls possibly lived a trained garrison of Etruscan soldiers, and for the first time we may uncover clues about the garrison, the role of Poggio Civitella in defence of Etruscan cities, in protection of trading routes. This site is immensely enlightening in advancing the study of Etruria. It is a reference point for the future and will reveal previously unrecorded knowledge.'

His infectious enthusiasm is demonstrated with two broken shards of terracotta he is holding in his dirt-encrusted hands. 'Here,' he grins at me, 'run your hands over these. We have just pulled them from the rubble – two pieces from a terracotta roof two and a half thousand years old.'

Archaeologists know a very great deal about Etruscans, the early inhabitants of Italy who developed their culture over 700 years from around the eighth century BC. Astonishing as it seems, when nothing more than primitive straw huts stood on the Palatine Hill in Rome, the Etruscans were entering a period of splendour and power, and by the sixth century BC were a technically advanced, civilised and refined people. All the more astonishing because the Romans were still little more than wild warring tribes brandishing swords. Rome was to learn many of her lessons in engineering, politics and religion – as well as the tactics of war – from the Etruscans. Ultimately, with their violent methods of aggressive expansion, the Romans destroyed the last Etruscan city in 40 BC.

Historians continue to ponder whether, had the Etruscans not persisted in neglecting to form a cohesive league, the course of history might indeed have been different; the magnificent Roman Empire might never have risen. But strangely, ancient Etruscans preferred independent cities, each ruled by its own king, or 'Lucumone', and instead of joining militarily to resist the advance of Rome, one by one they succumbed to her unstoppable aggression.

Perhaps the greatest Etruscan loss, which cleared the way for Roman expansion, was their defeat in a great sea battle in the Bay of Naples in 474 BC. The Etruscans had dominated the western seas for centuries, they were fearsome pirates, but the loss of their maritime fleet meant the loss of trade and a weakening of their power. With no seapower, and suffering the expansionist violence of Rome, they also had to respond to barbarian invaders from the north. Unable to fight on so many fronts against so many different enemies, their political vulnerability was exposed as they lacked a cohesive defensive league.

Many of the ancient Etruscan cities still exist today but are inaccessible to archaeologists because successive layers of society have built on top of them. Even so, excellent evidence exists of architectural monuments, the clever engineering of roads, tunnels, drainage canals, and thousands of inscriptions which we can read on graven stones, on artistic paintings on the walls of tombs, and on sculpted scenes on sarcophagi and cinerary urns. Italy's museums contain glorious artefacts found in the tombs – weapons, vases, goblets, mirrors, hair combs, extraordinary belt buckles and exquisite jewellery finely crafted in gold – all attesting to a great and cultured people. A people who not only possessed a language and a literature, but who held sumptuous and happy banquets accompanied by flute players. Etruscan women wore full-length, often transparent, chitons caught at the shoulder with golden clasps, their bracelets and earrings were exquisitely crafted, they dressed their hair with ivory combs and garlands of flowers and on their feet wore neat little slippers, delicately laced to the ankle, with delightfully pointed turned-up toes. Etruscans had their own religion, built temples to their gods and sought the will of those gods in the reading of signs by haruspices. But sadly, aside from some of their traditions which Rome claimed, all of this splendour perished with the advance of the conquering empire . . . or perhaps, after twenty-five centuries of silence, something may yet lie buried at Poggio Civitella. Even today, a single piece of exciting new evidence awaiting excavation by Professor Donati may change the whole picture of the amazing Etruscans.

I know I am not going to stumble on some Etruscan buried treasure. I am with those who are digging away the centuries of accumulated dirt and rubbish on top of the site so that Professor Donati and his team can number the stones, photograph and eventually reconstruct the fortress. But who cares? I am with my friends inside an Etruscan excavation which, I have now found out, began with the curiosity of a group of Montalcinesi, including Ivo and his friend Assunto, way back in 1950.

Ivo and Assunto were young men in their twenties when, after the turmoil of 1948 and the disorder which followed the arrests and sentences of an Italy grappling with dragging itself from the Fascist era, the parties to the left, similar to the left in the whole of Italy, had their backs to the wall. Conferences were held throughout the country, designed to bring the factions of the left together in order that, after the demise of Fascism, they could regroup. A sort of psychological tune-up was called for, and in Montalcino one of these conferences was addressed by a famous international archaeologist by the name of Ranuccio Bianchi Bandinelli, whose nickname was, appropriately, il Conte Rosso, the Red Count. Bandinelli was a highly regarded expert on Etruria and a learned Etruscan scholar of his times who, because

411

of his deep cultural understanding of Italy, had been chosen to accompany Mussolini and Adolf Hitler on a cultural tour of Italy a decade before.

As Assunto put it: 'The Red Count explained difficult concepts to us with crystal clarity and after the meeting we continued talking. The conversation strayed as he told us about his collaboration in a compelling archaeological paper which included his identification of an archaic site at Montalcino. Soon the wee hours of the night were joined to the dawning morning and we had not even noticed. Enthused by this brilliant scholar, we were rapaciously contaminated by an archaeological virus and next day our conversation about the dogmatic concepts of the left was put to one side and our fascination with this mysterious archaeological site grew. With youthful exuberance we planned an expedition, because we were curious to know if the site really existed, and if we could find it.'

Assunto admits he and his friends were ignorant of even the most elementary laws relating to archaeology and, having asked the owner of the land if they could explore, they set off one morning with crude digging equipment and zero experience of archaeology. Still groaning about it, Assunto recalls they faced brambles and bushes that seemed to have grown on the hill for the sole purpose of making penetration impossible. Their furious efforts left them with bodily marks which they do not remember with much affection to this day! At the end of a thrilling day, they gathered everything that looked interesting and sent it off to Professor Bandinelli, sat back and waited eagerly for his reply. It arrived speedily and is still jealously guarded by Assunto. The Red Count's letter included a few knuckle-rapping lines about infringing laws which govern interfering with archaeological sites without proper authority, about which Assunto and Ivo had been completely ignorant, but excused the interference because obviously they were not robbing the site, but were curious, wanting to deepen their knowledge of the history of Montalcino. But, he stressed, they must suspend activity immediately. He would report to the Superintendent of Archaeology at Florence, who would then send someone to examine the site. This proved significant, because Assunto and Ivo worked with him on the site and in a niche they unearthed an enormous pot. Hidden inside was a beautiful cup for drinking, called an oinochoe, and a kylix, a kind of vase for wine, and both were in bucchero, the black ceramic typical of Etruscans. These three pieces of antiquity were the first valuable finds and established the authenticity of the site, but left many questions.

The dig was closed after ten days, the representative from Florence went back to the University and the enthusiastic lads from Montalcino had to wait for better times. But the archaeological virus was virulent in Assunto and Ivo. They began to follow up stories from farmers close to Montalcino who reported strange openings, holes, crevices, shards of broken pottery, stories of peculiar stones and primitive statues and, as the years rolled by, they recorded and guarded treasures from underground openings and caves around Montalcino.

The two men had to wait forty-three years for better times in which to investigate Poggio Civitella, because it was not until 1993 that Ivo and Assunto's enthusiasm finally re-aroused the intervention of the University of Florence. In a country rich in archaeology with never enough funds for excavation, although the State does pour billions of lire into the exploration and documentation of archaeological digs, this led eventually to the first official documentation of the site. In 1993 Professor Donati arrived with a team of students from the University of Florence and in a few days established that they were studying a powerful fortress circled by a defensive wall, which had two more elliptical walls encircling the complex lower down the hill. The team returned for a few days each year for five years, making modest progress as funds allowed, but this year they are here for a whole month of digging.

The summit of Poggio Civitella has always interested archaeologists because it seems to have been levelled artificially, and an impressive ring of soil and rocks circles the summit. Earlier observation by archaeologists like Bandinelli, who were not able to excavate, led to the conclusion that it might have been a prehistoric site, but thanks to Bandinelli's prompting, the short investigation in 1950 and excavations each year since 1993, Professor Donati has established that here lay an Etruscan settlement of the sixth century BC. Inside rectangular dwellings they found fragments of domestic pots and of beautifully decorated ceramic vases, all evidence of the traditional female role in the home, as well as lamps, evidence of wool-spinning, and production and purification of metal. By these findings Professor Donati was able, after nearly fifty years, to confirm that the three precious pieces uncovered by Assunto and Ivo in 1950 were not accidental, but authentic finds from the habitation of the sixth century BC.

As the dig has progressed, Professor Donati has reconstructed some sixty metres of a ponderous wall around the summit, which was the topmost line of defence of the fortress and the wall earlier thought to be prehistoric. The wall is Etruscan, was erected in the fourth century BC, and in some places was still standing two metres high and reasonably intact. But Professor Donati then found he had to answer the question: What happened to the inhabitants of the dwellings on Poggio Civitella of the sixth century BC? According to his early findings, the site was abandoned for 200 years, possibly due to a crisis in agriculture, and later Etruscans returned to the site around the fourth century BC in order to build this potent fortress to control the territory of a great Etruscan metropolis. Its dominating position above important crossroads provided views which would have covered the whole of Etruria from the Tyrrhenian Sea to the Appenine Mountains, down to Lazio and across to Umbria.

'But whose fortress was it?' demands Professor Donati of me, with the searching look in his eyes which all professors fascinated with their own discoveries take on. 'This site is precisely equidistant between two powerful Etruscan cities, two seats of Lucumone power. In one direction is the city of Chiusi and in the other the city of Roselle – so who was it defending?' With the evidence from the dwellings of the sixth century BC and with knowledge of the early method of construction of the fortress, it seems to Professor Donati for the moment that the strategic role of this potent fortress was the protection of the Lucumone of Chiusi. There are many puzzling questions remaining to be solved and among them is the whereabouts of the dead. Most historians had asserted that Etruscans built villages on hilltops to facilitate defence, but Bandinelli pointed out that in fact Etruscan cities were often built on twin hills, with a river between them. On one hill they built the city for the living and across the stream was the city for the dead, the necropolis. This reasoning makes Poggio Civitella all the more archaeologically intriguing, because the question is still unanswered: Where did they bury the dead? Where is the necropolis for Poggio Civitella?

The official dig for this year is concluding and this is the last week students will be on the site together, so they are drawing a ground map of the summit of Poggio Civitella, taking measurements and wandering among the colossal stone slabs that seem to me to be lying haphazardly around the ground. The map shows partly dug-out stone slabs, but the students tell me they do not yet know what they were for. Funds are exhausted for this year, and although Professor Donati has some sixty metres of wall partially reconstructed to two metres in height, the wall was once five metres high; and although he has uncovered a small entrance with a passage, he still has not found the main gates into the fortress. The second and third elliptical rings of wall have not been touched. He walks over to study the irregular angles on the map the students are preparing.

'Will you look at these crazy Etruscans?' he groans. 'What headaches they give us. Why didn't they build straight lines like Romans? It is so hard to find everything, we need a helicopter so we can do some aerial work.' The students willingly respond to the joke, but are soon back in the pit shovelling dirt and heaving rocks, or brushing stones with small straw brooms. 'Rafaela!' he calls. 'Try tossing those rocks a little more scientifically. We're not in a quarry – even if it looks like it.'

Next year's work depends on sponsorship, and I am secretly delighted when Professor Donati tells me Castello Banfi and two private wine-growers have been financially supportive. The Bank of Monte Paschi di Siena and the Banca Toscana have also contributed funds, and smaller amounts have been gratefully received, but they must find more to guarantee continuance of work. 'We had a party of American archaeological students through this month. They are particularly interested to learn about an Etruscan dig so we had them studying the site and doing a bit of digging too.'

Professor Donati is called over to the edge of the site where the bobcat is clearing away soil and tangled roots, so I return to my position digging alongside Gabriele, who begins to chat about the finds Ivo and Assunto have made in fifty years. Always hampered by lack of proper excavating equipment, and aware they must not endanger a site by inadvertently destroying evidence which assists trained archaeologists, Ivo and Assunto worked patiently on.

Their youthful curiosity was never satiated in fifty years and they never lost faith in the existence of Etruscans at Montalcino. Their faith is being rewarded, not only by the intervention of Professor Donati but by the news Gabriele tells me will soon be announced: the Bank of Monte Paschi di Siena is donating L 300,000,000 towards the housing of the finds of Ivo and Assunto in a new Etruscan archaeological section of Montalcino's Civic Museum. Until now their treasures have more or less been stashed in cupboards – some were in cardboard boxes beneath Assunto's house for decades. The very valuable items found security in locked cabinets where few people see them. I am drawn once more to the unhappy conclusion that only the Bank of Monte Paschi di Siena is willing to substantially assist the causes of Montalcino. Thank goodness the bank is preserving the cultural patrimony of Sienese territory.

Foreigners living in Italy sometimes carry an irritating arrogance about themselves, as if deep down they believe where they come from gives them an inner superior knowledge about the way things *should* happen wherever they have willingly placed themselves. I am continually struggling against this, because I know it is a fallacy, yet, whilst digging away with Gabriele, the superior thought flickers fleetingly through my mind: Interesting in Italy how they consider it is okay for a fifteen-year-old boy to be excavating an Etruscan site. I dismiss this silly thought, annoyed with myself, but then jump into the fire. 'Are you coming back tomorrow?' I ask Gabriele, with all the airiness of an expert although coming from someone who is on an Etruscan dig for the very first time.

'Si, Signora,' he nods politely. 'I have been coming to Civitella with Ivo and Assunto, who is my grandfather, every day of my school holidays since I was eight years old.' His polite reply dumps me abruptly back with the inability of a stranger, even one who is trusted and privileged to be learning about Etruria, to *ever* comprehend what it is to be Montalcinese – indeed, what it is to be *Italian*.

The story of Poggio Civitella is slowly coming to light. Professor Donati may yet unearth a precious bronze statue for Ivo and Assunto to examine . . . and display in the new Museum. Maybe they will scramble over the rocks and stare, feeling a rush of tingling excitement at the rediscovery of archaic Etruscan life. Perhaps I will even be here when he locates the entrance gates to the fortress, or identifies where the necropolis lies and uncovers the tombs of the dead. Professor Donati may write a paper one day for the University of Florence about this potent triple-ringed Etruscan fortress, which will be a point of reference for international scholars. Like Assunto, I have been 'rapaciously contaminated' by this archaeological virus. I will listen and learn, literally, as history is unearthed stone by ancient stone.

AUTUMN

CHAPTER SEVENTEEN

Twenty Arrows in Half an Hour

'Isabella! Isabella!' Whirling round, I search behind, but nobody seems to be looking at me. Turning to the front I hear another urgent voice, but see no one. 'Isabella, up here!' Standing still and looking up, I see two heads poking between the shutters on opposite sides of the road. Lola's curly head is poking out on one side and on the other is Maria-Rosa, who lives across from her.

They have been having a conversation from their bedroom windows. Lola is talking urgently, but I am not listening to her words and stand dumb in the roadway, staring up. Maria-Rosa adds something about Pianello. I turn back to Lola. 'I'm sorry — what did you say? I didn't hear you.'

The reason I am dumbstruck is because they have just signalled a milestone which has been some years in emerging: Lola called me Isabella! I am not La Signora any more and, as if by justified expiration of time, a joint decision has been made. Maria-Rosa has offered to share with me the intimacy of first-name status. I am so overcome by this double opening into their friendship that I didn't listen to the questions.

'Tomorrow,' Lola repeats herself, 'we need you in Pianello, in the kitchen. Can you come early, because two hundred people are expected for lunch. Luigi too, he will be needed in the fortress for most of the day. Ask him to go down and see Ercole. Can he help siphon Rosso at the sede? Wear your Pianello scarf tomorrow. Fiorella is in charge, so she will tell you what to do.'

For days I have been observing the final preparations for the Sagra. This morning I watched men erect the timber stage in Piazza del Popolo, where The Lady of the Fortress will sit – right in front of Cosimo, of course. The crimson curtains draped across the tiers preclude the Florentine from participation, and it continues to be a fruitless campaign by the Roman-clad Medici to ever gain acceptance in Montalcino. Although I sympathise with his entombment, I find it hard to forgive him. He stares pompously from beneath the gloomy loggia pondering the past 450 years. The archery field, lush emerald with new growth, has been meticulously measured. Pegs and stakes are sunk deep into the soft earth, ropes isolate four avenues in which the arrows will be fired down the range, and ever-increasing metre distances from the target are chalked off in white. Target boards in the shape of wild boar are turned to the side, and the rope pulley to flick them round a second before the first arrows come flying down is tightly secured. Four medieval tents, gaily striped and peaked, are lined up along the grass, each in the identifying colours of the quartieri. From the fortress wall flutter more than a dozen flags, some displaying the quartieri colours, but also the green and white colours of Montalcino and the black and white shield of Siena. From every fortress tower fly Montalcinesi emblems and above the highest tower waves the ancient Standard of Montalcino.

For the four Presidents, Mayor Mauro, Andrea and everyone involved in planning the Sagra, it has been a horrendous two weeks of volatile meetings which initially appeared to be digressing from, rather than progressing towards, staging a successful pageant and tournament. The Presidents pressed doggedly on, desperately unwilling to succumb to pressure for cancellation of the Sagra and, along with Mayor Mauro, searched for ways to circumvent the massive problems, the most difficult of which was where to hold the feasting if they were forbidden to use the fortress.

'It seems to us,' one of the exasperated Presidents reasoned with the Mayor, 'that the crux of all the difficulties is the low number of people who drink excessively.' He went on to reflect that the exclusion of feasting in the fortress, the associated difficulty of insurance and safety, the request for quartieri to man all approach gates to the village and the stipulation for all wine to be sold only from the lower car park, in reality all stem only from the disruption caused by a few problem drinkers. 'So,' he wheedled concurrence from the Mayor, 'if we can put forward alternative suggestions which will alleviate the dangers posed by those few nuisance drinkers, surely you will agree to re-evaluate the Comune's requirements?'

Maurelia is still not sure how they did it, but the four quartieri

Presidents funnelled all of their concentrated brainpower into a think-tank and yesterday were again with Mayor Mauro, enthusing about the moderate concessions and dazzling solutions they put before him. 'But next year,' declared Mayor Mauro, 'we must bring in other changes. The Sagra is getting out of hand, and Andrea and the polizia are going spare trying to control things. We have outgrown our own festival and must move forward.'

'Si, si, Sindaco, we will have to do more thinking,' soothed the mentally-exhausted Presidents, but each of them has in mind that next year they will be facing a different Mayor . . . and that is a whole new ball game.

'Allora,' began Maurelia, explaining the Sagra changes to Pianello members last night, 'here is what will happen. First, we have agreed not to transport gas bottles into the fortress. That eliminates the possibility of disastrous explosions but means we have more work to do in order to cook everything over wood fires. Second, and this is vital, we will not sell any bottled wine from any stand. Wine will only be sold by the glass and the glasses will be plastic. This means we alleviate the problem of the few nuisances who buy bottles of Brunello which they are not used to drinking and then cause unpleasantness in the village. All the quarters have agreed not to uncork bottles for visitors, which should also solve the problem of drinkers propping themselves on other people's doorsteps. Thirdly, and this will be financed equally between all quartieri from the profits – and because of this concession we have secured co-operation from Mayor Mauro – the Comune will hire, and the quartieri will pay for, the attendance of extra police. Their job will be to visibly oversee the feasting in the fortress and deal with any nuisance drinkers. This means Andrea and the other polizia can concentrate on the wider picture, the traffic problems and visitors. And let's pray nothing goes wrong on Sunday, otherwise we will face horrendous restrictions next year regardless of who is Mayor of Montalcino.'

Finding my voice at last, I call up to Lola that Luigi and I will be ready to help at the Sagra tomorrow. 'Grazie, Isabella, grazie,' she grins down at me. I'm not sure which is the more wonderful, being accepted into Pianello as a fully active, loyal working member or witnessing La Signora vanish and being affectionately addressed on a first-name basis by Lola and Maria-Rosa. Either way, with these two symbolic notifications of our advancing state of acceptance in the life of our village, I speed home with the news for Luigi.

A milky globe, crisply outlined, hangs in a velvet sky flooding ghostly shadows into lanes and bathing the soaring fortress walls in a silvery glow. The towers and battlements stand boldly in stark silhouette. Flags barely flutter, catching only the occasional wafting breath from the face in the glowing moon. Creeping inside the fortress gates I stare at the dishevelled mess. The quartieranti will be back at dawn to assemble some kind of order here, to light the coal braziers and begin cooking for the feast. How do Italians manage to retrieve order from chaos? Things happen in spite of absolute abandonment of self-regulation. Somehow, when I come back tomorrow, the fortress keep will be functioning in a near-civilised manner. Tonight it looks as if one of those dreaded gas bottles has exploded and shot partially constructed timber stands, braziers, chopped wood, banners and tins of olive oil, cartons of wine, rounds of cheese, legs of prosciutto and handwritten menus skywards, and now everything has floated surreally down to settle haphazardly on an evacuated bombsite!

For an hour I have been sneaking around the quartieri because I want to invisibly observe what is happening on the night before the Sagra, and on the way to Borghetto sede the Standard of Montalcino, flying above the highest tower, lured me into the fortress. Standing chest-deep in this unfathomable mess, enclosed in midnight silence and surrounded by the protecting walls, I stare upwards at the flags. Half an hour ago I stood in the shadows of the scaffolding around Sant' Agostino and peered towards Ruga. All the sede lights were on, there were stacks of blue and gold banners against the wall, but I could not hear any voices from inside because the youngsters were not there. The noise was coming from round the corner. I listened to them laughing as they made up dastardly rhymes, singing stornelli which echoed round the stone walls of the courtyard outside Circolo.

At Travaglio I had to quickly turn a corner and hide under a gloomy archway before anybody spied me, because the quartiere is holding a street dinner in Via Donnoli and, by the sound of the rousing cheering and clapping, boisterously encouraging their archers to victory. Vasco, wobbling precariously on the edge of a chair, was leading the singing a couple of bars behind the chorus, because, with his usual passion for Travaglio, he was concentrating on unfurling a red and yellow banner. Just as well he did not see me or he would have had me on that chair with him in no time, and that would take some explaining in Pianello.

What brings dozens and dozens of young people to their quartiere to raise the flags, to chant and sing, to put on medieval costumes and, with passionate loyalty, support their archers in this tournament? Is it just a dazzling spectacle, just another image Italians cleverly reflect to the world of themselves sparkling in a mirror, making it impossible to know if you are watching the real thing or a glossy reflection of what they would like you to believe they are? Fleeting images of previous Sagre trigger glimpses of comprehension. One moment my mind is crystal-clear, but that recurring mist then sweeps it all away and fingers of fog creep in, leaving me a necklace of tangled thoughts. What *is* the sum total of all this?

Leaving the silent fortress, I step quietly down Via Panfilo del Oca and peep around the corner towards Borghetto sede. There is no one on the cobbled road, but six straw-covered demijohns of wine sit outside the door. Everyone is in the upstairs meeting room. Passing open windows, heads encased in crimson turbans dart back and forth as they try on their costumes. I creep past the sede and make my way towards Pianello, and as I turn into Via della Scuole the night is filled with glorious harmony. Riccardo's booming voice is familiar enough for me to distinguish, but Pianello youngsters are not in the sede either, they have gathered on a narrow terrace and, with their backs to me, are chanting their victory song across the moonlit Orcia Valley. It sounds like a haunting and mysterious ancient secret rite; they fervently plead to the gods for help. Pienza and San Quirico twinkle back across the hills and the cream-puff face in the silvery moon looks benevolently down as the joyful voices make their claim:

> *We of the great Pianello*
> *We come from Via Moglio*
> *We are the pride of the oak tree*
> *You all owe us respect.*

I do not have all the answers tonight, but, important as tomorrow's tournament is, deep inside I know this is not only about archery. Something is going on here which has been outside my circle of penetration for five years, beyond my life's experience. Like an illusive soap bubble it is twirling before my eyes. I am ready to pierce and enter the circle but do not want it to burst in case I lose the form. Tonight I am close enough to touch, balanced on the edge of comprehension.

A small boy of about four is next to me. I am sitting with my legs dangling over the front of the grandstand, peering between horizontal iron bars directly over the campo, but my young companion squats on his haunches, back straight, sitting upright like a rabbit. With eyes peeled he searches the field. He is vaguely familiar, and I must have seen him in the village. A Travaglio scarf is tied loosely around his shoulders but he is too intent on the campo to notice me smile at him. I turn around to look for his parents, but cannot identify them.

The beating of the drums tells us the pageant is approaching the gates to the campo, and first to appear, waving wildly and yelling instructions to the rows of drummers and trumpeters following him, is scarlet-faced Alessio. Perspiring in his green velvet pantaloons and buttoned waistcoat, he races a few metres ahead and at his signal the drummers change their rhythmic beat to a stirring drumroll. Silver trumpets rise to the sky and as Giancarlo takes his first step through the gate bearing the Standard of Montalcino, the resounding clamorous fanfare bursts over the campo. Giancarlo lengthens his stride and turns toward the grandstand. Flapping from the base of the Standard are the heraldic emblems of Ruga, Borghetto, Pianello and Travaglio, and rising from the very highest point above the crest is a living green leafy branch picked this morning from a holm oak tree, dancing about in the breeze.

I have followed the progress of this leafy branch since early morning, when an already anxious Alessio directed the drummers, trumpeters and Giancarlo bearing the Standard into the piazza, to form lines behind the banditore on his chestnut horse, for the reading of the proclamation. The familiar crest on a crimson banner cascaded down the stone walls of Palazzo Comunale and from the high window two silver trumpets were thrust out. The rallying call flowed over the piazza, echoing around the stone walls, and the banditore, dressed in his splendid olive-green fur-trimmed cape, gently guided the clopping hooves of his chestnut, turned to the expectant crowd and, unrolling the gilded scroll, read the now familiar annual proclamation:

'The citizens of the four quartieri of Montalcino are summonsed to each make an autumn offering to The Lady of the Fortress, to meet on the campo at the sound of the trumpets, bringing with you your most accurate and trusted archers . . . there they must display their skills and we will know who has the bravest archers of Montalcino.'

The trumpets and drums began again as Giancarlo raised the Standard above his head, and I turned and raced down to Pianello, where Fiorella was waiting for me. I was not able to listen to the draw for the archers, but I could hear the cheers rise up as each quarter was notified by the Captain of the Tournament which two of their three nominated archers will fire the arrows this afternoon. Luigi headed in the other direction, up to the fortress where the feasting had already begun.

Within minutes Fiorella had me spreading olive paste and parsley and basil sauce on what seemed like thousands of crostini. Then she called to me: 'Isabella! Can you help peel aglio? We need it soon for the pinci.' Peeling fistfuls of slithery garlic cloves, I was way behind in speed and could not believe we needed a full bucket of cloves for tomato and garlic sauce. 'Isabella,' panted Maurelia desperately, 'I have a party of six from Phoenix booked in. Ercole wants them to sit beside the New Zealanders. Can you watch for them arriving? Show them where to sit and explain the menu? Allora! Do South Africans speak English too, do you think?'

I was aware of distant trumpets and beating drums all morning as the banditore rode around the village making sure every citizen heard the proclamation. Being a Pianello worker this year, and not an enchanted spectator as at past Sagre, I cannot follow him, but I heard the drifting rhythm and knew where he was going. Halfway through the morning I explained to Fiorella that I had to dash up to Piazza Cavour. 'Do you mind, Fiorella? I'll only be a few minutes,' I promised. 'I'll be back before anyone arrives.'

A contadino farmer with a quiff of unruly hair straggling down from a peasant's narrow-brimmed felt hat, whose attire was probably not greatly exaggerated beyond his habitual, ambled into Piazza Cavour patiently leading a pair of staggeringly large white chianini cattle. Four enormous brown liquid eyes rolled lazily around as the two slow and gentle beasts, so loved by Tuscans, dispassionately followed the contadino, who mumbled indiscernibly into their floppy ears. These monolithic beasts are often paired in teams from early calfhood and, standing nearly two metres high and almost as wide, with long curving horns, their enormity at this short distance was startling. They stood motionless, apart from flicking tails, occasionally lifting drooping heads towards the farmer, who fondled their jaws grinding imaginary hay.

It worried them not one iota when a piano accordion began to play and a dozen girls dressed in floral skirts, straw hats resting on their shoulders, and young men in knee-breeches and waist-coats, wearing felt hats, formed a circle and ran quickly through a round of the trescone. Dancing the trescone is always a part of the Sagra, but this was a practice run before they reached the piazza. The farmer hitched an open gypsy cart behind the cattle, and the boys, after lifting the girls daintily into the cart, sat on hay bales, dangling their legs from the tailboard. The farmer pushed a handful of hay between gigantic masticating jaws and urged the slow-moving beasts towards Via Mazzini.

Even as they struggled to lift their hooves, reeling against the unexpected weight of the cart, I heard Alessio's panicking voice: 'Vai! Vai! Get out of here! I've got Borghetto coming down the hill, they will be here in thirty seconds!' He was frantically trying to assemble the four quartieri. Soon more than a hundred Montalcinesi dressed once more in an assortment of splendid medieval costumes – soldiers with glinting spears, hunters with nets draped over their shoulders, archers with bows and arrows, Lords with their Ladies, serfs shouldering axes – accompanied by rows of drummers and trumpeters would follow the chianini cattle on their annual pilgrimage to Piazza del Popolo. There they would present their autumn offering to The Lady of the Fortress, awaiting them on her crimson-draped podium.

As I watched these lumbering beasts jostle flanks into the narrow road, I understood why Mayor Mauro was terrified someone would be accidentally trodden on. Astonished visitors squealed in horror as the beasts lumbered along the roadway. Grabbing for their children, they scattered into doorways and tried to balance on windowsills. Amazingly docile, the animals plodded dispassionately behind the farmer, seeming not to be aware that today was different from any other workday in the Tuscan hills.

Back inside, Fiorella grabbed my arm and showed me the tables I would serve, then instructed me to set the antipasto on the plates and, as mezzogiorno pealed and the village bell began to strike 100 gongs, our 200 guests began filing through the door for pranzo. I was so preoccupied ferrying plates of food and bottles of wine that I ended up speaking a more than usually confused form of Italian to the Americans, and English to confused visiting Milanese. So much for Maurelia's bi-lingual plans. But somehow we satisfied 200 people with a scrumptious five-course Montalcinesi feast and they quickly left, because the afternoon procession which meanders through the village to the fortress and escorts the archers to the campo was about to commence.

Pianello ladies had the clean-up well in hand, but almost an hour passed before I could escape again. I told Fiorella I wanted to go to the fortress to see how Luigi was faring, and then I'd come straight back to help, but she said she was too exhausted to be worried about the clean-up. 'Go, go, we've got all afternoon to do that,' she assured me, then instructed me to be sure to pass a message to Ercole, who had gone up to relieve Lola half an hour before. It staggered me that these octogenarians were not dead on their feet.

Piazza Cavour was still teeming with visitors trying to squeeze into Via Mazzini to follow the departed pageant, so I quickly decided to take an indirect route through Ruga and Borghetto. Head down and puffing as I strode happily up the hill, my face was all smiles as I listened to the drummers and trumpeters making their way through the village. So much so that when I practically collided with the rear of a parked vehicle, I'm not sure who received the greatest shock, me or the two men standing beside a long box they had just unloaded on to the road. My radiant expression, surprise coupled with happiness, brought the cheeriest of buongiornos from my lips.

As I caught their looks of horror, my joyful smile froze and I noticed the elderly signora leaning against the doorway with a black lace shawl draped over her head. She was not smiling, nor were the men . . . and nor was the body at my feet! I was poised to leap like a frolicking lamb over a casket with gleaming brass handles! Instantaneously I recalled the tolling of the hospital bell yesterday, and those mournful notes only sound when someone has died. I had listened to them from my kitchen window – there is a different toll for a man or a woman – and remembered thinking how sad it was that someone had died right on the weekend of the Sagra. And here he was, stretched out right at my feet!

Choking on my disrespectful grin, I jumped back as the men each took a handle and carried the casket past the weeping signora who, awkwardly, was well-known to me. Giuseppe, for whom the bell tolled, had reached eighty-seven years of age and had evidently been brought home to spend one last night with his family. My face at last respectfully solemn, I was hazily aware of the blaring trumpets. The signora turned to follow her husband up the stairs, but I recovered my composure and, catching her arm, whispered in her ear; 'Coraggio, Signora.' She responded with the softest smile, saying, 'Grazie – but you must hurry, Signora, or you will miss the pageant too!' Racing uphill through Ruga into Borghetto, I arrived breathless beside the Church of Sant' Egidio just as Padre Don Guido emerged for the annual benediction.

The trumpeters and drummers announced the arrival of the Standard with the waving holm oak branch overtopping it, and behind them, winding up the narrow road, stretched the solemn medieval procession. Padre Don Guido raised his arms to bless the Standard and archers as they filed past, but I needed to stay ahead of them if I was to get to the fortress and then into the campo before the meandering pageant. I darted up Via Panfilo del Oca, watching furling clouds of smoke, which I had smelled lower down the hill, rising higher than the fortress towers and carrying the aroma of roasting wild boar. I pushed through the crowd streaming around the fortress who were hurrying out to take up positions along the roads to await the pageant.

Today the fortress resembled a giant kitchen and, as antici-pated, each festooned stand had been positioned in semi-orderly fashion and surrounded by smoking braziers cooking pork steaks and sizzling sausages over red-hot coals. Within the Pianello stand, ragù sauce simmered on wood-burning stoves and ladies who could scarcely lift their arms from fatigue were hand-rolling pinci. One of them was unstoppable Lola! Luigi is definitely not an octogenarian, but whilst Lola worked on he appeared dead on his feet, slumped over the stand with a Pianello banner draped over his shoulders. A purple wine-stained hand dug a fork into a plate of pinci – his first opportunity all day to rest his arms from pouring red wine.

From behind Travaglio's coal brazier, red-faced L'Arabo was rotating birds . . . not thrush, because I could see they were too large. They instantly reminded me the Sagra is always held in autumn to celebrate the return of migratory thrush, the abundance of bountiful food in the woods and the skill and bravery of the archers. I decided the dizzy birds must be pigeons and, nearby, furred wild hare with pert little pointed noses dangled upside down. What a feast has been taking place inside this fortress today! Braziers were still grilling carved-up slabs of polenta and, because many visitors have deserted the fortress to await the pageant, I could see that the mess which had surrounded me at midnight had indeed been retrieved from chaos and transformed to offer a continuous feast of the delicious cuisine of Montalcino.

When Lola heard I had not had time for pranzo, she thrust a prosciutto-filled panino at me and indignantly instructed me that she did not need relieving from her post. 'Ercole is already at the campo,' she said. 'You must deliver Fiorella's message to him there.'

The green tunics and red hats of the first row of drummers and trumpeters are passing the grandstand where I now sit with my small companion. I recognise many of these musicians disguised in velvet costumes – these are friends I share the piazza with every day. The drums roll, silver trumpets are lifted and blast a spine-tingling fanfare straight into our faces; the drummers then march forward, making way for the procession. The scrolls of the Comune are borne by two teenage boys wearing red turbans, and directly behind them come rows of soldiers at arms, long spears at their sides, shields protecting their chests, but steel helmets camouflage their identity. Their task is to guard the Magistrate, who follows in a long red and black cloak trimmed with white ermine, and precedes Giancarlo bearing the Standard. He raises it aloft and, at this symbolic movement, the grandstand explodes into emotional cheers for the sacred crest of Montalcino.

Now comes The Lady of the Fortress in rose velvet and white brocade, and her crimson-and-fur-clad Lord turns to the grandstand. I am astonished to see it is Luciano smiling up at me and, on his arm, his breathtakingly beautiful Lady is young Laura, who is studying economics at Arezzo University but has come home for the Sagra. Her fairytale face and noble bearing replicate the medieval princesses one recalls from history books and films. This is typically Luciano. Devastatingly handsome, he is sensually clasping svelte Laura by the arm. I can well imagine his words: 'So long as I can be the handsome Lord I will be there . . . So long as my costume is magnificent and the Lady is beautiful . . . but dai, I cannot possibly be a serf!'

Ladies-in-Waiting wearing delicate headdresses and gowns studded with pearls are followed by rows of boar-hunters with crossbows, and then the thrush-hunters in leather waistcoats and pantaloons. They trudge along in fur-edged leather boots as the nets slung expertly around their shoulders cascade and drape along the grass. Now the quartieri. Borghetto leads: white brocade and red velvet adorn their Lord and Lady. Now it's

Ruga; blue and gold, their emblem receives a mighty cheer from their quartieranti. Pianello Lord and Lady pass below me and my heart skips a beat. Cecilia, Riccardo, Maria-Teresa, Marco, so many of our youngsters take their place elegantly gowned in rich blue velvet and ivory. I know them all and soar with pride as the Pianello banner rises level with my head. But already Travaglio is approaching, last year's victors. The blood-curdling screams in my ear are deafening. It is my four-year-old companion. He screams over and over just one word: *'Travaglio! Travaglio! Travaglio!'* I am stunned by the apparent emotion already exploding inside this small boy.

Now comes the heart-stopping moment. Overwhelming pride spirals with the flourish of four heraldic banners, accelerating the excitement which is already at fever pitch. The air is filled with a crescendo of shouts and competitive chants, for in front of the crowd stand eight men, their symbolic archery costumes lifting them infinitely higher even than the pompous splendour of the parade. Trumpeters and drummers line up behind them and as the trumpet fanfare reaches its own deafening climax, the archers salute the cheering crowd. Lifting their long curved bows with one hand, and with the other drawing a single arrow from the leather sheath slung at their thighs, they dramatically raise the first arrow above their heads, pointed upwards to their passionate quartieranti.

'We are ready to prove our skills,' they are saying. 'We will defend you with these arrows. We are the greatest archers of Montalcino and our arrows will drive into the heart of the boar.'

Painfully aware, by dint of bursting eardrums, of the small boy's piercing screams, I follow his radiant eyes and of course they are riveted on Carlo and Pierluigi, last year's victors for Travaglio. And Carlo is looking straight back at him, smiling and offering him a barely perceptible nod. Carlo! This small boy is his four-year-old son, Federico, that is why he is familiar to me. His father is a champion Travaglio archer. Listening closely, I watch the few seconds of their exchange, but for me the striking revelation is that this little boy is not calling his father, he is not calling: 'Babo! Ciao, daddy, go for it, Dad, good luck in the competition.' He screams just one word, over and over: 'Travaglio! Travaglio! Travaglio!' and his screams hold more passion and emotion than I imagined a four-year-old could muster. Someone wraps their arms around him and I turn to see his mother kneeling behind him. My understanding of this little boy's passion turns to shock, for his young mother is draped in a Ruga scarf. She must have been born in Ruga, their child in Travaglio, yet this is not a competition between Federico's mother and father. This is his own emerging passion for his quartiere, for Travaglio.

Searching Massimo's face, I know he is calm. At this close range it is easy to see the outline of his powerful shoulders squashed into his medieval costume, but they are relaxed. His bulging biceps stretch the seams of his fitted white sleeves, but for the moment his muscles are slack. He smiles at the crowd, but I suspect he is not really hearing the shrieks of 'Pianello! Pianello! Pianello!' nor anything of the tumultuous explosion of chants and screams from thousands of quartieranti. The concentration in his eyes tells me he has already begun to close out the world, to enter into a state where only he, his bow and arrows and the target, exist.

Massimo is ready for this tournament. He has been training for months, making the sacrifice necessary to achieve excellence. He reached his peak after Apertura; his skill and concentration, focused and intact, have risen to an apex. Combined with his daily body-building sessions, this has melded with his crucially important mental fitness, and his persistence in training has carried him through the last few weeks without stress or tension, or the worrying disillusionment he felt last year. Then he had been so disheartened with the thought that if the young are not willing to make all the tremendous sacrifices, it will all come to an end and the ancient skills of the Montalcinesi will be lost. When Filippo, Samuele and Francesco had jumped mischievously up and down alongside him on the practice range last February, asking him to show them how to drive five perfect arrows into the heart of the boar, his fallen spirits and his determination had returned. He will continue to shoot for Pianello and he will nurture and encourage the young archers who battle so many distractions which he did not have.

'Isabella,' he had said to me a week ago, 'I had to let go of the self-destroying negatives. I have thrown myself into the months of work firing thousands of arrows down our range. I have made the personal sacrifices, I am centred and dedicated to my task, win or lose. I am mentally fit and will get through the rounds and I will drive every arrow straight and true for myself, for Pianello and for Montalcino. But remember, there will be eight great archers, and in the end it all comes down to twenty arrows in half an hour.'

I force myself to concentrate. What binds this thing together and knits it into a whole? What *is* it about this hill and the holm oaks that rouses the passion of the Montalcinesi? Is that tiny living branch of a holm oak waving above the Standard telling me something, or is the Sagra just a dazzling spectacle? Putting aside the enchantment of the first few Sagre I witnessed, the enthralling spectacle of medieval costumes, pageantry, stirring drums and heraldic trumpets, my drifting thoughts at midnight as I crept through the quartieri led me to believe obsessive passion for the Sagra had made the Montalcinesi reclusive, inward-looking, but as the blurred images at last begin to untangle, I realise I have it utterly back to front. Their obsession is with their inward-looking life – and the Sagra is clearly an emotional outlet for this obsession, expressed only within the defensive ring of stones around this village. Perhaps it is intelligible only to the initiated? But is it not an ancestral passion, stretching back through the centuries? Are they not affirming:

'Inside these walls we lack nothing and await nothing from the outside world. We are complete, contained within ourselves; the ring of defensive stones which encircles Montalcino is our emotional armour. It began halfway through the year 700 when we first sought to escape oppression, and we have battled with oppressive conquerors ever since. After the frenzied massacre by the Sienese of the Florentines in 1260, even while soulless corpses decayed on a hostile battlefield at Montaperti, the Sienese laid waste to Montalcino, cruel oppression by conquest. And we always knew we were the pawn in the game which ended in 1559. The French cared nothing for Montalcino, they abandoned us as soon as it suited them, but our mountain citadel posed a threat to both Siena and Florence. We cared not if the Florentines finally smashed the Sienese to a pulp, because we were the victim either way, but both were frightened we would become too powerful. They wanted to destroy Montalcino.'

This splendid autumn spectacle reflects their emotion, gives expression to the passion with which they refuse to recognise external power, be it necessary to cut off the heads of French soldiers who desecrate their village, or the heads of Spanish knights who come to lay siege, or be it Cosimo di Medici who, along with invaders plotted a Catholic Europe and drove them anti-clerical, so that even today visiting Bishops from Rome and Siena are perplexed at their belligerence.

My first clue to comprehension was when I awoke to something which has stared me in the face for all these years. Walking through the village, this question baffled me: Why is there no Renaissance in Montalcino? Why are there no grand palaces with perfectly proportioned loggias leading to exquisite gardens adorned with box hedges and fanciful fountains? Was Montalcino put to sleep in 1260 and reawakened after World War Two by the mysterious hammering of plumbers and electricians dragging it into the twentieth century? Is that why Cosimo, a suppressive conqueror, is forever alone under that loggia?

I had quickly grasped that the quartieri are an extension of the only enduring form of unity – the family – but do not the archers also symbolise survival, endurance, a fierce passion to triumph? For the fifth year in a row I stare intently at the eight archers poised on the campo. Yes! They are ready to *defend* Montalcino. They wear quartieri battle colours and carry weapons of war, as do the soldiers with threatening spears, serfs with axes and crossbows. All are capable of rising against a threatening enemy and spilling blood right at this moment, to fight for freedom from external abuse, external suppression and for their liberty on this hill, under the holm oaks, inside these walls.

The Lords and Ladies are seated in front of their tents. The Magistrate is ready, the Captain of the Tournament signals to Michele, whose job it is to release the rope pulley which will flick the targets face-on to the shooting range a second before the arrows begin to fire. A blanket of silent tension descends over the grandstand. Thousands of hearts stop beating as we watch two archers move into each firing range under their quartiere colours. My sharp gasp escapes into the silence as I realise Gabriele is not on the campo; Alessandro got the draw and will shoot alongside Massimo. My eyes sweep the grandstand in search of Gabriele, but instead they find Ercole. Ercole! The message! Oh no! My first day of real responsibility for my quartiere and I haven't delivered Fiorella's message. 'Tell him before the tournament,' she had instructed. I cannot possibly reach him and, in these electrical moments of hushed silence, I cannot bring myself to scream across the grandstand.

Four archers in battle colours face the targetless range, long curved bows firmly held in one hand as with the other they withdraw the first arrow from the leather pouch and raise it high above their heads. The Captain raises a baton, his eyes check each archer's poised arrow and, as the baton swoops down, simultaneously, with a rattle along the pulley, the four targets swivel and four wild boar now face the archers whose hands are moving to set the first arrow to the bow . . . and thousands of quartieranti erupt as one. A crescendo of hysterical screaming from the grandstand heralds the release of tension.

I do not think Massimo even hears the targets noisily swivelling, nor sees anything outside his narrowed line of vision down the range except the swooping baton. He has enclosed himself in a silent world, spent of fear, devoid of movement as if nothing else exists. He faces the boar. Raising the long curved bow and dropping his shoulders, uniting as one his arms and head, his eyes focus and I watch him gather the target in . . . the bow springs open . . . and the first arrow flies from his skilful hands, drives faultlessly along the range and sinks into the heart of the boar. The symbolism is revealed:

He is an archer, he is Pianello, he is Ilcinese and this hill is his life. Driving each arrow into the heart of the boar, each archer affirms the passion of the Montalcinesi that on this hill, under these holm oaks, inside these walls, they need only their liberty to be who they are.

My eyes are straining, trying to focus on the arrows which one after the other are flying like blurred missiles down the range. Fiorella's message, manifestly clear, runs through my mind: 'Luciana says yes – win or lose, *cena a casa sta sera, tutti insieme –*

tell everyone.'

A familiar chorus rises above the frenzied confusion all around me. Rising spontaneously to my feet, unable now to see the arrows flying down the range because tears of happiness sting my eyes, I wave my blue and white scarf at our archers and, throwing my fist into the air and screaming as loudly and passionately as I can, join in the chant: '*Pi . . . a . . . nello! Pi . . . a . . . nello! Pi . . . a . . . nello!*'

The undelivered message is for me as well. 'Luciana says yes, she has plenty of food, whether we win or lose, we'll have dinner at home in our sede this evening, all of us together, tell everyone.' I know this is not my hill, I know I can never be Ilcinese, nor even Montalcinese, but the search is over, I will run no further. I have found my home in Montalcino.

More About Pianello

Dear Reader,
Quartiere Pianello has begun work to raise the funds needed to restore San Pietro and renovate the sede, which will extend into the meeting room of San Pietro.

If you would like to contribute to the fundraising, your donation – which can be in various forms – will be acknowledged in a special way.

You can find out more about the fundraising as well as discover what is happening in Montalcino by visiting Isabella's websites at
www.montalcino-tuscany.com or www.montalcino-tuscany. it

You are invited to send your donation to:
The President
Quartiere Pianello
Via delle Scuole
53024 Montalcino (SI)
Italy

Glossary

About Montalcino

Montalcinese	A citizen of Montalcino
Montalcinesi	Plural
Palazzo Comunale	Equivalent to Town Hall or Village Hall
Quartiere	One quarter, or neighbourhood, of Montalcino
Quartieri	Plural
Quartierante	A member of a quarter, a supporter
Quartieranti	Plural
Sagra	A festival
Sagre	Plural
Sagra del Tordo	Festival of the Thrush – the annual festival
Travaglio	The names of the four quarters, or
Pianello	neighbourhoods
Borghetto	
Ruga	

Italian Words and Phrases

Accidente	Expression of stunned surprise, e.g., Crikey!, Damn!
Ape	Three-wheeler motorised work vehicle with rear tray
Bella figura	To make a good impression

444

Brodo	Stock cubes for soup
Cacciatore	Hunter – also Bar Cacciatore
Campo	Field with archery firing range for tournaments
Canai	Dog handler at the hunt
Cantina	Ground level of a house used for storage of wine, food, etc
Capitano del Arcieri	Captain of an archery squad on the firing range
Cara	Dear, feminine
Caro	Dear, masculine
Choro	Village choral group
Cena	Dinner
Cinghiale	Wild boar
Cittadino	A village dweller
Cittadini	Plural
Contadino	A farmer – land worker
Contadini	Plural
Etruria	Territory inhabited by Etruscans – roughly equivalent to present-day Tuscany
Hectare	One hectare = approximately 2.2 acres
Lira	Italian currency
Lire	Plural
Mariuccia	Bar Mariuccia and Pasticceria Mariuccia – the pastryshop
Mezzanotte	Midnight
Mezzogiorno	Midday
Nonna	Grandmother
Nonno	Grandfather
Passeggiata	Social ritual of strolling around greeting friends
Peperoncino	Chilli pepper

Piacere	Equivalent of 'Pleased to meet you.'
Piazzetta	Small piazza or communal square
Piazza	Communal square or central gathering place
Pranzo	Lunch
Ragazzi	Young people – males, or males and females
Sede	Headquarters of a *quartiere*
Straniera	A stranger – female
Stranieri	Strangers – males, or males and females
Tifosi	Fans or supporters – e.g., at football games
Vendemmia	Grape harvest
Via Cassia	Ancient road through the valley built by the Romans

Index